Praise for the Little Book of Magic *series:*

"Whether you are a beginner or an experienced healer, within these pages you will find the key to expand your path of spiritual growth and awaken the magick within."
—Bonnie Thompson, Crescent Moon Goddess

"There is, quite simply, no better book on the basics of healing magick anywhere for any price."
—Devon Cathlin, Publisher of *Rebel Planet* magazine

"A fascinating little book on altars that transcends the boundaries of religion and culture—the best reference book I've seen in years."
—Prairie Wind Stock, High Priestess

"Read this book, set your altar, and take control of your life. After all, what surrounds you is a reflection of you—use that to your advantage."
—Rev. Chameleon SilverCat, Wiccan Priestess

"A fascinating little book using this mysteriously ordinary tool that has been in our lives for hundreds of years—pendulums."
—Takira, High Priestess of the Whispering Willow

THE BIG LITTLE BOOK OF Magick

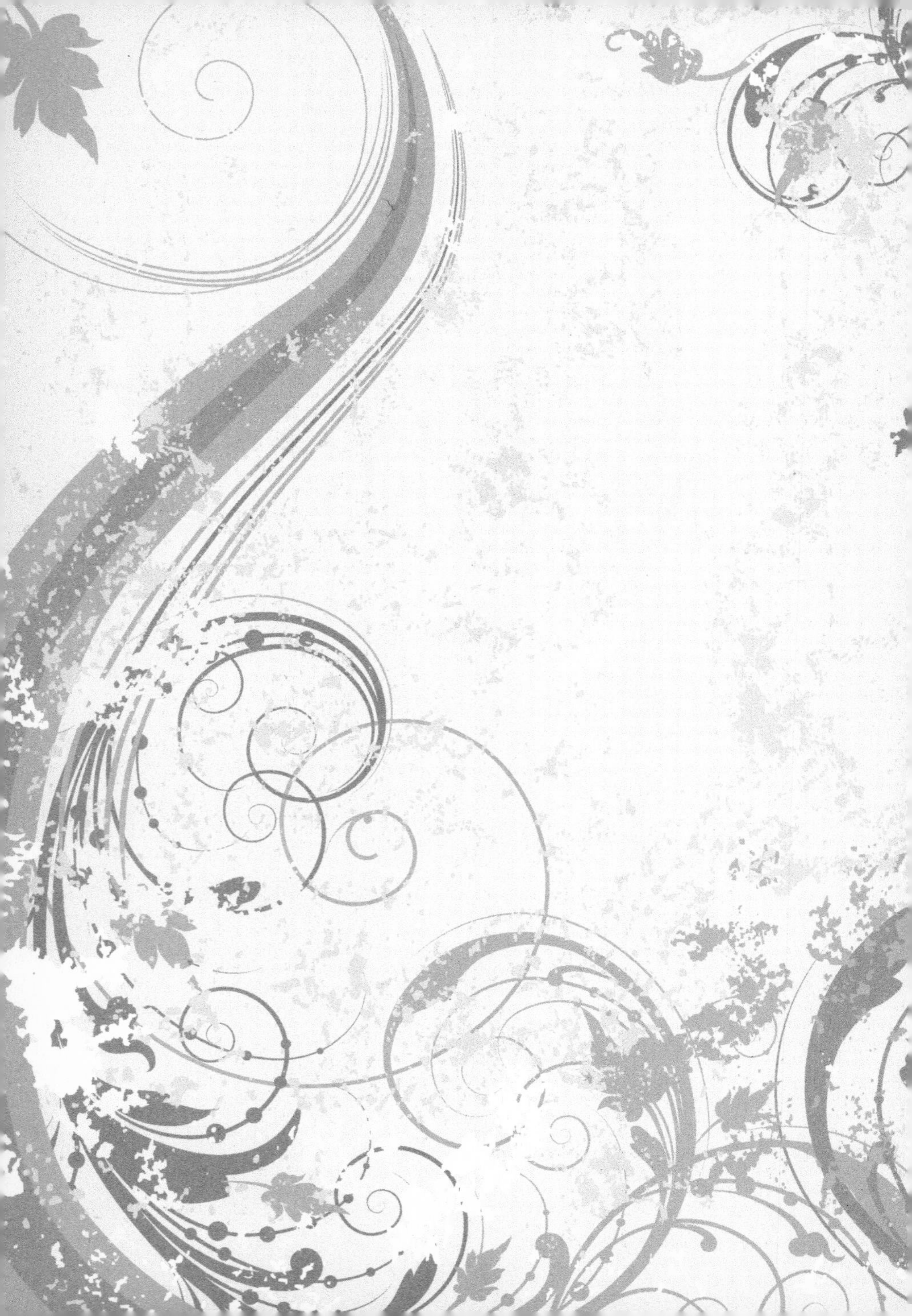

THE BIG LITTLE BOOK OF Magick

A Wiccan's Guide to Altars, Candles, Pendulums, and Healing Spells

D. J. CONWAY

CROSSING PRESS
Berkeley

The information in this book is not intended as a substitute for consulting with your physician or other licensed health-care provider. Any attempt to diagnose and treat an illness or condition should be done under the direction of a health-care professional. The publisher and author are not responsible for any adverse effects or consequences resulting from the use of any of the suggestions or preparations discussed in this book.

Published in the United States by Crossing Press, an imprint of the Crown Publishing Group, a division of Random House, Inc., New York.
www.crownpublishing.com
www.tenspeed.com

Crossing Press and the Crossing Press colophon are registered trademarks of Random House, Inc.

The books in this volume were originally published separately in paperback by Crossing Press, Berkeley, California, in 2000, 2001, and 2002.

Library of Congress Cataloging-in-Publication Data
Conway, D. J. (Deanna J.)
The big little book of magick : a Wiccan's guide to altars, candles, pendulums, and healing spells / D.J. Conway. — 1st omnibus ed.
p. cm.
Summary: "A Wiccan author explains how to enlighten and empower oneself using four different types of magick"—Provided by publisher.
Includes bibliographical references and index.
1. Magic. I. Title.
BF1611.C7245 2010
133.4'3—dc22
2010026555

ISBN 978-1-58091-005-7

Printed in the United States of America

Design by Chloe Rawlins

Cover image copyright © by iStockphoto.com / Cloudniners

Illustrations in Part IV by Petra Serafim

10 9 8 7 6 5 4 3 2 1

First Omnibus Edition

Contents

PART I

A LITTLE BOOK OF Altar Magick

The History of Altars

Altars have been used from almost the beginning of human civilization, as far back as the Paleolithic Age. Yet many people today do not understand exactly what an altar is outside of a religious structure, and do not believe they can set up personal altars in their homes. Nevertheless, on a subconscious level, we set up varieties of altars without giving any conscious thought to the process.

It is common to see groupings of family photos arranged on shelves, tables, or pianos. Many people place clusters of sentimental objects or collections of various kinds in glass-front cabinets or on shelves in various rooms of their homes. It is not uncommon to see displays of beer cans, thimbles, dragons, model cars, or similar objects. These are all done without conscious thought or planning except that we "want to." But why do we feel drawn to do this?

Why Do We Build Altars?

Carl G. Jung named the deepest part of our subconscious mind "the collective unconscious," and said that it connects every person to every single ancestor and provides access to everything that has been known in the past. It seems that the collective unconsciousness within each of us is persuading us to build a personal altar, such as our ancestors did. The problem is, we seldom stop our busy minds long enough to listen to the collective unconscious and learn from it.

The wall of beer cans is a type of informal attar to the gods Dionysus or Bacchus, both deities of the vine, wine, and good times. Model cars may well be a subconscious tribute to the fleet-footed Mercury or to Helios and his sun chariot. Thimbles are symbols of weaving goddesses such as Spider Woman, Ixchel, the Fates, and Athena. Collections of dragons, wizards, and the like are subconscious attempts to tap ancient magick and mystical knowledge. Groupings of family photos can be remembrances of the dead in the hope they will aid us, or sympathetic magick to link the dead with the living. A collection of frog figures may be a subconscious plea to ancient fertility goddesses.

This penchant for informal altars cuts across social and cultural lines. In fact, preparing an altar is a multicultural experience. Unknowingly, humans are constantly building altars around them. Perhaps we should give more thought to the process, thus learning how to enhance our daily lives and spiritual growth.

Early Altars

Archeologists have discovered the very earliest permanent sacred altars to be deep inside caves, with narrow, treacherous paths leading to them. Their difficult access made the journey a determined, conscious effort. The caves were highly spiritual places, not to be entered lightly, for they symbolized the eternal, everflowing womb of the Goddess and the cauldrons of primordial energy. Within them, people used magick for hunting and performed rites of passage including initiation. People and their tribal shaman visited these secret caves whenever their clan migrations brought them back to that area.

However, it is likely that the migrating people of the Paleolithic cultures also carried small Goddess images with them as they traveled from one area to another in search of wild game and other food. These people would create a temporary altar at the hearth they made inside each cave or rocky shelter they entered. The strange little rotund female figures they used to represent the Goddess were shaped with exaggerated belly, breasts, and buttocks to symbolize the Great Mother who gave birth to everything in the world. The faces of these figurines were only vaguely formed. Some figurines had their legs taper to a point that could be stuck into the ground, others had flat, widespread bottoms, so they could be placed on any fairly level surface. All were quite small, just the size for carrying easily from one place to another.

Later statues became slightly more sophisticated, but most still retained only the suggestion of facial features, like their earlier counterparts. Where the Goddess of Willendorf and those of Grimaldi, Lespugue, and Sireuil are very stylized and exaggerated in body form, the Minoan snake goddesses appear more human in proportion. In addition to being decorated with spirals or meanders (wavy lines), the Minoan figures now hold two recognizable snakes. This evolution of form continues until we find the beautiful, very human statues of Egypt, China, the Middle East, Greece, and Rome.

The earliest caves were decorated with vivid, life-like paintings of animals, handprints, and other symbols, all representing spiritual and magickal ideas concerned with sustaining life and bringing comfort in death. Later, when villages were established and the clans no longer roamed from place to place, human-built shrines became more elaborate. Although the shrine itself is a symbolic cave, the floors of some in the Minoan culture are carefully paved with seashells and roughly carved, colorful stones, with the walls painted just as vividly as those found in the mystical, secret caves. The symbolism's representation becomes more direct.

Altar Symbols

From the incised decorations on the surviving deity figures, the fabulous paintings on cave walls, and the remains of later shrines, archaeologists have learned that certain symbols held great meaning for our ancestors. Meanders represent water and the sacred snake of life. Lozenges stand for fertility, while the triangle means the feminine and regeneration, just as the cave itself did. The crescent represents the lunar cycle and energy. A cupmark cut into a stone held water, symbolizing the sacred water that flowed from the Goddess of life. Footprints painted on cave walls refer to the healing force and guidance of the Goddess, while hands are symbols of Her divine powers against evil.

Eyes, spirals, and coiled snakes represent the cosmic life force that is an endless source of energy. An X symbolizes death and regeneration, and is similar to both the butterfly and hourglass.

Archaeologists have found evidence of two types of shrine through every age: the permanent and the mobile. Two things become clear from the study of the religious practices of ancient cultures. The first type was originally a natural site, such as a special cave, grove of trees, hilltop, or power spot. What we would call the altar was usually a naturally formed rock that happened to be within the sacred place. Except for engravings on rocks or paintings on cave walls, the sacred place was not transformed in any way.

The second type of shrine indicates that these early people understood that any place could be made sacred by erecting a temporary altar. This simple portable altar, consisting of a Goddess statue, was of great value since Paleolithic clans seldom stayed in one place for very long. They needed a place to worship and to perform their sympathetic magick while they followed the migrating herds of wild game.

These two types of shrine persist even after people began to settle permanently in villages. It seems that although people gathered together in one place for special ceremonies, they liked the idea of having their own personal altars at home.

The elements of Earth, Water, and Fire were very important to the early migrating peoples. Their lives depended on fire for protection, warmth, and light; they considered that the earth provided their source of food; and they knew their existence depended upon a ready source of water. Much later, our ancestors added the element of Air to the list when they realized that this invisible substance was needed for breathing and that wind brought storms and rain. Spirit, the traditional fifth element, had always been important, for the elusive power of Spirit tied the living to the dead and held the promise of rebirth.

Today, we find the same symbolism in our modern places of worship. Some religions have a definite altar, while in others the altar has become only a raised platform for the minister and choir. Non-Christian religions often have special cabinets for their holy books. Sacred spaces are decorated with flowers, candles, and often pictures or statues of deities, saints, or gurus. Sometimes, holy water is kept by the door, and grape juice or wine is offered to the participants. Singing or chanting and prayer are usually part of the service.

But what do we do at home, in our private places? Statues of saints are common in Catholic households. A cross is a familiar symbol in other Christian homes. Non-Christian homes have statues or symbols of their deities, often surrounded by flowers, candles, and other symbolic offerings. These are consciously made altars, places we make sacred for our spiritual growth and comfort.

Those who do not attend any organized church or temple or do not profess any belief in any deities are still influenced by the collective unconscious mind to build altars. Subconsciously, they are drawn to build little informal altars of collections of items that appeal to them. With some thought and attention, these altars can add positive energy to our lives.

The Benefits of Building Altars

We need to realize that conscious intent in building an altar can create a positive, spiritual atmosphere that will improve our everyday lives. Altar building crosses all cultural lines and is not necessarily connected to any religion. Taking this action merely says that you wish to connect with the unlimited pool of cosmic energy that sustains the entire universe. This connection may be made to manifest certain desires in your life or simply to say "thank you" to a higher power for what you already have. An altar can be permanent, changeable, or temporary, according to your needs. The bottom line is that you should be building your altars with conscious intent and understanding of what you are doing.

Intentionally building an altar helps you to step outside yourself and whatever everyday troubles you may have. Using an altar helps you to elevate yourself in order to see your surroundings and conditions more clearly. It helps you to clarify what you want and why you want it. Although you may choose objects for your altar subconsciously, not completely understanding why you made the choice, the very act of creating an altar teaches you to listen to your subconscious mind and its messages. When you are centered, positive energy and happiness flow into your life. Isn't that what we all truly desire?

How to Erect and Prepare an Altar

Joseph Campbell said that a sacred place is a place where wonder can be glimpsed. Building an altar (or altars) in your home can fill your life with wonder, for the presence of an altar makes any place sacred. Creating an altar opens you to the spiritual dimension, whatever path you choose to take. It allows you to express your personal glimpse of the divine in whatever way you imagine it. It helps you to integrate the sacred into your personal life, for altars are places of centering and rebalancing. It draws on subconscious thoughts, making you receptive to the sacred in life.

Building an altar requires four stages of preparation: thinking out and clarifying your reasons for doing so, planning the project, acknowledging the emotions behind this decision, and actually building the altar. These steps are no different from what we should be doing when we make every major decision in our lives. The whole experience is a process of discovering more about yourself, how you perceive things, and what symbols and objects mean to you.

Placing an Altar

What do you need to create an altar and make a sacred space? Really, not much. There is no need to run out and spend lots of money. Begin with what you have on hand. Most people are pack rats of a sort and tend to accumulate items they like. Look closely at your possessions. You will be surprised at what you find.

The first thing you will need is something on which to arrange the symbols and objects you choose for your altar. An altar space can be anything: a small shelf, a table, a covered box set in a corner, the top of a dresser, or one corner of the coffee table. The important thing is simply a flat surface, which does not need to be large or elaborate.

If you wish your altar to be private, arrange it in a place not readily visible to everyone, perhaps in your bedroom. If you wish to energize certain rooms of your home and do not care about your altars being seen, you can place them wherever you wish.

It is not unusual to find tiny altars in kitchens today. These may contain shiny copper molds, pictures of the family and pets, or perhaps a small statue of the Virgin Mary or the goddess Kuan Yin. At one time, the hearth and cooking area was the most important part of every house, for it was here that the precious fire was kept burning and the food for survival cooked. And it was here that one could find a small statue of the Goddess and perhaps a kitchen deity. The symbolism is the same as eight thousand years ago, when people placed Goddess statues in the grain bins so that the food supply would never run out and so that occupants of the house would prosper.

According to the Chinese art of placement, called *feng shui,* situating an altar so that it faces the main door will permit the *ch'i,* or energy, to freely enter the house. This may go back to the centuries-old thought that the threshold of a house should be protected, and that sacred objects set near the entrance build a demarcation between the outer public world and the inner private one.

Feng shui is thousands of years old and still used, with remarkable results. The energy forces said to be promoted by this art are believed to determine or change the outcome of health, prosperity, and luck. If you wish to place your altars according to *feng shui,* consider these suggestions. The Chinese say that rectangular and square shapes are very *yang,* or masculine, in nature and spin off energy, while circular shapes are *yin*, or feminine, and hold energy in balance. Both *yin* and *yang* objects should be used in the art of placement; wind chimes, mobiles, or small fountains will increase energy within the home.

The Chinese also carefully consider directions when placing altars. The south is connected with professional success, fortune, and fame, also with the color red and images of birds. The west is for creativity, joy, and children; the color white and an image of a tiger will increase energy in these aspects. East is associated with health and growth; use green and a dragon here. The north is connected with money, career, and business, as well as the color black.

For information on the use of colors, the elements, objects, symbols, and the directions, see page 13.

Choosing Altar Symbols

Now that you have decided what you will use for your altar and where you will set it, you need to consciously choose what you will place on it. You may wish to have all goddess statues, or you may choose to have both god and goddess images. Perhaps you will have saints instead, or no images at all. Every altar will reflect the personality and spirituality of the person who erects it.

Using the four elements on an altar will bring the energies associated with these elements to your sacred space. Fire can be a candle; Air, incense; Earth, a stone or flowers; Water, a fountain or water in a vase. Or each of these elements might be portrayed in a picture that speaks to you. By placing the elements on your altar, you are subconsciously asking that balance come to your space and life.

Certain flowers and the wood of trees have traditional meanings and can be used to symbolize specific energies. So can objects, such as a pyramid, box, animal figurine, or stone. Or you may decide to incorporate images and objects that remind you of a person you wish to remember or an event or action you desire to accomplish. Listen with your heart, and choose what feels right to you.

If you burn candles on your altar, be certain that the candle is firmly set in a metal holder and is well away from anything flammable. The last thing you want is a devastating fire ruining your home. Incense is also a potential problem if not handled with care. Stick incense should be placed in a can of sand or a holder large enough not to tip over. Cone incense should be placed in an unbreakable, heat-resistant holder or on a bed of sand. If you burn paper requests at your altar, use a metal bowl or cauldron.

Beginning on page 87, there are several examples of altars erected for a specific purpose and the objects placed on them. These altars are eclectic, and not especially based on any religion or lack thereof. Feel free to change them to incorporate your own ideas and desires.

Maintaining an Altar

It is a good idea to cleanse your altar periodically. Dust does accumulate, as does pet hair. Some people feel that need to cleanse their altar weekly by smudging or burning incense and sprinkling holy water. Others only clean when their instincts say it is necessary, or after negative people have been in the house and have touched the altar.

Try to cleanse your altar separately from your ordinary housecleaning so you can concentrate on the action and not shatter the vibrations built up around the altar. Remove any dead flowers, clean up incense ashes, and trim candle drips. Rearrange or replace any items you wish.

If children are visitors or permanent residents, they will probably rearrange things on the altar. Take this in stride and be patient. As long as the children are not destructive, arranging an altar can be an enthralling pastime for them.

Altars can be erected in celebration, commemoration, to mark life's turning points, or to heal grief. They are also valuable in helping you to focus energy on a specific part of your life that you would like to improve or change. Grief altars are helpful in working through emotional pain, whether that pain arises from the loss of a loved one to death, divorce, or some other end of a relationship. Event altars keep you focused on a goal, such as paying off a mortgage or saving money for a long-desired trip. Altars are reminders of where we need to focus our attention, and that the spiritual is intertwined with the mundane and is never separate from it.

It does not matter how you view the word "spiritual" in relationship to altars. Spiritual simply means acknowledging that there is a Power or Force greater than you. You may call it Goddess, God, or the Big Bang. Building an altar is a way of consciously reminding yourself that a powerful force of energy runs through the universe that anyone can tap into with a little effort. Whether you do positive or negative things with that force is up to you. However, remember that the type of energy you give out is what you get back, so it is safer and more productive to do only positive things.

Perhaps one of the most important things to remember about building an altar is that it should be done with joy, anticipation, and a sense of wonder. By your actions you are drawing spiritual energy into your everyday life. This cannot help but make changes for the better.

So build your altar as it pleases you, and be prepared for your life to open and expand in a way you never thought possible.

Symbols and Sacred Objects

Through the centuries, humans have used many different symbols and objects as part of their individual and collective spiritual worship. Since the collective unconscious mind of every human, as described by Carl Jung, is connected to the symbols used by our ancestors through genetic memory, these objects and symbols still have deep meaning for us.

The subconscious mind does not speak in words, but only in nonverbal symbols. By using symbolic objects on your altars, you are communicating with your subconscious mind, the conduit through which flow psychic messages, spiritual communications, and extrasensory perception, all the little nudges and gut feelings that help us deal with life's difficulties. To open the door to the collective unconscious, one must enter through the subconscious mind. Until you establish a dialogue using symbols, the subconscious mind will not allow you to reach that deeper source of information.

Today, many people are attracted to ancient deities from around the world. This attraction may be to the deities of their ancestors, or it may come from a past life to which they still have strong ties. Renewing a relationship with the powers represented by these old goddesses and gods by placing representations of them on altars may help these people improve their lives.

For those who have no attraction to ancient deities, I have provided lists of angels, archangels, and saints. Petitions to these spiritual beings have brought about success and guidance in many people's lives.

By using any of the following images and objects on your altars, you are strengthening the spiritual energies that collect about your sacred places. By intensifying the energies, you deepen your spiritual experience and hasten the creation of your desires.

Sacred Animals

All around the world, various creatures have always represented certain deities and/or magickal qualities. Using statues, photos, or drawing of animals on your altar can help you to invoke a specific energy you wish to manifest in yourself or in your life. These animals can be actual creatures, or they can be what are known as fabulous beasts, such as the unicorn.

Following is a list of creatures, both physical and fabulous, whose magickal-spiritual qualities have been known and used by many cultures. Sometimes called shamanic or totem animals, their astral (nonphysical) equivalents frequently appear in meditations, shamanic journeys, and dreams. They act as guides and portents of things to come.

ADDER, SNAKE Wisdom, cunning, defense, psychic energy, creative power, pure divine energy, beginning and ending, and understanding.

BADGER Tenacity and unyielding courage.

BAT Gaining direction in difficult circumstances; avoiding obstacles, barriers, and troublesome people. In China, the bat is a symbol of good fortune and happiness; in Europe, a companion creature of the goddess Hel.

BEAR Stamina, harmony, protecting the self and the family, dreams, intuition, transformation, and astral travel. The bear was sacred to the Greek goddesses Callisto and Artemis.

BEE Responsibility, cooperation, prosperity, and planning for the future. In the Indo-Aryan and Greek Orphic teachings, bees were thought of as souls. They were called the Little Servants of the Goddess by early matriarchies. Bee was also the title of Aphrodite's high priestess on Mount Eryx. The Greek goddess Demeter was sometimes called "the mother bee."

BLACKBIRD This bird denotes joy.

BOAR, SOW, PIG Cunning, intelligence, revenge, defense, knowledge of past lives, magick, protection of family, cooperation, prosperity, and health, death, and rebirth. The sow, in particular, represents magick, the Underworld, and deep knowledge of the Crone aspect of the Goddess. The sow was sacred to Astarte, Cerridwen, Demeter, Freyja, and the Buddhist aspect of the Goddess called Marici.

BULL, COW The bull is a symbol of strength, potency, alertness, protection of the family, and knowing when to be aggressive. The cow represents gentleness and balance, but also fierce mother love and the life-giving and sustaining power of creation. In the beginning of human religious symbology, the bull was a lunar symbol of the Great Mother, with the horns emblematic of the crescent moon. Later, the bull became a symbol of sun gods such as Attis and Mithra, both associated with Cybele. The cow was associated with the Egyptian goddesses Hathor and Neith, and the Norse goddess Audhumla.

BUTTERFLY Reincarnation, beauty, love, transformation, joy, and freedom. To the ancient Greeks, the butterfly represented the soul. In Ireland, Cornwall, Mexico, and Siberia, white butterflies are still believed to be the spirits of the dead.

CAT (DOMESTIC) Independence, discrimination, stealth, resourcefulness, healing, love, self-assurance, seeking hidden information, seeing spirits, and receiving protection when faced with a confrontational situation. In ancient Egypt, the cat was considered to be a lunar creature and was sacred to Bast and Isis. In other cultures, it was sacred to Artemis, Diana, and Freyja.

CHEETAH Swiftness, speed, and developing self-esteem; making events happen quicker.

COBRA To the ancient Egyptians, the cobra symbolized spiritual and divine wisdom and protection. The Hindus saw the cobra as a representation of the kundalini force that rose through the seven chakras of the astral body.

COCK Self-confidence.

COYOTE Cunning, shapeshifting, stealth, opportunity, creativity, and new life.

CRANE From China to the Mediterranean, the crane represented justice, longevity, dignity, wisdom, discipline, vigilance, and reaching deeper mysteries and truths.

CROCODILE To ancient Egyptians, this creature represented mindless fury and evil. However, they also said the crocodile could provide knowledge.

CROW Trickery, boldness, skill, cunning, alertness, prophecy, and shapeshifting. A companion of the Celtic goddess Morrigan, the crow symbolized the creative power and spiritual strength found through the Crone aspect of the Goddess. The raven is similar.

DEER, HIND, DOE A messenger from the Otherworld, the appearance of the deer traditionally signaled a guide for adventures of mystical value. This creature also represented contact with spirit guides and the gods; abundance, dreams, intuition, and psychic powers.

DOG, HOUND Devotion, companionship, loyalty, willingness to follow through, alertness, and discovering hidden knowledge and the truth. Sacred to Underworld goddesses, dogs also represented our own subconscious judgment. Myth says that the Celtic god Nodens, a healer, could shapeshift into a dog. The Norse god Odin rode on his Wild Hunt with a pack of hounds, carrying out the wishes of the goddess Hel.

DOLPHIN, PORPOISE Intelligence, communication, friendships, eloquence, freedom, speed, prudence, change, balance, and harmony. Sacred to the Greek goddess Themis, this creature also symbolized active seedforms within the sea-womb of creation.

DOVE, PIGEON Often the symbol of a spiritual messenger between worlds, in the past this bird also represented peace and love, a meaning it still holds today. It was sacred to Aphrodite, Astarte, and Venus.

DRAGON This fabulous creature is a universal symbolic figure found in most cultures around the world, and has several, sometimes contradictory, meanings. The dragon represents cunning, knowledge, riches, protection, the ability to rise above and conquer obstacles, and instruction in spiritual matters.

DRAGONFLY Dreams, breaking down illusions, mystic messages of enlightenment, and seeing the truth in any situation.

EAGLE Wisdom, long life, taking advantage of opportunities, keen insight, strength, courage, seeing the overall pattern of life, connecting with powerful spiritual beings, and the ability to reach spiritual heights.

EEL Avoiding trouble.

ELEPHANT A sacred creature to the Hindus, the elephant represents the power of the libido, removal of obstacles and barriers, confidence, patience, tackling a new situation, strength, wisdom, and eternity.

FALCON Astral travel and healing.

FISH To many Mediterranean and Asian cultures, fish in general symbolized sexuality and fertility. They also represent the subconscious mind and divination

FOX The Greek god Dionysus was said to shapeshift into a fox on occasion; his Lydian priestesses wore fox skins and were called Bassarids. The fox denotes intelligence, cunning, wisdom, remaining unobserved, and avoiding trouble.

FROG Moving quickly, keeping a low profile, fertility, a new cycle of life, and initiation and transformation. The Egyptian frog goddess Hekat was connected with birth.

GOOSE New beginnings, inspiration, happiness in general, happy marriage, children, creativeness, and spiritual guidance in one's destiny.

GRIFFIN Great magick, power, facing the inner self, spiritual enlightenment, and understanding the relationship between psychic energy and cosmic force.

HARE, RABBIT Transformation, receiving hidden teachings and intuitive messages, quick thinking, divination, fertility, swiftness, and avoiding traps or dangerous situations. Hares and rabbits were sacred to lunar goddesses.

HAWK Keen insight into situations, being observant, omens and dreams, and recalling past lives. In Egypt, the hawk was thought to represent the soul. Sacred to the god Horus, the hawk symbolized the inner vehicle for transformation. The hawk was also an animal of Apollo.

HEDGEHOG Self-defense.

HERON Dignity, watching for opportunities, patience, and the generation of life.

HIPPOPOTAMUS Birth of new ideas, pregnancy, life, and strength. The Egyptian hippopotamus goddess Ta-Urt also represented righteous fury.

HORSE Associated in several cultures with death and the Underworld, the horse was frequently sacred to ocean deities. It was considered to be a vehicle for journeying to the Underworld, where one could contact spirits of the dead. It also symbolized freedom, friendships, stamina, faithfulness, and a journey.

HUMMINGBIRD Love and happiness.

IBIS A bird of the Egyptian god Thoth, the ibis was symbolic of magick, spells, writing, and recordkeeping.

LEOPARD, PANTHER Swiftness, cunning, strength, aggressiveness, and perseverance. These animals were sacred to the Greek god Dionysus.

LION, LIONESS The male lion represents relaxation, strengthening family ties, power, majesty, courage, energy, releasing tension and stress. The lioness symbolizes strong, protective mother love, the ability to care for one's self and family, and the strength to defeat aggressors. The lioness was sacred to such goddesses as Hathor, Sekhmet, and Cybele, while the lion belongs to such male deities as Apollo, Chrysocomes, the Arabic Shams-On, and Mithra.

LIZARD Escape from danger, dreams, mental creations, keeping a low profile, and asking for guidance in difficult situations.

LYNX Intelligence and long journeys.

MAGPIE Boldness.

MONKEY Ingenuity when dealing with problems.

MOUSE Being inconspicuous.

OCTOPUS Symbolizes the unfolding of the creative-destructive process.

OTTER Magick, friendship, joy of life, finding inner treasures or talents, gaining wisdom, and recovering from a crisis.

OWL To the ancient Egyptians, the owl symbolized death, night, and cold. However, to the Greeks, it represented wisdom, the moon, lunar mysteries, and initiations. This bird also symbolizes alertness, wisdom, magick, keen insight into obscure events, unmasking deceivers, dreams, shapeshifting, clairvoyance, and a messenger of hidden secrets. The owl was sacred to such goddesses as the Eye Goddess of the Mediterranean, Athena, Lilith, Minerva, Blodeuwedd, Anath, and Mari.

PEACOCK Dignity, self-confidence, watchfulness, and divine justice. It was sacred to the goddesses Hera and Sarasvati.

PEGASUS Poetic inspiration, astral travel, and changing evil into good. It was sacred to the Greek goddess Medusa and to the Muses.

PHOENIX Renewal, rebirth, and spiritual growth.

QUAIL Good luck and victory.

RACCOON Creativeness when faced with a new problem.

RAM, SHEEP Keeping your balance in upsetting situations, fertility, and new beginnings.

RAT Slyness and being able to move inconspicuously.

RAVEN This bird has long been considered a messenger from the spirit world and a guide to oracles and teachers of magick. Sacred to Celtic goddesses such as Rhiannon and Morrigan, the raven represents great magick, divination, eloquence, spiritual wisdom, prophecy, a change in consciousness, intelligence, and communicating with the Otherworld.

SALMON Great magick, journeys, endurance, and spiritual wisdom.

SCARAB BEETLE Vitality, new life, and learning about past lives.

SEAGULL Taking advantage of opportunities.

SEAL Guidance when facing a separation or divorce, protection from gossip.

SNAIL This creature, with its spiral-shaped shell, represents the action of the primordial spiral of energy upon matter.

SPHINX Initiation and the end of a cycle.

SPIDER Creativity, new life, beginning a new project, and becoming pregnant. As a weaver, the spider symbolizes the spiraling energy of primordial matter and the Divine Center in the web of illusion.

SQUIRREL Harmony with life, patience, endurance, changing with the times, preparing for the future, and moving to a higher level of consciousness.

STAG This horned creature represents the animal passions within each human.

STORK Sacred to the goddess Juno, the stork represents a messenger of new ideas and birth.

SWAN Dream interpretation, mystical knowledge, developing intuitive abilities, dignity, and following instincts. Sacred to such goddesses as Aphrodite, Venus, Sarasvati, and the Norse Valkyries, the swan also symbolizes a messenger from the Goddess and the satisfaction of a desire.

TIGER Power, energy, facing an unpleasant situation and doing something about it.

TURTLE, TORTOISE Keeping alert for danger; patience, perseverance, long life. In the Far East, the turtle symbolized the cosmos and seeds of unformed matter that would subsequently manifest.

UNICORN Purity of spirit, a link between the physical and spiritual realms, fame, prosperity, strength of mind, and developing personal power.

VULTURE Cycle of death and rebirth, spiritual counsel, destruction followed by rebirth, and prophecy. Sacred to the Egyptian goddesses Nekhbet and Mut.

WHALE Music, long life, family, friends, developing psychic and telepathic abilities, intuition and rebirth, and embracing the opposites of existence.

WOLF This animal represents cunning, intelligence, independence, avoiding trouble, and escaping pursuers, the ability to pass by danger invisibly, outwitting those who wish you harm, strength to fight when necessary, wisdom, dreams, intuition, transformation, strong protection, strength, and spiritual guidance. To the Egyptians and Romans, the wolf represented valor; the wolf-god Wepwawet was a companion of Isis and Osiris. Among the Norse, it symbolized the destructive powers of chaos; Odin had two great wolves by his side at all times. The wolf was sacred to the Roman Lupa or Feronia and was a symbolic animal of the Vestal Virgins.

WREN Divination, joy, and finding your niche in life.

Ritual Objects

Throughout human history, certain symbols and physical objects have been used in ritual and art to represent spiritual ideas. Many of these physical and artistic metaphors are still being used in modern religions and are powerful symbols for spiritual development. They often appear spontaneously in dreams and visions.

Any object becomes sacred when it is used consciously for the proper reasons on the altar. The following list suggests items you might wish to use. However, any object that has meaning for you is just as appropriate.

ANKH A life symbol of a cross with a loop on top, the ankh was used by the ancient Egyptians to represent eternal life and resurrection. The crook or crozier, also known as the Shepherd's Cross, is a similar symbol. The Egyptian god Osiris, in his role as Shepherd of Souls, carried a crook, as did the Greek Hermes. Use it to represent divine guidance and spiritual seeking.

ARROWS This emblem signifies divine intervention of both healing and killing power. To the Balkans god Perun, the arrow denoted lightning, long a symbol of illumination. A symbol of the god Apollo, the arrow also represents supreme power and the sun's fertile rays. Mars, Tyr, and Mithra were also associated with the arrow. Use the arrow to symbolize the direct path you plan to take.

BASKET A sign of fertility, passion, and birth, a basket of ivy in ancient Greece symbolized the Bacchanalian mysteries of Dionysus. In ancient Egyptian hieroglyphs, it represented the wholeness of divinity. Ceremonies to the Egyptian goddess Isis and the Greek Artemis featured sacred baskets. Place a basket on your altar to symbolize gathering what you need in life.

BOWL A symbol of the universal womb, the bowl represents both nurturing and giving. Use it to hold special stones or paper requests.

BOX With a lid, this is a female symbol connected with the subconscious mind and the unknown. A box without a lid represents life or gifts coming to you; it represents the universal womb. As with the basket and bowl, you can place in the box requests written on pieces of paper or jewelry that you wish to empower.

BREASTS Breasts symbolize the source of life power and life-giving fluids from the Great Mother. Some of the earliest sacred images were little models of two breasts with a stem that could be pushed into the ground, thus holding the image on an altar or personal hearth. Breasts represent everyday material needs being met.

BRIDGE Traditionally, the bridge is a link between heaven and earth, or between the subconscious and conscious minds. Bifrost was the astral bridge that spanned the heavens between Asgard and Midgard in Norse myth, while for the Israelites the bridge symbolized the

Covenant between God and His people. An image of a bridge can represent the bridging of differences, making a transition from one cycle of life to another, or moving to a higher plane of consciousness.

BRIDLE This is a symbol of control over the physical body and the emotional things that would motivate a person to react without clear thinking.

CADUCEUS Most people are familiar with the wand with two entwined serpents as the emblem of the Greek god Hermes and healing. However, this emblem existed long before the Greeks used it. The Sumerian goddess Inanna is shown holding the caduceus as she stands under the Tree of Life. The double-headed snake was one of the emblems of Ningishzide, a healer god who was one of Ishtar's lovers. The caduceus is also found on stone tablets in India, in paintings by Native Americans, and in Aztec art. To the Romans, it was a symbol of moral equilibrium, while to Buddhists it represents the axis of the world with the kundalini of the chakras entwined about it.

CANDLES Lighted candles symbolize personal spiritual enlightenment. When choosing a color, check the list on Colors and Elements for the meaning.

CAULDRON Long a holy object, the cauldron represents the belly-vessel of rebirth and transformation. It was associated with many goddesses, one of whom was the Celtic Cerridwen. Use a small cauldron to symbolize the churning, primordial matter from which you can draw energy to manifest your desires.

CAVE A womb symbol of the Goddess, the cave represents that which is concealed, something incubating, or the entrance to the subconscious mind.

CHALICE, CUP Similar to the cauldron, the chalice has several meanings. Its primary meaning is rebirth and illumination. However, a filled chalice represents the bounty of life coming to you from a higher power, while an empty chalice is the receptacle for offerings. To rid yourself of negative emotions and feelings, gently blow into an empty cup, mentally emptying yourself of your problems. Then, turn the cup upside down on the altar. This symbolizes your turning your problems over to a higher power to be solved and transformed.

CHILD The image of a child symbolizes the future with its potential as yet unrealized, the deeply hidden treasure in the mystic center of each human, or the beginning of a new cycle.

CIRCLE An ancient symbol, the circle represents the return from multiples to unity, from time to timelessness, from body-obsessed consciousness to the spiritually centered subconscious. Jung calls the circle the ultimate state of Oneness, for it has no beginning and no end. Engravings of circles and cups can be seen in Paleolithic caves and Neolithic graves. The Gnostics used a drawing of a snake with its tail in its mouth to represent the circle; this symbol was called the ouroboros and it represented the cycles of time, life, the universe, death, and rebirth.

The Native Americans made and still make circular medicine wheels. Permanent circles often marked holy places and sacred sites, such as Stonehenge and the Chinese Temple of Heaven.

To several ancient cultures, the black circle represented the sun god during his nightly passage through the Underworld. Sometimes, instead of the sun god, it symbolized his dark twin brother, a secret, very wise god who held knowledge about all worlds.

Modern Wiccans and magicians draw a circle about their ritual area to symbolize protection from negative astral forces and to represent moving beyond the material world's vibrations.

CLOVER OR TREFOIL Long before Christianity arose, the clover, or any three-leafed plant, was an emblem of the Triple Goddess; among Christians, it became the symbol of the Trinity. All trinity symbols date back to the time of the Goddess religions when they represented the Maiden, Mother, and Crone aspects of the Goddess. As far back as the civilization in the Indus Valley (c. 2500–1700 BCE), the trefoil emblem signified a triple deity.

COBWEB Associated with the Fate goddesses and weaving, the cobweb is the spiral shape of the creative matrix that leads inward to the center where matter is destroyed before being reformed. Minerva, Athena, and Spider Woman are associated with spiders and cobwebs.

COLUMN, TREE, LADDER, OBELISK Symbolic of the connection between heaven and earth, or gods and mortals, this emblem has been pictured as a ladder, column, World Tree, sacred mountain, obelisk of the sun god, or tent pole of the shamans. It is much the same symbol as the bridge. When in pairs, the columns signify the balancing of opposing forces.

CORNUCOPIA This horn of plenty, usually filled with fruits and vegetables, symbolizes strength, abundance, and prosperity.

CRESCENT The crescent is a lunar and Goddess symbol. It represents the world of changing forms that goes through a cycle to repeat itself endlessly.

CROMLECH Whether part of a circle or monolithic stones or standing alone, the cromlech stands for fertility, health, and spiritual enlightenment. A cromlech is an arrangement of stones, consisting of a cap stone on top of surrounding stones.

CROSS Now a Christian symbol, the cross is actually a very ancient symbol, meaning much the same as the column. However, the crosspiece of the emblem signifies the balance of the four elements. The cross was associated with the Phoenician goddess Astarte, the Greek deities Artemis and Aphrodite, and the Aztec goddess of rain.

CROWN In cultures as far apart as India and northern Europe, the crown symbolized the sacred marriage between the Goddess and Her consort. This emblems signifies light, achievement, success, and spiritual enlightenment.

CUBE The three-dimensional equivalent of the square, this symbol represents the material world of the four elements. It is also associated with stability. A box with a lid can be a cube into which you place your requests on slips of paper.

CURL, LOOP, ROPE As with the knot, this emblem means binding and unbinding, especially in a magickal or spiritual sense.

CURTAIN, VEIL The veil represents the ethereal door between the worlds of matter and spirit. Seven veils were associated with the goddesses Ishtar and Isis.

DICE These represent gambling with the Fates; taking chances.

DISK A sun emblem, the disk symbolizes matter in a state of transformation. Associated with the sun, the disk also signifies celestial perfection.

DOOR, GATE, PORTAL Any door signifies the entrance to the path leading to spirit, an initiation, or the opening of a new talent or way of life. In addition, the door represents the ability to pass from the earth to the astral plane, from one cycle of life to another, or to another level of spiritual knowledge. Similar to circles, doors also symbolize a separation of the physical and the sacred, signaling to the subconscious mind that a mindset transition must be made. The two-faced Roman god Janus, deity of the past and the future, ruled over doorways of all kinds. Altars were frequently placed near doors in ancient Greece, Rome, and Mexico.

DRUM This instrument symbolizes divine ecstasy in ritual. In Africa, the drum is associated with the heart, while other cultures that practice any form of shamanism believe it is a mediator between earth and heaven.

DWARF The personification of forces that remain outside the realm of consciousness, this figure represents the guardian of the threshold between the conscious and subconscious minds, and the guardian who protects us from being exposed to more than we can understand or assimilate.

EAR OF CORN Associated with many harvest deities, including Ceres and Demeter, an ear of corn represents the disintegration of life followed by rebirth. It also symbolizes the germination and growth of ideas. Maize or grains or corn represent prosperity and fertility.

EGG Eggs dyed red were an important part of early Goddess worship and ritual, especially in spring. In ancient Egypt, the hieroglyph of an egg represented the potential seed of rebirth. Several creation myths tell the story of the World Egg. This symbol signifies immortality and the potential for life renewal.

EYE Thousands of statues of the Eye Goddess have been excavated from third-millennium Sumer, where this aspect of the Goddess was very sacred. In Egypt, the eye was associated primarily with the god Horus. The eye is associated with intelligence, spiritual light, intuition, and truth that cannot be hidden. It also represents judgment by the Goddess.

FAN Femininity, intuition, and change. The fan is an emblem of the Chinese deity Chung-Li Chuan, one of the Eight Chinese immortals.

FEATHER, PLUME In Egypt, the feather of truth was associated with the goddess Maat. It represents faith, contemplation, and reincarnating souls. Many goddesses, including Juno, were associated with feathers, which represent change.

FLOWER Flowers are usually connected with spring and rebirth or renewal. For a more complete explanation of flowers, read the Flowers chart on page 58.

FOUNTAIN The main portion of the fountain is associated in a minor way with the World Tree, while the flowing water represents the life force within all things. The fountain symbolizes blessings, wisdom, purification, renewal, and comfort arising from the Divine Center.

GEODE A womb symbol similar to the cave.

GLOBE, SPHERE Representing the world soul and the human soul, the globe or sphere symbolizes wholeness. If it is depicted with wings, it represents spiritual evolution.

GOBLET The same as the chalice and cauldron.

GRAIN, WHEAT, CORN This emblem represents life and the sustaining of it, and the harvest.

GRAPES Associated with such gods as Dionysus, grapes represent fertility and sacrifice.

HAND Handprints are among the first symbols found in ancient, sacred Paleolithic caves. There, red marks of individual hands are found among wavy lines for water and crescent-shaped horns of fertility. In the shrines of matriarchal Catal Huyuk in seventh-millennium Anatolia, handprints, along with butterflies, bees, and the heads of bulls, decorate the walls. In Catal Huyuk, the hand probably represented the hand of the Goddess and action or manifestation, while in ancient Egypt, when combined with an eye, it signified clairvoyant action. In present Islamic cultures, the hand is still sacred and symbolizes protection, power, and strength.

HARP Similar to the World Tree or mystic ladder, the harp is another symbol of the bridge between heaven and earth.

HEART The ancient Egyptians believed that thoughts and morals arose from the heart, the center of physical life and a symbol of eternity. Thus, this symbol represents moral judgment, and pure, true love.

HEXAGRAM OR SIX-POINTED STAR The six-pointed star is comprised of two overlapping triangles oriented in opposite directions, and is found around the world. It is known as the Seal of Solomon, David's Shield, or the Star of David (in Judaism). The hexagram represents the combination of male and female.

HONEY To the Greek Orphists, honey was a symbol of wisdom. In India, it symbolizes the higher self.

HORNS Originally a fertility and lunar symbol, to early cultures horns also represented strength, power, and prosperity. The Egyptian hieroglyph of the horn signified elevation, prestige, and glory. The word *horned* may be derived form the Assyro-Babylonian *garnu* of the Phoenician words *geren*, *garnuim*, or *kerenos*. The horned Apollo Karnaios resembles the horned Celtic god Cernunnos.

HORSESHOE Originally a symbol of the Goddess, the horseshoe represents the ending of one cycle and the beginning of another.

HOURGLASS This emblem symbolizes the cycle and connection between the upper (spiritual) and lower (physical) worlds, creation and destruction.

JAR, URN Long a sacred object in many cultures, a pot or jar represents the universal womb of the Goddess and the Oneness that proceeds from the Great Mother. It symbolizes the potential for transforming anything placed inside it. In China, the jar represents good luck. Isis was frequently portrayed with a jar about her neck, just as the Hindu goddess Kali was shown with pots and jars.

Many sacred ceremonies involved the use of water jars to signify the presence of the deities. These ceremonies included the Osirian Mysteries of Egypt, the Babylonian rites of the god Nabu, the Cabirian Mysteries for Demeter and Cabirius, and the Greek festival of Anthesteria for Dionysus.

KEYS The symbol is associated with many deities from a variety of cultures. Hecate and Persephone held the keys to the Underworld and the universe. Athena was said to control the key to the city of Athens. The Babylonian god Marduk is said to have made the keys to heaven and hell that only Ishtar could use. In Rome, women in labor were given keys to hold for an easy childbirth. The Egyptian god Serapis was believed to have the keys to both the earth and the sea. Ancient spiritual mysteries speak of keys as the symbol of knowledge, a task to be performed, or a successful question or spiritual journey. Keys are still used as a symbol of warding off evil spirits, and represent the means of solving a mystery or performing a task. They are also symbols of locking and unlocking, or binding and loosening.

KNIFE While the sword symbolizes spiritual heights, the knife represents vengeance, death, and sacrifice; it also alludes to the means to end a cycle.

KNOT The knot has two meanings: unity, stopping progress, or binding up energies when it is tied, but also releasing energy when untied. It is closely associated with weaving and the woven web of life. This symbol, with its weaving connotations, was connected with the Greek Fate goddesses and the Norse Norns.

In ancient Egypt, Isis was said to loosen or bind the knot of life, while Hathor wore a *menat*, the knotted headband or necklace. All the Egyptian holy mysteries were called "she-knots." The knot can be found in the Egyptian circle of eternity, the loop of the ankh, and the cartouche that circles the name of a pharaoh. Priestesses of the Goddess in Crete wore a knot of hair at the back of their heads and hung a knot of cloth at the entrance to the shrines.

In Rome, it was forbidden for anyone to wear anything knotted or tied within the precinct of Juno, who was the goddess of childbirth; knots were thought to cause a difficult birth. Muslims will not wear knots when they take their pilgrimage to Mecca. According to rabbinical law, Jews are not to tie knots on the Sabbath. One of the Chinese emblems of good luck is the Buddhist "endless knot" of longevity. Among the Celts, the knot was a protective device to trap negative or evil energies.

Tie knots in strings or yarn to bind up negative energy. Or use intricate drawings of knotwork to release energy when it is needed.

LABYRINTH The labyrinth takes its name from the ancient Minoan labrys, or double ax. However, the idea and use of the labyrinth in drawings goes back much further than Crete. Such designs are found on the walls of Paleolithic caves, where the ritual participants had to crawl through narrow openings and traverse narrow passageways to reach the sacred center of the cave itself. This symbol represents the spiritual path leading back to the Divine Center, regeneration through the Goddess by the process of initiative rebirth. Focus on a drawing of a labyrinth while tracing the path with your finger. This will draw you toward the spiritual center of your being.

LABRYS, DOUBLE AX A Goddess and moon symbol widely used in Minoan Crete, the labrys was sacred as a ritual tool. It was also a sacred image of the Amazons, who used it both in battle and as a ritual tool. It symbolizes the renewing of the life cycle and the soul through sacrifice, or death and regeneration.

LAMP This emblem symbolizes spiritual intelligence and enlightenment. The Hermit of the tarot cards is shown holding a lamp or lantern, denoting his offering of guidance and higher instruction. Deities associated with the lamp were Juno Lucina and Diana Lucifera.

LEAF To the Chinese, the leaf means happiness.

MASK In ancient times, the mask was worn during Mystery rituals to signify the spiritual metamorphosis conferred by the rite itself. This emblem represents secrecy, hidden meanings, and shapeshifting.

MIRROR A Goddess and moon symbol whose meanings include revealing the truth, intuition, and the psychic realm, and the imagination. Mirrors were also known as soul-catchers or soul-carriers; Celtic women were buried with their mirrors that they believed carried their souls.

MOON Originally a symbol of many goddesses and a few gods, the moon later came to symbolize the rhythm of life and the universe, the passage of time, and the power of rebirth. The moon represents creation, ripeness, cycles of life, spiritual disciplines, and initiations.

NECKLACE At one time a sexual symbol of the completeness of the Goddess, the threaded, beaded necklace later came to mean the unity of diversity, or the continuity of the past lives of a human. The goddesses Freyja and Ishtar wore special necklaces.

NEST This symbol represents the foundation or beginning of a life, event, or path.

OAR This mundane object represents action, controlling the direction life is taking, and stability within an unstable situation.

OBELISK Primarily a symbol of ancient Egypt, the obelisk was an emblem of the sun god and considered to be a solidified ray of the sun. Physically, it was a slender, four-sided, tapering column that could be hundreds of feet high. Obelisks frequently stood beside the doors of temples. The door to the temple of the goddess Astarte at Byblos was flanked by a pair of obelisks.

PALACE, CASTLE This emblem represents the sacred place within, or the Divine Center.

PAPYRI, BOOK Whether a rolled scroll or a bound book, the symbol means knowledge and an unfolding of the Akashic Records. These Records are a spiritual compilation of all the lives of every person.

PEACH To the Asians, the peach symbolizes immortality.

PEARL Considered one of the eight Chinese emblems, the pearl signifies the sacred center. To Muslims, it represents heaven or paradise.

PENTACLE, PENTAGRAM A pentacle is a five-pointed star, once the symbol of all things feminine and the great Earth Mother. In Egyptian hieroglyphs, it means to "rise up" or "cause to arise," and it was associated with both Isis and Nephthys. The pentacle was also a symbol of the Babylonian Ishtar and the Celtic Morrigan. To the Gnostics, it represented the sacred number five, while for Pythagoreans it meant harmony of the body and mind. The five-pointed star was also associated with the Virgin Mary in her aspect of Stella

Maris (Star of the Sea). This symbol represents the repulsion of evil, or protection.

PINECONE A product of the pine tree, which symbolizes immortality, the cone represents psychic oneness. It was one of the symbols of both Astarte in ancient Byblos and the sacrificed savior Attis. The sacred wand of Dionysus, called the *thyrsus*, was tipped with a pinecone, as was that of the Roman Bacchus.

PLAIT, BRAID Long associated with rope and knots, the braid represents the intertwining of relationships or creative matter.

POMEGRANATE The Greek Underworld goddess Persephone was linked with the pomegranate, thus giving it the meaning of the dead lying in sleep before rebirth. Deities associated with this fruit were Persephone, Dionysus, Adonis, Attis, and the Crone aspect of the Goddess.

PUMPKIN An emblem of Li Tieh-Kuai, one of the Chinese Immortals, the pumpkin represents a link between two worlds. It can also mean an upheaval in the usual order.

PYRAMID Similar in meaning to the triangle, the pyramid is actually a hollow mountain. It symbolizes rebirth, regeneration, and creation.

RAINBOW Similar to the bridge, ladder, and obelisk, the rainbow represents the connection between earth and the sky, or the mundane world and the sacred. The Greek goddess Iris carried messages from the gods to humans on this celestial bridge. In the Middle East, the rainbow symbolized the veils of Ishtar and, in the Far East, the illusive veils of Maya. Among the Pueblo and Navajo Indians, the rainbow was known as the road of the spirits and gods.

RING Similar to the circle, the ring represents continuity and wholeness. When associated with the Fates, it symbolizes the eternally repeated cycle of time.

SCALES First seen in Chaldean carvings, the scales symbolize justice, cause and effect, the divine assessment of a life. Deities associated with this emblem were Maat and Astraea.

SCEPTER Related to the magick wand, the thunderbolt, the phallus, and Thor's hammer, the scepter represents fertility, purification, and the ability and willpower to make changes.

SCISSORS A symbol of both life and death, scissors were associated with the Fates and other deities who ruled over the length of life.

SCYTHE Connected with the god Saturn and with the moon, the scythe represents reaping the harvest, or the harvest when the life-path is finished.

SHEAF, BUNDLE Related to knots, the sheaf symbolizes unification and strength, but also limitation because of the binding.

SHELL To Chinese Buddhists, the shell is one of the eight emblems of good luck. It is related to the moon, the sea, and all sea deities. The spiral form of the shell represents the life force moving toward the sacred center.

SHIELD Protection, identity.

SHIP The journey through physical life, or the inner, spiritual journey.

SIEVE Sorting out, purifying, discarding the useless.

SPIRAL Connected with both the snake and the labyrinth, the spiral is an ancient sacred symbol. Spirals appear on Paleolithic sacred sites and objects, and represent the awesome powers of death and rebirth, a process Pagans and Zirceans believe is held only by the Goddess. The spiral signifies the unfolding of potent, creative energy.

SQUARE Symbolic of the four elements, the square represents order and direction. It is considered to be of feminine nature with strong connections to the earth. Egyptian hieroglyphs used the square to mean achievement. Carl Jung believed this symbol signified the unachieved state of inner unity. The square represents definition, stability, and firmness.

STAFF Support, authority.

STAR To many cultures, the star signified the dead; in Judaism it is believed that each star has a guardian angel. The Aztecs said that stars were the regenerated spirits of fallen or sacrificed warriors. The star symbolizes spirit shining in the darkness of the labyrinth and a beacon to guide the pilgrim on the journey through the subconscious.

SWASTIKA Although not likely to appeal to most people today, this symbol had a long history of deep, spiritual meaning before it was perverted by the Nazis. The name actually comes from the Sanskrit words su, "good," and asti, "being." Connected with both the sun and the moon, it signifies movement and regenerative power.

SWORD Strength, defense.

THUNDERBOLTS Celestial fire, illumination, chance, destiny, associated with Zeus, Jupiter, Shiva, Pyerun, and Thor.

TOWER Rising above the physical, ascent of the spirit.

TRIANGLE This was an early symbol of the feminine principle. In Paleolithic times, skulls were often buried under triangular rocks, representing the Goddess's power of rebirth. For the Pythagoreans, the Greek letter delta (a triangle) symbolized cosmic birth. The triangle was associated with the Hindu goddess Durga, the Celtic Triple Goddess, the Greek Moerae, the Nordic Norns, and the triple Roman Fortunae. The triangle symbolizes body, mind, and spirit, and therefore represents the Triple Goddess.

TRUMPET Fame and glory; warning; elements of Fire and Air.

VASE An ancient symbol of repose, life, and fertility, vases with breasts have been dated back to the sixth millennium BCE. During rituals, these breast-vases were filled with a liquid that was sprinkled through the nipples onto the offering and worshippers. The Chinese goddess Kuan Yin often holds a vase in one hand.

WATER Primal matter, universal possibilities.

WHEEL The wheel differs from the circle in that it has spokes that divide it. To the Romans, the wheel was an emblem of the goddess Fortuna, who ruled the fate or changing fortunes of humans. The wheel of the Hindu goddess Kali is the wheel of karma. The Buddhists call the wheel the Holy Wheel of Life, while the Celts used an eight-spoked wheel to represent their sacred year with its eight sacred festivals. Today, the wheel is commonly seen as one of the Major Arcana cards in tarot decks, where it represents the changing cycles of fortune. Frequently, the wheel is a solar symbol and connected with sun gods. It signifies spiritual advancement or regression, and the progression of karma, which is payment of good and evil done in a life.

WINGS In many ancient carvings and drawings, wings denoted the divine and were added to figures of deities or sacred objects. Wings represent ideas, thoughts, spirituality, imagination, mobility, and enlightenment.

YIN/YANG SYMBOL This Asian symbol is a circle divided into half-white and half-black by a curving S. It represents perfect balance.

Colors and Elements

Most world cultures recognized the elements of Earth, Air, Fire, and Water, and used their colors and powers in magickal and spiritual practices. These elements were usually connected with the cardinal directions—north, east, south, and west. The elements are forces and energies that make up the universe and everything in it. They also influence human personalities and are employed in the practice of magick. When used singularly, the proper elemental color is placed in the appropriate direction. When used all together, the elemental colors are arranged in the appropriate directions at the edge of a sacred circle.

The Celts, particularly those in Scotland, used red in the east for the rising sun, white in the south for noon, gray in the west for twilight, and black in the north for midnight. In Scotland, they were called the Four Airts or Airs and were based on the prevailing winds in Britain. The Scottish Gaelic words for the cardinal directions were *aiet*, east; *deas*, south; *iar*, west; and *tuath*, north. The Druids said that the center was ruled by *nyu*, or spirit. In later Western cultures the correspondences became Air, yellow, east; Fire, red, south; Water, blue, west; Earth, dark green or black, north; and Spirit, white, center.

In this tradition, the east represents knowledge, harmony, the intellect and ideas, freedom, revealing the truth, finding lost things, travel, and psychic abilities. The south signifies change, perception, spiritual illumination, cleansing, sexuality, energy, authority, healing, and purification. The west is associated with the emotions, healing, plants, communion with the spiritual realm, purification, the subconscious mind, love, friendships, marriage, fertility, happiness, dreams, and the psychic on an emotional level. The north represents endurance, responsibility, stability, thoroughness, and purpose in life. The center represents enlightenment, finding your life path, spiritual knowledge, and seeing and understanding karmic paths in life.

In other cultures, both placement and choice of color differed. The Hindus used what are called *tattwas* symbols to represent the elements. A yellow square represented north and Earth; a silver crescent, west and Water; a blue circle, east and Air; a red triangle, south and Fire; and a black or indigo ovoid, the center and Spirit.

In the Western Hemisphere, the native peoples had many differing traditions about colors. The ancient Mayas, for example, used red in the east, yellow in the south, black in the west, and white in the north. Other ancient Mexican cultures had a different classification—green and Water in the east, blue and Air in the south, yellow and Earth in the west, and red and Fire in the north, and many colors together in the center.

The Native American tribes further north had still different groupings of color. The Navajos used white in the east, blue in the south, yellow in the west, and black in the north, while the Zuni had yellow in the east, red in the south, blue in the west, white in the north, and all colors in the center. However, the Cheyenne of the Plains believed that red was in the east, yellow in the south, white or blue in the west, and black in the north. Other Plains tribes used yellow in the east with the totem animal eagle; red in the south with mouse; black in the west with bear; and white in the north with buffalo.

Traditional Colors

Colors, separate from the elements, have also played an important part in the religion and magick of many cultures. Today, color is primarily used in candle burning and for the cloth that is sometimes spread over the altar or shelf.

BLACK This color absorbs and removes anything negative. It is used for reversing or binding negative forces, releasing, breaking up blockages, and unsticking stagnant situations. Black is also used to create confusion and discord among your enemies or repel dark magick and negative thought forms. According to Marija Gimbutas, Neolithic cultures thought black to be the color of fertility. One of the most powerful colors available, black represents protection, mystery, and the ability to become "invisible." However, be careful how you use it. If you use black for selfish, evil purposes, the energy can backlash upon you.

BLUE To the Navajo, blue is the fertile, nurturing power of the earth, while in Tibetan Buddhism, it represents both emptiness and potential. The hue of this color plays an important part in its use. Light blue is for truth, inspiration, wisdom, protection, healing, understanding, good health, happiness, inner peace, fidelity, patience, harmony, and contacting the Higher Self. Royal blue is for loyalty, group success, occult knowledge, and expansion.

BROWN This color can be used to attract money, establish financial success, and influence Earth elementals. It is also used for balance, concentration, ESP, intuition, study, to fulfill basic material needs, to ground and center, and communication with nature spirits. To some cultures, brown represents the cycle of life, running from the brown earth in the spring to the withered vegetation in the autumn. To the ancient Romans, the color symbolized humility.

GOLD OR CLEAR LIGHT YELLOW Gold helps with good fortune, intuition, understanding, divination, fast luck (if circumstances are out of your control), and contacting higher influences. It is also useful for happiness, healing, money, and gaining knowledge. This color is primarily associated with male deity powers.

GRAY A neutral color, it symbolizes the art of meditation and the state of existence just before rebirth.

GREEN This color can bring a fresh outlook on life or can balance an unstable situation. It also aids with abundance, fertility, good fortune, generosity, material gain, wealth, success, renewal, marriage, balance, healing, and communication with nature spirits. In ancient Egypt, this color represented both life and death, and was associated with the god Osiris. To the Romans, green belonged to the goddess Venus and love; for many centuries, brides wore green.

INDIGO This shade is a Saturn color of a purplish blue that is almost black. Use it for meditation, balancing out karma, and neutralizing another's magick. It is also useful to stop gossip, lies, and undesirable competition.

MAGENTA This is a very dark but clear red with a deep purple tint to a dark cranberry color. It can be very difficult to find. This color has a very high vibrational frequency that makes things happen fast. It is best to burn a magenta candle together with other colors. Burned alone, it is for quick changes, spiritual healing, and exorcism.

ORANGE A powerful color, use orange only if you are prepared to face major changes. It is good for adaptability, encouragement, stimulation, attraction, sudden changes, prosperity, creativity, enthusiasm, success, energy and stamina, and mental agility. It also discourages laziness, helps to gain control, draws good things, and changes luck.

PINK This color represents the purest form of true love and friendship. It is helpful with affection, romance, spiritual awakening, healing, honor, and family love. It helps to banish hatred, depression, and negativity.

PURPLE OR VIOLET Use this color with caution, for purple is very powerful and the energies are difficult to handle. It aids with success, idealism, higher psychic ability, wisdom, progress, deliberate action, protection, spirit contact, breaking bad luck, driving away evil, divination, great magickal knowledge, removing jinxes and hexes, success in court cases, business success, and influencing people who have power over you. This color has long been associated with priests and priestesses.

RED Use red for energy, strength, sexual potency, physical desire, passionate love, courage, willpower, good health, and to protect against psychic attack. Considered to be a sacred color all over the world, for millennia, red was associated with life, the womb, birth, and blood. Only with the rise of patriarchal cultures did red become a symbol of combat and the gods of war. To the Hindus, red belongs to the goddess Lakshmi, deity of good luck and prosperity.

SILVER OR CLEAR LIGHT GRAY Silver is associated with victory and stability, helps with meditation, developing psychic abilities, and neutralizing any situation, removes negative powers, and repells destructive forces. It is primarily associated with female deity powers.

WHITE A highly balanced spiritual color, white helps with spirituality and greater attainments in life, purity, truth, sincerity, wholeness, power of a higher nature, contacting spirit helpers, balancing the aura, confusing enemies, helping with pregnancy and birth, raising the vibrations, and destroying negative energies. Through the Neolithic period, white was considered the color of death and clean-picked bones. In Asia, white is still the color of mourning. However, in the West, by the time of the Greek states, white had become associated with purity and innocence. In ancient Egypt, white was one of the colors of the cycle of life, along with black, red, and green. The Druids wore white robes, representing their spiritual connection with the Otherworld. Thus, this color also symbolizes initiation, spiritual light, and mystical knowledge. Whenever in doubt about a candle color, use white.

YELLOW This brilliant color helps with intellect, imagination, power of the mind, creativity, confidence, gentle persuasion, attraction, concentration, inspiration, mental clarity, knowledge, commerce, medicine, and healing. To several Native American tribes, yellow represents reproduction and growth. However, Buddhism uses this color for robes to symbolize renunciation of worldly matters.

Asian Colors

The Chinese have five elements—Wood, Fire, Earth, Metal, and Water. Their interpretation of color meanings is also different from those in the West. They placed green in the east for spring and the elements of Wood; red in the south for Fire and summer; white in the west for Metal and autumn; black in the north for Water and winter; and yellow in the center for Earth.

With *feng shui* (the art of placement) such a popular practice, you might be interested in utilizing Asian colors for your altars.

BLACK Deception, dishonesty, slander, penance, and evil influences. The color of the element of Water, winter, and the north. Use with great caution when combining it with red. Deception, penance.

BLUE Self-cultivation, consideration, and thoughtfulness.

GOLD One of the colors of the element of Metal, autumn, and the west. A very fortunate color, said to attract success, wealth, strength, and a good reputation.

GRAY Travel and helpful people.

GREEN The color of the element of Wood, spring, and the east. Rebirth, new growth, family, harmony, health, peace, posterity, and longevity.

PINK Marriage.

PURPLE OR VIOLET Truth and spiritual growth. It is a visionary color.

RED The color of the element of Fire, summer, and the south. Happiness, good fortune, a long and stable marriage, prosperity, and spiritual blessings. A revitalizing color, red is excellent for those who lack energy.

WHITE One of the colors of the element of Metal, autumn, and the west. Children, helpful people, marriage, mourning, peace, purity, and travel.

YELLOW The color of the element of Earth and the center. Blessings, developing the intuition, great wisdom, and ambition. Some sources say this color is used to remember the dead and guard against evil.

Stones

Gemstones and minerals have been used by most world cultures for centuries for their healing and magickal properties. They were employed in ritual worship and worn as talismans. Talismans are actually a form of portable altar that we carry with us. The following list by no means describes all the known and used stones. Also see stones listed by color (page 124) and by magickal powers (pages 125–133).

AGATE Strength and courage. It also balances energies. Blue Lace Agate can remove blockages from the nervous system and promote calmness. Moss Agate is an opener for the crown and brow chakras, thus connecting the physical with the spiritual. It can also protect the aura, cleanse the environment, and help one to balance logic with intuition. It can be used to attract enlightenment and luck, while helping to open psychic abilities and facilitate contact with spiritual guides. Brown Agate helps one to become grounded when one's energies and emotions are flying everywhere. Orange and Brown Agate also aids in grounding and stabilizing.

AMBER This fossilized resin has a wide range of magickal uses. By helping to stabilize brainwave patterns, it can change negativity to positivity, both in thoughts and surrounding vibrations. It also calms, protects, repels psychic attack, gently revitalizes, and aids in releasing karmic problems and influences.

AMETHYST A major stabilizing and grounding stone, it balances the aura and cleanses it. It also improves meditation and breaks negative patterns. On the spiritual level, amethyst aids in developing psychic abilities and helps to open spiritual dimensions.

BLOODSTONE Although not a stone of great beauty, bloodstone brings renewal and harmony, and enhances talents and creativity. It is also valuable when attempting to contact deceased ancestors.

CARNELIAN This reddish orange stone raises the mood, aids in seeing into the past, grounds, and protects. It is also helpful in stabilizing the energy in an atmosphere and repelling psychic attacks or ghosts.

CHRYSOCOLLA Comparable to lapis lazuli, this stone can sooth grief, ease tension and heartache, given inner strength, and balance the emotions.

CHRYSOPRASE Green in color, this stone can balance the attitudes, heal heartache and old traumas, and help one to accept one's self.

FLUORITE The green-colored stone helps with concentration, gives the ability to see through illusions, and calms the nervous system. The purple-colored fluorite aids in psychic development, grounds, calms, and protects.

GARNET Red garnet draws earth energy. It can attract a compatible mate, protect against negatives, give courage, and regenerate.

HEMATITE This gray-black stone is useful for grounding, calming, reducing stress, and dispelling negativity.

LAPIS LAZULI Known and used for centuries, this stone has many uses. It can be used to gain wisdom in understanding spiritual mysteries, bring success in relationships, protect from psychic attack, release past pain, and raise the mood.

MALACHITE A green stone, it helps to change situations, release negative experiences, inspire hope, create an unobstructed path to goals, and prevent attack by negative vibrations. It also connects the physical plane to the spiritual.

OBSIDIAN Black obsidian is very useful in grounding, calming, protecting, shielding from negative thoughtforms, and collecting scattered energy. It can also aid in making psychic contact and dealing with past lives.

ONYX Black onyx will absorb negativity, protect, reduce stress, banish grief, enhance self-control, and draw good fortune.

PYRITE This glittering, gold-colored stone aids the memory and intellect, protects from all negativity, and grounds the energies.

QUARTZ CRYSTAL A very powerful, all-healing, transpersonal stone, clear quartz cleanses the atmosphere, helps with clear thinking, aids in contacting spirit guides, enhances psychic abilities, energizes, harmonizes, and dispels negativity.

ROSE QUARTZ A pink stone connected with the heart and love, it balances, relieves depression, and rejuvenates. It is also helpful for acceptance, forgiveness, learning self-love, healing emotional pain, and attaining inner peace.

TIGER'S EYE This stone, with its golden brown color, aids in recognizing karmic ties, manifesting ideas into reality, protecting, balancing, and stimulating wealth.

TOURMALINE All colors of tourmaline can inspire, balance the energies, and clear the aura. Green tourmaline, also called verdelite, transforms negative energy into positive, draws prosperity and creativity, calms fears, attracts love, and dispels fear. Watermelon tourmaline helps to heal past emotional scars, stabilizes, attracts love, and protects.

TURQUOISE A powerful stone and master healer, it protects, calms, draws prosperity and good luck, absorbs negativity, and increases psychic abilities.

Trees

Using the wood, leaves, and fruit products from certain trees can also enhance your altar energies. Most trees were sacred to specific deities in one culture or another. Even today, these trees are valued for their scents, their energy patterns, and their magickal qualities. Acorns and pinecones can be used to decorate the altar during certain seasons of the year, as well as for specific purposes. Clusters of leaves make eye-pleasing bouquets, particularly in the autumn, with their variety of colors and textures. Wood can be made into wands or purchased in the form of boxes or other objects.

APPLE In Greek legend, Gaea, the Earth Mother, gave an apple and its tree to the goddess Hera as a wedding gift. When an apple is cut crosswise, a five-pointed star, symbol of many goddesses, is seen inside. This fruit symbolized immortality to the Norse and the Greeks, and earthly desires to the Christians. It represents beauty, goodness, renewal, death, and rebirth. Use it to represent the ending of one cycle of life and the beginning of another.

ASH This tree has been considered sacred by several ancient cultures. Among the Norse, it is associated with Yggdrasil, the World Tree, which had its roots in the well of wisdom. The Irish Druids fashioned the wood into wands and spear shafts, while in Greece it was considered a tree of the god Poseidon. It symbolizes grandeur and prudence.

BAY In ancient Greece, the bay tree was sacred to Apollo and often made into crowns or wreaths as rewards. It was believed to ward off evil spirits and protect property. Bay twigs with leaves were used by Roman priests to sprinkle holy water.

BIRCH This tree has always been associated with the Goddess. It is a symbol of the returning summer. Sprigs of birch were worn on the Summer Solstice and other ancient holidays.

CEDAR A symbol of immortality and sacred to Osiris, the evergreen cedar was used for coffins in ancient Egypt. The Romans fashioned statures of cedar, and many Native American tribes use it in purifying smudges. To help ground yourself, place the palms of your hands against the ends of cedar needles.

CHERRY The cherry tree was particularly sacred to Far Eastern cultures, where it was a symbol of immortality. The Chinese goddess Hsi-Wang Mu guarded the celestial cherries that only ripened every one thousand years. Doorway guardians, who warded off evil spirits, were carved of cherry wood. In Japan, Kono-Hana-Sakuya-Hime was goddess of the cherry tree.

CYPRESS To the Greeks, cypress was sacred to the Underworld deities such as Persephone; they also associated it with Cronus, Apollo, the healer Asclepius, Cybele, Aphrodite, Artemis, Hera, Athena, and the Fates. The cypress symbolizes death and returning to the abyss of regeneration; the Greeks buried their dead heroes in cypress coffins, and the Egyptians also fashioned cypress into mummy cases. A variety of cypress in Japan, called *hinoki,* is used for Shinto ritual fires.

ELDER Sacred among the Celts, this tree was associated with the White Goddess and the Summer Solstice. Wands of elder wood can drive out negativity and evil spirits.

ELM This tree symbolizes dignity.

FIG Called the "fruit of heaven," the fig tree has been sacred throughout the Middle East as a symbol of life and plenty. It was sacred to the Roman goddess Juno.

FIR Burning the needles of this evergreen tree will cleanse the atmosphere and bless your entire house.

HAWTHORN This tree has long been associated with fairies and Otherworld beings. It is considered unlucky to bring the flowers into the house except on May 1. It symbolizes hope.

HAZEL The Druids taught that this tree symbolized wisdom, knowledge, poetry, fire, beauty, and fertility. They ate its nuts to gain inspiration and eloquence.

HOLLY Considered a lucky tree, holly is said to ward off evil spirits. The ancient Persian followers of Zoroaster made an infusion of holly leaves and berries for their religious rituals. The Druids believed it to be sacred as a plant symbolizing death and regeneration, while the Norse thought it sacred to the Underworld goddess Hel, who ruled over the dead. In both the Celtic and Norse cultures, holly was used in celebrations of Winter Solstice and hung in the homes of common people as protection against evil spirits. Holly was also given as a friendship gift during the Roman Saturnalia in December.

JUNIPER This was a sacred tree to the Celtic Druids, who burned juniper berries and thyme as an incense. It symbolizes protection.

MISTLETOE This parasitic plant, which grows primarily on oaks, has been held as sacred throughout ancient European cultures. It was considered a tree by the Druids, who cut it with great ceremony by using a golden sickle. Both the Greeks and Romans connected it with the Underworld. Its power of death followed by rebirth is shown in the Norse myth when the god Baldur was slain by an arrow of mistletoe and was subsequently reborn. Take care using the plant, as the berries are poisonous to both animals and humans. Nevertheless, mistletoe symbolizes the sweetness of kisses and affection.

OAK Considered the most sacred of all trees in Europe and the Mediterranean, the Greeks said it was the first tree with roots that ran down into the Underworld. Because of its magickal qualities of strength, long life, endurance, and immortality, oak groves in the oracular shrine of Dodona were sacred to Zeus and to prophecy. The Roman goddess Diana had a shrine in a great forest at Nemi, where a perpetual fire of oak wood was kept burning; her priest, called King of the Wood, ruled there. The Celts worshipped in oak groves and used acorns in their prophesying. Oak was sacred to the Norse god Thor because lightning, caused by his mighty hammer, frequently struck oak trees. Oak was also sacred to Cybele, Jupiter, and Herne the Hunter. As late as the nineteenth century in England, Christians often gathered under "Gospel Oaks" to hold their meetings. This tree symbolizes courage and hospitality.

ORANGE An emblem of fertility in China, it was the custom to give twelve oranges as gifts on the New Year. This conveyed wishing the recipient happiness and prosperity.

PALM In Egypt, palm fronds were frequently laid on coffins or offered to the goddess Hathor. Among the Greeks and Romans, the palm frond was a symbol of victory. Nike, the Greek goddess of victory, was often portrayed holding a palm branch, and the palm was also sacred to Astarte, Isis, and Aphrodite. The Greek word for palm is the same as that for "phoenix," which ties this tree to the Underworld, death, and rebirth. Carvings from ancient Babylon show the palm tree as the Tree of Life.

PEACH In many Eastern cultures the peach symbolized long life and immortality. At one time, Chinese children wore peach pits as amulets, and peach boughs were hung over doorways for protection.

PEAR Pear wood was often used to carve goddess statues in the early Mediterranean cultures. The pear was sacred to the Greek goddesses

Hera and Aphrodite, and to the Roman goddess of vegetation, Pomona. In China, the pear represented longevity.

PINE TREE The pine has religious significance in several Mediterranean and Far Eastern cultures because of its connection with immortality, rebirth, and fertility. It represents the life force in Japan and China. Japanese Shinto shrines and ritual tools are made from pine. In the Mediterranean region, during ancient ceremonies honoring the goddess Cybele, this tree represented the body of her consort Attis, who was annually slain and then reborn. Among the Greeks, Etruscans, and Romans, the pinecone was a symbol of fertility and abundance. This tree was also sacred to Artemis, Aphrodite, and Dionysus, who held a pinecone-tipped wand. Burn pine needles to cleanse and purify your home.

POMEGRANATE This fruit was considered sacred to many Mediterranean and Middle Eastern goddesses, such as Astarte, Demeter, Aphrodite, Hera, and Persephone. Because its many seeds represented fertility, the womb, and rebirth, it was used in the Greek Eleusinian Mysteries.

POPLAR A tree of the Earth Goddess and Persephone of the Underworld, poplar was said to have regenerative qualities. Myth says that this tree grew at the entrance to Calypso's cave and that Hercules wore a wreath of its leaves when he traveled into the Underworld. It symbolizes courage.

ROWAN This tree is also known as American Ash in the Western Hemisphere. A tree of the Goddess, rowan is thought to bless the property on which it grows.

SPRUCE The Navajo Indians of North America made brushes and wands of spruce for use in their sacred rituals.

WILLOW This tree was connected with the moon and water, and had the qualities of both creativity and death. It was sacred to Hecate, Circe, Hera, Persephone, and to Apollo in his aspect as the god of poetry and prophecy. The Chinese Kuan Yin is said to use a willow wand to sprinkle the water of life. Many Prairie Indian tribes considered willow to be symbolic of seasonal rebirth. In Ireland, priests, priestesses, and artisans sat in willow groves to gain inspiration.

YEW This tree has long been associated with Underworld deities and was connected with both immortality and death. It was sacred to the goddess Hecate, who ruled with Persephone and Hades in the Greek Underworld. One of the five magickal trees of Ireland, yew symbolized the Triple Goddess in Her death aspect. A sacred tree of the Druids, yew was associated with death, rebirth, and the Winter Solstice. The berries are poisonous, and the tree itself symbolizes sorrow.

Herbs

While today herbs and spices are primarily used in cooking or for their scents, for centuries many were considered to be sacred and were used in rituals and worship ceremonies throughout the world. Herbs may be used on the altar as bouquets, in plant form, or dried and sprinkled over burning coals for incense.

Do not eat herbs unless you are absolutely certain of the effect they will cause on the body.

BASIL In India, basil is still grown near homes and temples as protection. It is sacred to the god Vishnu and the goddess Lakshmi. The Greek Orthodox Church uses basil to make holy water and sets basil in pots around the altar. Basil is a good herb for exorcising negativity from the home. Small amounts may also be sprinkled in the corners of rooms for added protection.

BAY LAUREL An herb long associated with deities such as Apollo, bay laurel will stop unwanted interference in your life, and protect you against evil.

CATNIP This herb is associated with the goddesses Bast, Sekhmet, and Freyja. It brings courage, love, and happiness.

CHAMOMILE Roman chamomile smells like fresh apples. It is associated with gaining a marriage proposal and bringing gambling luck.

CLOVE Besides being used to banish evil, cloves are used to build friendships and gain desires.

DANDELION Helps with clairvoyance and purifies.

DRAGON'S BLOOD This is actually the powdered resin of a shrub and was once considered to be extremely rare and valuable. It is good for removing hexes and attracting love and money.

FERNS The Druids classed ferns as sacred trees and gathered the uncurled fronds of male fern at Summer Solstice to use for good luck. All ferns attract fairies and give protection.

FRANKINCENSE This was considered to be one of the most sacred scents by ancient Greeks, Romans, Persians, Babylonians, Assyrians, and Egyptians. It was also one of the Jewish offerings on the Sabbath. Use it for exorcism, protection, and purification.

GARLIC Although garlic is frequently used only in cooking, because of its strong odor many ancient cultures believed it had valuable properties of protection against evil. The Egyptians used it for swearing oaths. It was left as an offering at crossroads to the Greek goddess Hecate, while the Romans ate it for strength and endurance, and assigned it to Mars.

GINGER Most people connect the smell of this herb with cookies, pies, and pastries. However, its oldest uses are for love, money, success, and power.

HYSSOP This herb's name in Greek means "holy herb." Hyssop has a long history of being used to cleanse and purify sacred places.

JASMINE FLOWER Love; money; strengthens psychic abilities.

JUNIPER BERRIES Traditionally, this shrub was grown near dwellings for protection, particularly against thieves. However, it is also used to attract love and to develop psychic abilities.

LAVENDER Love; money; attracts helpful spirits.

LEMON VERBENA This plant is helpful in getting rid of unwanted lovers.

LILY OF THE VALLEY Poisonous, so do not eat or leave where children or pets can find it! Known to attract peace and knowledge, it is easier to use the oil than the plant.

MARIGOLD These flowers added to pillows give clairvoyant dreams.

MARJORAM A common cooking herb, marjoram helps with protection when soaked together with mint and rosemary, and the water sprinkled about the house.

MINT The Druids burned mint leaves to cleanse a space.

MUGWORT A sacred herb to the Celtic Druids, this plant is strongest when picked on a full moon or during the Summer Solstice. Rub the leaves on ritual tools to increase their power.

MYRRH Another sacred herb from ancient times, myrrh aids in purification, protection, and strengthening spirituality.

NUTMEG The whole nutmeg is traditionally carried for luck in gambling and lotteries, while the powdered form is useful for love, prosperity, and fertility.

ORRIS ROOT This root, in powdered form, is sprinkled about to attract the opposite sex.

PATCHOULI An herb highly valued by Hindus, patchouli can break any spell, bring back a lost love, attract money, and defeat enemies. It is also useful in healing grief.

PARSLEY Given to soldiers as a sign of victory, this herb was also thought to be sacred to the dead in both Greece and Rome.

PEPPERMINT Purification; love; increases psychic ability.

PINE Pine needles have a clean, refreshing scent and are used for purifying an atmosphere. It was sacred to such deities as Mars.

ROSE PETALS Love; happiness in the home.

ROSEMARY The modern name of this herb connects it with the Virgin Mary, although it was known and used in the Mediterranean cultures long before Christianity arose. Its name means "dew of the sea." The Greeks associated it with remembrance, and students wore a sprig of rosemary to help improve their memory. The Romans made crowns of rosemary for their household deities and burned it to purify an atmosphere to ward off evil. A symbol of remembrance and fidelity, it is also useful for exorcisms and to keep a lover faithful.

RUE In Europe during the Middle Ages, rue was strewn on floors for its scent, a custom begun by the Greeks and Romans, who believed it gave protection from evil spirits. The word *rue* comes from the Greek word *reuo*, which means "set free." Thus, this herb became a Christian symbol for repentance. Among the Druids, rue was used for defense against magickal spells. When burned, it starts things moving.

SAFFRON This expensive herb, which is the pollen from crocus flowers, was highly prized from the Mediterranean area to Tibet and India. The Greeks and Romans used it for its scent, which was said to be cleansing. When a worshipper brought a gift to a temple in India, they received a dot of saffron paste on the forehead. Because of saffron's association with humility and purity, Buddhist monks dyed their robes the color of saffron.

SAGE A symbol of wisdom and long life to the Romans, this herb was gathered ceremoniously, with a gift of bread and wine left as an offering to the plant. Native Americans use sage for smudging and cleansing.

SAINT-JOHN'S-WORT An herb sacred to the Druids, it was worn in Ireland for invincibility and in Scotland as a charm against fairy glamour. Its other magickal associations are attracting happiness and healing, courage, love, and protection. It also is said to aid with divination.

SANDALWOOD An herb widely used in India, yellow sandalwood is associated with protection, exorcism, and spiritual growth; red sandalwood is associated with exorcism, healing, protection, spirituality, and gaining your wish.

THYME The name of this herb is derived from the Greek, meaning "to burn a sacrifice." It was considered a holy incense throughout the Mediterranean cultures. However, the Romans believed thyme was an aphrodisiac and offered it to Venus. The Druids used this plant to repel negativity and depression. In Medieval Europe, thyme was associated with increasing energy and bravery. Used in pillows, it is said to cure nightmares.

VERVAIN Also called holy herb and verbena. When burned, this herb repels psychic attack. However, it is also useful for purification, gaining love, and attracting wealth.

WORMWOOD Removes hexes; repels black magick; aids with the psychic.

YARROW Primarily used for divination and love spells, this herb is said to have the power to keep couples happily married.

Oils

Oils are best used to anoint candles before lighting them. When wishing to attract something, rub the oil on the candle from the wick to the end. When wanting to repel something, rub from the end to the wick. A few drops of an essential oil can also be placed directly on the top of votive candles. If you put a votive candle in a small cast-iron cauldron to burn, drop the oil in the bottom of the cauldron first. This not only allows the scent to be released with the burning candle, but also helps to keep the wax from sticking to the cauldron. Never drink any essential oils.

AMBER Use for happiness and love.

BAYBERRY Long associated with prosperity and money, bayberry is also useful in gaining control of a situation.

BERGAMOT A spicy oil, it can aid in attracting money, happiness, and optimism.

CARNATION This oil is most helpful in healing spells, for it draws in strength and protection. Legends associate this oil and the flower with Venus and the warrior Ajax.

CEDAR Oil made from the cedar tree will remove hexes, purify, and heal.

CINNAMON A scent of richness and money, this oil can also be used for purification and to gain energy.

CLOVE Basically a healing oil, clove will also stimulate creativity.

DRAGON'S BLOOD Protection; purification; removes hexes; exorcism.

FRANGIPANI Traditionally, this is an oil for attracting love and the perfect mate.

FRANKINCENSE AND MYRRH This combination is valuable for purification, protection, healing, and great spirituality.

GARDENIA A sweet-smelling oil, gardenia is used for peace, love, healing, harmony, and happiness.

HELIOTROPE This oil attracts wealth and gives protection.

HIGH JOHN THE CONQUEROR Aids in all endeavors; strengthens the mental abilities; protection; removes hexes.

HONEYSUCKLE The oil of this flower both attracts money and strengthens psychic abilities.

JASMINE Some people believe that only the extremely expensive, pure jasmine oil will attract love, money, and psychic dreams. However, I have found the less expensive oil works just as well. A symbol of sensuality, the name is said to come form the Persian word *yasmin*.

JUNIPER Used for protection.

LAVENDER This flower oil is primarily used for healing and love.

LILAC Use to ward off evil and to protect.

LOTUS A sacred flower and oil in ancient Egypt and India, this oil brings protection and purification, while promoting spirituality.

MAGNOLIA This oil is best for establishing a sense of oneness with nature.

MUSK Although primarily used to attract the opposite sex and promote sexual love, musk can also draw in prosperity.

MYRRH This oil will break hexes, heal, aid psychic development, and protect.

PATCHOULI This oil promotes love and purification.

PEPPERMINT An oil of great energy, it can stimulate creativity and attract money.

PINE This oil can protect and cleanse.

ROSE An oil of love, rose also cleanses the atmosphere of a room.

ROSEMARY Energy; protection.

SAGE The oil of purification also aids in finding wisdom and truth.

SANDALWOOD Primarily an oil of great spirituality and cleansing.

VANILLA This oil attracts sexual love.

VETIVER A powerful oil to be used sparingly, it removes hexes, attracts money, and can stimulate love.

VIOLET Use this oil to gain luck and love. It is also helpful in finding wisdom to resolve a problem.

YARROW Courage; exorcism; strengthens the psychic.

YLANG YLANG This is an oil of love and harmony.

Flowers

Flowers have been used as offerings to deities and placed at gravesites for millennia, in a wide variety of cultures. In Rome, when the *Lares*, or property guardians, were honored in early December, flowers were placed at all the boundary stones on a piece of property. Certain flowers have long been associated with particular qualities and spiritual meanings. During the Victorian era, the meanings of flowers changed from spiritual to romantic symbols. Flower meanings became a secret code of love, a means of sending nonverbal messages. Many flowers are also considered to be magickal herbs, you can use a flower's symbolism to enhance your altars.

Dreams of flowers in general can mean several things. To dream of gathering flowers means a delightful surprise is coming your way. A basket of flowers portends a wedding or birth, while a wreath of flowers represents a new love. A garden symbolizes spiritual blessing. To smell flowers in a dream is a sign you should grasp an opportunity that will soon present itself.

ALYSSUM This flower symbolizes sweet virtue.

ANEMONE Also known as the windflower from the Greek *anemos* (wind), tradition says that Aphrodite created the blossom in remembrance of her lover Adonis. The Greeks associated it with Zephyr, god of the west wind, while the Christians believed it sprang up at the foot of the cross from Jesus' blood. It symbolizes abandonment or being forsaken.

ASTER The name of this flower means "star," for it was said to spring from stardust that the goddess Virgo sprinkled on the earth. Known in England as starwort, after 1637, the name changed to Michaelmas daisy. In Europe, tradition says the aster will drive away evil spirits. It symbolizes beginnings that lead to greater things.

BLUEBELL In Scotland, this flower is known as Deadmen's Bells. A tradition says that if you hear a bluebell ring, it is a death knell. These flowers are associated with fairies and enchantment. They symbolize constancy.

BUTTERCUP This wildflower is a symbol of radiance and brightness in a person, or a childlike appreciation of life.

CAMELLIA Originally from southern and eastern Asia, this flower symbolizes loveliness.

CARNATION The name comes from the Greek *dios* (divine) and *anthos* (flower). The Greeks used carnations, whose name meant "divine flower," to make ceremonial crowns. The red blossom symbolizes passion, while the white represents pure devotion.

CORNFLOWER Also called the Bachelor's Button, this flower symbolizes gentleness of manner and hope in solitude. Greek tradition says that a centaur was healed by this flower after Hercules shot it with a poisoned arrow. It received its other name, Bachelor's Button, during the Middle Ages in England when girls tucked a blossom under their aprons to ensnare the bachelor of their choice.

CHRYSANTHEMUM A solar symbol associated with completion and fullness of life, this flower was a traditional autumn offering flower in the Far East, where it was cultivated (in China) for over 2,400 years before being brought to the West. In Italy, chrysanthemums are associated with death. This flower symbolizes truth and hope in dark times.

DAFFODIL Giving a daffodil symbolizes chivalry. The name is derived from the Old English affodyle, which means "an early arrival." The Romans introduced this flower to Britain.

DAHLIA When the conquistadors came to Mexico, they found that the Aztecs ate dahlia tubers as a treat; the Aztecs called this flower *cocoxochitl*. It represents the instability of perfect physical beauty.

DAISY The present name of this flower is derived from the Old English daeges ege, meaning "day's eye." As a symbol of innocence, the Christians believed it was sacred to Mary Magdalene and St. John.

FOXGLOVE The name comes from the Old English name *foxes glofa,* or "fingers of a glove." The ancients thought the markings of the flowers were the fingerprints of fairies and associated this flower with them. The Victorians thought this flower symbolized insincerity. The seeds contain digitalis and are poisonous.

GARDENIA In China, this flower represented feminine grace, subtlety, and artistry, while in the southern states of the U.S., it meant hospitality. At one time, it was known as Cape Jasmine, because of a species found in South Africa. During the nineteenth century, this flower was frequently worn by gentlemen on their evening jackets. The gardenia symbolizes sweetness.

GLADIOLUS At one time this flower, also known as flags, grew wild in the Middle East. One species grows only in the spray of Victoria Falls in Africa. It symbolizes natural grace.

HEATHER This flower grows wild in northern England and Scotland and was said to be a traditional fairy food. The red variety symbolizes passion, while the white means protection from passion.

HELIOTROPE Although variations of this flower were discovered in Peru in the eighteenth century, one variety has been known in Europe for millennia. It represents devotion.

HOLLYHOCK Brought to Europe by the Crusaders, this flower was originally grown for the taste of its leaves in food. In the eighteenth century, new strains were brought from China. The name is derived from holy plus hoc (mallow). It has several meanings: fertility, creation, abundance, and ambition.

HONEYSUCKLE The botanical name of this flower means "goat flower." Shakespeare mentions it under the name woodbine. A symbol of plighted troth, this flower is associated with weddings.

HYACINTH The blue flower symbolizes dedication, while the white one represents admiration. Named after the youth who loved Apollo, hyacinth also represents young love.

IRIS A symbol of reconciliation and joining, the iris was associated with the Greek goddess of the same name. However, the Egyptians knew of this flower long before and carved images of it into the temples at Karnak. In Japan, this flower is known as *ayame*. Louis VII had irises with him during the Second French Crusade in 1147; from this came the name *fleur de Louis* or fleur-de-lis.

IVY Although not technically a flower, this plant is listed in Victorian flower codes as symbolizing tenacity. Wear a leaf over your heart to attract a love.

JASMINE Known in the East as a symbol of good luck and increase, the flower was brought to Europe by Vasco da Gama, the explorer, in the sixteenth century. The Chinese call this plant *yah-hsi-ming*. Italian brides sometimes wear a sprig of jasmine at weddings. The name is derived from the ancient Persian word *yasmin*. Traditionally, this flower is used in magick for love, money, and to strengthen psychic abilities. It symbolizes elegance.

LAVENDER This flower is widely used to scent drawers and clothing, but is also useful in gaining love, money, and helpful spirits. The name comes from the Latin word *lavare*, "to wash." The Romans added a sprig of lavender to the laundry and also placed it between sheets and blankets. A symbol of devotion, this flower was placed in homes to avoid marital discord.

LILAC Native to Turkey, this flower's name comes from the Arabic *laylak* or the Persian *nylac*, which means "blue." The purple flower represents first love, while the white one symbolizes innocence. These flowers were once thought to ward off the Black Death.

LILIES An ancient seal from the Minoan culture portrays priestesses bearing temple gifts of lilies and figs. Another seal shows the Goddess descending into a field of lilies where priestesses are dancing. It was sacred to the Cretan goddess Britomartis because of its powerful association with the feminine. The Greeks believed that the lily sprang from Hera's breast milk dropped upon the earth. The Romans called this flower *rosa Junonis*, which means "Juno's rose." The Christians connected it to Mary because it symbolized purity.

LILY OF THE VALLEY This flower is also called Our Lady's Tears and Liriconfancy. In Greece, priestesses to Hera made offerings of lilies of the valley to invoke her presence. It symbolizes modesty.

LOTUS Possibly the flower with the oldest spiritual meanings, the lotus was sacred to cultures from ancient Egypt to those of China and Japan. Before Buddhism was brought to China, the lotus represented summer, purity, fertility, spirituality, and creative power.

A symbol of spiritual purity and the sacred center, the opened lotus was considered sacred in both Buddhism and Hinduism. The bud represented fertility and potential.

In ancient Egypt, this flower symbolized the sun and the resurrection of the god Horus. It was so sacred that it is found painted and sculpted on temples and tombs.

In India, the Hindu goddess Lakshmi is connected with the lotus. When associated with Lakshmi, this flower symbolizes the *yoni*, or womb of creation. Many Hindu deities are portrayed sitting on the lotus, which in this instance represents divinity and spirit.

MARIGOLD The flowers are said to promote psychic dreams. This flower was first called "golds" in England. Later, when it was used to adorn statues of the Virgin Mary, it became known as "Mary's gold." It symbolizes constancy and endurance in love in some sources, while in others, it stands for grief or cruelty.

ORCHID This flower symbolizes luxury and ecstasy.

PANSY Also called heartsease, one definition of this flower is broken hearts and disappointment in love. However, another definition lists the symbolism as thoughts exchanged between lovers. The name comes from the French word for "thought," as it was believed that this flower could grant telepathic ability.

PEONY Known and revered from the Mediterranean to the Far East, the peony has long been connected to healing and magick. The plant, flower, and seed were used as protection against evil spirits and natural disasters, particularly storms and shipwrecks. According to the Chinese, this highly prized flower was of the yin, or female, principle. Paeon, the Greek physician to the gods and a student of the healer Asclepius, was associated with the peony, which took his name. This flower represents the ability to keep a secret.

PERIWINKLE The Italians call this blue flower the "flower of death," while the French knew it as the "violet of sorcery," and the Virgin's flower. It is associated with death because of the tradition that souls of the dead live within the blossoms. It symbolizes a long relationship.

POPPY Long associated with sleep, forgetting, and rejuvenation, the poppy was an important part of Egyptian funerary rites. Although the Greeks knew of its narcotic, healing properties, they also offered it at shrines to Demeter and Artemis for fertility, and to Persephone in her death aspect. Their god Morpheus, the god of dreams, was said to use poppy wreaths. The red poppy represents consolation, the pink one, sleep, and the white one, time.

PRIMROSE Another flower associated with fairies, tradition says to lay one at your doorstep so the fairies will bless your house. Climbers in Switzerland carry the flowers to ward off vertigo. It is a symbol of beginning love, birth, and children.

ROSE One of the most meaningful flowers in the West, a single rose primarily represents achievement and perfection. It can also mean the mystic center, the heart and love, spiritual rebirth, and the soul itself. The yellow rose represents home and domestic happiness; the red stands for beauty and passionate love. Sometimes called the flower of light, the white rose symbolizes purity and silence in the West, but death in Asia.

Ancient Greek myth says that the rose and the anemone sprang into being when the blood of Adonis, the beloved of the goddess Aphrodite, was shed on the ground. The rose was also sacred to Athena. Whenever Hecate was shown wearing a garland of roses, it symbolized the beginning of a new cycle of life. When a chariot containing a statue of Cybele was pulled through Rome during a specific ritual, the Romans tossed roses into the conveyance in her honor. Later, the Christians would honor the Virgin Mary with roses in much the same way. Deities associated with this flower were Aphrodite, Eros, and Venus. The rose has long been used as a magickal herb for love and happiness in the home.

SNOWDROP This flower is a symbol of hope and renewal.

SUNFLOWER A plant sacred to the sun deities, Inca priestesses wore gold replicas of this flower. Sunflower seeds were used as offerings in Inca rituals. The botanical name comes from that of the Greek sun god, Helios. It symbolizes adoration.

SWEETPEA Although the botanical name comes form the Greek word for "pea," this plant is poisonous if ingested. This flower represents tenderness and lasting pleasure. Tradition says that this good omen should be presented at weddings to the married couple.

TULIP This flower is a native to Persia and was brought to Europe in 1559 by a man who saw them in a walled garden in Constantinople. The name comes from the Turkish *tulbent* (turban). Red symbolizes a declaration of love, while yellow means your love is hopeless. Other sources say the tulip is a lucky charm bringing good luck and fame.

VERVAIN, VERBENA Both an herb and a flower, vervain has been held sacred by many cultures that considered it a plant of enchantment and mystery. In Egypt, it was a symbol of the tears of Isis. Greek priests carried it in their robes and used it to cleanse the altars of Zeus. Celtic Druids and ancient Persians believed that vervain not only purified, but also helped with visions and divinations. Christian churches used it to make holy water. As one of the most sacred of Celtic herbs, vervain was placed on altars as an offering. Other names for this herb are verbena and holy herb. Burn it to repel psychic attack. Other uses are for purification, to attract wealth, and to find love.

VIOLET Used in ancient love philters, this flower symbolizes faithfulness, modesty, and a steady love.

YARROW This flower has been known and used for millennia in religious rituals. The earliest archaeological finding of yarrow pollen was in Neanderthal graves. It has always been associated with healing and the stopping of bleeding. The Celtic Druids used yarrow in many of their ceremonies, as well as for healing. The name is derived from the Anglo-Saxon *gearwe*, which means "to prepare." One Chinese method of divination originally used fifty stalks of dried yarrow. Presented to a new bride, yarrow is said to bring happiness. Wear it to break spells and to protect.

ZINNIA This flower symbolizes thoughts of absent friends. In 1519, when the conquistadores were exploring Mexico, they found zinnias, which they called *mal de ojos*.

Deities

The following lists of ancient deities give the esoteric meanings connected with these archetypal figures of power. These major deities are divided according the their country or area of origin and usage. You may wish to choose a goddess or god to whom you are attracted and who portrays the magickal and spiritual qualities you want to represent on your altar. The lists do not contain all the deities known to these ancient cultures.

Egyptian

AMEN/AMUN/AMMON God of reproduction, fertility, agriculture, prophecy. Associated with the ram and the goose.

ANUBIS God of death, endings, wisdom, surgery, hospital stays, finding lost things, journeys, and protection. Considered a messenger from the gods to humans, he was associated with the jackal and sometimes the dog.

BAST The cat-headed goddess of all animals, but especially cats. She symbolizes the moon, childbirth, fertility, pleasure, joy, music, dance, marriage, and healing.

BUTO Cobra goddess of protection.

HATHOR A mother and creatress goddess, protectress of women. Symbols include the moon, marriage, motherhood, artists, music, happiness, and prosperity. She is associated with the cow, the frog, and the cat.

HORUS God of the sun and the moon, he stands for prophecy, justice, success and problem solving. Associated with the falcon and the hawk.

IMHOTEP God of medicine and healing.

ISIS The supreme Egyptian goddess, who was honored for 3,000 years. In later times, her worship spread to Greece and Rome. Meanings include magick, fertility, marriage, purification, initiation, reincarnation, healing, divination, the arts, and protection. Associated with the cat, the goose, and the cow.

MAAT Goddess of judgment, truth, justice, and reincarnation. Associated with ostrich feathers.

NEITH A warrior goddess and protectress, she represents magick, healing, mystical knowledge, domestic arts, and marriage. Two arrows were among her symbols. She was associated with the vulture.

NEPHTHYS The dark sister of Isis. Magick, protection, dreams, and intuition. The basket was one of her symbols.

OSIRIS The supreme Egyptian god. Fertility, civilization, agriculture, crafts, judgment, architecture, social laws, power, growth, and stability. Associated with the hawk and the phoenix.

PTAH God of artisans and artists, builders and craftsmen. Associated with the bull.

SEKHMET The dark sister of Bast, a lion-headed goddess. Physicians and bonesetters; revenge, and power. Associated with the lioness.

TA-URT/TAURET The hippopotamus goddess. Childbirth, maternity, and protection.

THOTH God of books and learning, and the greatest of magicians. Writing, inventions, the arts, divination, commerce, healing, intuition, success, wisdom, truth, and the Akashic Records. Associated with the ibis.

Middle Eastern

ADDAD Canaan, Babylon, Assyria, Syria, Mesopotamia. God of storms, earthquakes, floods, and furious winds. Associated with lightning and the bull.

ADONIS Semitic god. Harvest, death, and resurrection. Associated with the boar.

AHURA MAZDAH Persia and Zoroastrianism. God of universal law, purification, and goodness. One of his symbols was the winged disk.

ASSHUR Assyria, Babylon. Supreme god represented by a winged disk. Fertility, protection, victory, and bravery. Associated with the bull.

ASTARTE Known as Ashtart in Phoenicia. Queen of Heaven. The moon, astrology, victory, revenge, and sexual love. Among her symbols were the eight-pointed star and the crescent.

DUMUZI/TAMMUZ Mesopotamia, Sumeria. Called the Anointed God. Harvest and fertility.

EA/ENKI Mesopotamia, Babylon, Sumeria. Creator god of carpenters, stonecutters, and goldsmiths; patron of all the arts. Associated with the goat, the fish, the eye, and the vase.

ENLIL/BEL Sumeria, Babylon, Assyria. King of the gods. Destructive winds, hurricanes, floods, storms, and the laws.

INANNA Canaan, Phoenicia, Sumeria, Uruk, Babylon. Queen of the Heavens. Defense, victory, love, fertility, destiny, prosperity, and justice. Associated with the star, the serpent staff, and dogs.

ISHTAR Lady of Heaven. Patroness of priestesses; sexual love, fertility, revenge, resurrection, marriage, initiation, overcoming obstacles, and social laws. Associated with the lion, the serpent staff, the dragon, the eight-pointed star, the dove, the double ax, the rainbow, and the bridge. She had a rainbow necklace similar that that of the Norse god Freyja.

LILITH Protectress of all pregnant women, mothers, and children. Associated with the owl.

MARDUK God of fate, courage, healing, justice, the law, and victory. Associated with the bull.

MARI/MERI/MARRATU Syria, Chaldea, Persia. Goddess of fertility, childbirth, the moon, and the sea. One of her symbols was the pearl.

MITHRA/MITHRAS Persia; god of many Middle Eastern cultures. The sun, warriors, contracts, predictions, wisdom, sacred oaths, prosperity, and spiritual illumination. Associated with the disk or circle and the cave.

SHAMASH/CHEMOSH Mesopotamia, Sumeria, Babylon, Assyria. God of the sun, divination, retribution, courage, triumph, and justice.

SIN Mesopotamia, Ur, Assyria, Babylon, Sumeria. God of the moon, the calendar, destiny, predictions, and secrets. Associated with lapis lazuli and the dragon.

TIAMAT Mesopotamia, Babylon, Sumeria. Goddess of destruction, karmic discipline, death, and regeneration. Associated with the dragon and the serpent.

Greek

APHRODITE Goddess of love, sensuality, passion, partnerships, fertility, renewal, the sea, joy, and beauty. Associated with the swan, dove, poppy, rose, apple, and pomegranate.

APOLLO God of the light of the sun, healing, oracles, poetry, music, inspiration, magick, and the arts. Associated with the arrow, bay laurel, and the raven.

ARES God of war, terror, courage, raw energy, and stamina.

ARTEMIS Virgin Huntress. Goddess of wild places and wild animals, protectress of young girls. Magick, psychic power, fertility, childbirth, sports, contact with nature, and mental healing. Associated with dogs, the stag, horse, acorn, crescent, and juniper.

ATHENA/ATHENE Goddess of Athens. Freedom and women's rights; patroness of career women; patroness of craftsmen. Wisdom, justice, writing, music, the sciences, invention, weaving, architects, and renewal. Associated with the owl, horse, intertwined snakes, the olive, and oak.

CYBELE A Phrygian Great Mother goddess of the earth and caverns, associated with the god Attis. Goddess of the natural world and wild beasts. The moon, magick, wildlife, and the dead. Originally worshipped in the form of a black meteorite, Cybele's worship spread to ancient Greece and Rome. Associated with the lion, bees, pomegranate, violets, pine, cypress, the cave, bowl, and pearl.

DEMETER Goddess of the Eleusinian Mysteries. Protectress of women; crops, initiation, renewal, fertility, civilization, the law, motherhood, and marriage. Associated with corn and wheat.

GAEA/GAIA Earth Goddess. Oaths, divination, healing, motherhood, marriage, and dreams. The Oracle at Delphi was originally hers, before Apollo took over. Associated with the laurel.

HADES God of the Underworld. Elimination of fear of the dead. Associated with gemstones.

HECATE A Thracian Triple Goddess of the moon and the Underworld with great power. Patroness of priestesses. The moon, prophecy, averting evil, riches, victory, travelers, crossroads, transformation, purification, and renewal. Associated with the snake, dragon, dogs, and cauldron.

HELIOS God of the actual sun, riches, and enlightenment.

HEPHAESTUS God of blacksmiths, metalworkers, craftsmen, and volcanoes. Associated with pottery.

HERA Queen of the Gods. Use her image when facing infidelity and insecurity, and also for marriage and childbirth. Associated with the peacock, cow, pomegranate, marjoram, lily, apple, flowers, willow, the sickle, and double ax.

HERMES Messenger of the Gods. Commerce, good luck, orthodox medicine, occult wisdom, music, merchants, and diplomacy. Associated with the ram.

HESTIA Virgin Goddess of the hearth. The home, dedication to duty, and discipline. Her name was mentioned by the Greeks in all their prayers and sacrifices.

NIKE Goddess of victory. Associated with the palm branch.

PAN God of male sexuality, animals, fertility, farming, medicine, and soothsaying. Associated with goats, fish, and bees.

PERSEPHONE Queen of the Underworld. The seasons, crops, and overcoming obstacles. Associated with the bat, willow, narcissus, pomegranate, sheaf, corn, and cornucopia.

POSEIDON God of the seas and all sea animals. Storms, hurricanes, earthquakes, horses, rain, human emotions, sailors, and weather. Associated with the horse, fish, dolphin, and bull.

THEMIS Goddess of law and order. Associated with the scales.

ZEUS God of the Heavens. Rain, storms, lightning, wisdom, justice, the law, riches, and the heart's desires. Associated with the eagle, oak, and lightning.

Roman

BACCHUS/LIBER God of good times, wine, and fertility. Associated with the goat and vine.

CERES The Grain Goddess. Crops, initiation, protectress of women, and motherhood. Associated with corn and wheat.

DIANA Goddess of the woodlands and wild animals. Childbirth and women. Associated with deer, dogs, and the stag.

FAUNUS/LUPERCUS God of nature and woodlands. Farming, music, dance, and agriculture. Associated with the goat, bees, and fish.

FORTUNA Goddess of fate, oracles, and chance. Associated with the wheel and cornucopia.

JANUS God of two faces representing the past and the future. Beginnings and endings, new cycles, and journeys. Associated with doors.

JUNO Queen of Heaven. Women's fertility, childbirth, the home, and marriage. Associated with the peacock, goose, and the veil.

JUPITER King of Heaven. Storms, rain, honor, riches, friendships, the heart's desires, and protection. Associated with lightning.

MARS God of war, terror, revenge, and courage. Associated with the woodpecker, horse, wolf, oaks, and laurel.

MERCURY Messenger of the Gods. God of commerce, cunning, success, magick, travel, and merchants. Associated with the caduceus.

MINERVA Goddess of women's rights and freedom. Artisans, craftsmen, renewal, and protection. Associated with spinning and weaving, the owl, horse, snake, spear, and pillar.

NEPTUNE Sea god of earthquakes, storms, ships, the seas, and horses. Also associated with the bull and the dolphin.

SATURN God of abundance, prosperity, and karmic lessons. Associated with the sickle, corn, and the vine.

VENUS Goddess of love, fertility, and renewal. Also associated with the dove.

African

ALA/ALE Nigeria. Earth Mother and creator goddess. Community laws, morality, and oaths.

ASA Kenya. God of mercy, surviving the impossible or insurmountable.

FA Dahomey. God of personal destiny.

FAMIAN Guinea. God of fertility and protector against demons.

KATONDA East Africa. God of judgment, and against all odds, and divination.

MBABA MWANA WARESA Zulu. Goddess of the rainbow and crops.

MUKURU Southwest Africa. God of rain, healing, and protection.

MUNGO Kenya. God of rain.

NYAME West Africa. God who prepared the soul for rebirth.

OGUN West Africa. God of iron and warfare, removal of difficulties, and justice.

OLORUN Yoruba. God of truth, foreseeing, and victory against odds.

RUBANGA Banyoro. God of fertility, children, harvest, health, and rebirth.

SHANGO Nigeria. God of storm and war.

WELE Bantu. God of rain, storms, creativity, and prosperity.

YEMAYA Yoruba. Goddess of women and children.

Celtic

ANGUS MAC OG Ireland. God of love. Associated with birds.

ANU Ireland. Goddess of fertility, prosperity, and health. Associated with cows.

ARIANRHOD Wales. Goddess of beauty and reincarnation. Associated with the wheel.

BADB Ireland. Goddess of wisdom, inspiration, and enlightenment. Associated with the cauldron, crow, and raven.

BEL Ireland. God of the sun, healing, science, success, and prosperity.

BLODEUWEDD Wales. Goddess of wisdom, lunar mysteries, and initiation. Associated with flowers and the owl.

BRAN Wales. God of prophecy, the arts, leadership, music, and writing. Associated with the raven.

BRANWEN Wales. Goddess of love and beauty. Associated with the cauldron.

BRIGIT/BRIGID Ireland. Goddess of all feminine arts and crafts. Healing, inspiration, learning, poetry, divination, and occult knowledge. Associated with weaving.

CERNUNNOS Known to all Celt areas. God of the woodlands and wild animals. Fertility, physical love, reincarnation, and wealth. Associated with the serpent, stag, ram, and bull.

CERRIDWEN Wales. Goddess of regeneration, initiation, inspiration, magick, poetry, and knowledge. Associated with the cauldron and the sow.

THE DAGDA Ireland. High King of the Tuatha De Danann, the ancient Irish deities. Patron of priests; the arts, prophecy, weather, reincarnations, knowledge, healing, and prosperity.

DANU Ireland. Goddess of prosperity, magick, and wisdom.

DIANCECHT Ireland. God of healing, medicine, and regeneration. Associated with herbs and the snake.

EPONA Britain, Gaul. Goddess of horses, dogs, and prosperity.

LUGH Ireland, Wales. God of crafts, the arts, magick, journeys, healing, initiation, and prophecy. Associated with the raven, stag, and dog.

MACHA Ireland. Goddess of war, cunning, sexuality, and dominance over males. Associated with the raven and the crow.

MANANNAN MAC LIR/MANAWRYDAN AP LLYR Ireland, Wales. God of magick, storms, sailors, weather forecasting, merchants, and commerce. Associated with the pig, apple, and cauldron.

MORRIGAN Ireland, Wales. Patroness of priestesses. Goddess of revenge, magick, and prophecy. Associated with the crow and raven.

OGMA Ireland. God of poets and writers, physical strength, inspiration, and magick.

SCATHACH/SCOTA Ireland, Scotland. Goddess of martial arts, blacksmiths, prophecy, and magick.

Norse

AEGIR God of the sea, brewing, prosperity, sailors, and weather.

AUDHUMLA Goddess of motherhood, child-rearing, and home crafts. Associated with the cow.

BALDUR/BALDER God of the sun, reconciliation, gentleness, reincarnation, and harmony.

FREYJA/FREYA Mistress of cats and a shapeshifter. Goddess of love, sex, childbirth, enchantments, wealth, trance, wisdom, good luck, fertility, writing, and protection. Associated with the horse, cat, and amber.

FREYR/FREY The god of Yule. God of fertility, love, abundance, horses, sailors, happiness, and weather. Associated with the boar.

HEIMDALL God of the rainbow, beginnings and endings, and defense against evil. Associated with the bridge.

HEL Queen of the Underworld. Revenge, fate, and karma.

IDUNN/IDUN Goddess of immortality, youth, and long life. Associated with the apple.

LOKI A trickster and shapechanger. God of earthquakes, fire, cunning, deceit, daring, and revenge. Associated with the wolf and snake.

NJORD God of the sea, fishing, sailors, prosperity, and journeys.

ODIN/ODHINN King of the Gods. God of runes, poetry, magick, divination, storms, rebirth, knowledge, weather, justice, and inspiration. Associated with the wolf and raven.

THOR/THORR Protector of the common person. God of thunder, storms, law and order, strength, weather, and trading voyages. Associated with the goat, oak, and lightning.

TYR The bravest of the gods. God of victory, justice, the law, honor, and athletes.

Russian-Slovenian

BABA-YAGA Goddess of endings, death, and revenge. Associated with the snake.

DAZHBOG God of the sun, fair judgment, and destiny.

DIIWICA Goddess of the hunt and the forests, hounds, victory, and success. Associated with the horse and dog.

DZIDZILEYLA/DIDILIA Goddess of marriage, fertility, and love.

MATI SYRA ZEMLYA Goddess of the earth, crops, fertility, oaths, justice, divination, and property disputes.

PERUN God of storms, purification, fertility, oracles, defense against illness, victory, and oak forests. Associated with the cock, goat, bear, bull, and lightning.

SVANTOVIT Four-headed god of divination, prosperity, victory, and battles. Associated with the horse.

Indian

AGNI God of fire, rain, storms, protector of the home, new beginnings, and justice.

BRAHMA God of creation and wisdom; often portrayed as having four heads, each facing different directions. Associated with the swan.

BUDDHA The Enlightened One, the Awakened One, the Way-Shower.

CHANDRA/SOMA Moon god of psychic visions and dreams.

DURGA Goddess of nurturing, protection, and defense. Associated with the lion and bowl.

GANESHA Elephant-headed god of beginnings, writing, worldly success, learning, prosperity, journeys, and overcoming obstacles. Associated with the elephant and flowers.

INDRA King of the Gods. God of fertility, reincarnation, rain, the rainbow, the law, opposition to evil, creativity, and the sun. Associated with the elephant, horse, dog, and lightning.

KALI/KALI MA Goddess of Death. Goddess of regeneration, sexual love, and revenge; protectress of women. Associated with the wheel, knot, braid, and snake.

KRISHNA God of erotic delights and music, and savior from sin. Associated with the star.

LAKSHMI Goddess of love, beauty, creative energy, agriculture, good fortune, prosperity, and success.

SARASVATI Goddess of the creative arts, science, and teaching. Associated with the lotus and crescent.

SHIVA Demon-Slayer. He is shown with a third eye in the center of his forehead and four arms. God of fertility, physical love, medicine, storms, long life, healing, righteousness, and judgment. Associated with cattle, the bull, elephant, serpent, lightning, and the hourglass.

TARA Goddess of spiritual enlightenment, knowledge, and compassion. In Tibet, Tara has twenty-one forms and colors; the most familiar forms being the Green Tara for growth and protection, and the White Tara for long life, health, and prosperity.

VISHNU God of peace, power, compassion, abundance, and success. Associated with the lotus, serpent, and shells.

Chinese

CHUANG-MU Goddess of the bedroom and sexual delights.

ERH-LANG God of protection from evil.

FU-HSI God of happiness, destiny, and success. Associated with the hat.

HSUAN-T'IEN-SHANG-TI God of exorcism of evil spirits.

KUAN YIN Goddess of fertility, children, motherhood, childbirth, and mercy. She is often portrayed holding a child in one arm and a willow twig or lotus blossom in her other hand. Associated with the willow.

K'UEI-HSING God of tests and examinations, protector of travelers.

LEI-KING God who punished the guilty that human laws did not touch.

LU-HSING God of salaries and employees. Associated with deer.

SHEN NUNG God of medicine.

SHOU-HSING God of longevity and old people. Associated with the peach.

T'AI-YUEH-TA-TI God of fortune, payment of karmic debt, and prosperity.

TSAI SHEN God of wealth. Associated with the carp and cock.

TSAO-WANG God of the hearth and kitchen. He is said to guard the hearth and family, allotting next year's fortune.

TWEN-CH'ANG God of literature and poetry.

YAO-SHIH Master of healing and psychic abilities.

Japanese

AMATERASU Sun goddess of harvest, fertility, and light. Associated with weaving.

BENTEN Goddess of good luck and protection from earthquakes.

BENZAITEN Goddess of love.

BISHAMONTEN God of happiness.

DAIKOKU God of prosperity.

EBISU God of work.

FUKUROKUJU God of happiness and long life.

HOTEI OSHO God of good fortune.

INARI Fox-goddess of merchants, business, and prosperity. Associated with the fox and rice.

JIZO BOSATSU Protector of women in childbirth, and children.

JUROJIN God of happiness and long life.

KISHIMOJIN Goddess of children, compassion, and fertility.

Native North American

AGLOOLIK Eskimo. God of hunters and fishermen.

ATAENTSIC Iroquois/Heron. Goddess of marriage and childbirth.

IOSKEHA Iroquois/Heron. God who defeats demons and heals diseases.

ONATHA Iroquois. Goddess of wheat and harvest.

SPIDER WOMAN Navajo. Goddess of charms and magick.

TIRAWA Pawnee. God of hunting, agriculture, and religious rituals.

WAKONDA Lakota. God of all wisdom and power.

YANAULUHA Zuni. The great medicine god. Civilization, animal husbandry, healing, and knowledge.

Mayan

HURUKAN God of fire, the whirlwind, hurricanes, and spiritual illumination.

ITZAMNA God of knowledge, writing, fertility, regeneration, and medicine. Associated with the lizard.

IXCHEL Goddess of childbirth, medicine, pregnancy, and domestic arts, especially weaving.

KUKULCAN God of learning, culture, the laws, and the calendar.

YUM CAAX God of maize, fertility, riches, and life.

Aztec

CHALCHIHUITLICUE Goddess of storms, whirlpools, love, and flowers.

CHANTICO Goddess of the home, fertility, and wealth. Associated with snakes and gemstones.

COATLICUE Goddess of famines and earthquakes. Associated with snakes.

ITZCOLIUHQUI God of darkness, volcanic eruptions, and disaster. Associated with obsidian.

ITZPAPLOTL Goddess of fate and agriculture.

MAYAUEL Goddess of childbirth. Associated with the bowl, turtle, and snake.

QUETZALCOATL God of wind, life breath, civilization, the arts, and fate.

TLALOC God of thunder, rain, fertility, and water. Associated with lightning and the pitcher or vase.

TOZI Goddess of midwives, healers, and healing.

Incan

CHASCA Goddess of girls and flowers.

INTI Sun god of fertility and crops. Associated with corn.

MAMA QUILLA Goddess of married women and the calendar.

PACHACAMAC God of the arts and occupations, and oracles.

VIRACOCHA God of the arts, the sun, storms, oracles, moral codes, and rain.

Angels and Archangels

Angels have been known around the world and in many cultures outside of or prior to Christian influence, or before Christianity was ever formed. They have been called by many names, but their descriptions are remarkably similar. They are always described as messengers from the spirit world, helpers, and guardians of those who recognize and call upon them.

CAMAEL Visions, discretion, courage, exorcism, purification, and protection.

GABRIEL Resurrection, mercy, truth, hope, visions, divination, and herbal medicine.

HANIEL Love, beauty, and creativity; protection against evil.

METATRON Spiritual enlightenment and mystical knowledge.

MICHAEL Truth, knowledge, divination, protection, repentance, deliverance from enemies, victory in battle, and protection from police harassment. Patron of police officers, paratroopers, and mariners.

PERSONAL GUARDIAN ANGEL Protection, guidance in all things, and help with spiritual wisdom.

RAPHAEL Healing, harmony, success, honor, contacting your guardian angel, safe journeys, reuniting with loved ones, and curing all disease.

RATZIEL Illumination, guidance, and destiny.

SANDALPHON Seeing the guarding angel; stability, guidance, and protection.

TZADQUIEL Spiritual love and good fortune.

TZAPHKIEL Spiritual development, overcoming grief, and balancing or changing karma.

URIEL Teaching, insight, stability, and endurance.

Saints

Certain Christian saints are called upon for specific help. This usually takes the form of prayers and an offering of a candle when the petition is made. The Vatican Council of the Catholic Church addressed this devotion to the saints in their Constitution on the Church, No. 90, saying that the saints were helpful friends in heaven. These devotions usually consist of saying prayers, lighting candles, and offering flowers or incense.

THE INFANT JESUS OF PRAGUE Health matters, surgery, guidance, and wisdom.

OUR LADY OF FATIMA Protection from evil and the anger of adversaries, and freedom from any situation that restricts and binds.

OUR LADY OF GUADALUPE Peace, sickness, luck, and help in any situation.

OUR LADY OF THE IMMACULATE CONCEPTION Sickness and fertility.

OUR LADY OF LORETTO Sickness and regaining health.

OUR LADY OF MERCY Peace, health, justice, and release from jail.

OUR LADY OF MOUNT CARMEL Protection from accidents or sudden death.

ST. AGABUS Patron of psychics and clairvoyant visions.

ST. AGATHA Breast diseases, rape, and volcanic eruptions. Patroness of nurses.

ST. AGNES Fidelity, finding a suitable mate, and relationships.

ST. AGRICOLA OF AVIGNON Protection against misfortune, bad luck, and plagues. Patron of rain.

ST. ALBINUS Gallstones and kidney disease.

ST. ALEXIS Keeping enemies away.

ST. ALPHONSUS LIGUORI Rheumatic fever, arthritis, gout, joint and muscle ailments, osteoarthritis.

STS. ALODIA AND NUNILO Patronesses of child abuse victims and runaways.

ST. ALOYSIUS Patron of fishermen.

ST. ANN Help with deafness and blindness, and with special requests. Patroness of women, particularly those in childbirth.

ST. ANTHONY Finding lost items, marriage or love problems, financial problems, and getting a job. Considered a wonder worker.

ST. APOLLONIA Patron of toothaches and dentists.

ST. ARTHELIUS Patroness of kidnap victims.

ST. BARBARA Protectress of women; love, help against those trying to break up a marriage, clearing a path through obstacles, release from prison, and driving away evil. Patroness of prisoners, architects, the military, and stoneworkers.

ST. BARTHOLOMEW Learning the truth, protection from violence, and surgery. Patron of surgeons.

ST. BENEDICT Fever, kidney disease, poisons, contagious diseases, safe delivery in childbirth, sick animals, business success, and protection from storms.

ST. BERNARDINE OF SIENA Gambling addictions.

ST. BLAISE Diseases in both humans and animals, especially throat diseases. Patron of veterinarians.

ST. BRIGID OF KILDARE Childbirth, fertility, protection from fires, healing, agriculture, inspiration, learning, poetry, prophecy, and love. Patroness of blacksmiths, dairy workers, and physicians.

ST. CADOC OF WALES Glandular disorders.

ST. CAPISTRANO Repelling enemies.

ST. CLARE OF ASSISI Understanding, help with difficulties, and overcoming drug and alcohol problems.

ST. CATHERINE OF ALEXANDRIA Beauty, fertility, a peaceful death, love, jealousy, healing, fortunate birth, visions and dreams, and public speaking. Patroness of teachers and jurors.

ST. CATHERINE OF SIENA Patroness of nursing homes, fire protection, and unmarried women.

ST. CECILIA Success in composing, music, poets, and singers.

ST. CHRISTOPHER Protection from accidents and sudden death, safe travel, fever, storms, and nightmares. Patron of unmarried men, bus drivers, and motorists.

ST. CIPRIANO Protection while traveling, homeless people, earthquakes, fire, bad neighbors, liars, deceitful lovers, and keeping one out of jail.

ST. CLOTILDE Adopted children and widows.

STS. COSMAS AND DAMIAN Sickness, correct diagnosis of diseases, and removal of obstacles. Patrons of barbers, druggists, physicians, and surgeons.

ST. DENIS Headaches.

ST. DISMAS Patron of prisoners, thieves, death-row inmates, and undertakers.

ST. DOROTHY OF MONTAU Miscarriages.

ST. DYMPHNA Insanity, nervous disorders or any mental problems, family harmony, and epilepsy.

ST. ELMO Appendicitis, intestinal disease, and seasickness.

ST. EXPEDITE Settling disputes and changing things quickly.

ST. FABIOLA Infidelity and physical abuse. Patroness of divorce and widows.

ST. FLORIAN Protection of the home against fire and flood, help in danger and emergencies. Patron of firemen.

ST. FRANCIS DE SALES Deafness. Patron of writers and journalists.

ST. FRANCIS OF ASSISI Understanding, peace, spiritual wisdom, and help with problems. Patron of all animals and birds, gardens, firemen, merchants, and garment makers.

ST. FRANCIS XAVIER CABRINI The poor, being accepted when you move, health, education. Patroness of emigrants.

ST. GEORGE Courage, conquering fear, overcoming jealousy; skin diseases, and mental retardation. Patron of soldiers.

ST. GERARD MAJELLA Fertility, pregnant women, mothers with small children, being falsely accused, channeling, prophecy, healing, and seeing the truth. Patron of pregnant women.

ST. GERTRUDE OF NIVELLES Getting rid of rats and mice. Patron of cats.

ST. GILES Patron of the physically disabled.

ST. HELEN OF JERUSALEM Love and overcoming sorrow. Patroness of archaeologists.

ST. HIPPOLYTUS Patron of horses.

ST. HULBERT Patron of dogs, hunters, and rabies sufferers.

ST. IGNATIUS OF LOYOLA Protection against burglars and evil spirits. Patron of soldiers.

ST. JAMES THE GREATER Conquering enemies, removing obstacles, justice, arthritis, and rheumatism. Patron of manual laborers.

ST. JOAN OF ARC Courage, spiritual strength, and overcoming enemies.

ST. JOHN THE BAPTIST Good luck, crops, and protection from enemies. Patron of tailors.

ST. JOHN BOSCO Temporal needs, students, and trouble with children. Patron of editors.

ST. JOHN GUALBERT Patron of foresters and park services.

ST. JOHN THE DIVINE Friendship. Patron of art dealers, editors, and publishers.

ST. JOSEPH Protection, finding a job, selling a house, married couples. Patron of carpenters and bakers.

ST. JUDE Hopeless cases, court troubles or getting out of jail; drugs.

ST. LAWRENCE A peaceful home and family, and financial assistance. Patron of the poor.

ST. LAZARUS Sickness, diseases of the legs, drug addiction, and getting prosperity.

ST. LEONARD Burglary, prisoners of war, and women in labor.

ST. LOUIS BERTRAND Learning languages, and protection from evil and accidents.

ST. LUCY Eye problems, repelling legal problems, settling court cases, protection from hexes, help when your back is against the wall. Patroness of salespeople and writers.

ST. LUKE Patron of painters, physicians, or surgeons.

ST. MADRON Pain.

ST. MARTHA Domestic problems, money troubles, keeping a lover or husband faithful, bringing in a new love, and conquering enemies. Patroness of housekeepers and servants.

ST. MARTIN DE PORRES Financial needs, health, and harmony. Patron of the poor and animals.

ST. MARTIN OF TOURS Repelling evil, protection from enemies; money, lucky, and a successful business.

ST. MARY MAGDALENE Patroness of repentant prostitutes, perfumers, and hair stylists.

ST. MATTHEW Patron of bankers, bookkeepers, customs agents, security guards, and tax collectors.

ST. MICHAEL Total protection.

ST. NICHOLAS OF MYRA Patron of dock workers, children, brides, merchants, unmarried women, and travelers.

ST. PATRICK Prosperity, good luck, spiritual wisdom, guidance, and protection against snakebite.

ST. PAUL Courage, overcoming opposition, and a peaceful home. Patron of authors, journalists, publishers, and travelers.

ST. PEREGRINE LAZIOSI Health problems, particularly cancer.

ST. PETER Success, good business, strength, courage, good luck, and removing obstacles. Patron of bridge builders and masons.

ST. PHILOMENA Pregnant women, destitute mothers, fertility, trouble with children, happiness in the home, money problems, mental illness, and real estate. Patroness of any desperate situation.

ST. RAYMOND NONNATUS Stopping gossip and protection of unborn babies. Patron of midwives.

ST. RITA Bleeding, desperate situations, parenthood, infertility, and marital problems.

ST. RITA OF CASCIA Loneliness, abusive relationships, healing wounds and tumors, and deliverance from evil. Patroness of hopeless cases.

ST. SEBASTIAN Justice, court cases, overcoming rivals, removing obstacles, and obtaining good fortune. Patron of athletes, gardeners, potters, stonemasons, and soldiers.

ST. TERESA OF AVILA Headaches and heart attacks.

ST. THERESE OF LISIEUX Alcohol and drug problems, spiritual growth, protection against black magick, and tuberculosis.

ST. THOMAS AQUINAS Improving the memory and passing school exams. Patrons of scholars and students.

ST. VITUS Exorcism of evil spirits and curing epilepsy. Patron of comedians and dancers.

VIRGIN MARY The mother of Christ. Love, kindness, protection, and intercession for any need.

Building Special Altars

The object of any altar is for it to symbolize what you want to attract into your life. Your altar should be pleasing to you, not necessarily to anyone else. To make your altar more powerful, concentrate on your objective while arranging the objects on it, then visit the altar frequently. The following examples are only suggestions to give you ideas for your own creations. See page 13 for more information on the meaning of objects and symbols.

An altar need not be anything fancy. It can be a small table, a shelf in the kitchen or bathroom, or some other available space. In fact, you may decide to prepare different altars for different rooms. If you use candles on your altars, be certain that they can burn without creating a fire hazard. Do not burn candles under another shelf, near curtains or hanging fabrics, and always put candles in a nonflammable, unbreakable holder.

The deities listed do not include all the appropriate deities or saints who can help with the problem for which you are building your altar. You may not wish to include any deity statue, or you may wish to have several. The choice is yours.

There is no proper place on an altar to place any object. Work with arrangements until the altar is pleasing to your eye and your soul. Candles may be used on any altar, as may incense. Consult the list of colors on page 39 to choose an appropriately colored candle. If you wish, anoint it with a corresponding oil before burning it. You may have as many candles as you wish on an altar, either all of the same color, or a combination of several appropriate colors. The color white can be added safely and effectively to any altar arrangement. Never leave wilted flowers on an altar; replace them whenever necessary.

An altar may be left unchanged for a long period, or rearranged and changed whenever you feel it is necessary. An altar is a very personal, individual expression and should not reflect the desires of another person.

Love

When building an altar to attract love into your life, you should never specify a particular person. This not only limits your choices, but may well bring about a relationship that is not the one you expected. Also, you do not want to create negative karma by trying to make an uninterested person love you. You most definitely should not try to separate a couple.

Examples of altar objects: Statues or pictures of a cat or dove; symbol of a basket or heart; the colors pink and green; the stones rose quartz, garnet, and lapis lazuli; the herb ginger; the tree mistletoe; the oil and incense violet; the flower red carnation.

Examples of deities: Aphrodite, Inanna, Haniel, St. Martha.

Suggested arrangement: Place the cat statue next to a small basket with a red heart inside. The colors may be used in an altar cloth and/or the candles. You may wish to write out on a piece of paper the characteristics you value in a love relationship, then put the paper into the basket with the heart. Sprinkle ginger lightly over the items in the basket, or place a piece of mistletoe in with the heart. Arrange the stones near the statue, with the incense nearby. Use a small vase for the red carnation.

Prosperity

Your first prosperity altar may be for short-term financial relief. However, you also need to concentrate on long-term prosperity. To achieve this, you need to work for good opportunities to come your way, ones that will help you achieve what you desire. Nothing comes free, so do not expect to win a huge lottery.

Examples of altar objects: Statues or pictures of a pig or dragon; symbols of a box and a cauldron; the colors brown, green, or gold; the stones turquoise, moss agate, or tiger's eye; the tree fig; the herb ginger; the oil and incense patchouli; the flower hollyhock or jasmine.

Examples of deities: Fortuna, Freyr, Raphael, St. Anthony.

Suggested arrangement: Place the cauldron in the center of your altar space and place inside it the stones and a little of the herb. The box can hold a list of the reasons you want to increase your prosperity. By making this list, you convince your subconscious mind that you have a need and the right to ask for the opportunities to increase your wealth. The colors may be used in altar clothes and/or candles. Hollyhock blossoms can be floated in a shallow bowl and jasmine placed in an elegant vase.

Protection

Protection altars can be built for protection against specific dangers or simply to protect against negative thoughts coming from jealous or hateful people. If your altar is for protection from a specific, threatening person, such as an ex-spouse, ex-lover, or harmful family member, try to place a photo of the offending person under the deity or animal statue that symbolizes divine wisdom and the power to overcome the threat.

Examples of altar objects: Statues or pictures of a tiger or wolf; symbols of a ring or circle; the colors black and indigo; the stones amber, carnelian, and black obsidian; the tree holly; the herb basil or bay; the oil and incense lavender; the flower peony.

Examples of deities: Heimdall, Thor, Guardian Angel St. Michael, St. Christopher.

Suggested arrangement: Place the statue in the center of the altar so that the animal figure has a prominent place. Around it, position the stones, keys, and either a ring or a drawing of a circle. Holly twigs and the herb may be placed at both ends to produce protective energies. Place the incense, candle, and flowers to make an eye-pleasing arrangement.

Thanksgiving

Thanksgiving altars can be built for a number of reasons: recovery from an illness, finding a wonderful friend or lover, success in obtaining a good job or home, escape from a potential danger, and so on.

Examples of altar objects: Statues or pictures of a unicorn or blackbird; symbols of a shell or the yin/yang symbol; the color white; the stones clear quartz crystal and chrysoprase; the tree cedar; the herb, oil, and incense myrrh; the flower of a white rose.

Examples of deities: Buddha, Bishamonten, Metatron, and the Virgin Mary.

Suggested arrangement: Choose a nice vase for the rose and set it in the center of the altar. Around it, arrange the stones, symbols, and animal statue. To represent the tree, you may have any object made of cedar, or else burn cedar incense. If you use a cedar box or bowl, you may want to write out on a small piece of paper why you are thankful, and place that inside the cedar container.

Spiritual Growth

Altars for spiritual growth are not that common, as most people are usually more intent on improving their lives in other areas. However, there will come a time when only spiritual growth on your part will improve your life and bring it into balance. This altar is excellent for meditation on self-discovery and your personal life path.

Examples of altar objects: Statues or pictures of a goose or raven; a symbol representing a bridge or wings; the colors magenta or purple; the stones amethyst and clear quartz crystal; the tree pine or another evergreen; the herb hyssop or mugwort; the oil and incense lotus; the flower lily.

Examples of deities: Tara, Isis, Metatron, St. Francis of Assisi.

Suggested arrangement: Either place a picture of the bridge or wings to the rear center of the altar or fasten it to the wall directly behind the altar. In front of the picture, place the animal statue and the stones, with the pine or evergreen arranged around them. The herb may be tucked among the pine boughs, and the lily can be floated in a shallow bowl next to the candles and incense.

Finding a Job

Although you must be sincere in your efforts and desires to obtain a good job, you do not have to be absolutely specific in every detail. You want to create opportunities for yourself. Once the opportunities present themselves, it is up to you to make the effort of applying for the job and doing your best once you get it.

Examples of altar objects: Statues or pictures of a bat, coyote, or frog; symbols of breasts, a box or cube; the colors black and orange; the stones bloodstone and malachite; the tree bay; the herb thyme; the oil and incense ginger; the flower aster or ivy.

Examples of deities: Ganesha, Ebisu, Ptah, Sandalphon, St. Joseph.

Suggested arrangement: Write out the type of job you wish in a small piece of paper. Place the paper either in the center of your altar or inside a box there. Set the stones on top of the paper or box. Twine the ivy around the box, or place the asters nearby in a vase. Sprinkle a little thyme and bay leaves over the altar. Place the black candle (for absorbing negativity) on one side of the altar and the orange (for action and increasing the intellect) on the other. Place the animal statue near the paper or box, to watch over it.

Making a Decision

Sometimes you feel you cannot make a decision because you feel inadequate or do not have all the facts. A decision-making altar will help bring the information and courage you need if you meditate before it once a day.

Examples of altar objects: Statues or pictures of an elephant, eagle, or bee; symbols of an ear of corn or an eye; the colors gold, red, and yellow; the stones fluorite and pyrite; the tree apple; the herb sage or catnip; the incense clove; the flower aster or chrysanthemum.

Examples of deities: Horus, Ganesha, Ratziel, St. Sebastian. In the Far East, the elephant with an upraised trunk symbolizes good fortune; in India, the elephant-god Ganesha is said to remove obstacles. Therefore an elephant of any kind is symbolic of moving ahead in life by making the right decision.

Suggested arrangement: Surround your animal statue with the stones, and place the vase of flowers nearby. An apple can represent the apple tree. Place it together with the ear of corn to symbolize abundance. Sprinkle the herbs before the animal statue, and use the colors in candles.

Recovering from Divorce

Most divorces do not end amicably. They tend to sour with bitterness, recrimination, and sometimes threats by one or both parties. The parties involved forget the old saying: the best revenge is to live a good life. You need to move beyond all these negatives and let go of the past in order to accept the future. Never put a photo of the divorced partner on your altar, only your own photo. This altar is for *your* healing from the divorce. Choose a photo where you are smiling and happy, a symbol of what you will have in the future.

Examples of altar objects: Statues or pictures of a badger or bear; symbols of a mask, knots, door, scepter (wand), or square; the colors red or black; the stones brown or orange and brown agate, amber, or chrysoprase; the tree holly or juniper; the oil and incense patchouli; the herb mint; the flower anemone or chrysanthemum.

Examples of deities: Anubis, Buto, Uriel, St. Fabiola.

Suggested arrangement: Place your smiling photo in the center of the altar, representing your central importance in your new life. Put the animal statue, symbols, stones, and herbs in a semicircle before it. These items will be a daily reminder that you are guided and protected as your forge a new existence for yourself. Arrange the bouquet of flowers on one end of the altar, the candles and incense on the other, for balance.

Healing

This altar may be for you, another person, or a pet in need of healing. In fact, you can arrange groups of photos of friends and family who need divine healing energies. This altar may be an ongoing, changeable altar that becomes a source of hope and inspiration to many.

Examples of altar objects: Statues or pictures of a phoenix or dog; symbols of the caduceus, arrows, ring, jar, or yin/yang; colors light blue and green; stones of hematite and clear quartz crystal; the tree holly or oak; the herb rue; the oil and incense pine; the flower bachelor's button or lilac.

Examples of deities: Brigit, Yao-Shih, Imhotep, Raphael, Saints Cosmas and Damian.

Suggested arrangement: If you have only one photo of someone needing healing, place it in the center of the altar. If you have several photos, arrange them in a line across the altar so you can clearly see each one. Place the animal statue, stones, herb, incense, candles, flowers, and symbols around or among these photos. This will keep the flow of healing energy moving among the sick people at all times.

In Memory of Lost Loved Ones

Some people already have "altars" to lost loved ones, although they may be unaware of this. Pictures of deceased friends and family may cover the top of the piano or table in the living room. This is an excellent way to remember loved ones, as well as to remind others of their continued existence in our hearts and in another realm.

If you are having difficulty coming to terms with the loss of someone, whether recent or not, a special altar holding shared objects, photos, and other mementos can help. When you feel the hurt has been healed, you can move the photos to stand among others of beloved family and friends, living and deceased.

Examples of altar objects: Statues or pictures of a deer, hawk, or raven; symbol of a star, peach, or pumpkin; the colors white and royal blue; the stones bloodstone and black onyx; the herb rosemary; the tree yew or pomegranate; the oil and incense lily; flowers rose and periwinkle.

Examples of deities: Osiris, Ishtar, Tzaphkiel, the Virgin Mary.

Suggested arrangement: Arrange the altar in whatever way seems best to you. This is a symbol of your personal grief over the loss of someone dear to you. Add or remove personal mementos as time passes and your degree of grief changes. There will come a time when the deep hurt lessens, and you will not be grieving before this altar so much. The pain never completely goes away, but you will learn how to handle it better.

Dedication to God/Goddess/Saint

Some people find they can move through life with more ease if they have one special altar dedicated to a deity or saint of their choice. This altar is one that you should visit daily for help with your everyday life. Commune with the deity or saint through meditation and prayer.

Examples of altar objects: Statues or pictures of your chosen deity or saint; the colors, white, gold, and silver; the stones clear quartz crystal, black obsidian, amethyst, lapis lazuli, malachite, and rose quartz; the flowers sunflower or red and white roses; the oil and incense rose.

Examples of deities: Use any deity that you choose.

Suggested arrangement: Place the deity or saint statue in the center of the altar as the prominent object. Arrange the stones, candles, and flowers about this statue in whatever way seems best to you. Requests written on paper can also be placed on the altar.

PART II

A LITTLE BOOK OF Candle Magick

Candles and Fire in Religious History

Humankind has always held a deep respect for fire and its power. This respect for and curiosity about fire probably began when humans first became brave enough to take fires caused by lightning back to their camping places to use for warmth and cooking. Some archaeologists place this occurring about 250,000 to 500,000 years ago. Until humans learned how to start fires on their own, these early people were very careful to keep such "captured, sacred" fire burning at all times.

It was not long before humans discovered that fire had two aspects: the sacred and the mundane. Shamans kindled their fires in specific ways with special woods. They used this fire to light mysterious caves and sacred power sites that only certain people entered for mystical rituals. These holy fires helped the shaman and other initiated participants connect with the spiritual worlds where they received messages and first learned healing and magick. Later, they learned other secrets, such as metalworking. Because fire could be either creative or destructive, those who handled fire were considered to be divinely touched.

Early myths and legends tell of various divine beings who either stole fire from heaven, as Prometheus did, or who gave this wonderful gift to humans so they could survive and worship the deities. Many deities from cultures around the world are associated with fire in one or more of its forms, such as the hearth, volcanoes, and lightning.

Much later in their history, humans developed more portable forms for using sacred fires. First came the torch, then the oil lamp and candles. All holy places were lit by these miniature forms of fire, as were private home altars. Priests and magicians taught that the flame of oil lamps and candles represented the spirit's highest potential and that the smoke carried the worshipper's prayers and desires into the spiritual realm.

Herbs were either burned as incense or added to the candles. The herbs not only gave off a pleasant scent, but also often were chosen for their ability to trigger altered states that led the priest or magician into a higher state of consciousness. Accompanied by prayer, chants, dance, and/or deep concentration, the priests and magicians learned that they could manifest their desires. Thus, magick was discovered.

Magick continued to thrive and be accepted as a viable method for making life better until much later, when religions declared that magick was not possible and was only superstitious nonsense. However, these same religions continued to light their sacred places with the holy flame in one form or another.

Modern Fire Rituals

Even today, fire rituals are still used in many cultures and religions around the world. Nearly every religion uses candles, lamps, or incense to mark their religious centers and ceremonies.

In Latin America, people still use candles to mark Halloween. They prepare an altar or a gravesite with pictures of departed loved ones and light candles that represent the spirits of the dead. In the United States and Europe, people celebrate this same seasonal festival with candles inside hollowed-out pumpkins; however, these candles are to chase away spirits, not honor them.

The Catholic religion uses an ever-burning flame, hung above the altar, to alert worshippers of the presence of the communion host. Catholic churches also have racks of votive candles, which can be lit by those presenting petitions and desires to Mary or one of the saints. Devotional candles are very popular with the worshippers of several religions. These lights may be in the form of votive, taper, or novena candles, which are offered to a particular saint, deity, or Loa (a deity in certain African religions) in a petition for their help.

To mark birthdays, several cultures use a tall candle measured into twenty-one segments. This candle is blessed and lit on the first birthday of a child. Then, it is relit on each consecutive birthday and allowed to burn down to a mark; this is repeated until the child turns twenty-one. This is enacted in the form of a petition to a deity so that the child may have a happy, healthy life. The candles commonly placed on top of a birthday cake have much the same meaning.

As far back as very ancient history, funerals have also used fire in many forms. Cremation was believed to release the soul immediately into the afterworld. Torches and candles often lined a processional path to the burial site or place of cremation, symbolically guiding the soul to the invisible door that led to Valhalla, heaven, or whatever the culture believed to be the Otherworld.

Likewise, candles are often used at weddings, this time with a different connotation. The flame of the candles traditionally signals the presence of deities who will bless the union, as well as remind the bride and groom that the element of Spirit should be present in the marriage.

Hanukkah is a Jewish festival known also as the Feast of Dedication or the Festival of Lights. It commemorates the victory of the Maccabees over the Syrian Greeks. The Talmud says that after the Temple was cleansed and rededicated, only one small cruse of holy oil was found to use for relighting the perpetual fire. Miraculously, this oil burned for eight days. Today, this festival is marked by lighting one candle each day, until eight candles are lit.

Another tradition found in several cultures says that when a house has known happiness and prosperity, then that dwelling is inhabited by a good spirit. When the family moves, they can carry this spirit with them by lighting a large candle from the hearth. The hearth in the new home is then lit from this candle, thus providing a welcome for the good spirit.

Several Yule or Christmas customs also use the sacred flame, although we have forgotten much of the significance behind these seasonal rituals. The lights on the modern Christmas tree have replaced the candles once used to signify rebirth. The electric light in the window was at one time a candle that helped departed loved ones return to join in the festivities. The Yule log in the fireplace symbolizes the death of the old year and the birth of the new year; it also represents the old tradition of the rebirth of the sun.

In a great many public gatherings, you will see people holding candles. Known as vigilance candles, these are used to remember a specific person or event and to create unity and change. Little do these participants realize that they are performing a type of magick. This multitude of candles actually directs the people's spiritual energy to a desired goal.

Why are candles still so popular? I believe it is because of genetic memories that lie buried deep within the superconscious mind of every human. These memories call to us over the distance of centuries; they affect our subconscious responses to life. Fire has always been sacred. Genetic memories remind us that it still is. In response, we are drawn to candles, whether we use them in ritual or simply light them on a birthday cake or the table for a special dinner.

Candle burning as a ritual attracts us. It is easy to do, primal in meaning, and a powerful form of sympathetic magick. Since magick is not a religion, a person of any religion can use it. The altar, deity-named candle or candles, and the ritual itself can be rearranged to suit your personal faith. Candle burning is comforting, as it helps us to realize we can do something about the things in our lives that we find annoying or distressing. It is spiritual in its meaning and often draws the user into a more spiritual state of mind. Powerful in its results, this form of simple magick has centuries of use behind it. It does not require fancy robes, expensive tools, or vast metaphysical knowledge to perform. It is a magickal tool of the common person who desires to make her/his life better.

The Purpose of Rituals and Magick

Because of the effectiveness of magick, and the simplicity of candle magick in particular, it has been feared by many people throughout its long history, even though candles are part of many contemporary religions.

Most candle magick is done by people who say they do not believe in magick. Candles are lit in a room simply because someone thinks it "feels" good to do it. Certain aromatic candles are used to cleanse the atmosphere and give calmness to the occupants of the house or apartment. Candlelight dinners create a romantic mood. A birthday cake with lighted candles celebrates another year of life. These are all magickal, psychic, and psychological rituals that speak to the human heart. Yet they are performed by people who have no conscious intention of doing magick.

Our lives are filled with rituals, the majority of them of mundane nature. Ritual is any repeated act. We routinely do certain things every day with the expectation of certain results. We brush our teeth, take a bath, eat meals, watch the news, work, and some of us may go to a religious gathering. Therefore, we are all acquainted with rituals and can understand what they are. Rituals give cohesion to our lives. It is only when ritual is connected with magick that the confusion begins.

Joining Rituals and Magick

Actually, there is nothing that mysterious about magick. Magick is simply the altering of events through willpower. Ritual magick is the taking of energy from another plane of existence and weaving that energy, through certain actions, into a desired physical form on this plane of existence. A magician deliberately seeks these pools of otherworld energy, tapping into them and adding their power to the energy for manifestation that each person holds within her/himself. Because humans have a difficult time relating to abstract ideas, we call these energy pools God and/or Goddess. This otherworld energy needs two catalysts from the human magician in order to create a desire: human willpower and a deep desire to accomplish a specific goal. You cannot halfheartedly do magick for something; it will not work. You must want very much the results you are striving to create; you must be totally involved in the candle ceremony—body, mind, emotions, and spirit. That is why it is easier to do magick for yourself than for others.

To do magick properly, however, may take some rethinking. The original magick of affecting an event through willpower has degenerated, in most modern minds, to the acts of a stage magician, who does sleight-of-hand tricks and affects no events. There is no similarity between ritual magick and stage magick.

To prepare yourself for performing magick, you have to rethink what is possible or impossible. Magick cannot be placed under a microscope or proved in a laboratory. It lives in the mind of the user, manifesting itself in the results. When you realize that certain actions bring results, nothing is impossible.

One of the biggest hurdles to using magick is the erroneous belief that to be spiritual you cannot be concerned with material things. In defining materialism, one must understand that there is a difference between being concerned with material well-being and being controlled by material things and miserliness. It is not wrong to use magick to have a better life. In fact, if a person's life is in a negative cycle because of lack of money or health or even love, there is no way that person can concentrate on being spiritual. When you are content with your physical life, you are more open to expanding your spiritual life. Above all things, magick is practical.

However, it is wrong to use magick to willfully harm or control others or take something that belongs to another person. Many people are surprised to learn that there are ethics in the use of magick. Magicians know that negative actions build negative karma. No matter what excuse one uses for such behavior, the result is always the same: If you use negative magick, you have to pay for what you do. No bad deed goes unpunished, even if it takes some time for that punishment to fall upon the perpetrator.

Candle Magick

This is true even of the little magick of candle burning. Think very carefully about your desire before you burn candles to get it. Never take one person away from another, or try to make someone love you or give you money. By naming a specific person in a spell, you are limiting your chances of success. Use candle magick to attract the perfect loving person for you or to bring you positive opportunities to get the money you need. You must never interfere with the free will of another person.

Neither should you do spellwork to harm physically or materially destroy someone. There are other, safer methods of bringing justice down upon evil people. For example, use your candle magick so that the law will catch and convict rapists, abusers, and murderers. Burn a candle for the swindler and con artist to be caught by his/her own actions.

This does not mean you should be a doormat about protecting yourself and your loved ones. If you are in fear of your life, do everything physically and magickally within your power to eliminate the menace. Be creative in doing protective spellwork. It is essential to think through your reasons for doing magick.

Although some rituals will produce immediate results, most of them will not. It is not uncommon for a spell to take quite some time to manifest your desire. You will need to repeat the spell over a period of time, since the goal is difficult to manifest and must build up the energy it uses before manifesting. Because of this, many people who try candle-burning magick do not believe it works. They see no results in a week or a month and thus give up. Some spells need several months before their effects are seen. The time spent in empowering the more difficult spells over a period of time also gains you the biggest rewards.

Candle magick is not an instantaneous magick. It will not solve your problems overnight. However, it is a powerful tool for manifestation of your desires.

Candles and Colors

When you feel ready to try candle magick, start out with a small goal that you want to reach. By starting small, you gain confidence and experience at candle-burning magick. Use any supplies you have on hand to begin with, and get acquainted with the procedures in the rituals. However, it is not a good idea to use candles that have been burned for any other reason.

Altars and Other Essentials

An altar (see page 4) is an essential piece of equipment for candle rituals. Although you can use any table or available flat surface, it is very inconvenient to have to clear away all ritual candles and tools each time you need to go about your everyday affairs. This moving of candles will also interrupt the magickal energy flow. For this reason, you need to have a separate small area on which to burn your ritual candles and where you can meditate upon the purpose of your spellwork. This can be a shelf attached to the wall or a small table that will fit into one corner of a room. If possible, it is best to have this shelf or table in a room that is not readily available to visitors or anyone who might question what you are doing or who might feel free to touch or rearrange your project.

If you use a shelf, be certain that it is not under any other object, such as another shelf. The heat from the candles can scorch wood or start a fire by igniting nearby papers or books. If you use a table, position it away from draperies and other flammable materials. It is best not to have any cloths or scarves on the shelf or table. If a candle falls over, it could ignite such combustible material. Candle wax is also very difficult to get out of cloth or carpet. If you want to protect the altar top, cover it with a marble board, a metal sheet, or a thick piece of tempered glass. This protective covering also makes it easier to clean up drips of candle wax.

Eventually, you will want a few more essential items for candle-burning magick: an assortment of colors and types of candles, a number of metal holders, a candle snuffer, and perhaps a statue or two representing the deities of your spiritual path. If you use incense, you will need a holder for the sticks and cones. In a pinch, a can of sand will work for both types of incense and will provide safety from fire. You will also at some time want to include a variety of oils and small stones to enhance the power of the spells.

There are several kinds and colors of candles that are traditionally used in candle-burning magick. Lists and meanings vary from book to book. You can be as elaborate or as simple as you wish in your choices of candles and their colors. You can even burn more than one type of candle at a time if you wish. The important thing is to choose a type and color of candle that symbolizes the desire you want to manifest.

Types of Candles

Traditionally, different kinds of candles are used for specific rituals. The most common types are the six-inch straight and the small votive candles, which can be used in place of the more elaborate types of candles. Other types of candles are explained later in this section.

There are always three main types of candles used in a ritual: the altar candle or candles that symbolize whatever deity you want to call upon; the astrological candle that represents you or another person; and the candle that signifies the desire you are trying to achieve. Using a nail or a small knife, inscribe identifying initials or zodiac symbols onto the astrological candles. If you do not know names, you can scratch on J for judge or OW for other woman, for example. This helps you to avoid confusion. If you do not know a person's astrological sign, choose one that most closely represents a type of person, such as Libra for a judge or Aries for someone with an aggressive attitude.

ADAM AND EVE OR IMAGE CANDLES These candles are made in nude male and female forms, as well as a variety of colors. The figures are primarily used in spells for love and/or relationships. They are usually burned to bring love into your life. However, they can also be used to draw back a wayward lover, send away an undesirable lover, or banish an illness. Although mentioned in old Scottish records, wax images have been used as far back as ancient Egypt and Babylon.

ALTAR, JUMBO, OR PILLAR CANDLES These are tall, thick candles that come in various colors, usually red, white, or black. They are used as altar or deity candles since they burn too slowly to use in any other capacity. Although white is the most popular color, you may use any color that symbolizes the deities or powers with which you want to communicate. You need these candles to burn longer than the other candles, as they are lit first and extinguished last. There can be two altar candles on the altar, one on each side, or just one in the center. Some people use a seven-day candle in a glass container with a particular saint painted on the glass. Frequently, altar candles are one white and one black candle. It is not safe to leave pillar candles burning unattended, as the melted wax, which gathers in the center, can collapse one side of the candle and possibly start a fire.

ASTRAL OR ZODIAC CANDLES These colored candles represent you and any other persons included in the spell. You may use colors from the list on page 115, or choose colors that seem right to you.

CAT CANDLES This candle in the figure of a seated cat is used according to the color. Black will banish bad luck, break jinxes or hexes, and bring in good luck. Red helps with love. Green is used to get money or to heal, especially pets. The cat candle in black is the most popular and is often called the black cat candle.

CROSS OR CRUCIFIX CANDLES Primarily used for protection and banishing, this type of candle can be burned as an offering to a deity, saint, or Loa. This candle will often have a rose at the crosspieces or a prayer written on it.

DEVOTIONAL CANDLES These come in a heat-resistant glass container, usually with pictures of saints or Loas on the glass. A type of novena candle, they are burned when asking a petition from the deities.

DOUBLE-ACTION OR REVERSING CANDLES Made with two colors of wax, these are used for dual purpose or reversing spells; only the lower half of a candle is dipped into another color of wax. For example, a green candle with the lower half dipped in black is for bringing in prosperity and repelling negativity and bad luck. Red dipped in black defeats the influence of anyone who is destroying your marriage or a relationship. White with black reverses all spells against you. Sometimes you can find Triple-Action candles, or candles dipped into three different colors of wax.

MEMORIAL CANDLES These are usually the very largest of the votive candles that come in a glass. Ordinarily they are lit at midnight or sunrise to honor a birthday or anniversary or to remember a deceased loved one.

MUMMY CANDLES This is a candle made in the form of a mummy figure in a coffin. It is used to ward off illness, death, or any dangerous situation. The skull candle works in much the same manner.

SATAN OR DEVIL-BE-GONE CANDLES This candle is made in the image of the Christian Devil. It is not for worshipping this entity, but for performing exorcisms or clearing houses of negative vibrations or spirits. It is always burned with an astral candle to represent the person or persons being harassed. The astral candle must be large enough to last longer than the Satan candle when burned.

SEPARATION CANDLES This jumbo red candle is completely dipped in black wax so that all of the red color is covered. This candle should be used with extreme care and only after much honest thought, since it separates one person from the enthrallment or bondage of an undesirable person. This may be advisable when your daughter is caught in an intensive abusive relationship or marriage, or your father or mother are being conned by a swindler for all of his or her money. The break-up candle with a snake coiled around it is used for the same purposes.

SEVEN-DAY NOVENA This purchased candle has white or colored wax poured into a tall, heat-resistant glass container, often with a picture of a saint on the glass. However, you can sometimes find these without the picture. The word *novena* means "new beginning" in Latin. You are to write your desire nine times on a piece of paper and tape it to the candle bottom before burning, or at least place it under the candle. Certain saints are called upon for specific help: St. Anthony for a job; St. Capistrano to repel enemies; St. Jude for any court troubles; the Sacred Heart for marriage; St. Clara for any addiction problems, whether alcohol or drugs; St. Michael for total protection. Sometimes, you can also buy a seven-color, seven-day novena candle, although these are difficult to find. With this candle, one color is burned each day for seven days.

Some novenas are performed as nine-day rituals and use the ten- or fifteen-hour votive candles instead of one large glass-enclosed candle. The novena is begun in the last quarter of the moon's waning phase and ends nine days later in the first quarter of the waxing moon. Nine of the votive candles are burned at a time, with replacement candles being lit from the old candle when one is close to burning out. To perform this ritual correctly, you must never let any of the candles go out before a replacement is lit.

SEVEN-KNOB CANDLES Made of seven thick knobs, one on top of the other, these candles are meant to have one knob burned per day while you concentrate on your desire. The most common colors are black for banishing or releasing spells sent against you; red for setting energy into motion or removing obstacles to finding love; and green for money, manifesting, or favorable court action. Occasionally, you can find other colors of seven-knob candles: brown for delaying a court case or giving you your day in court; yellow to remove bad luck; purple for defeating psychic attack or eliminating minor health problems; blue to stop quarreling, confusion, or depression; orange for removing obstacles to a successful business or career; white to grant you a secret wish. Because it takes seven days to finish the ritual, it can be extremely powerful.

SKULL CANDLES Made in the shape of a skull, these candles are used not for hexing, but for healing serious, deadly, or terminal diseases. They are always burned with an astral candle.

The first thing you should do after purchasing candles and taking them home is to gently clean them of any dust and debris. Do this by wiping them with a paper towel or soft cloth. If the candle is particularly dirty, you may have to wipe it with a mild soap and water solution. If it has any imperfections, carefully trim and smooth it with a knife. Then store each color of candle separately in a box or drawer. Do not put all the candles willy-nilly in the same place. It is not a good idea to store different colors directly touching each other, as the colors may bleed onto each other.

If you like to make your own candles, this will add even more energy to your spells. However, candle making is a time-consuming effort, far beyond the reaches and desires of most people. If you make your own candles, do not use the remains of old candles. The old wax still holds within it vibrations from other spells or situations. These vibrations will contaminate any spells you do with these candles.

It is also a good idea to check each candle for the power and type of vibration it holds. Purchased candles have been repeatedly handled by a number of people before they get to you. Some of these people may leave undesirable vibrations on whatever they touch. To check for this, hold a pendulum (see page 216) over each candle. If the pendulum swings forward and backward or in a clockwise direction, the candle's power is strong and its vibration positive. If the pendulum swings side to side or in a counterclockwise direction, the power is weak and the vibration negative. To remove negative vibrations and strengthen the power, pass the candle through frankincense incense smoke. Then test it again with the pendulum. Repeat until you get a positive answer with the pendulum.

If you plan to let candles burn out, you need to use a marble board or a thick piece of tempered glass on your altar and set each candle into a metal container or holder. This will prevent any accidents that might cause a fire. Porcelain and glass holders or containers will occasionally break from the heat.

Before you burn the small votive candles, remove the metal tab from the bottom of the candle to avoid cracking the glass container into which you put it. Better yet, coat the bottom of a small metal cauldron with an appropriate oil and set the votive candle inside to burn. Small cast-iron cauldrons are best because they take heat well. The oil will keep the wax from sticking. You should always clean away all old wax before using a holder or cauldron for another spell. If you burn seven-day candles that come in a glass container, they are ordinarily safe from breakage. If you feel uneasy about them, however, set the candle into a metal cauldron or onto a marble board.

If you burn request papers after a candle spell is finished, do not burn the paper in a cauldron or holder that still has candle wax in it. This will cause a dangerous flame that is difficult to extinguish and will be strong enough to set off smoke alarms and probably burn marks into your altar. It can also set fire to surrounding objects.

Messages and Symbols

After you have worked with candle magick for a time, you will recognize certain patterns of candle-flame behavior that have traditional meanings. Even in the absence of drafts, the flames of some candles will wave and dip. This is a type of communication. If the flame bends to the north, it symbolizes that something of a physical nature is occurring. To the east, a mental aspect of the spellwork is happening. To the south, much physical energy is around the event. In the west, there are heavy emotions involved.

Some candles will also sputter and crackle, another traditional form of communication. Softly chattering candles indicate things of a personal nature are being affected. Frequent sputters mean a person of authority is influencing what happens. A candle that has strong crackles means arguments and quarrels are likely.

The strength of a candle flame also has meaning. A candle that puts out a strong, steady flame is a good sign. It indicates that a lot of power and energy are being projected into your spell. When you use figure candles, it symbolizes that one person strongly influences and possibly controls the other. A jumping flame represents raw emotions and perhaps heated arguments. A weak flame is an indication that you are facing resistance and opposition against gaining your desire. In this case, you must repeat the spell several times in order to overcome this opposition.

If a spell calls for you to burn candles for a specified length of time, then put them out and reburn them later. Do not blow out the candles. Snuffing the flame with a candle snuffer or your fingers seals the energy into the spell instead of blowing it away.

Tradition also says you should not strike a sulfur match to light ritual candles. A lighter can be used to initially light the altar candles. Then, light a simple white candle from the altar candle and ignite the other candles with this.

If you repeat a spell using the same candles for the same purpose for several days in a row, you need to carefully trim off any drips or imperfections before beginning each ritual. This includes cleaning off any dust that might have gathered. You especially should do this with the altar or deity candles that you use for all your rituals. You want the energy of the candle spell to be as perfect as possible.

Spellwork

Very few spells last forever and must be worked at on a regular basis. Most spells, in fact, will need to be renewed, or repeated, if you desire the effects to be permanent and continuing. To sustain the magickal effects, you should repeat the candle spells quarterly, in the proper phases of the moon. Some spells need to be repeated because they require a buildup of energy to "mature." Among these spells are those for faithfulness, marital and family happiness, healing of certain diseases, and a successful business.

You have to put feeling, effort, and time into your candle spells. Then you must have patience while you give the spell energy the time to grow and manifest what you desire.

Before you ever begin a candle spell, you need to make a list of everything you will need. This way you can be certain you have everything on hand. Then comes the most important part of any spellwork: writing down in detail exactly what you desire to manifest from the spell. Besides setting parameters for the spell, this will help you concentrate on the actual spell itself.

Setting parameters is very important in spellwork. For example, if you are working for an increase in money, you certainly do not want it to come about through an auto accident, lawsuit, an insurance claim, or a fall. You simply want the opportunity to make money honestly without harming yourself or anyone else.

When spellworking for love, always work with the goal of "a perfect love for me" in mind, never a specific person. Controlling another person and forcing him/her through magick to love you is very bad for your spiritual health, as well as your mental and emotional well-being. Not only are you limiting your happiness, which could be greater with someone else, but you are also limiting the opportunity to have the very best person for you come into your life. I have never seen a love spell directed at a specific person ever turn out happily. The forced person resents the control and will eventually break away.

The same principle applies when doing spellwork for justice or protection, although here it is safe to mention names if you are absolutely certain. You must not, however, specify punishment. When the person in question pays the price for her/his misdeeds, you do not want to be in the messy middle of it and possibly even entangled in her/his fate. Direct the spell's energy toward having the guilty party's own actions bring justice down upon her/him. Let the guilty one be caught and punished by her/his own words and deeds. In this manner, you are not involved in any way, yet have helped the scales of justice be balanced. Transfer all your hatred, sadness, and strong emotions into candle magick. In this way, you can manifest your deepest desires and rid yourself of unhealthy emotional and mental turmoil, which will be changed into positive energy. After all, the best revenge is to live a good and prosperous life.

When doing candle magick, do only one spell at a time. Choose the most important need in your life and work on that first. Then, go on to another type of spell to manifest a different desire or need. You need to keep your energy centered on one thing at a time, or the spell's energy will be scrambled and the magick will dissipate before manifesting anything.

For the best results, time your rituals to the phases of the moon. For even more success, use both the correct moon phase and a particular day of the week that corresponds to your desire. The dedicated magicians often go so far as to time spells to a certain planetary hour on a certain day (see page 134).

Remember, candle magick does not bring instantaneous results. It takes time for the opportunities to come that will manifest your desires.

Colors

Colors are very important in candle-burning magick. However, some people have been taught to be prejudiced against certain hues. If, for example, you are not comfortable with black candles, substitute a dark blue one. Black, however, is not an evil color and definitely has its place in magick. It is the most powerful color for absorbing negative vibrations and protecting. White candles can be substituted for any color, except magenta. White, though, is not as powerful for some spells as colored candles are. To read about the meanings associated with basic candle colors, see page 39.

Astral or Zodiac Colors

Here, as with other candle colors, lists vary from writer to writer, so I have given choices for each sign. If the color given for your astrological sign does not appeal to you, choose a color that does.

ARIES Red, white, pink.

TAURUS Green, pink, red, yellow.

GEMINI Yellow, silver, green, red, blue.

CANCER White, green, brown.

LEO Gold, orange, red, green.

VIRGO Gray, yellow, gold, black.

LIBRA Royal blue, light brown, black.

SCORPIO Black, red, brown.

SAGITTARIUS Dark blue, purple, gold, red.

CAPRICORN Red, black, dark brown.

AQUARIUS Light blue, dark blue, green.

PISCES Aquamarine, royal blue, white, green.

Planetary Colors

As with other color charts, planetary colors can differ greatly, depending upon the writer and the magickal system they follow. Candles in these colors can be used on the appropriate days or to call upon certain energy forces. Refer to the Days of the Week section following and page 137 for more information.

EARTH Browns, tans.

JUPITER Royal blue, purples, bright blue.

MARS All shades of red.

MERCURY Yellows, orange, yellow-green.

MOON Silver, pink, cream, light gray, white, pale blue.

SATURN Black, very darkest blue, very darkest purple, dark brown.

SUN Gold, orange, deep yellow.

VENUS Pink, green, pale blue, all pastel colors.

Colors for the Days of the Week

Candles used to symbolize a day of the week are similar to planetary candles, in that they are burned to invoke a particular planetary energy power.

SUNDAY Yellow, gold; the Sun.

MONDAY White, silver, light gray; the Moon.

TUESDAY Red; Mars.

WEDNESDAY Purple, yellow; Mercury.

THURSDAY Blue; Jupiter.

FRIDAY Green; Venus.

SATURDAY Black, purple; Saturn.

Seasonal Colors

Spring is yellow and corresponds to the element of Air and the east. The time period is from the Spring Equinox in March until the Summer Solstice in June. The element of Air symbolizes mental pursuits.

Summer is red and corresponds to the element of Fire and the south. The time period is from the Summer Solstice in June until the Autumn Equinox in September. The element of Fire symbolizes the physical and action. Some sources say Fire represents spirit.

Autumn is blue and corresponds to the element of Water and the west. The time period is from the Autumn Equinox in September until the Winter Solstice in December. The element of Water symbolizes the emotions.

Winter is dark green and corresponds to the element of Earth and the north. The time period is from the Winter Solstice in December until the Spring Equinox in March. The element of Earth symbolizes material things.

Basic Elemental Colors

Most world cultures knew of and used the colors and powers of the elements. However, the placement and choice of color often differed. The ancient Mayans used: east, red; south, yellow; west, black; and north, white. Other ancient Mexican cultures had a different classification: north, red; west, yellow; south, blue; east, green; and center, many colors together.

EAST Air; yellow. Knowledge, inspiration, harmony, herbs, intellect, ideas, travel, freedom, revealing the truth, finding lost things, movement, and psychic abilities.

SOUTH Fire; red. Change, freedom, perception, visions, spiritual illumination, learning, love, will, sexuality, energy, authority, healing, destruction, and purification.

WEST Water; blue. Plants, healing, emotions, absorbing, communion with the spiritual, purification, the subconscious mind, love, friendships, marriage, fertility, happiness, sleep and dreams, and the psychic.

NORTH Earth; dark green. Wealth, prosperity, surrendering self-will, empathy, incorporation, business, employment, stability, success, and fertility.

CENTER White. Enlightenment, finding your life path, spiritual knowledge, and seeing and understanding karmic paths in life.

Traditional Asian Colors

Many Asian cultures have different magickal meanings for colors. For example, they wear white for mourning the death of a loved one instead of black, as Western cultures do. With *feng shui* becoming so popular, many people will be interested in utilizing Asian colors. The five Chinese elements are very different from Western ones. Instead of Earth, Air, Fire, and Water, they are Wood, Fire, Earth, Metal, and Water. In China, one of the charts of the elements lists: north, black; west, white; south, red; east, green; and center, yellow. To read about the meanings associated with traditional Asian colors, see page 42.

Traditional Native American Colors

The following list of color definitions is according to the Seneca tribe. Other Native American groups have their own beliefs of color meaning, which may differ.

The Navajo culture believed that different colors represented the elements: east, white; south, blue; west, yellow; and north, black. Among the Zuni it was east, yellow; west, blue; south, red; north, white; and center, all colors. The Cheyenne of the Plains used east, red; south, yellow; west, white; and north, black.

BLACK Hearing, harmony, listening.

BLUE Intuition, teaching, serving.

BROWN Knowing, self-discipline.

GRAY Honoring, friendship.

GREEN Will, living.

ORANGE Learning, kinship.

PINK Creativity, working.

PURPLE Wisdom, gratitude, healing.

RED Faith, communication.

ROSE Seeing, motivation.

WHITE Magnetism, sharing.

YELLOW Love, overcoming challenges.

The Uses of Incense, Herbs, Oils, and Stones

Although candle magick will get you results merely from burning a candle or candles, it works more efficiently if you add a few other ingredients to your spell. Oils, herbs, incenses, and small stones are easily obtained from local stores, the Internet, or mail order catalogs. If you purchase stones locally, rock shops are usually cheaper than most New Age stores. (See the Resources section on page 417 for more information.)

The reason for using oils, herbs, and stones as part of your spellwork is not only to add the psychic energies of these materials to your work, but also to help you concentrate more deeply on the spell.

Preparing Your Candles

As you prepare the candles, place each item on your altar in a certain position, and do each step of the candle-burning spell in a specific order. Your mind should be totally concentrated on what you are doing.

As you rub the candles with the appropriate oil, concentrate on the purpose you have in mind. Roll the oiled candle in the appropriate crushed herbs, still thinking of your goal. The herbs do not have to coat the candle thickly to be effective. As you place each stone on the altar, continue to think of the purpose of your spell. See every object on the altar as another stone in the foundation of your success. The incense evokes subconscious memories that connect you with ancient magickal practices.

Use an appropriate oil on each candle. This may mean that you use three or four different oils in any candle-burning ritual. It also helps to burn a compatible incense that represents the general idea of the ritual itself.

To simply set out candles without deep thought on why you are doing it takes away from the energy the spell will create. If you cannot be focused on your work, you will not obtain satisfactory results.

If the spell calls for candles to be burned only a certain length of time and then snuffed until the next night, please do not blow out the candles. Use a candle snuffer or your fingers to extinguish them. This seals the energy of the spell, instead of dissipating it.

Do not eat any of the herbs or drink any of the oils called for in candle magick. This can be extremely dangerous, if not deadly!

Incense

It really does not matter if you use incense in powered form, cones, or sticks. You are using incense to set a particular magickal atmosphere. Included here is a list of appropriate scents long known for certain magickal energies, scents that are often burned as part of ritual. However, you can always substitute the all-purpose scents of lotus, frankincense, or frankincense and myrrh combined in either stick or cone form.

BALANCE Jasmine, orange, rose.

BANISHING, RELEASE Cedar, clove, patchouli, rose, rue, vervain.

BINDING Apple, cypress, dragon's blood, pine, wormwood.

BLESSING, CONSECRATION Carnation, cypress, frankincense, lotus, rosemary.

CHANGES Dragon's blood, peppermint.

CONTACTING AND WORKING ON THE ASTRAL Frankincense.

CREATIVITY Honeysuckle, lilac, lotus, rose, vervain.

DETERMINATION, COURAGE Allspice, dragon's blood, musk, rosemary.

DIVINATION, CLAIRVOYANCE Acacia, cinnamon, honeysuckle, lilac, nutmeg, rose, thyme, yarrow.

ENERGY, POWER, STRENGTH Allspice, bay, carnation, cinnamon, dragon's blood, frankincense, ginger, lotus, musk, pine, thyme, rosemary, verbena.

EXORCISM Basil, bay, cedar, frankincense, lavender, myrrh, pine, rosemary, vervain, yarrow.

GOOD LUCK, FORTUNE, JUSTICE Bayberry, cedar, cinnamon, honeysuckle, jasmine, lotus, mint, nutmeg, strawberry, vervain, violet.

HAPPINESS, HARMONY, PEACE Apple blossom, basil, cedar, clove, cypress, fir, gardenia, jasmine, juniper, lavender, lilac, lily of the valley, lotus, myrrh, orange, patchouli, rose, rosemary, vetiver, vervain, ylang-ylang.

HEALING Carnation, cedar, cinnamon, clove, cypress, eucalyptus, gardenia, lavender, lotus, myrrh, orange, peppermint, rose, rosemary, sandalwood.

INSPIRATION, WISDOM Acacia, clove, cypress, fir, laurel, lily of the valley, rosemary, sage.

LOVE Amber, apple blossom, frangipani, gardenia, honeysuckle, jasmine, juniper, lavender, marjoram, musk, patchouli, rose, strawberry, vanilla, vetiver, violet, ylang-ylang.

MEDITATION Acacia, bay, cinnamon, frankincense, jasmine, myrrh, nutmeg, wisteria.

MONEY, PROSPERITY, WEALTH Bayberry, bergamot, cinnamon, honeysuckle, jasmine, musk, vetiver.

PROTECTION, DEFENSE Basil, bay, bayberry, carnation, cinnamon, citronella, cypress, dragon's blood, fir, frankincense, jasmine, juniper, lilac, lily of the valley, lotus, marjoram, patchouli, pine, rosemary, sandalwood, vervain, violet.

PSYCHIC ABILITIES, OPENING PSYCHIC CENTERS Ambergris, honeysuckle, lemon, lotus, mimosa, nutmeg, wisteria.

PURIFICATION, CLEANSING Basil, bay laurel, cedar, cinnamon, citronella, dragon's blood, eucalyptus, frankincense, lavender, marjoram, myrrh, peppermint, pine, rosemary, sage, thyme, vervain.

REMOVING HEXES Cedar, myrrh, vetiver.

SPIRITUALITY Frankincense, lotus, myrrh, sandalwood.

SUCCESS Ginger.

VISIONS Acacia, bay laurel, frankincense, lotus.

WILLPOWER Rosemary.

Herbs

Herbs are often used to coat oiled candles. To do this, crush the chosen herbs into small pieces and put the powdery mixture onto a paper towel. Then roll the oiled candle in this mixture. The herbs do not have to coat the candle entirely to be effective.

Herbs can also be burned on small charcoal blocks found in religious or New Age stores. The charcoal mentioned here is not the kind you use for a barbecue. A little goes a long way with herbs, so use a light hand when burning them. Also make certain you have adequate ventilation in any closed room in which you burn them. To read about the meanings associated with various herbs, see page 51.

Oils

Candles are frequently rubbed with scented oil from wick to end (to attract something) or from end to wick (to repel something). As you do this, concentrate on the purpose you have in mind. Candles can be used with only the oil, or oil and herbs. If called for, roll the oiled candle in the appropriate crushed herbs, still thinking of your goal. To read about the meanings associated with basic oils, see page 56.

Planetary oils are used when you desire to strengthen certain planetary energies in your life or in more advanced magickal spells.

JUPITER Anise, lime, magnolia, nutmeg, sage, sandalwood.

MARS Allspice, carnation, dragon's blood, ginger, honeysuckle, peppermint, pine.

MERCURY Bayberry, lavender, lemon grass, lily of the valley, peppermint.

MOON Coconut, eucalyptus, gardenia, jasmine, lotus, myrrh, sandalwood, water lily, white rose, wintergreen.

SATURN Black orchid, hyacinth, patchouli, water violet.

SUN Cedar, clove, cinnamon, frankincense, juniper, rosemary, rue.

Stones

When using stones to amplify your candle magick, there are two ways to choose them. You may use the general description by color to choose the stones you need, or you may use the more specific list by magickal description.

Stones do not need to be faceted, fancy, or expensive to work. Stones found in a natural state or tumbled until smooth can be just as effective as expensive ones.

There are certain stones that can be used with any candle burning. Clear quartz crystal is so powerful and all embracing that you can substitute it for other stones or add it to groupings of other stones to amplify their energy. Fluorite also amplifies the energies of other stones, regardless of its color. Carnelian will speed up the manifestation of your desire. Lodestone will help in any ritual where you are attempting to attract something into your life. The little-used spectrolite can manifest results in any situation that may require a "miracle" to see results.

It is important to wash your stones carefully before use. A few stones in the following lists should not be washed with water or put into salt for cleansing. Calcite is an example of a stone that should not be washed, and turquoise should not be placed in salt. Also, hold them in the smoke of frankincense or frankincense and myrrh incense to give them positive vibrations. Also see stones listed by type on page 43.

Stones by Color

BLACK Binding; defense by repelling dark magick; transforming negative spells and thoughtforms into positive power; general defense; release from feeling bound.

BLUE Harmony; understanding; journeys or moves; healing.

BROWN Contacting Earth elementals; success; amplifies all Earth magick and psychic abilities; common sense.

GREEN Marriage; relationships; balance; practical creativity, particularly with the hands; fertility; growth; money.

INDIGO Discovering past lives; understanding karmic problems; balancing out karma; stopping undesirable habits or experiences.

ORANGE Change your luck; power; control of a situation.

PINK Healing; true love; friendship.

PURPLE Breaking bad luck; protection; psychic and spiritual growth; success in long-range plans.

RED Courage to face a conflict or test; energy; taking action.

WHITE Spiritual guidance; being directed into the right paths; calmness; becoming centered; seeing past all illusions.

YELLOW Power of the mind; creativity of a mental nature; sudden changes.

CLEAR QUARTZ CRYSTAL Psychic work; helps with divination; amplifies the power raised during all spellwork.

LODESTONE OR MAGNET Drawing power; ability to attract what you desire.

MOONSTONE Gaining occult power; soothing the emotions; rising above problems; Moon deities.

PYRITE OR FOOL'S GOLD Money, prosperity, total success; Sun deities.

Stones by Magickal Powers

ABUSE, SURVIVING Iolite, jasper, kunzite, lapis lazuli, obsidian, smoky quartz, rhodocrosite, spinel, tourmaline.

ACCIDENTS, PREVENTING Carnelian, chalcedony, malachite, spinel, topaz, turquoise.

ANGER Chrysocolla, jade, marble, peridot, rhodonite, ruby, serpentine, topaz.

ARTISTS Aventurine, emerald, quartz crystal, tourmaline.

ASTRAL TRAVEL Moss agate, carnelian, galena, lodestone, meteorite, petrified wood, quartz crystal, sapphire, shell, zircon.

ATTRACTING THE PERFECT MATE Aventurine, lapis lazuli, malachite, rose quartz, ruby.

AUTHORITIES OR GOVERNMENT, INFLUENCING Bloodstone.

BAD HABITS Agate, amazonite, citrine, obsidian.

BALANCE Agate, amethyst, aquamarine, aventurine, calcite, carnelian, chrysoprase, emerald, ivory, jade, kunzite, lepidolite, lodestone, malachite, moldavite, moonstone, obsidian, onyx, opal, quartz crystal, rhodocrosite, serpentine, sodalite, spectrolite, sugilite, tanzanite, thulite, tiger's eye, topaz, tourmaline, turquoise, vanadinite, obsidian.

BEAUTY Alabaster, chalcedony.

BINDING TROUBLESOME PEOPLE Agate, beryl, bloodstone, chrysoprase, coral, emerald, hematite, jet, malachite, black obsidian, black onyx, pyrite.

BLOCKAGES, REMOVING Aventurine, calcite, jasper, kunzite, malachite, quartz crystal, rhodocrosite, ruby, sapphire, shell, sodalite, obsidian.

BURGLARS, DETERRING Topaz.

BUSINESS Amethyst, citrine, garnet, jade, malachite, marble, obsidian, opal, quartz crystal, sard, serpentine, spinel, tourmaline.

CALMING Adularia, agate, amber, amethyst, aquamarine, aventurine, chrysoprase, coral, fossils, ivory, jade, kunzite, lapis lazuli, lepidolite, marble, onyx, peridot, quartz crystal, rhodocrosite, rhodonite, serpentine, sodalite, tanzanite, topaz, tourmaline, zircon.

CHANGE OF LUCK Aquamarine, aventurine, azurite, bloodstone, chalcedony, citrine, fluorite, garnet, hawk's eye, hematite, iolite, lapis lazuli, malachite, moonstone, peridot, petrified wood, pyrite, rhodonite, sardonyx, staurolite, tiger's eye.

CHANGES Amethyst, obsidian, peridot, quartz crystal, smoky quartz.

CHANGING VIBRATIONS Agate, quartz crystal.

CHILDREN Coral, lapis lazuli, quartz crystal.

CLEANSING Azurite, lapis lazuli, opal, peridot, quartz crystal, selenite.

COMMUNICATIONS Agate, amazonite, aventurine, beryl, chrysocolla, garnet, lapis lazuli, malachite, moldavite, sodalite, spinel, tourmaline, turquoise.

CONCENTRATION Carnelian, fluorite, quartz crystal, spinel, topaz, tourmaline.

CONFLICTS Agate, tourmaline.

CONSCIOUSNESS-ALTERING Quartz crystal.

CONTROL Garnet, hawk's eye, jet, onyx, sapphire, thulite.

COURAGE Agate, diamond, hematite, jade, ruby, serpentine.

COURT CASES, LAWYERS, INFLUENCING THE LAW Amethyst, aquamarine, chalcedony, hematite, jade, lodestone, sard, serpentine.

CREATIVITY Agate, amazonite, amethyst, apatite, aquamarine, aventurine, chrysocolla, chrysoprase, emerald, jade, lapis lazuli, malachite, obsidian, onyx, opal, quartz crystal, sapphire, serpentine, sodalite, spinel, topaz, tourmaline, turquoise.

CYCLES IN LIFE Obsidian, tiger's eye.

DARK MAGICK, DEFEATING Amethyst, holey stones, mica, obsidian, onyx, peridot, petrified wood, pyrite, quartz crystal, sapphire, sard, topaz, tourmaline.

DECEPTIONS, UNCOVERING Moonstone.

DEFLECTING NEGATIVITY Beryl, jasper, quartz crystal.

DEMONIC POSSESSION, REMOVING Jet, black obsidian.

DEPRESSION, RELIEVING Garnet, jade, jet, lapis lazuli, serpentine, topaz.

DESTINY Peridot, quartz crystal.

DISCRIMINATION Agate, spinel.

DIVINATION, SCRYING Agate, amethyst, hawk's eye, beryl, cat's eye, crocidolite, emerald, fluorite, mica, moonstone, obsidian, quartz crystal, rhodocrosite, tiger's eye, tourmaline. (See Psychic Abilities.)

DREAMS, PROPHETIC Agate, amethyst, emerald, jade, quartz crystal, rhodocrosite, serpentine.

END OF THE ROPE, TOTALLY DISCOURAGED Malachite.

ENEMIES, DEFEATING Aquamarine.

ENERGY, GAINING Agate, andalusite, beryl, goldstone, jasper, quartz crystal, rhodocrosite, rhodonite.

ENERGY SHIELD Tektite or meteorite, rhodocrosite, tourmaline.

EVIL SPIRITS, REPELLING Agate, bloodstone, carnelian, crocidolite, jade, jasper, malachite, obsidian, onyx, serpentine, tourmaline.

EXCESSIVE ENERGY, REMOVING Fluorite.

FAMILY PROBLEMS Carnelian, sard.

FEAR Amber, aquamarine, aventurine, chrysocolla, citrine, coral, fossils, obsidian, tourmaline.

FEMININE ENERGIES Chrysocolla, jade, moonstone, turquoise.

FERTILITY See Pregnancy and Creativity.

FIRE, PROTECTING AGAINST Topaz.

FRIENDS Agate, geode, iolite, lapis lazuli, ruby, sard, topaz, tourmaline, turquoise, zircon.

GAINING SPIRITUAL BLESSINGS Amethyst, apatite, citrine, diamond, emerald, lapis lazuli, moldavite, opal, pearl, petrified wood, sapphire, sugilite, black tourmaline.

GAMBLING LUCK Aventurine, lodestone.

GIVING THANKS Citrine, lapis lazuli, pearl, quartz crystal, sapphire, sugilite.

GOALS, MAKING Adularia, amethyst, azurite, calcite, chrysoprase, citrine, diamond, hawk's eye, hematite, iolite, snowflake obsidian, peridot, rhodocrosite, sodalite, topaz, watermelon tourmaline.

GOD Amethyst, ammonite, quartz crystal.

GODDESS Amethyst, ammonite, jet, moonstone, quartz crystal, shell.

GOOD LUCK Agate, amethyst, aventurine, carnelian, holey stones, lodestone, onyx, opal, petrified wood, sapphire, sard, staurolite, tiger's eye, topaz.

GRIEF Obsidian, tourmaline.

GROUNDING Agate, fluorite, obsidian, smoky quartz, serpentine, tiger's eye, zircon.

GUARDIAN ANGELS Quartz crystal.

GUILT, RELEASING Chrysocolla, tourmaline.

HALLUCINATIONS, CONTROLLING Jasper.

HAPPINESS Moss agate, amazonite, amethyst, garnet, marble, ruby, sapphire, sard, zircon.

HARMONIZING Aventurine, calcite, coral, jade, lapis lazuli, lepidolite, obsidian, quartz crystal, serpentine, sodalite.

HEALING Moss agate, amazonite, amber, amethyst, aquamarine, beryl, bloodstone, boji stones, carnelian, chrysocolla, citrine, emerald, flint, fluorite, garnet, hematite, jade, jasper, lapis lazuli, malachite, pearl, rhodocrosite, ruby, sapphire, tourmaline, turquoise.

HIGHER TEACHINGS Azurite, fluorite, jade, quartz crystal, ruby, sapphire, spectrolite, ugilite, tourmaline.

HOPE Amazonite.

HOUSE, HOME Garnet, jade, marble, sard, serpentine.

ILLUSIONS, SEEING THROUGH Amethyst, azurite, chalcedony, pyrite, sodalite.

ILL-WISHING, REPELLING Carnelian, coral, sard.

IMPROBABLE SITUATIONS, HANDLING Spectrolite.

INFORMATION, GAINING Azurite, quartz crystal, sapphire.

INNER GUIDANCE Bloodstone, quartz crystal.

INSOMNIA, TREATING Agate.

INSPIRATION Amazonite, amethyst, aquamarine, azurite, garnet, onyx, peridot, pyrite, quartz crystal, sapphire, tourmaline.

INSPIRING CREATIVITY Amazonite, amethyst, apatite, chrysocolla, citrine, tsavorite garnet.

INTELLECT Agate, amber, jade, lapis lazuli, rhodocrosite, serpentine, topaz, tourmaline.

INTOLERANCE, REMOVING Beryl, morganite.

INTUITION Amethyst, aquamarine, azurite, citrine, malachite, opal, peridot, quartz crystal, ruby, sapphire, sodalite, topaz, tourmaline.

JEALOUSY, DISSOLVING Peridot.

JOB, CAREER Carnelian, lapis lazuli, obsidian, scapolite.

JUSTICE Amethyst, jade, serpentine.

KARMA Calcite, citrine, jade, jet, obsidian, onyx, quartz crystal, serpentine, shell, tiger's eye, topaz.

LAWSUITS See Court Cases, Lawyers, Influencing the Law.

LAZINESS, CURING Beryl.

LEADERSHIP Iolite, opal, ruby, spinel.

LONG LIFE Moss agate, beryl, onyx.

LOVE Aquamarine, aventurine, calcite, coral, emerald, lodestone, malachite, moonstone, rose quartz, ruby, zircon.

MARRIAGE Aquamarine, sard.

MEDITATION Amethyst, azurite, calcite, coral, emerald, fluorite, geode, jade, malachite, moldavite, obsidian, quartz crystal, serpentine, shell, sugilite, tanzanite, turquoise.

MEMORY Amethyst, beryl, carnelian, coral, emerald, opal, rhodocrosite, topaz.

MONEY Agate, amber, bloodstone, calcite, lodestone, malachite, obsidian, opal, spinel, tourmaline, zircon.

MOVES Bronzite, jade, serpentine.

NATURAL DISASTERS, SURVIVING Spinel.

NEGATIVE VIBRATIONS, SHIELDING AGAINST Hematite, jade, serpentine.

NEW BEGINNINGS Agate, emerald, opal, tourmaline.

NIGHTMARES, TROUBLED SLEEP, REMOVING Chalcedony, garnet, holey stones, jasper, topaz.

OBSTACLES, OVERCOMING Agate, hematite.

OPPORTUNITY Garnet.

PAST LIVES Amethyst, coral, fluorite, fossils, garnet, geode, hematite, jasper, malachite, moonstone, obsidian, opal, petrified wood, quartz crystal, rhodocrosite, shell, staurolite, tiger's eye, tourmaline.

PATIENCE Danburite, spectrolite.

PERSONAL POWER Agate, cinnabar, jasper, obsidian, opal, plasma, quartz crystal, ruby.

POVERTY, REVERSING Sapphire.

PREGNANCY Dioptase, lapis lazuli, rose quartz.

PRIVACY Jasper, sapphire.

PROPHECY Amethyst, bloodstone, moonstone, obsidian, opal, quartz crystal, tiger's eye, topaz, tourmaline.

PROSPERITY Agate, amber, aquamarine, aventurine, bloodstone, cat's eye, chalcedony, citrine, crocidolite, emerald, garnet, jade, malachite, marble, opal, pyrite, sapphire, yellow topaz, green tourmaline, turquoise, green zircon.

PROTECTION Eye agate, amethyst, aquamarine, aventurine, beryl, bloodstone, calcite, carnelian, cat's eye, chalcedony, chrysoprase, emerald, epidote, flint, garnet, hematite, holey stones, iolite, jasper, jet, lapis lazuli, malachite, moonstone, black obsidian, obsidian, black onyx, pearl, petrified wood, pumice, pyrite, ruby, sapphire, sard, sunstone, tiger's eye, black tourmaline, turquoise, zircon.

PSYCHIC ABILITIES, GAINING Agate, amethyst, apatite, azurite, beryl, crocidolite, heliodor, jet, moonstone, opal, quartz crystal, sapphire, sodalite, spinel, sugilite, tanzanite, tiger's eye, tourmaline, turquoise.

PSYCHIC ABILITIES, STRENGTHENING Adularia, moss agate, Apache tear, apatite, aquamarine, beryl, fluorite, jet, moonstone, peridot, blue topaz, purple tourmaline.

PSYCHIC ATTACK, STOPPING Obsidian, smoky quartz, turquoise.

PUBLIC SPEAKING Carnelian, emerald. (See Communications.)

PURIFICATION Aquamarine, quartz crystal, tourmaline.

REGENERATION Alexandrite, garnet, quartz crystal, tourmaline.

RELATIONSHIPS Chrysocolla, pyrite, sapphire.

RELEASING Apatite, aventurine, chalcedony, chrysocolla, chrysoprase, jade, moonstone, morganite, petrified wood, quartz crystal, sodalite, tourmaline.

RESPONSIBILITY Aquamarine.

SECRET ENEMIES, REVEALING Moonstone.

SECURITY Agate, petrified wood.

SELF-CONFIDENCE Amazonite, aventurine, bloodstone, carnelian, chalcedony, citrine, garnet, iolite, ivory, quartz crystal, rhodonite, sard, spinel, tourmaline.

SELF-LOVE Calcite, ivory, quartz crystal.

SEXUAL ATTRACTIVENESS Obsidian, opal, sodalite, sunstone.

SOLVING PROBLEMS Jade, quartz crystal, serpentine.

SOUL FRIENDS Amethyst, quartz crystal.

SOUL MATES Quartz crystal.

SPEECH See Public Speaking.

SPEED UP MANIFESTATION Carnelian, quartz crystal.

SPIRIT GUIDES, TEACHERS Moss agate, citrine, diopside, lapis lazuli, moonstone, obsidian, opal, pearl, quartz crystal, spinel, sugilite, topaz, tourmaline, zircon.

SPIRITUAL AWARENESS Amethyst, apatite, calcite, emerald, hiddenite, labradorite, lepidolite, moonstone, onyx, pearl, quartz crystal, rhodonite, sphalerite, sugilite, tiger's eye, vanadinite.

SPIRITUAL GROWTH Amber, amethyst, citrine, diamond, emerald, lapis lazuli, ruby, sapphire.

SPIRITUAL MATES Quartz crystal.

STAMINA Jade, labradorite.

STUBBORNNESS Agate, beryl, goshenite, tiger's eye.

STUDYING Carnelian, quartz crystal, topaz, tourmaline.

SUCCESS Andalusite, obsidian, sard.

SURVIVAL Chrysocolla, flint, fossils, jade. (See Abuse, Surviving.)

TELEPATHY Quartz crystal, spinel.

TENSION AND STRESS, REMOVING Agate, amethyst, hematite, jade, lapis lazuli, moonstone, obsidian, peridot, pyrite, quartz crystal, rhodonite, serpentine, zircon.

THIRD EYE Moss agate, amethyst, azurite, quartz crystal, sodalite, tiger's eye.

TIME TRAVEL Galena, fossils, geode, lodestone, quartz crystal.

TRANCE Quartz crystal, sapphire, spinel.

TRANSFORMATION Alexandrite, amethyst, ametrine, azurite, fluorite, garnet, jasper, malachite, onyx, quartz crystal, ruby, shell, tourmaline.

TRAVEL Coral, quartz crystal.

TRUTH Agate, calcite, chrysoprase, emerald, galena, geode, pearl, pyrite, quartz crystal, sapphire, tiger's eye, topaz.

UNWANTED SITUATIONS, HANDLING Iolite, malachite.

USELESS SACRIFICES, STOPPING Quartz crystal.

VICTORY Agate, chrysoprase, diamond, jet.

VISIONARY Adularia, agate, amethyst, holey stones, malachite, quartz crystal.

VISUALIZATION Aventurine, quartz crystal.

VITALITY Moss agate.

WILLPOWER Hematite, pyrite.

WRITERS Amethyst, aventurine, garnet, sapphire, spinel, tourmaline.

Timing by the Moon and Days

To ensure the greatest probability of success for your candle rituals, you should time them to correspond with certain phases of the moon and do them on specific days of the week. To help you determine the correct dates for all the moon's phases, buy a good astrological calendar that gives accurate moon measurements.

Moon Phases

The full moon is when the moon is completely lit, big and round. When the moon is growing in size, it is referred to as the waxing moon. The waxing moon cycle runs from the day after the new moon until the day of the full moon. The day and night of the full moon is the strongest part of this cycle. This is the time to do spellwork for beginning new projects, prosperity, growth, love, success, harmony, peace, and all positive energy projects. Basically, the waxing moon is for increase, growth, building, and gain.

The new moon is when no light is seen from the moon at all; it is completely dark. When the moon is decreasing in size, it is referred to as the waning moon. The waning moon cycle runs from the day after the full moon until the day of the next new moon. The day and night of the new moon is the strongest of this cycle. This is the time for dissolving any negatives, protection, neutralizing hostile situations, removing bad habits, and terminating unhealthy relationships or situations. The waning moon is for decrease, destruction, banishing, binding, and removal.

Days of the Week

Each day of the week is traditionally connected with a specific planet, deity, and function. Monday is the Moon; Tuesday, Mars; Wednesday, Mercury; Thursday, Jupiter; Friday, Venus; Saturday, Saturn; and Sunday, the Sun. By carefully studying the religious pantheon of your choice, you can correspond any deities to the days of the week, instead of using the listed deity interpretations.

Using moon phases and planetary days and hours in magickal rituals goes back to ancient Babylon and perhaps beyond. Many ancient cultures knew of the seven closest planetary bodies and considered them important and powerful enough to influence the lives of humans. These planets were also said to correspond to the days of the week and the hours of each day. Although moon phases are crucial to the power raised in a candle spell, using the correct day and hour will further enhance the buildup of energy to manifest your desire. However, you do not have to use days and hours if you do not wish to do so.

The idea behind using planetary days and hours is that you are connecting with a stronger energy for use in candle rituals. To use this system, decide which planet best symbolizes the type of ritual you plan to do. Then, from the charts in this section, select the proper day and hour in which to do the ritual. When reading the hour charts, always make adjustments for daylight saving time.

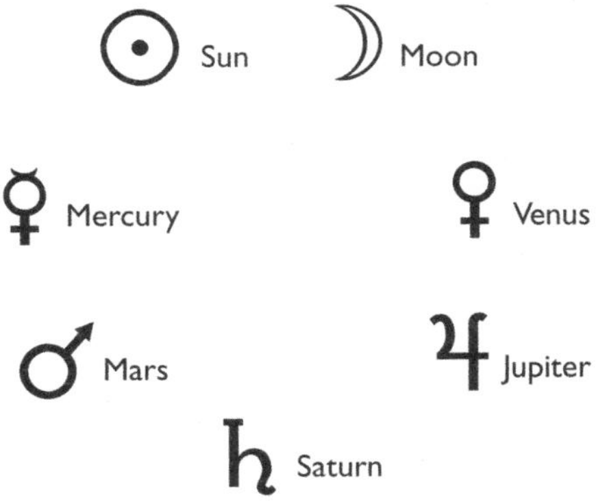

Planetary Symbols

A.M.	Mon	Tues	Wed	Thurs	Fri	Sat	Sun
1:00	☾	♂	☿	♃	♀	♄	☉
2:00	♄	☉	☾	♂	☿	♃	♀
3:00	♃	♀	♄	☉	☾	♂	☿
4:00	♂	☿	♃	♀	♄	☉	☾
5:00	☉	☾	♂	☿	♃	♀	♄
6:00	♀	♄	☉	☾	♂	☿	♃
7:00	☿	♃	♀	♄	☉	☾	♂
8:00	☾	♂	☿	♃	♀	♄	☉
9:00	♄	☉	☾	♂	☿	♃	♀
10:00	♃	♀	♄	☉	☾	♂	☿
11:00	♂	☿	♃	♀	♄	☉	☾
12:00	☉	☾	♂	☿	♃	♀	♄

A.M. Hours

P.M.	Mon	Tues	Wed	Thurs	Fri	Sat	Sun
1:00	♀	♄	☉	☾	♂	☿	♃
2:00	☿	♃	♀	♄	☉	☾	♂
3:00	☾	♂	☿	♃	♀	♄	☉
4:00	♄	☉	☾	♂	☿	♃	♀
5:00	♃	♀	♄	☉	☾	♂	☿
6:00	♂	☿	♃	♀	♄	☉	☾
7:00	☉	☾	♂	☿	♃	♀	♄
8:00	♀	♄	☉	☾	♂	☿	♃
9:00	☿	♃	♀	♄	☉	☾	♂
10:00	☾	♂	☿	♃	♀	♄	☉
11:00	♄	☉	☾	♂	☿	♃	♀
12:00	♃	♀	♄	☉	☾	♂	☿

P.M. Hours

Planetary Colors and Powers

JUPITER Colors are royal blue and purples. Stones are lapis lazuli, amethyst, turquoise, and sapphire. Incenses are lilac, nutmeg, and cedar. Use on Thursday for good luck, winning over great odds, honor, more of what you have in abundance, social pleasures, family reunions, male fertility, to get a raise or promotion, health, friendships, the heart's desires, trade and employment, group enterprises, legal matters, harmony, accomplishment, and expansion of things in your life.

MARS Colors are all shades of red. Stones are bloodstone, garnet, red agate, ruby, and red topaz. Incense is dragon's blood. Use on Tuesday for power over enemies, overcoming obstacles, courage, conflict, surgery, physical strength, opposition, defense, endurance, victory, politics, difficulties in lawsuits, to seek paroles, peaceful separations, gambling, athletics, to change the weather, to divert storms, destruction, and protection.

MERCURY Colors are orange, pale yellow, violet, and multicolored. Stones are carnelian, fire opal, and agate. Incense is white sandalwood. Use on Wednesday for creativity, mental sharpness, memory, business, medicine, diplomacy, counseling, changes, divination, eloquence, speed, speech, writing, poetry, and healing of nervous disorders.

MOON Colors are silver, lavender, cream, light gray, pearl-white, and pale blue. Stones are moonstone, clear quartz crystal, beryl, and pearl. Incenses are white rose, myrtle, mugwort, camphor, lily, jasmine, and lotus. Use on Monday for travel, visions, divinations, dreams, magick, love, agriculture, domestic life, medicine, luck, feminine aspects, calming and controlling emotions, journeys for pleasure, plant growth, female fertility, birth, and healing women's problems. Avoid performing spells during a lunar eclipse.

SATURN Colors are black, very darkest blue, very darkest purple, and dark brown. Stones are onyx, jet, pearl, and star sapphire. Incenses are poppy, myrrh, civet, and storax. Use on Saturday for knowledge, familiars, death, reincarnation, protection, binding, overcoming curses, retribution, duties, responsibilities, finding lost objects, to reveal secrets, recovering stolen goods, to collect a debt, to influence others, intuition, overcoming blocks and removing obstacles.

SUN Colors are gold and deep yellow. Stones are zircon, jacinth, goldstone, yellow topaz, and yellow diamond. Incenses are heliotrope, orange blossom, cloves, frankincense, ambergris, musk, cinnamon, and vanilla. Use on Sunday for health, healing, confidence, hope, prosperity, leadership, happiness, personal fulfillment, life-energy, promotion, swift success, new money, instant action, theatrical success, release from captivity, support of those in power, political influence, friendships, active change, and creativity. Avoid performing spells during a solar eclipse.

VENUS Colors are green, pale blue, and pink. Stones are amber, malachite, jade, peridot, coral, emerald, and turquoise. Incenses are apple blossom, musk, verbena, rose, and red sandalwood. Use on Friday for love, marriage, harmony, music, pregnancy, friendship, pleasure, artistic creativity, fertility, partnerships, sex, spiritual harmony, children, the emotions, and instincts.

Candle Spells

Before you begin a candle spell, be certain you have all the needed materials on hand. Choose the spell you wish to use, and make a list of all candles and their colors, any oils, herbs, stones, and anything else that will be needed. If you cannot find seven-knob or seven-day candles, use seven of the straight or votive candles instead.

If a candle spell is for more than one burning or to be continued for a certain number of days, try to repeat the spell at the same time each day. When you are finished with any candle burning, carefully gather up the remaining wax and paper ashes and safely dispose of them.

When anointing candles, always use only a small amount of oil. Then, wipe your hands carefully before proceeding with the ritual. To use oil in a seven-day, glass-enclosed candle, simply put a few drops on the top of the candle and carefully spread it around.

Herbs can be used with candle burning in three simple ways. After oiling a candle, you can roll it lightly in crushed herbs (see page 122), or you may sprinkle the herbs in a circle around the lit candles. If you use incense to be burned on charcoal, you may sprinkle the herbs on the coals. Only a small amount of herbs is required for any of these procedures. If you do not care for the incense, herbs, and oils listed, you can always substitute other appropriate ones from pages 120–123. Frankincense, combined frankincense and myrrh, and lotus are good all-purpose incenses.

Many of the herbs can be found right in your kitchen. Herbs such as basil, allspice, nutmeg, ginger, cloves, cinnamon, and sage are commonly used in cooking. Finding lemon verbena need not be a problem if you have a small area for growing this herb. The dried leaves can also be used in a delicious tea without harmful effects. However, although it is easily cultivated by even the blackest of gardening thumbs, lemon verbena tends to spread and will take over existing flowerbeds unless you vigorously keep it within bounds.

Check for the correct phase of the moon and the proper day for candle magick. If the phase of the moon is not a good one for the type of ritual you will be doing, reschedule the spellwork for a more appropriate time. If you have an emergency and need to take action immediately, by all means do the ritual whatever the moon phase. There will be some benefit, although it will be less powerful. When the moon next enters the more auspicious phase, repeat the ritual for better results.

Although some candle spells specifically call for a seven-day ritual, all candle burning with straight or votive candles always has a more powerful effect if repeated three, five, seven, or nine times.

Write out your desire so you can see if you have it clearly in mind. You want to create opportunities to gain what you desire, instead of depending on random chance to fulfill it. For example, you do not want your spell for money to be fulfilled through an injury or death. In this case, state that you wish a positive opportunity to gain money to come your way.

Remember the law of karma. If you deliberately harm someone or break up a relationship so you can have one of the partners, you will eventually pay a heavy price for such unethical behavior. Besides doing the spell for the wrong reasons, such as greed, jealousy, or revenge, you are also limiting yourself and interfering with the free will of another. Think how you would respond if someone tried to manipulate and control you through magick.

Setting Up a General Altar

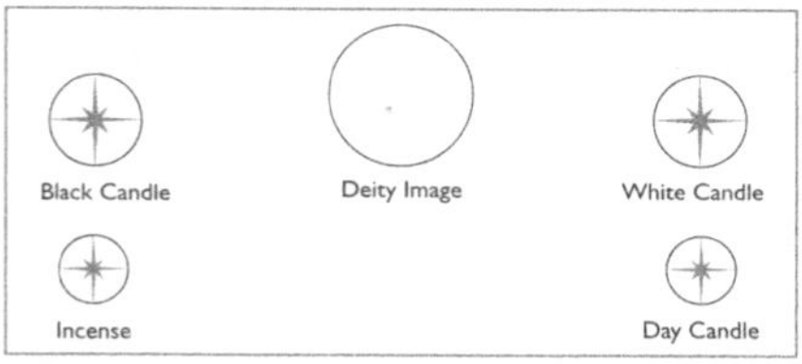

It is best to set up your general altar (see page 9) and meditate there before you ever begin to do candle magick. This helps to build up an atmosphere of power around your altar, an atmosphere that will enhance your spellwork and make it more effective.

Choose a table, chest, or shelf that is not in the central living area and is in a place where it will not be disturbed. Also check for anything nearby that might be a fire hazard.

You will need either a white pillar or seven-day candle to set in the central back portion of your altar, or one white pillar candle and one black one, one to set on each end of the altar toward the back. Traditionally, the black candle sits on the left side of the altar, the white on the right. If you use the two altar candles, you can place an image, picture, or symbol of a deity between them, in the central rear portion of the space.

Have a lighter and a plain white candle available at all times for lighting the other candles; never light the other candles with the lighter. You will also find it convenient to keep nearby a nail or other sharp instrument for carving names onto candles, a supply of small squares of papers, and a metal cauldron or bowl for burning them. Put the incense holder on the left side of the altar. If you want to burn a candle to symbolize the powers of a particular day, place it in a holder on the right side. This leaves the center of the altar open for your candle-burning spells.

Use metal or nonflammable holders for all your candles, especially the ones you leave to burn out completely.

If you want to place a picture of a person or pet (such as for healing) on the altar during your rituals, you can easily make what is called a placket to enclose it. A placket is two square or rectangular pieces of cloth or felt, sewn together on three sides only. This leaves a kind of pocket. You can slip a photo, letter, or paper inside on which a person's name is written, and keep it safe from candle wax, oil, dust, and prying eyes. You can make plackets in several colors if you wish, although white is considered to be an all-purpose color. You will find it convenient to have several plackets on hand for your work.

If possible, leave this basic altar set up at all times. By meditating near it, you build a store of energy there before you begin to do candle spells. Always light your altar candles first, then the incense, then the day candle. Extinguish the candles in the reverse order. The incense is left to burn out.

Whenever a chant is given in a candle spell, you can substitute an appropriate psalm or other text according to your belief system.

Unless stated differently in a spell, use the six-inch straight or small votive candles.

Abundance

Change Your Luck

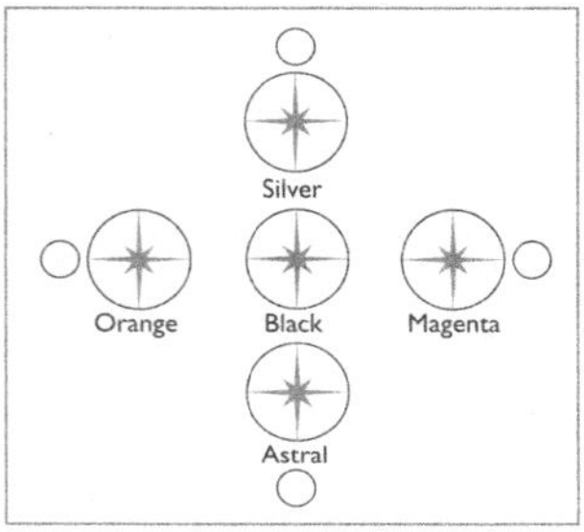

CANDLES Straight or votive candles in the following colors: your astrological color, one orange (sudden change), one silver or light gray (neutralization of bad luck), one black (remove bad luck), and one magenta (to hurry the luck-changing process).

OIL Lotus.

HERBS Basil.

INCENSE Lotus or frankincense.

STONES Four pieces of carnelian or four clear quartz crystals.

OTHER SUPPLIES None.

TIMING The full moon.

DAY Thursday.

ADVICE Changing your luck is sometimes the only way to obtain prosperity, health, love, or a new job. You need to rid yourself and your life of negative vibrations before positive vibrations can enter.

SPELLWORK Light the altar candles and the incense. Anoint the black candle from the end to the wick; the others from the wick to the end. Place the black candle in the center of your altar. Set your astrological candle in front of the black, with the other candles joining it in a circle around the central black candle. Place a stone beside each of these four candles.

Light the astrological candle and say: *"This is me and everything that represents me."* Light the black candle and say: *"This is my bad luck. It now leaves me. I shed no tears over the parting."* Light the silver candle and say: *"This neutralizes any remnants of bad luck. They dissolve into nothingness."* Light the orange candle: *"This represents the changes for good that are coming into my life. I welcome them with open arms."* Light the magenta candle: *"This is the astrological energy that I need to speed up the change."*

Sit for at least five minutes, repeating to yourself: *"I welcome change. I welcome the incoming good."* Do not allow any thoughts of failure or bad situations to enter your mind during this time.

Leave the candles to burn out completely. Dispose of the wax afterward.

Attract Money

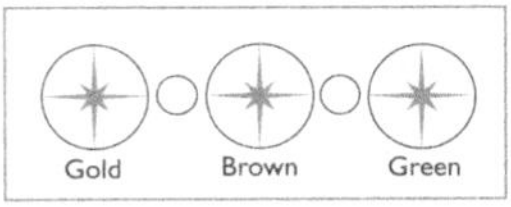

CANDLES Straight or votive candles: one green (material gain), one brown (attract money), and one gold (financial benefits).

OIL Bergamot or cinnamon.

HERBS Nutmeg.

INCENSE Cinnamon or honeysuckle.

STONES Agate and garnet.

OTHER SUPPLIES Small nail.

TIMING The full moon or the waxing moon cycle.

DAY Sunday.

ADVICE The Attract Money spell is not for long-term prosperity or for an unlimited supply of money. It is for a specific amount of quick money to pay off the bills piling up on the table.

SPELLWORK Light the altar candles and the incense. Using the nail, inscribe the brown candle with three dollar signs representing money: $$$. Below this, carve in the amount you need. Anoint the candles from the wick to the end. Set the brown candle in the center of your altar with your astrological candle behind it. Set the gold candle on the left of the brown candle and the green candle on the right. Place the agate between the gold and brown, and the garnet between the brown and green. Light the candles from left to right. Say the chant five times. Leave the candles to burn out completely. Dispose of the wax afterward.

CHANT *One, two, three, four,*
Money knocking on my door.
Five, six, seven, eight,
A jingling purse is my fate.

Gain Prosperity

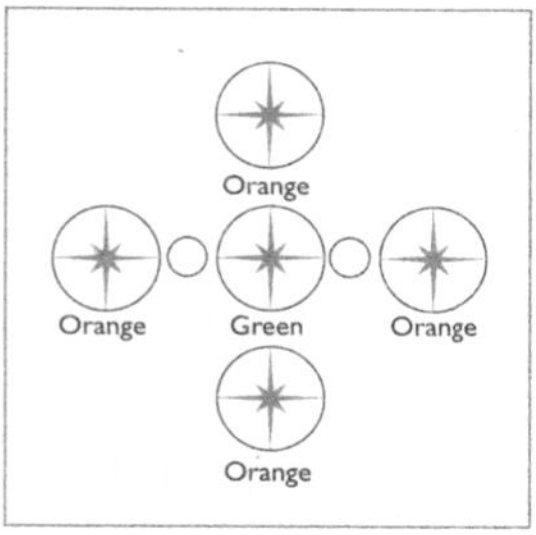

CANDLES A green (material gain) seven-day, glass-enclosed candle or a double-action green candle. Four orange (attraction, sudden changes, success) straight or votive candles.

OIL Bayberry or bergamot.

HERBS Vervain.

INCENSE Bayberry or jasmine.

STONES Bloodstone and malachite.

OTHER SUPPLIES Small nail.

TIMING On the full moon or the waxing moon cycle.

DAY Thursday.

ADVICE Prosperity gained through the use of magick will continue only as long as you use it responsibly. It also needs to be renewed at regular intervals.

SPELLWORK Light the altar candles and the incense. Using a nail, carve a dollar sign into the green portion of the double-action candle or into the top of the glass-enclosed candle. Inscribe a lightning bolt into each of the orange candles. Anoint the double-action candle and the orange candles from the wick to the end, or just the top of the enclosed candle. Set it in the center of your altar. Arrange the orange candles around the central green candle. Place the malachite on one side of the central candle, the bloodstone on the other. Light the central green candle, then the orange ones. Say the chant. Leave the candles to burn out completely. Dispose of the wax afterward. If you wish, you may burn four new orange candles each day until the seven-day green candle is gone.

CHANT *Worries gone, finances clear,*
Security comes for one full year.
I wrap myself in prosperity.
As I will, so shall it be.

Influence Someone to Repay a Debt

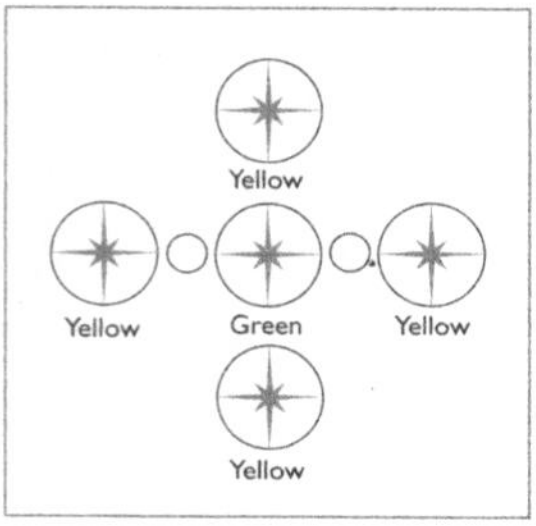

CANDLES A green (material gain) seven-knob candle or seven green straights or votives and four yellow (gentle persuasion) straight or votive candles.

OIL Jasmine.

HERBS Clove.

INCENSE Ginger, jasmine, or allspice.

STONES Hematite and tiger's eye.

OTHER SUPPLIES None.

TIMING On the full moon or the waxing moon cycle.

DAY Saturday.

ADVICE Be certain the debt is actually owed to you before doing this spell. If you think someone owes you a debt, but it is not true, you will find yourself being forced to pay back any debts you owe. This spell also works for people who borrow things and don't bother to return them.

SPELLWORK Light the altar candles and the incense. Inscribe the name of the person who owes you the debt on the seven-knob green candle. Anoint the candles from the wick to the end. Set the green candle in the center of your altar. Set the yellow candles around the green one, with the stones inside this circle. Light the green candle first, then the others. Say the chant seven times. Leave the yellow candles to burn out completely. Dispose of the wax afterward. Burn only one knob of the green candle each night. If you wish, you may burn new yellow candles each night until the seven-knob candle is gone.

CHANT *What was given in trust shall be freely returned. What was mine shall be mine again.*

Career or Job

Increase Personal Power

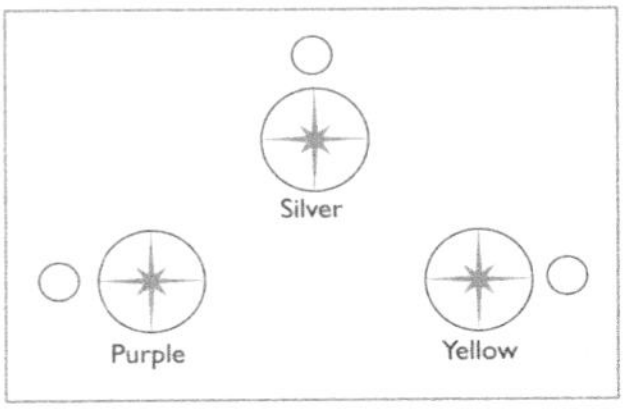

CANDLES Straight or votive candles in the following colors: one silver (victory, stability), one yellow (confidence, concentration), and one purple (success, wisdom).

OIL Carnation.

HERBS Red sandalwood or rue.

INCENSE Carnation, frankincense, or pine.

STONES Agate, jasper, and black obsidian.

OTHER SUPPLIES None.

TIMING On the full moon or the waxing moon cycle.

DAY Thursday.

ADVICE Increasing your personal power is a positive action only when you are trying to build up your self-esteem or want to stand up to someone who is manipulating or bullying you. It is not a positive action if you use this spell to gain power so that you can control others.

SPELLWORK Light the altar candles and the incense. Anoint the candles from the wick to the end. The candles are set out in a triangular pattern with the silver at the top, the yellow at the bottom right, and the purple at the bottom left. Place the black obsidian near the silver candle, the jasper near the yellow, and the agate near the purple. Light the candles in the same order, beginning with the silver. Say the chant. Leave the candles to burn out completely. Dispose of the wax afterward.

CHANT *Power of the self, I seek.*
Strength to be bold, not weak.
Courage to stand straight and tall,
Power to overcome all.

Conquer Fear

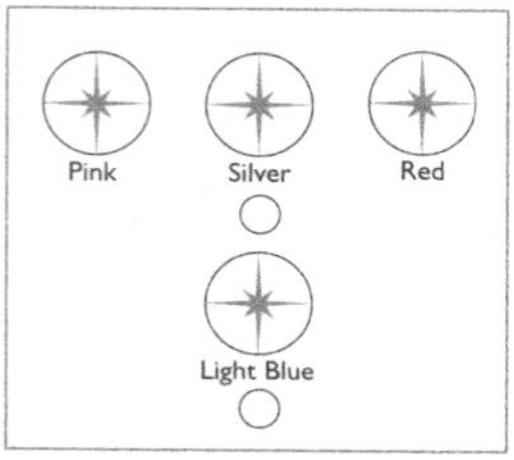

CANDLES Straight or votive candles in the following colors: one silver (stability), one light blue (inspiration, inner peace, contacting the Higher Self), one pink (banish depression), and one red (strength, courage).

OIL Musk.

HERBS Sage.

INCENSE Allspice, dragon's blood, or musk.

STONES Amber and black obsidian.

OTHER SUPPLIES None.

TIMING On the full moon or the waxing moon cycle.

DAY Saturday.

ADVICE This spell is particularly useful when you fear public speaking, facing someone who has intimidated you in the past, flying on a plane, or tackling a new project. Although you are working to eliminate fear, you are doing this by drawing in the necessary cosmic energy to help you conquer this fear.

SPELLWORK Light the altar candles and the incense. Anoint the candles from the wick to the end. Set the silver candle near the center of your altar with the light blue in front. Place the red on the right side, the pink on the left. Put the black obsidian in front of the silver candle and the amber in front of the light blue one. Light them in any order. Meditate for several minutes on absorbing the energy coming from the candles. Visualize yourself facing your fear and being triumphant. Say the chant. Leave the candles to burn out completely. Dispose of the wax afterward.

CHANT *All fear is washed away,*
Only courage with me will stay.
I am in control of my destiny.
As I will, so shall it be.

Find a New Job

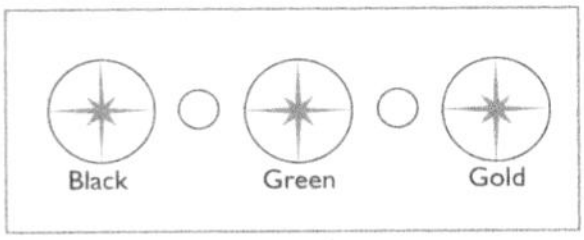

CANDLES Straight or votive candles in the following colors: one black (break up blockages, remove negatives), one gold (fast luck, happiness), and one green (success, material gain).

OIL Pine or peppermint.

HERBS Dragon's blood or ginger.

INCENSE Jasmine, peppermint, or pine.

STONES Carnelian and lapis lazuli.

OTHER SUPPLIES None.

TIMING On the full moon or waxing moon cycle.

DAY Thursday.

ADVICE No magickal spell will work unless you do your part to help. This means you must actively seek a new job, not sit back and wait for it to fall into your lap.

SPELLWORK Light the altar candles and the incense. Anoint the black candle from the end to the wick; the others from the wick to the end. Place the black candle on the left, the green in the center, and the gold on the right. Put the carnelian between the black and green candles, and the lapis lazuli between the green and gold candles. Light the candles in the same order as you set them out. Say the chant. Sit for several moments, thinking of the type of job you want. Leave the candles to burn out completely. Dispose of the wax afterward.

CHANT *Doors to new opportunities open before me.*
No obstacles stand in my way.
Only the best of employment comes to me.
Good luck draws a new day.

Attain Success

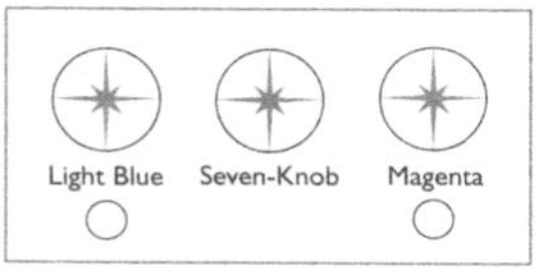

CANDLES Orange seven-knob candle. Seven straight or votive candles in each of the following colors: light blue (inspiration, patience, inner peace) and magenta (fast action, success). If you cannot find an orange seven-knob candle, substitute seven orange straights or votives, one to be burned each day.

OIL Peppermint.

HERBS Ginger or vervain.

INCENSE Ginger or rosemary.

STONES Sard and black obsidian.

OTHER SUPPLIES None.

TIMING On the full moon or the waxing moon cycle.

DAY Thursday.

ADVICE The definition of success varies from person to person. Decide what success means to you personally before you do this spell.

SPELLWORK Light the altar candles and the incense. Anoint the candles from the wick to the end. Set the orange seven-knob candle in the center of your altar. Inscribe "harmony" on the light blue candle and "success" on the magenta candle. Place the light blue candle on the left of the seven-knob candle and the magenta on the right, with the piece of sard in front of the blue candle and the black obsidian in front of the magenta. Light the seven-knob candle first, then the others. After one knob has burned, extinguish all the candles. Repeat the spell the next day when you again relight the candles. Say the chant. Allow the seven-knob candle to burn down one knob, while leaving the other candles to burn out completely. Dispose of the wax afterward.

CHANT *Success is beautiful. I attract success.*

Opportunities are bountiful. I attract opportunities.

A new cycle of life begins. I accept the new cycle.

Inspire Creativity

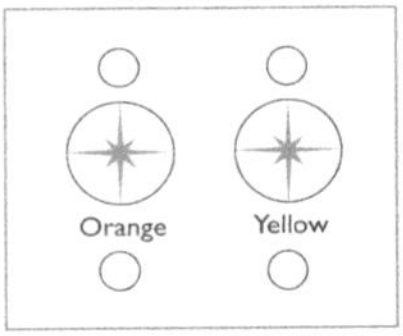

CANDLES Straight or votive candles in the following colors: one orange (creativity, enthusiasm) and one yellow (creativity, imagination, inspiration).

OIL Lilac or rose.

HERBS Rose petals.

INCENSE Lilac, lotus, or rose.

STONES Amethyst, chrysocolla, black onyx, and turquoise.

OTHER SUPPLIES None.

TIMING On the full moon or the waxing moon cycle.

DAY Wednesday.

ADVICE Creativity is more than writing, painting, or music. It can be coming up with a new idea for a birthday party, some innovative business method, or how to redecorate your home. Pregnancy can also count as creativity, so this spell can be used to get pregnant.

SPELLWORK Light the altar candles and the incense. Anoint the candles from the wick to the end. Place the orange and yellow candles side by side in the center of your altar. Put the black onyx behind the orange candle and the turquoise in front of it. With the yellow candle, place the chrysoprase behind and the amethyst in front of it. Light the candles. Say the chant. Meditate on the particular reason you need creativity. Leave the candles to burn out completely. Dispose of the wax afterward.

CHANT *The universe is filled with endless ideas of creativity.*
I attract them to me like a magnet.
My mind and dreams are open to these ideas.
They flow in like a stream of clear water.

General Life Path

Overcome a Bad Habit

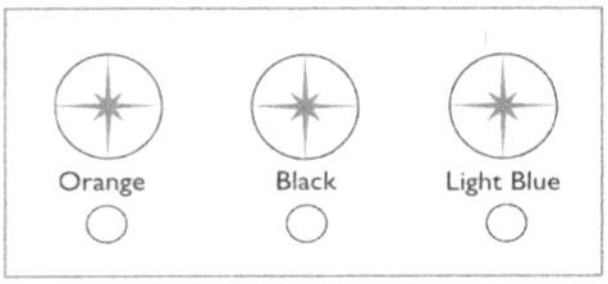

CANDLES Straight or votive candles in the following colors: one black (remove anything negative), one light blue (good health, happiness, inner peace), and one orange (sudden changes, success).

OIL Cedar or peppermint.

HERBS Basil or bay laurel.

INCENSE Dragon's blood, peppermint, or cedar.

STONES Jade, rhodonite, or topaz.

OTHER SUPPLIES Small nail; small piece of paper.

TIMING On the new moon or the waning moon cycle.

DAY Tuesday.

ADVICE This is one spell you cannot do for another person. No habit can be broken unless there is a sincere desire to quit.

SPELLWORK Light the altar candles and the incense. Inscribe the name of the habit on the black candle. Anoint it from the end to the wick and set it in the center of your altar. Write "peace" on the light blue candle and "success" on the orange candle. Place the orange candle to the left of the black candle and the light blue on the right. Put the jade in front of the orange candle, rhodonite in front of the black, and topaz in front of the light blue. Light the black candle first, then the others. Say the chant nine times. Leave the candles to burn out completely. Dispose of the wax afterward.

CHANT *I walk away from harmful things.*
I walk into the Light.
I draw my strength from endless Love,
And from this win my fight.

Stop Arguments

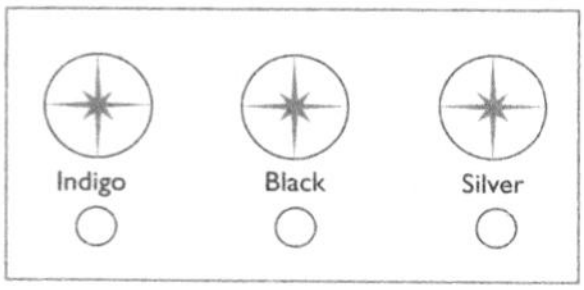

CANDLES Straight or votive candles in the following colors: one black (remove negatives), one indigo (balance out karma, stop lies), and one silver (neutralize the situation, repel destructive forces).

OIL Patchouli.

HERBS Patchouli.

INCENSE Allspice, cedar, or patchouli.

STONES Bloodstone, black obsidian, and black onyx.

OTHER SUPPLIES Small nail.

TIMING On the new moon or the waning moon cycle.

DAY Tuesday.

ADVICE This spell should not be used to gain the upper hand over someone, but rather to sincerely bring peace and harmony.

SPELLWORK Light the altar candles and the incense. With the nail, inscribe the names of the quarreling parties on the black candle and set it in the center of your altar. Be sure to include your own name if you are involved. Anoint the black candle from the end to the wick; the others from the wick to the end. Place the indigo candle on the left and the silver one on the right. Place the stones in front of the candles: black obsidian in front of the black, black onyx in front of the indigo, and the bloodstone in front of the silver one. Light the black candle first, then the others. Say the chant. Sit for several minutes, visualizing the quarreling parties completely bathed in white light. Leave the candles to burn out completely. Dispose of the wax afterward.

CHANT *Peace, harmony, friendship, and joy.*
Only these shall surround you.
Only these shall remain with you.
Peace, harmony, friendship, and joy.

Settle Disturbed Conditions in a Home

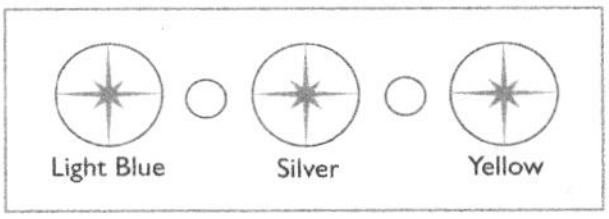

CANDLES Seven straight or votive candles in the following colors: light blue (harmony in the home), silver (neutralize a negative situation), and yellow (gentle persuasion, healing). One candle of each color is burned each night for seven nights. A seven-knob candle in each color may be substituted, with one knob burned each night.

OIL Patchouli.

HERBS Frankincense or myrrh.

INCENSE Frankincense or patchouli.

STONES Hematite and agate.

OTHER SUPPLIES None.

TIMING On the full moon or the waxing moon cycle.

DAY Tuesday.

ADVICE Disturbed conditions, such as constant dissension and general unhappiness, can vary in intensity, depending upon the seriousness of the events occurring. These conditions make those who live in the home uncomfortable and irritable.

SPELLWORK Light the altar candles and the incense. Anoint the candles from the wick to the end. Set the candles in a straight line with the light blue on the left, silver in the middle, and yellow on the right. Place the hematite between the blue and silver, and the agate between the silver and yellow. Light the candles from left to right. Say the chant. Leave the candles to burn out completely. Dispose of the wax afterward.

CHANT *Your (My) home is filled with peace and love.*
No negatives shall enter there (here).
Harmony shall reign with peace and love.
This I decree for one full year.

Learn the Truth About a Situation or Person

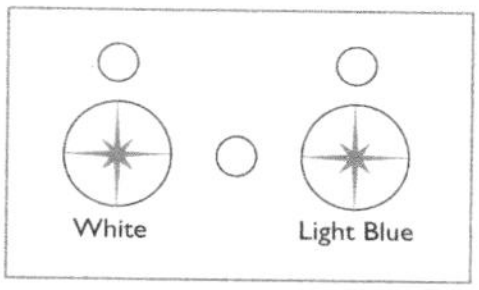

CANDLES Seven straight or votive candles in the following colors: white (truth, purity) and light blue (truth, wisdom). One candle of each color is to be burned each night for seven nights.

OIL Carnation.

HERBS Sage or yellow sandalwood.

INCENSE Clove, cypress, or sage.

STONES Chrysoprase, a geode, and tiger's eye.

OTHER SUPPLIES None.

TIMING On the full moon or the waxing moon cycle.

DAY Monday.

ADVICE This spell is not to be used for snooping or to satisfy curiosity. It is of value when you need to know the hidden truth of a person for business reasons or if you are romantically involved.

SPELLWORK Light the altar candles and the incense. Anoint the candles from the wick to the end. Set the white and blue candles side by side in the center of your altar. Place the chrysoprase behind the white candle and the tiger's eye behind the blue one.

Set the geode between the two candles. Light the candles. Say the chant. Leave the candles to burn out completely. Dispose of the wax afterward.

CHANT *Whatever the truth may be,*
Reveal it to me.
Give me the knowledge to use truth wisely.
Grant me clear sight.

Release Situations or People from Your Life

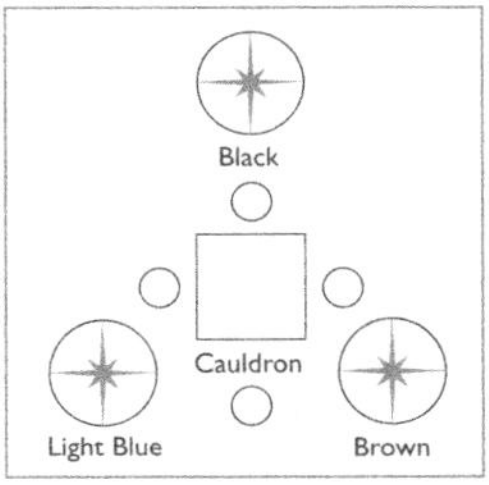

CANDLES Straight or votive candles in the following colors: one black (remove negative forces), one light blue (happiness, wisdom, inner peace), and one brown (ground and center).

OIL Lilac or patchouli.

HERBS Lemon verbena.

INCENSE Patchouli or cedar.

STONES Aventurine, jade, petrified wood, and clear quartz crystal.

OTHER SUPPLIES Small metal cauldron; small piece of paper.

TIMING On the new moon or the waning moon cycle.

DAY Saturday.

ADVICE Think carefully before deciding to remove situations or people from your life. If they are creating adverse or negative effects, then they deserve to be removed, but not if it is merely a retaliatory whim of the moment. Remember, to help the spell, you must also do your part to take action.

SPELLWORK Light the altar candles and the incense. Anoint the black candle from the end to the wick; the others from the wick to the end. The candles are arranged in a triangular shape with the cauldron in the center. Set the black candle at the back of the cauldron, the light blue in front and to the left and the brown in the front and to the right. Set the stones around the cauldron. Write on the paper the situations or people you want to move out of your life. Light the candles in the same order as you set them out. Say the chant. Light the paper from the black candle and drop it into the cauldron to burn. Allow the candles to burn completely out. Dispose of the wax and ashes.

CHANT *I cut all ties that bind me.*
All negatives that block my way
Shall disappear as morning dew
In the light of a brand-new day.

Accept a Situation

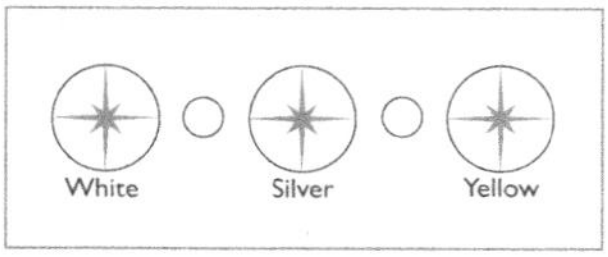

CANDLES Straight or votive candles in the following colors: one yellow (mental clarity, confidence), one silver (neutralize a situation), and one white (purity, truth, sincerity).

OIL Gardenia.

HERBS Frankincense.

INCENSE Rose, orange, or musk.

STONES Sard and amazonite.

OTHER SUPPLIES None.

TIMING On the full moon or the waxing moon cycle.

DAY Tuesday.

ADVICE This spell is to be used when you know you should not walk away from a situation, but see it through. This is not for control of the situation, but to help you cultivate an attitude of acceptance and nonhostility until either the problem is resolved or you can walk away from it.

SPELLWORK Light the altar candles and the incense. Anoint the candles from the wick to the end. Place the candles in a straight line from left to right: white, silver, and finally the yellow. Put the sard between the white and silver candles, and the amazonite between the silver and yellow ones. Light the candles from left to right. Say the chant. Leave the candles to burn out completely. Dispose of the wax afterward.

CHANT *I accept my karma to be in this time and place.*
Give me the strength and courage to endure what I must.
Grant me the peace and wisdom I need to endure.

Find Happiness

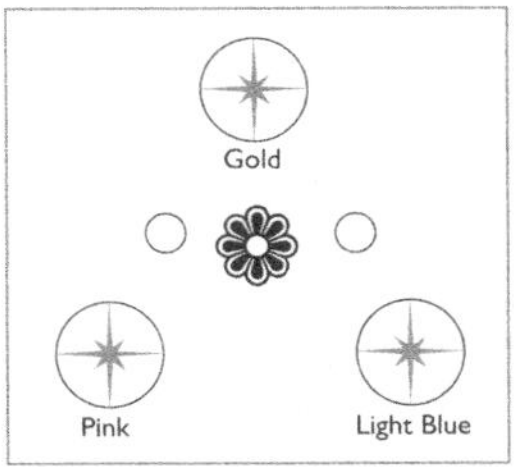

CANDLES Straight or votive candles in the following colors: one pink (friendship, spiritual healing), one light blue (inner peace, harmony, patience), and one gold (healing, happiness).

OIL Lily of the valley.

HERBS Saint-John's-Wort.

INCENSE Jasmine or rose.

STONES Moss agate and amethyst.

OTHER SUPPLIES Small nail; a flower you like.

TIMING On the full moon or the waxing moon cycle.

DAY Friday.

ADVICE All happiness must come from within yourself. It is not someone else's responsibility to make you happy. This spell helps you to see the truth within yourself and to come to terms with that.

SPELLWORK Light the altar candles and the incense. Using a nail, inscribe the word "love" on the pink candle, "peace" on the light blue one, and "success" on the gold candle. Anoint the candles from the wick to the end. Place the flower in the center of your altar; it should be a flower that in some manner represents happiness to you. Set the candles in a triangular shape with the gold one at the top, the pink at the bottom left, and the light blue at the bottom right. Place the agate between the gold and pink candles, and the amethyst between the gold and blue ones. Light the gold candle first, then the others. Say the chant three times. Leave the candles to burn out completely. Dispose of the wax afterward.

CHANT *Open my life to happiness and joy.*
Fill my life with the wonder of peace and love.
Open my eyes to the incoming happiness.
Make me aware of all the good that comes into my life.

Consecrate a Talisman

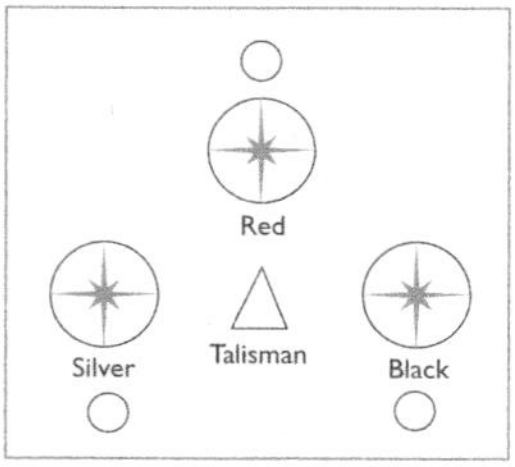

CANDLES Straight or votive candles in the following colors: one red (willpower, strength), one silver (stability), and one black (binding all negative forces).

OIL Frankincense or lotus.

HERBS Frankincense or yellow sandalwood.

INCENSE Lotus or frankincense.

STONES Bloodstone, black onyx, and black obsidian.

OTHER SUPPLIES The jewelry or item you plan to use as a talisman.

TIMING On the full moon or the waxing moon cycle.

DAY Monday.

ADVICE A talisman acts like a good luck charm. It is something you wear or carry with you to help you cope with life and the unexpected.

SPELLWORK Light the altar candles and the incense. Anoint the black candle from the end to the wick; the others from the wick to the end. Place the red candle with the bloodstone above it at the top point of a triangular pattern. Set the silver candle and the black obsidian in front of it and to the left, and the black candle with the black onyx in front of it and and to the right. Hold the talisman in the incense smoke for several minutes. Then place it in the center of the triangle. Light the red candle, then the black, followed by the silver. Say the chant. Leave the talisman in place until the candles have burned completely out. Leave the candles to burn out completely. Dispose of the wax afterward. Wear or carry the talisman until the next full moon, when it should be reconsecrated.

CHANT *I bind you with protection and light,*
So that protection and light is all that you return to me.
This is my will. So shall it be.

Reach a Decision

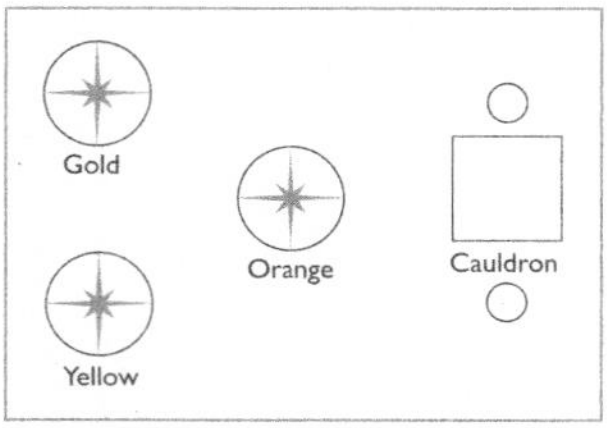

CANDLES Straight or votive candles in the following colors: one yellow (intellect, confidence), one orange (success, energy), and one gold (intuition, fast luck).

OIL Lotus.

HERBS Rue.

INCENSE Sage, acacia, or lotus.

STONES Agate and clear quartz crystal.

OTHER SUPPLIES Small metal cauldron; small piece of paper.

TIMING On the full moon or the waxing moon cycle.

DAY Tuesday.

ADVICE Before doing this ritual, take time to think out all the possibilities of your decision carefully. Afterward, you must do everything you can to take action. This spell will bring you wisdom to help make the correct decision, not have it made for you.

SPELLWORK Light the altar candles and the incense. Anoint the candles from the wick to the end. Although the candle pattern will be a triangular shape, the point of the triangle will point to the right where the cauldron sits. Set the gold candle behind the yellow one. Then place the orange candle to the center right of these candles. Put the cauldron to the right of the orange candle. Situate the clear quartz crystal above the cauldron and the point toward it, the agate below the cauldron. Write out exactly what decision you need to make and place the paper inside the cauldron. Light the gold candle, then the yellow, and finally the orange candle. Say the chant three times slowly. Light the paper from the orange candle and drop it into the cauldron to burn. Leave the candles to burn out completely. Dispose of the wax and ashes afterward.

CHANT *Grant me the wisdom to make a choice.*
Give me the spiritual guidance to do what is right.
Fill me with courage to take the right stand.
Grant me the wisdom to make my decision.

Start a New Venture

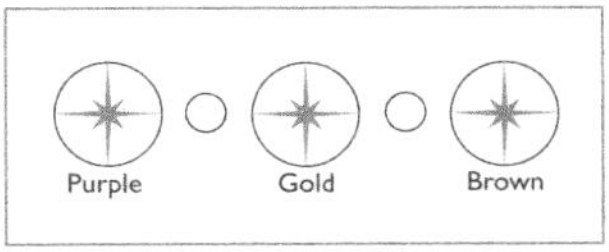

CANDLES Straight or votive candles in the following colors: one purple (success in business, wisdom), one gold (good fortune, fast luck, money), and one brown (financial success, balance).

OIL Cinnamon.

HERBS Nutmeg.

INCENSE Cinnamon, rosemary, or clove.

STONES Agate and emerald.

OTHER SUPPLIES None.

TIMING On the full moon or the waxing moon cycle.

DAY Thursday.

ADVICE Do not perform this candle ritual until you have settled on only one new venture. If you do this spell while thinking of several possibilities, you will get a muddled, unclear answer or result.

SPELLWORK Light the altar candles and the incense. Anoint the candles from the wick to the end. Set the candles in a straight line, purple on the left, gold in the middle, and brown on the right. Put the agate between the purple and gold candles, and the emerald between the gold and brown ones. Light them from left to right. Say the chant.

Meditate on the new venture you want to undertake. Leave the candles to burn out completely. Dispose of the wax afterward. This ritual and meditation may be repeated each night, if you wish, until the next new moon.

CHANT *A new road opens before me.*
A new cycle begins its round.
I step out in courage and wisdom.
To me success is bound.

Peaceful Divorce

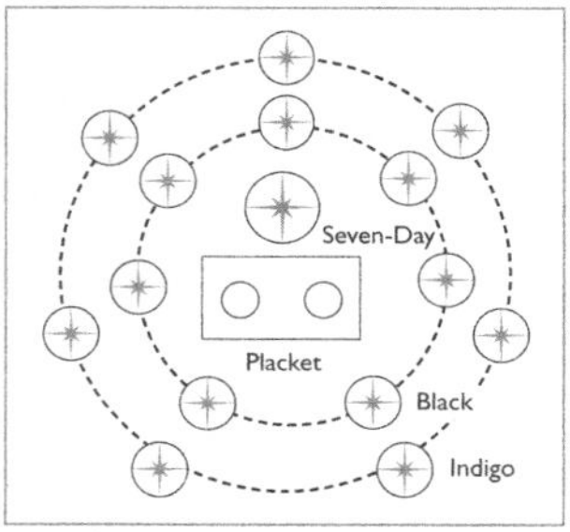

CANDLES A seven-day candle in light blue (inner peace, harmony), plus seven straight candles each of black (protection, binds negative forces) and indigo (balance out karma). You can use seven light blue straight candles instead of the seven-day candle, and burn one each day with the other colors.

OIL Patchouli.

HERBS Lemon verbena.

INCENSE Patchouli or vervain.

STONES Sodalite and chalcedony.

OTHER SUPPLIES Seven new straight pins; placket with photo of divorcing couple.

TIMING On the new moon or the waning moon cycle.

DAY Tuesday.

ADVICE It is extremely unusual for a divorce to end amicably. Somewhere during the process, animosities inevitably seem to arise. Try to be as fair as possible, leaving aside thoughts of revenge, even though you may feel you have just cause. You should aim instead for a fair, swift, and peaceful separation. Only then can your life come back into balance and open up new opportunities for you.

SPELLWORK Light the altar candles and the incense. Anoint the top of the seven-day candle and put it in the center of your altar. Anoint the black candles from the end to the wick; the others from the wick to the end. Place the placket containing a photo, if possible, or at least a paper with both names on it before the seven-day candle. Lay the chalcedony and sodalite on top of the placket. Make a circle of the black candles around the placket and seven-day candle. Carefully push a straight pin in each indigo candle about halfway down. Then arrange the indigo candles around the black candles in another circle on the outside of the black ones. Light the seven-day candle first, then the black candles, and finally the indigo ones. Say the chant. Leave the seven-day candle burning at all times, but extinguish the other candles after an hour. Relight them each day at the same time and again say the chant.

CHANT *These pins I do not wish to burn.*
'Tis (name)'s mind I wish to turn.
May she/he not know peace or rest
Until she/he grants my request.

Celebrate a Birth

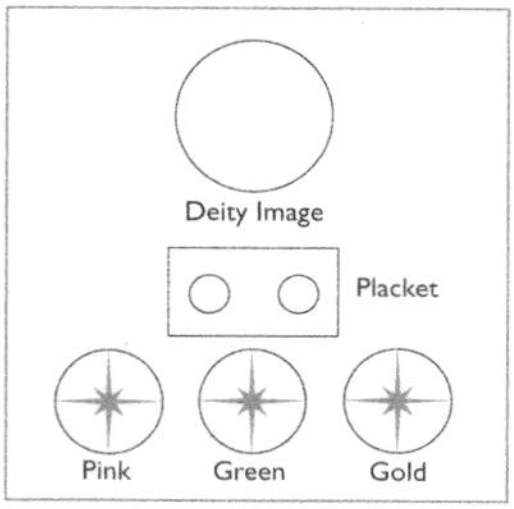

CANDLES Straight or votive candles in the following colors: one pink (love, spiritual awakening, family love), one green (fresh outlook on life), and one gold (happiness, good fortune).

OIL Rose.

HERBS Rose petals.

INCENSE Frankincense or myrrh.

STONES Lapis lazuli and rose quartz.

OTHER SUPPLIES Placket with a photo or name of the new baby.

TIMING Preferably, on the full moon or the waxing moon cycle.

DAY Monday.

ADVICE This ritual can be performed at any time within a month after the birth. If you adopt a child, you can use this same ritual when you receive the child. Receiving an adopted child counts as a birth, for it truly is just that.

SPELLWORK Light the altar candles and the incense. Anoint the candles from the wick to the end. Put a placket containing a photo of the child or the name on a piece of paper before the deity image on your altar. Place the lapis lazuli and rose quartz on top of the placket. Arrange the candles in a straight line, pink on the left, green in the middle, and gold on the right. Light the candles from left to right. Say the chant. Leave the candles to burn out completely. Dispose of the wax afterward.

CHANT *We light these candles in joy for the new life in our midst.*

May love and goodness always surround her (him, or child's name).

May Light always guide her (him, or child's name).

May good health and prosperity always fill her (his, or child's name) life.

May happiness and contentment always be on her (his, or child's name) doorstep.

We welcome you, child of Light and love.

Celebrate a Wedding Anniversary

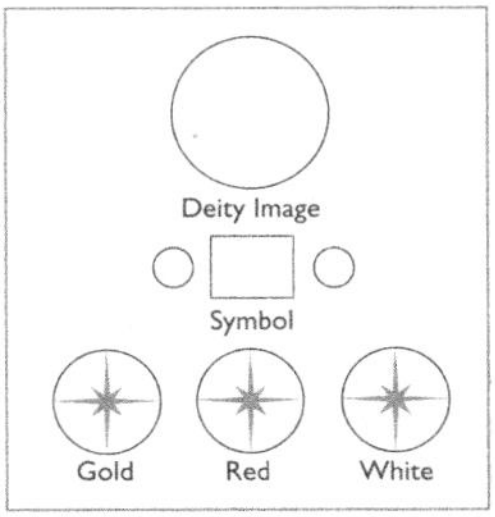

CANDLES Straight or votive candles in the following colors: one gold (good fortune, understanding), one red (physical desire, good health), and one white (sincerity, wholeness).

OIL Rose.

HERBS Rose petals.

INCENSE Frankincense or myrrh.

STONES Aquamarine and sard.

OTHER SUPPLIES A photo of the couple, or some symbol important to them.

TIMING On the full moon or the waxing moon cycle.

DAY Friday.

ADVICE This candle ceremony can be performed as a private affair for the couple or can be done during a gathering of sympathetic and understanding friends and family. Every anniversary of a relationship that survives the constant ups and downs of life is reason for celebration.

SPELLWORK Light the altar candles and the incense. Put a symbol of the marriage in front of the deity image on your altar. This symbol can be a photo of the couple, a spiritual wedding gift that has special meaning to them, saved flowers or cake from the wedding itself, or simply a nice card with their names carefully done in calligraphy. Place the aquamarine to the left of this symbol and the sard to the right. Anoint the candles from the wick to the end. Arrange the candles in a straight line before this, gold on the left, red in the center, and white on the right. Light the candles from left to right. Say the chant. Leave the candles to burn out completely. Dispose of the wax afterward.

CHANT *True love found us and brought us together.*
True love bound our hearts together as one.
May true love always fill our hearts and our days
As we continue our journey through life.

In Memory of a Deceased Loved One

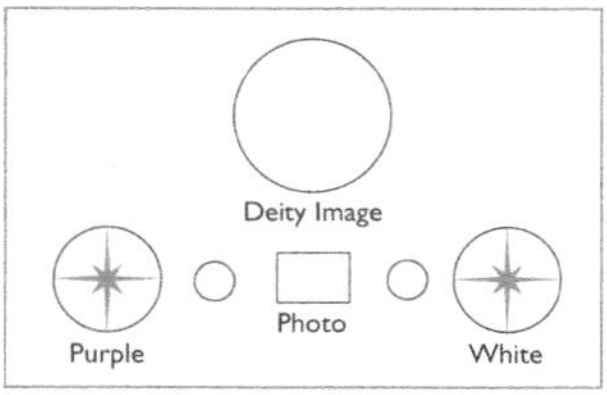

CANDLES Straight or votive candles in the following colors: one purple (spirit contact, spiritual healing) and one white (purity, truth, wholeness).

OIL Patchouli.

HERBS Patchouli.

INCENSE Patchouli or lotus.

STONES Four pieces of clear quartz crystal.

OTHER SUPPLIES Photo of the deceased person.

TIMING This spell can be used on the loved one's birthday, the day of their death, or on a full moon or during a waxing moon cycle.

DAY Saturday.

ADVICE It takes a very long time for the heart and mind to heal after losing someone. The pain never completely goes away, but it does become more bearable with time. A remembrance, such as this candle ritual, is a good healing method. Holding back the sorrow and tears is never healthful. Allow anyone present to cry and express him- or herself. Just keep a full box of tissue on hand. Such remembrances often bring remaining family and friends closer together.

SPELLWORK Light the altar candles and the incense. Place a photo of the deceased person before the deity image on your altar. Put one clear quartz crystal to the left and right of the photo. Anoint the candles from the wick to the end. Set the purple candle on the left of the photo, and the white candle on the right. Light the candles. Say the chant. Leave the candles to burn out completely. Dispose of the wax afterward.

CHANT *Gone from this Earth, but not forgotten.*
Gone from our sight, but not from our hearts.
Memories comfort our sorrow.
We know we shall meet again.

Giving Thanks

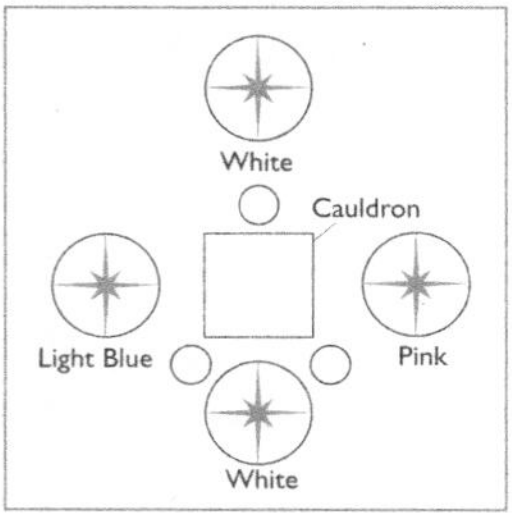

CANDLES Straight or votive candles in the following colors: two white (truth, sincerity), one light blue (inner peace, harmony, contacting the Higher Self), and one pink (affection, healing).

OIL Lotus or frankincense.

HERBS Sage.

INCENSE Frankincense or myrrh.

STONES Amethyst, clear quartz crystal, and iolite.

OTHER SUPPLIES Small metal cauldron; small piece of paper.

TIMING On the full moon or the waxing moon cycle.

DAY Sunday.

ADVICE Giving thanks for little things, as well as big ones, helps one to grow spiritually and have a better insight into life in general. This ritual can be worked once a month or whenever an important event occurs. It is especially nice to do after having a successful candle ritual manifestation.

SPELLWORK Light the altar candles and the incense. Write on the paper exactly what you are thankful for. Set the cauldron with the paper inside it in the center of your altar. Place the amethyst, clear quartz crystal, and iolite around the cauldron. Anoint the candles from the wick to the end. The white candles go behind and in front of the cauldron, while the blue candle is set on the left side and the pink on the right. Light the candles. Say the chant. Leave the candles to burn out completely. Dispose of the wax and ashes afterward.

CHANT *I give thanks to the Goddess (God)*
For the blessings showered upon me.
I ask for continued blessings.
So it is. So shall it be.

Healing

General Healing 1

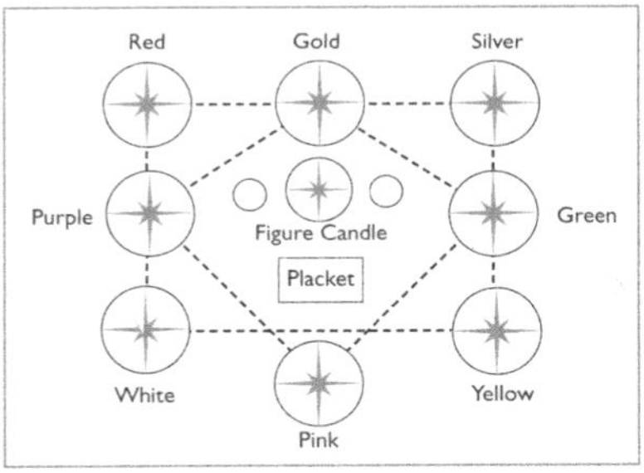

CANDLES A red or blue figure candle to represent the sick person. Red figure candles are easier to find than blue ones. Nine candles each of the following colors: gold, green, pink, purple, red, silver, yellow, and white.

OIL Carnation, myrrh, or lavender.

HERBS Frankincense.

INCENSE Lotus or lavender.

STONES Amber and turquoise.

OTHER SUPPLIES Small nail; placket with photo or name.

TIMING Waxing moon cycle.

DAY Sunday (health, healing), Thursday (good health), Monday (emotional medicine), or Wednesday (physical medicine).

ADVICE Always make certain the person for whom the healing is done actually wants to be healed. Some people subconsciously do not want a healing. Their illness gives them leverage to control those around them. With such a person, no amount of healing will take effect.

SPELLWORK Light the altar candles and the incense. Using a nail, carve the sick person's name or initials into the figure candle. Anoint the candles from the wick to the end. Arrange the turquoise and amber on each side of the figure candle. A placket containing a photo of the sick person, or a paper with their name, is placed in front of the figure candle. The other candles are arranged in two interlocking squares around the figure candle.

On the inside square, the gold candle is set behind the figure, the green to the right, the pink in front of it, and the purple to the left. On the outer square, the red goes between the gold and purple, silver between gold and green, yellow between green and pink, and white between pink and purple.

To begin the spell, anoint the figure candle with lavender, carnation, or myrrh oil from the wick to the bottom. Lay it on its back on a paper towel in the center of your altar. Light the surrounding candles, beginning with those in the inner square. Say the chant. Pray or meditate, visualizing great rays of white light streaming down upon this candle. Leave the other candles to burn out.

On the second day, stand the figure candle on its feet, facing the altar. Again anoint it with healing oil, say the chant, and visualize the white light. Light the surrounding candles and meditate. Leave the other candles to burn out.

On the third day, anoint the figure candle again and stand it facing the altar. This time, light the candle and the surrounding candles. Say the chant. Pray or meditate again, visualizing the sickness leaving the person's body and being burned to nothing in the brilliant white light. This time leave all the candles to burn out. Dispose of the wax.

You can repeat this spell twice more for a count of nine days. If you do this, always start each spell-cycle of three days with a fresh figure candle.

CHANT *Healing comes from the Light.*
You are filled with Light.
Healing comes from Universal Love.
You are filled with Universal Love.
All shadow of disease disappears under the Light.
You are healed and whole again.

General Healing 2

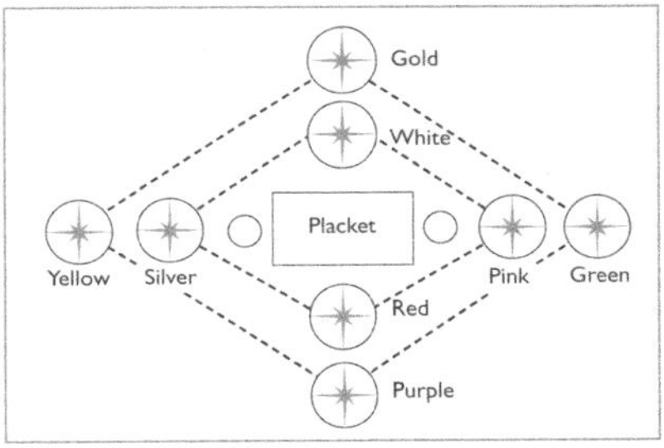

CANDLES Straight or votive candles of the colors of: one gold (healing, happiness), one green (renewal, balance), one pink (spiritual awakening, healing), one purple (drive away evil, healing), one red (energy, courage, good health), one silver (neutralize a situation, remove negatives), one yellow (confidence, healing), and one white (wholeness, balance the aura).

OIL Clove or gardenia.

HERBS Myrrh.

INCENSE Jasmine or myrrh.

STONES Beryl and fluorite.

OTHER SUPPLIES Placket with photo of the sick person.

TIMING On the full moon or the waxing moon cycle.

DAY Sunday (health, healing), Thursday (good health), Monday (emotional medicine), or Wednesday (physical medicine).

ADVICE Always make certain the person for whom the healing is done actually wants to be healed. Some people subconsciously do not want a healing. Their illness gives them leverage to control those around them. With such a person, no amount of healing will take effect.

SPELLWORK Light the altar candles and the incense. Place the placket containing the sick person's photo or a paper with their name in the center of your altar. Set the beryl to the left side of the placket and the fluorite to the right. Anoint the candles from the wick to the end. The candles go in a doubled square around this. On the upper left corner of the square, arrange the gold and white candles, the upper right the pink and green. On the lower right, set the red and purple candles, and on the lower left, set the yellow and silver ones. Light the candles, beginning with the upper left ones and working clockwise around the square. Say the chant. Leave the candles to burn out completely. Dispose of the wax afterward.

CHANT *I call in the Light of healing,*
To fill the body, mind, and spirit of (name).
The Light cannot be denied its healing powers.
No one and nothing can stop it from its cleansing path.
I draw down the Light! I draw down the Light!

General Healing 3

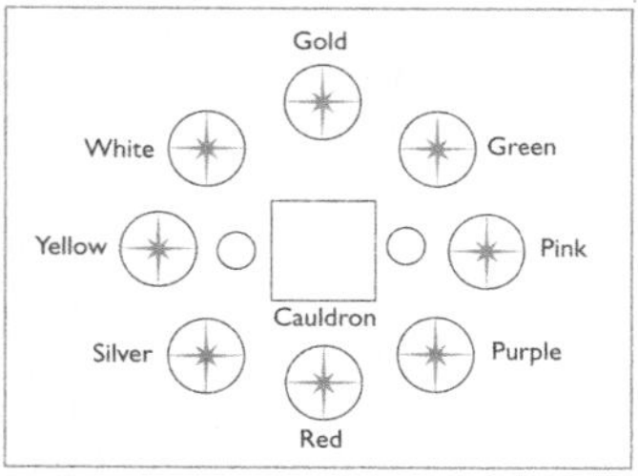

CANDLES Straight or votive candles in the following colors: one gold (healing, happiness), one green (renewal, balance, healing), one pink (spiritual healing, banish depression), one purple (spiritual protection and healing), one red (energy, willpower, good health), one silver (remove negative powers), one yellow (power of the mind), and one white (purity, wholeness).

OIL Gardenia.

HERBS Rue.

INCENSE Sandalwood or gardenia.

STONES Lapis lazuli and tourmaline.

OTHER SUPPLIES Small metal cauldron; paper with the sick person's name.

TIMING On the full moon or the waxing moon cycle.

DAY Sunday (health, healing), Thursday (good health), Monday (emotional medicine), or Wednesday (physical medicine).

ADVICE Concerning a person to be healed, read the advice in General Healing 1 (page 171).

SPELLWORK Light the altar candles and the incense. Write the sick person's name on the paper. Place the cauldron in the center of your altar, with the paper inside it. Set the lapis lazuli on the left of the cauldron and the tourmaline on the right. Anoint the candles from the wick to the end. Arrange the candles in a circle around it, beginning with the gold one behind the cauldron and working clockwise. Light the candles in the same order in which you placed them. Say the chant nine times. Leave the candles to burn out completely. Dispose of the wax afterward.

CHANT *Life and healing the Goddess (God) brings.*
Accept the healing! Welcome the healing!

Regain Health

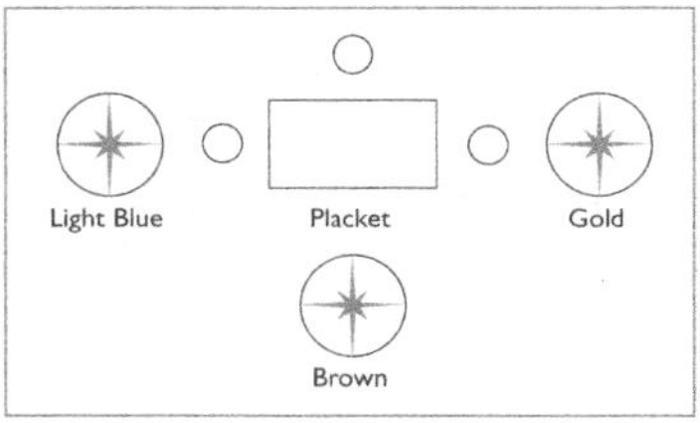

CANDLES Straight or votive candles in the following colors: one light blue (inner peace, good health), one brown (balance, grounding), and one gold (healing, happiness).

OIL Carnation.

HERBS Red sandalwood.

INCENSE Carnation or rose.

STONES Bloodstone and boji stones.

OTHER SUPPLIES Placket containing a photo or paper with the person's name.

TIMING On the full moon or the waxing moon cycle.

DAY Sunday (health, healing), Thursday (good health), Monday (emotional medicine), or Wednesday (physical medicine).

ADVICE Sometimes, after a person is healed of a disease, he or she still needs to regain lost ground before he or she is totally well again.

SPELLWORK Light the altar candles and the incense. Place the placket in the center of the altar, with a boji stone on each side of it (boji stones always come in pairs), and the bloodstone behind it. Anoint the candles from the wick to the end. Put the brown candle in front of the placket, the light blue one on the left, and the gold one on the right. Light the candles in the same order you arranged them. Say the chant. Leave the candles to burn out completely. Dispose of the wax afterward.

CHANT *Strength return to the body.*
Peace return to the mind.
Contentment return to the soul.
Balance and energy return to [name]'s life.

Recovery from Surgery

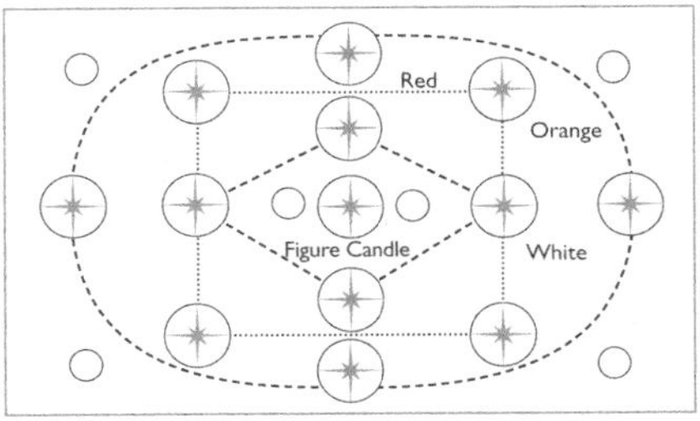

CANDLES One red figure candle. Straight or votive candles in the following colors: four red (energy, willpower, good health), four orange (stamina, encouragement), and four white (balance the aura, raise the vibrations).

OIL Lilac.

HERBS Pine needles.

INCENSE Cedar or sandalwood.

STONES Carnelian and boji stones.

OTHER SUPPLIES Small nail.

TIMING On the full moon or the waxing moon cycle.

DAY Tuesday.

ADVICE Surgery always damages the body's aura, thus leaving it open to potential disease of another kind. This ritual will seal the aura and help the patient to recover faster.

SPELLWORK Light the altar candles and the incense. Using the nail, mark the red figure candle in the same place as the surgery, duplicating the site of the scar as closely as possible. If it was a tonsil-lectomy, mark both sides of the neck. Lay the figure candle in the center of your altar and lightly rub the boji stones over the mark or marks. Anoint the candles from the wick to the end. Stand the figure upright in the center of your altar and place one boji stone on each side of it. Arrange the white candles at four sides around this figure. (See the diagram.) Next, arrange the orange candles in a square around the white ones. Finish by setting the red candles in a square around the orange ones. Light the figure candles, followed by each square of candles in the same order in which you set them out. Say the chant five times. Leave the candles to burn out completely. Dispose of the wax afterward.

CHANT *What was harmed is mended.*
What was cut is healed.
What was removed is balanced.
The Light of healing mends all, balances all.
Complete healing is accomplished through the Light.

Purification

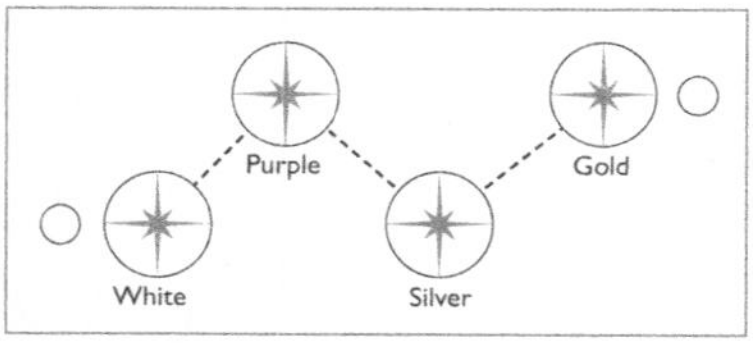

CANDLES Straight or votive candles in the following colors: one white (purity, spiritual contact), one purple (spirit contact, drive away evil), one silver (remove negative powers), and one gold (higher influences, healing).

OIL Pine.

HERBS Rosemary.

INCENSE Frankincense, pine, or rosemary.

STONES Aquamarine and tourmaline.

OTHER SUPPLIES None.

TIMING On the full moon or the waxing moon cycle.

DAY Sunday.

ADVICE If you have undergone an illness, an extremely emotional experience, been around very negative people, or through a traumatic event, you need to consider using this ritual to purify your aura. Negative experiences of any kind frequently leave a number of very small holes in the aura, which open you up to even more negative experiences.

SPELLWORK Light the altar candles and the incense. Anoint the candles from the wick to the end. Set the candles out in a zigzag line, like a lightning bolt laid horizontally on your altar. Place the candles in this order, beginning on the left: white, purple, silver, and gold. Set the aquamarine to the left of the white candle and the tourmaline to the right of the gold one. Light the candles in the same order you arranged them. Say the chant. Leave the candles to burn out completely. Dispose of the wax afterward.

CHANT *Swift as lightning, pure Love and Light flow through my body.*

All negatives are burned away in this universal power.
Willingly, I stand before this altar as a cleaned vessel,
Waiting for the inflow of positive energy.

Banish Serious or Terminal Illness

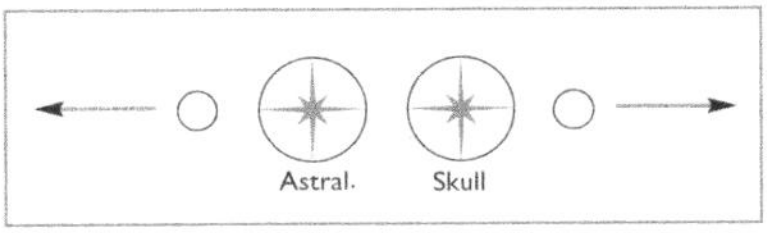

CANDLES Black skull candle, astrological candle for the person for whom the healing is being done.

OIL Myrrh or patchouli.

HERBS Rue.

INCENSE Frankincense, combined frankincense and myrrh, patchouli, or vervain.

STONES Black obsidian and black onyx.

OTHER SUPPLIES Small nail.

TIMING On the new moon or during the waning moon cycle.

DAY Saturday.

ADVICE As with any healing, make certain the sick person actually wants to recover. If she/he feels that her/his time has come, do not interfere with karma, but instead work for a peaceful passing.

SPELLWORK Light the altar candles and the incense. Using a nail or other sharp instrument, carve the sick person's name and the name of her/his disease onto the black skull candle. Carve only the person's initials on the astrological candle. Anoint the skull candle from the end to the wick, the astrological candle from the wick to the end. In the center of the altar, place the skull candle and an astrological candle representing the sick person, side by side, touching. Place the onyx near the astrological candle and the obsidian near the skull candle.

Light the skull candle first, then the astrological candle. While concentrating on the sick person, say the chant. Leave the candles burning. The skull candle will burn longer than the astrological candle, so you must have others ready. Just before the astrological candle burns out, light another astrological candle. An astrological candle must be burning at all times until the skull candle is completely burned out.

Each day move the candles one inch farther apart until the skull candle is burned out or they reach the farthest points on the altar. Each time you move the candles, repeat the chant. If the candles are still burning after you have moved them as far as you can, leave them there until the skull candle is out. Dispose of all the wax.

If, at the end of this process, the skull candle has burned out only the inside, leaving an outer shell, the threat remains. You will have to repeat the candle spell.

CHANT *Be gone, you darkened specter.*
Be gone, all illness and fear.
Healing and Light only may come.
This I declare, for one full year.

Love

Stop Interference in Your Love or Marriage

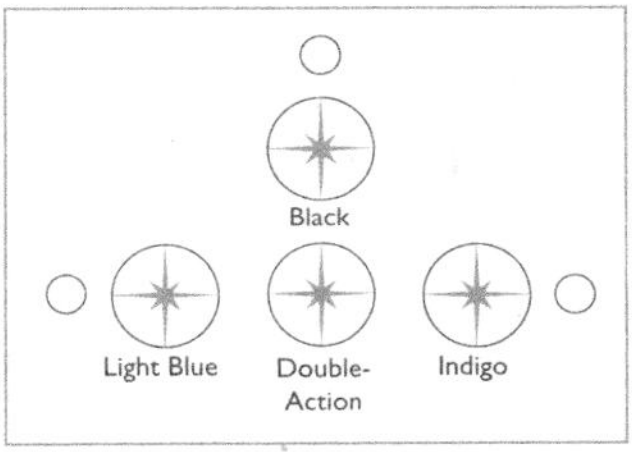

CANDLES A red and black double-action candle. Straight or votive candles in the following colors: one black (bind negative forces, break up blockages), one light blue (inner peace, harmony), and one indigo (stop another's actions).

OIL Frangipani.

HERBS Bay laurel.

INCENSE Frangipani or pine.

STONES Moonstone, chrysocolla, and pyrite.

OTHER SUPPLIES A small steel or iron nail.

TIMING On the full moon or during the waxing moon.

DAY Friday.

ADVICE Interference may come in the form of family, friends, or outsiders. Decisions must be made by the couple about continuing a relationship with the offending parties if they will not cease their interference.

SPELLWORK Light the altar candles and the incense. Using the nail, carve two hearts into the red portion of the candle; put your initials inside one heart, your lover's initials inside the other. Then stick the nail into the candle where the red wax meets the black wax. Anoint the black candle from the end to the wick; the others from the wick to the end. Set the black candle behind the double-action candle, with the pyrite behind it. Set the light blue candle and the moonstone on the left of the double-action candle and the indigo candle and the chrysocolla on the right. Light the double-action candle first, then the other candles. Say the chant. Burn the double-action candle down to the nail. Allow the other candles to burn out completely. Then dispose of the central candle and all wax from the others.

CHANT *No one can come between us.*
The troublemakers receive back their own words and actions.
We walk only in the Light.

Heal an Unhappy Marriage or Relationship

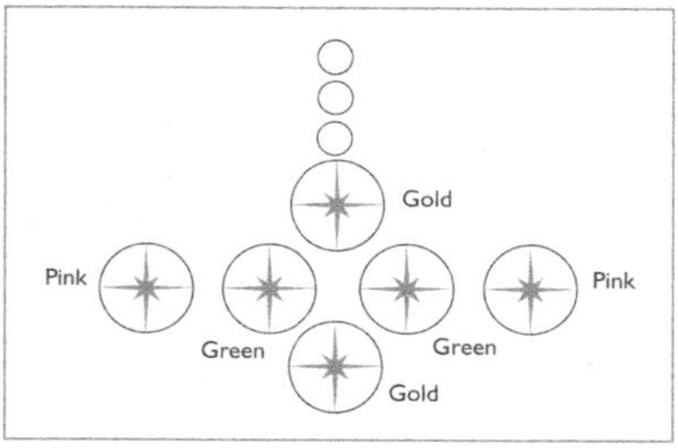

CANDLES Straight or votive candles in the following colors: two green (good fortune, balance, marriage), two gold (happiness), and two pink (true love, honor).

OIL Rose.

HERBS Rose petals or yarrow.

INCENSE Apple blossom, allspice, or sandalwood.

STONES Agate, amethyst, and lapis lazuli.

OTHER SUPPLIES Small nail.

TIMING On the full moon or the waxing moon cycle.

DAY Friday.

ADVICE Healing an unhappy relationship may come in many forms. It may mean that all differences are resolved, or one partner must continue to endure the situation because the other will not change. Or, it may mean that separation is the only healing that can come to a troubled partnership.

SPELLWORK Light the altar candles and the incense. Using a nail, inscribe each of the green candles with initials of one member of the couple. Anoint all the candles from the wick to the end. Set them side by side in the center of your altar. Behind them, place one gold candle, with the stones in a vertical line behind the gold candle. Place the other gold candle before the green candles. One pink candle is set on the right, and the other on the left. Light the green candles first, then the other candles. Say the chant. Leave the candles to burn out completely. Dispose of the wax afterward.

CHANT *All that was broken is mended.*
All that was wrong is made right.
All darkness and hurt are banished.
All that remains is the Light.

Win the Love of a Man

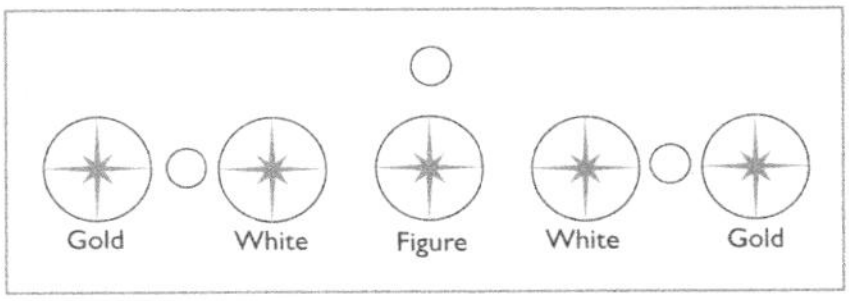

CANDLES Straight or votive candles in the following colors: one red male figure candle (physical desire, love), two gold (happiness, fast luck), and two white (sincerity, spirituality).

OIL Vanilla.

HERBS Catnip or ginger.

INCENSE Vanilla or ylang-ylang.

STONES Lodestone, aventurine, and malachite.

OTHER SUPPLIES Small nail; small piece of paper.

TIMING On the full moon or the waxing moon cycle.

DAY Friday.

ADVICE Do not use this spell to force someone to love you. Control over another will only bring you heartache and misery. The controlled person will always resent your action subconsciously and will constantly try to move away from you. This spell is best used when a person is in love with you, but is hesitant to make a commitment.

SPELLWORK Light the altar candles and the incense. Using a nail, carve the initials of the man into the red figure candle. Write your name on the piece of paper. Anoint all the candles from the wick to the end, and set the figure candle in the center of your altar. Place a gold (on the outside) and a white candle to both the left and right of this figure. Put the aventurine between the left-hand candles, and the malachite between the right-hand ones. Set the lodestone behind the figure candle and on the paper containing your name. Light the figure candle first, then the others. Say the chant seven times. Leave the candles to burn out completely. Dispose of the wax after the figure candle has burned out.

CHANT *Love and warmth I offer thee.*
Hear me, lover. Come to me.

Win the Love of a Woman

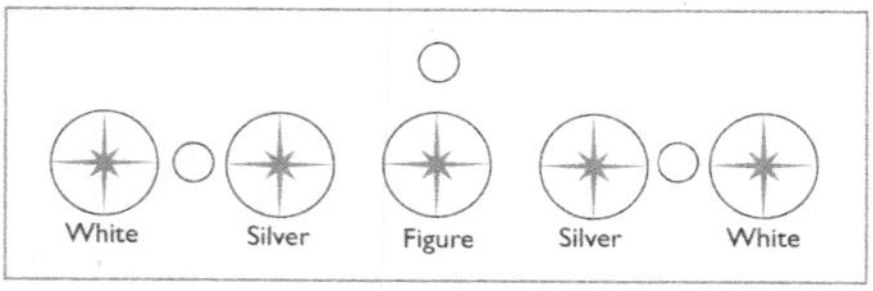

CANDLES Straight or votive candles in the following colors: one red female figure candle (physical desire, love), two silver (help from feminine deities), and two white (sincerity, spirituality).

OIL Rose.

HERBS Rose petals.

INCENSE Frangipani or rose.

STONES Coral, lodestone, and rose quartz.

OTHER SUPPLIES Small nail; small piece of paper.

TIMING On the full moon or the waxing moon cycle.

DAY Friday.

ADVICE See the advice on the previous spell.

SPELLWORK Light the altar candles and the incense. Using a nail, carve the initials of the woman into the red figure candle. Write your name on the piece of paper. Anoint all the candles from the wick to the end, and set the figure candle in the center of your altar. Place a silver and a white (on the outside) candle to both the left and right of this figure. Put the coral between the left-hand candles, and the rose quartz between the right-hand ones. Set the lodestone behind the figure candle and on the paper containing your name. Light the figure candle first, then the others. Say the chant seven times. Leave the candles to burn out completely. Dispose of the wax after the figure candle has burned out.

CHANT *Love and protection I offer thee.*
Hear me, lover. Come to me.

Find the Perfect Mate

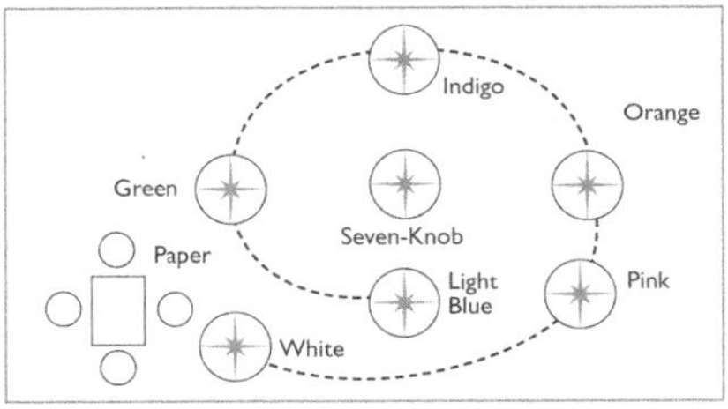

CANDLES A red seven-knob candle, plus seven straight or votive candles in the following colors: light blue (inner peace, harmony), green (good fortune, marriage), indigo (balance out karma), orange (success, energy), pink (true love, romance), and white (sincerity, purity).

OIL Musk.

HERBS Rue.

INCENSE Musk or patchouli.

STONES Moss agate, clear quartz crystal, lapis lazuli, and rose quartz.

OTHER SUPPLIES Small piece of paper with your name on it.

TIMING On the full moon or the waxing moon cycle.

DAY Monday or Friday.

ADVICE This love spell is the safest and best to use, as it does not target any particular individual. Instead, it reaches out into the universe to bring you the best and perfect mate for you.

SPELLWORK Light the altar candles and the incense. Anoint the candles from the wick to the end. Place the red seven-knob candle in the center of your altar. Set the other candles in a spiral around the red candle, beginning with the light blue on the inside in front of the seven-knob candle and ending with the white on the outer end of the spiral. Place the paper containing your name next to the white candle. Put the stones, one at each side, around the paper. (See the diagram.) First, light the red candle, then the others. Say the chant three times. Extinguish all the candles when the red candle has burned one knob. Relight all the candles at the same time each night for seven nights and repeat the chant each time. The last night, leave the candles to burn out completely. Dispose of the wax afterward.

CHANT *One to seek her/him, one to find her/him.*
One to bring her/him, one to bind her/him.
Heart to heart, forever one.
So say I, this spell is done.

Release an Unwanted Admirer or Lover

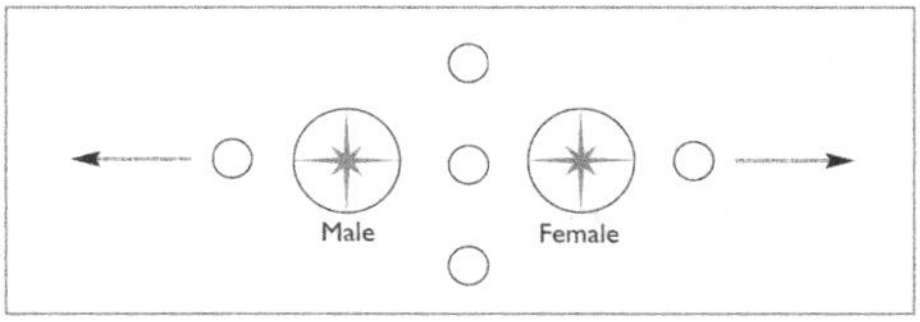

CANDLES Two red figure candles, the sexes representing the sexes of the two people involved.

OIL Patchouli.

HERBS Lemon verbena.

INCENSE Patchouli or rue.

STONES Spectrolite, jade, clear quartz crystal, agate, and malachite.

OTHER SUPPLIES Small nail.

TIMING On the new moon or the waning moon cycle.

DAY Tuesday.

ADVICE Sometimes you find yourself in a relationship, friendship, or situation with a person that is not good for you. It can be a problem to get possessive people to let go. This spell will make it easier to move them out of your surroundings. However, you must do your part by calmly stating, if possible, that the relationship or friendship is ended, and that you are definitely not interested.

SPELLWORK Light the altar candles and the incense. Using a nail, carve the appropriate initials into each figure candle. Anoint the candles from the wick to the end. Place the figure candles back to back on the altar. Place the clear quartz crystal between the two figures. Set the spectrolite centered behind the figures, the agate on the left, the jade on the right, and the malachite in front of them. Light the candles. Say the chant nine times. Burn the candles for one hour each day. Each day, move the figures farther apart, still facing away from each other. On the last day, leave the candles to burn out completely. Dispose of the wax.

CHANT *Peacefully, we walk away.*
No pain or sorrow remain.
Separately, we live our lives,
Never to join again.

Protection

Stop Slander and Gossip

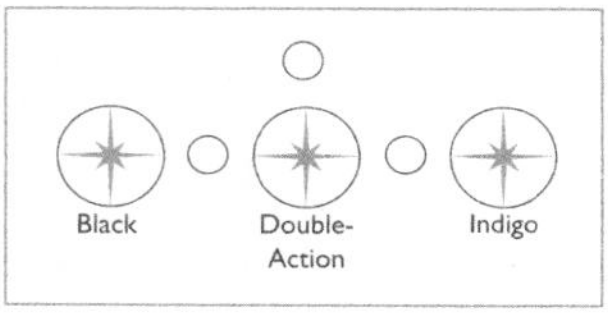

CANDLES A black and white double-action candle, plus straight or votive candles in the following colors: one black (remove negative energies) and one indigo (stop gossip and lies).

OIL Juniper or lilac.

HERBS Clove or marjoram.

INCENSE Cypress or pine.

STONES Aquamarine, hematite, and agate.

OTHER SUPPLIES A small nail; piece of shiny foil.

TIMING During a waning moon.

DAY Tuesday.

ADVICE Although this spell will stop gossip, you must remain alert that by your actions and words you do not set up another situation that will bring more gossip your way. Also, do not gossip yourself.

SPELLWORK Light the altar candles and the incense. With the nail, carve an eye inside a triangle on the white part of the candle. Anoint the black candle from the end to the wick; the others from the wick to the end. Then stick the nail into the double-action candle right where the black wax starts. Place the candle on shiny foil and light it.

Put the stones around the candle. Set the black candle on the left of the double-action candle and the indigo one on the right; light them. As the white wax drips down and covers the black wax, the gossip will return to the one who sent it. Say the chant three times. Burn the candle down to the nail. Then dispose of the candle and all wax from it.

CHANT *Your mouth is stopped.*
Your eyes see naught.
Your thoughts are bound.
Your words turn 'round.
No longer will you bother me.
This is my will. So shall it be.

Rid Yourself of Negatives

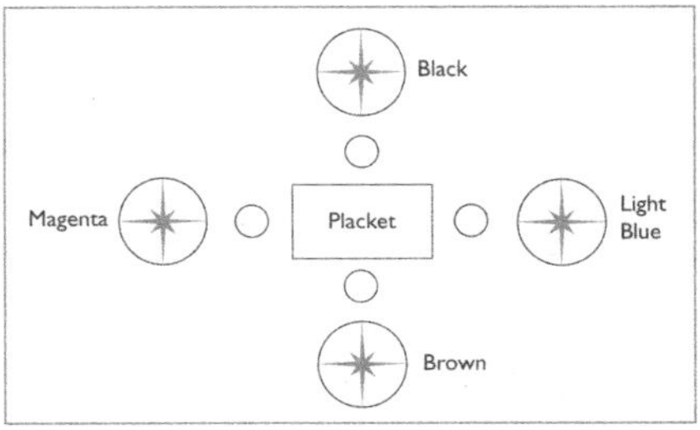

CANDLES Straight or votive candles in the following colors: one black (remove negative energies, protection), one light blue (inner peace, harmony, contacting the Higher Self), one brown (balance, grounding), and one magenta (exorcism, healing, fast action).

OIL Pine.

HERBS Basil.

INCENSE Cedar or vervain.

STONES Two pieces each of hematite and smoky quartz.

OTHER SUPPLIES Placket with your photo.

TIMING On the new moon or the waning moon cycle.

DAY Tuesday or Saturday.

ADVICE Ridding yourself of negatives may require you to give up certain friends, activities, and habits. Think carefully about this before performing this ritual.

SPELLWORK Light the altar candles and the incense. Place the placket containing your photo in the center of your altar. Put a piece of hematite behind and in front of the placket, with a piece of smoky quartz on each side. Anoint the black candle from the end to the wick; the others from the wick to the end. Set the black candle behind the placket, with the light blue on the right side, the brown in front, and the magenta on the left. Light the candles in the same order as you arranged them. Say the chant five times. Leave the candles to burn out completely. Dispose of the wax afterward.

CHANT *All negatives go out of my life.*
Only positive enters.
I turn from the path of darkness,
And walk only in the way of Light.
I am cleansed. I am purified. I am changed.

Binding Troublesome People

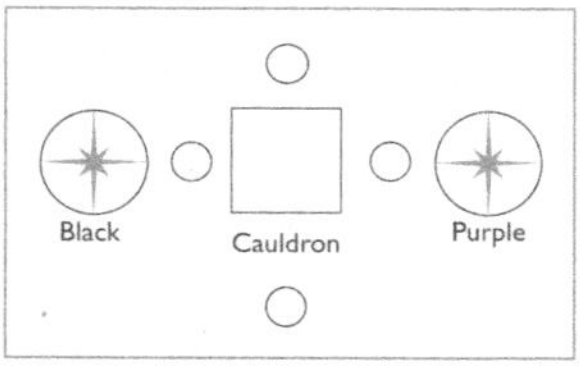

CANDLES Straight or votive candles in the following colors: one black (cause confusion to enemies, protection) and one purple (drive away evil, spiritual protection).

OIL Patchouli.

HERBS Patchouli.

INCENSE Cypress or pine.

STONES Jade, lapis lazuli, and two pieces of black onyx.

OTHER SUPPLIES A small metal cauldron; a small piece of paper.

TIMING On the new moon or the waning moon cycle.

DAY Saturday.

ADVICE Sometimes nice little spells simply do not make an impression on certain types of malicious, harmful people. Then you must be willing to do whatever is required to protect yourself from harassment, revenge, or whatever nasty tactics are being used. Binding them, or preventing them from doing mischief, is one way to protect yourself.

SPELLWORK Light the altar candles and the incense. Put the cauldron in the center of your altar. If you know for certain the names of the offending people, write them on the paper. If you are unsure, simply write "all my enemies." Place the paper inside the cauldron. Anoint the black candle from the end to the wick; the purple from the wick to the end. Set the black candle to the left of the cauldron, the purple candle to the right. Place the lapis lazuli behind the cauldron and the jade in front of it, with one piece of black onyx on the right side of the cauldron and another piece on the left of the cauldron. Light the candles and say the chant slowly five times. After the candles are burned completely out, burn the paper with the names. Dispose of the wax and ashes.

CHANT *Darkness is ended.*
Interference is done.
Enemies are shackled.
My battle is won.

Release One from Enthrallment

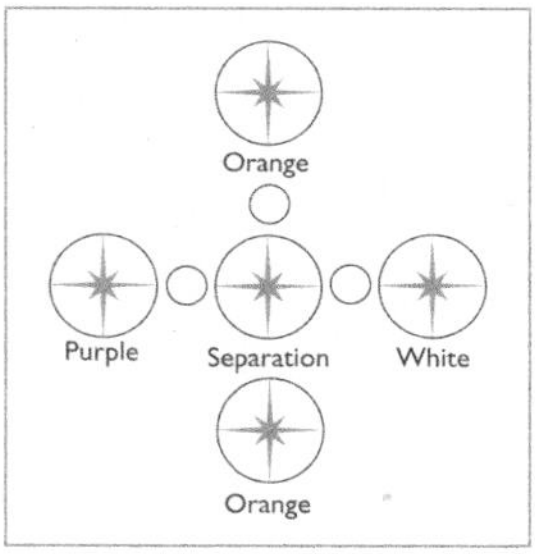

CANDLES A separation candle, which is a large red jumbo candle dipped completely in black. Straight or votive candles in the following colors: one purple (break bad luck, influence people), one white (power of a higher nature, truth), and two orange (sudden changes, success).

OIL Cedar or dragon's blood.

HERBS Dragon's blood.

INCENSE Patchouli or myrrh.

STONES Chalcedony, tourmaline, and malachite.

OTHER SUPPLIES Small nail.

TIMING On the new moon or the waning moon cycle.

DAY Tuesday.

ADVICE The only time this break-up spell is justified is when a loved one is being hurt by the person with whom he/she has a relationship. This can be a daughter who is involved with an abuser, alcoholic, or drug addict, or a family member who is blind to one who is conning him/her out of his/her money and possessions.

SPELLWORK Light the altar candles and the incense. Using a nail, carve the initials of the enthralled person into the separation candle. Anoint the candles from the wick to the end. Place the separation candle in the center of your altar, with the purple candle on the left and the white candle on the right, with an orange candle behind and in front. Put the chalcedony behind the separation candle with the malachite on the right and the tourmaline on the left. Light the separation candle first, then the other candles. Say the chant slowly three times. Leave the candles to burn out completely. Dispose of the wax afterward.

CHANT *All that was joined is now severed.*
All that was wrong is now right.
All that was shadowed is brightness.
The truth is revealed by the Light.

Release from Psychic Attack or Ill-Wishing

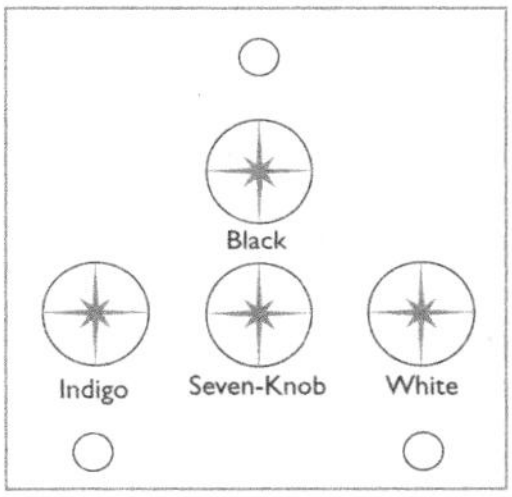

CANDLES A purple (drive away evil, spiritual protection) seven-knob candle (or seven purple straight or votive candles), plus seven each of the colors black (absorb and remove negative energies), indigo (neutralize the magick of others), and white (spiritual protection).

OIL Patchouli or frankincense.

HERBS Patchouli.

INCENSE Cedar or myrrh.

STONES Smoky quartz, turquoise, and black obsidian.

OTHER SUPPLIES Small nail.

TIMING On the new moon or the waning moon cycle.

DAY Saturday.

ADVICE Psychic attack is usually perpetrated knowingly by people, while ill-wishing is the continual repeating of negative statements to you or about you. Both can cause all kinds of problems. These energies should be returned to their senders.

SPELLWORK Light the altar candles and the incense. Carve your initials into the purple seven-knob candle with a nail, anoint it from the wick to the end, and set it in the center of your altar. Anoint the black candle from the end to the wick; the others from the wick to the end. Place the black candle and the black obsidian behind the seven-knob candle. Set the white candle and the clear quartz crystal on the right side, and the indigo candle and the turquoise on the left. Light the seven-knob candle, then the other candles. Say the chant seven times. Burn only one knob of the purple candle each night. Leave the other candles to burn out completely. Use fresh black, indigo, and white candles each night. Dispose of the wax afterward.

CHANT *All evil returns to the maker and source.*
The rebound hits with a tenfold force.
My enemies have no power o'er me.
As I will, so shall it be!

Remove Negative Vibrations or Spirits from a Home

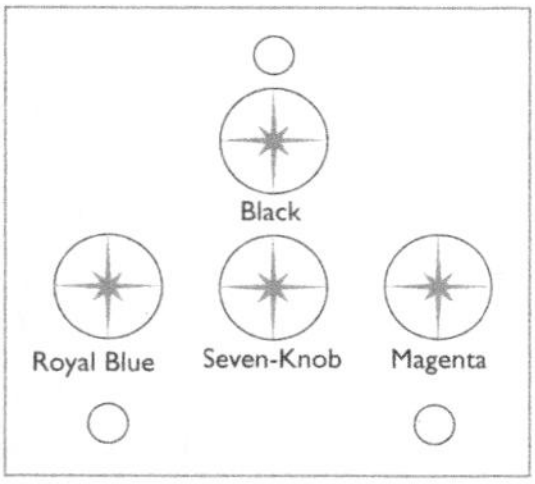

CANDLES A purple (drive away evil, spiritual protection) seven-knob candle (or seven purple straight or votive candles), plus seven each of the colors black (absorb and remove negative energies), royal blue (happiness, calling upon occult power), and magenta (fast action, exorcism).

OIL Vetiver or yarrow.

HERBS Vervain or patchouli.

INCENSE Frankincense, myrrh, or patchouli.

STONES Agate, clear quartz crystal, and bloodstone.

OTHER SUPPLIES Holy water. Bless water yourself in full moonlight by asking Goddess/God to make it pure, or see if you can obtain it from any Catholic Church.

TIMING On the new moon or the waning moon cycle.

DAY Saturday or Tuesday.

ADVICE Negative vibrations or a spirit may already occupy a house or apartment when you move in, especially if a previous occupant was troubled in spirit or led a negative lifestyle. These forces can range from mildly irritating to outright disruptive and dangerous. It is a good idea to cleanse any new place of residence, or recleanse your present dwelling place on a monthly basis. On rare occasions, an earthbound, dangerous spirit will require an expert to remove it.

SPELLWORK Light the altar candles and the incense. Anoint the black candle from the end to the wick; the others from the wick to the end. Place the seven-knob candle in the center of your altar. Set the black candle and the bloodstone behind the seven-knob candle, with the magenta candle and agate on the right side, and the royal blue candle and clear quartz crystal on the left. Light the seven-knob candle first, then the others. Say the chant nine times. Take the bottle of holy water and sprinkle each corner of every room in the house or apartment, ending up at the front door. Open the door and order the spirit or vibrations to leave at once. Then close the door and sprinkle it also. Burn only one knob of the central candle each night. Leave the other candles on the altar to burn out completely, replacing them with fresh candles each night. Dispose of the wax afterward.

CHANT *This is a place of Light and Love.*
No darkness or evil can remain here.
By the power of the Goddess (God),
I order all darkness to leave at once!
Out with the darkness! In with the Light!

Remove Negative Vibrations or Spirits from a Person

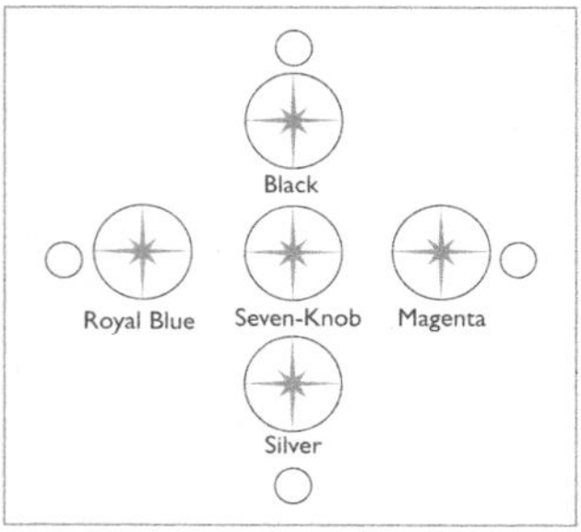

CANDLES A purple (drive away evil, spiritual protection) seven-knob candle (or seven purple straight or votive candles), plus seven each of the colors black (absorb and remove negative energies), royal blue (happiness, calling upon occult power), magenta (fast action, exorcism), and silver (neutralize negative powers, repel destructive forces).

OIL Vetiver or patchouli.

HERBS Vervain or patchouli.

INCENSE Frankincense, myrrh, or patchouli.

STONES Agate, clear quartz crystal, black onyx, and black obsidian.

OTHER SUPPLIES Holy water; small nail.

TIMING On the new moon or the waning moon cycle.

DAY Saturday or Tuesday.

ADVICE Determining personal possession can be a tricky decision. Some types of temporary or permanent mental illness can be mistaken for possession. So can certain types of willful behavior. If you are uncertain, consult an expert in the field. At no time should you ever use force of any kind to exorcise a person or inflict any type of physical or mental punishment!

SPELLWORK Light the altar candles and the incense. Using a nail, carve the initials of the troubled person into the purple seven-knob candle. Anoint it from the wick to the end and place it in the center of your altar. Anoint the black candle from the end to the wick; the others from the wick to the end. Place the black candle and the black obsidian behind the seven-knob candle, with the magenta candle and agate on the right side, the silver candle and the black onyx in front of it, and the royal blue candle and clear quartz crystal on the left. Say the chant seven times as you sprinkle the "possessed" person with the holy water. Even though this spell may appear to work the first time you do it, repeat it for the remaining six nights. Each night burn only one knob of the purple candle. Leave the other candles to burn out completely, replacing them with fresh candles each night. Dispose of the wax afterward.

CHANT *By the power of Light, I cast out all evil and darkness.*

By the power of Light, I call upon only goodness to dwell in this body.

By the power of the Goddess (God), I set you free!

Bring Pressure to Bear on an Enemy

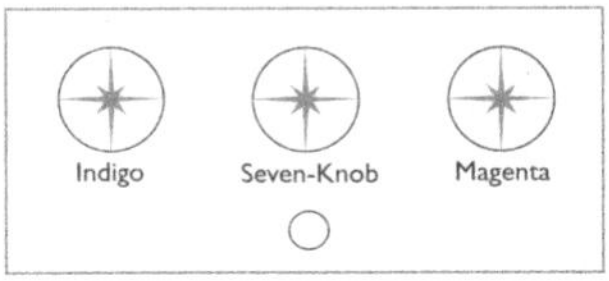

CANDLES A purple seven-knob candle (or seven purple straight or votive candles), plus seven each of indigo (balance out karma, stop another's actions) and magenta (fast action, spiritual healing).

OIL Pine.

HERBS Bay laurel or clove.

INCENSE Dragon's blood, pine, or patchouli.

STONES Aquamarine.

OTHER SUPPLIES Small nail.

TIMING During a waning moon.

DAY Saturday or Tuesday.

ADVICE Sometimes the only way to stop enemies is to put them under pressure from their own lives. Then they have no time to worry about you.

SPELLWORK Light the altar candles and the incense. With a nail, carve the initials or name of the enemy into the purple seven-knob candle. Anoint the candles from the wick to the end. Place the aquamarine in front of the seven-knob candle with the indigo candle on the left and the magenta one on the right. Light the seven-knob candle first, then the others. Say the chant. Sit quietly and visualize yourself building a thick stone wall between you and your enemy. Take your time with this, for when you can feel that this wall is there, your protection will be complete. Everything negative sent to you will rebound upon the sender. Each night burn only one knob of the purple candle. Leave the other candles to burn out completely, replacing them with fresh candles each night. Dispose of the wax afterward.

CHANT *One to seek her/him. One to find her/him.*
One to bring her/him. One to bind her/him.
Stone to stone, forever one.
So say I. This spell is done.

Uncross a Person

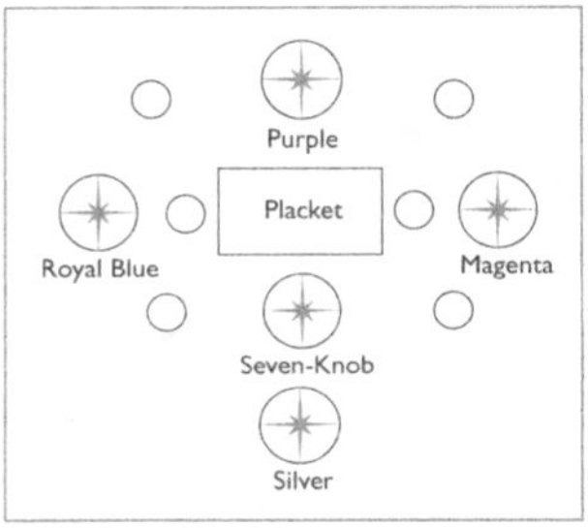

CANDLES A black seven-knob candle (or seven black straight or votive candles), plus seven each of royal blue (occult power), magenta (exorcism, fast action), purple (drive away evil, remove hexes), and silver (neutralize negative powers).

OIL Cedar or patchouli.

HERBS Dragon's blood or wormwood.

INCENSE Cedar, myrrh, or patchouli.

STONES Holey stone, mica, clear quartz crystal, black obsidian, black onyx, and sard.

OTHER SUPPLIES Placket with photo; holy water. To make or obtain holy water, see the "Remove Negative Vibrations from a Person" spell.

TIMING On the new moon or the waning moon cycle.

DAY Saturday.

ADVICE Active hexing or putting a magickal curse on a person is vastly different from ill-wishing someone. Hexing is a willful act, requiring thought and determination. This can have devastating effects on the life of the person hexed, such as loss of job and money, a turn of ill health, trouble in relationships, and any number of other negative occurrences. To remove a hex, it requires seven nights (preferably at midnight) and deep concentration and determination on the part of the hexed person and the person helping.

SPELLWORK Light the altar candles and the incense. Anoint the black candle from the end to the wick, the others from the wick to the end. Place the placket containing the photo of the hexed person in the center of your altar. In front of it set the black seven-knob candle with the black obsidian on the left and the black onyx on the right. Put the purple candle behind the placket, and the silver one in front of the black seven-knob candle. Set the royal blue candle to the left of the seven-knob candle with the magenta one to the right. Place the remaining stones, one beside each of these last candles. Light the seven-knob candle first, then the other candles. Say the chant as you sprinkle the hexed person with holy water. Each night burn only one knob of the black candle. Leave the other candles to burn out completely, replacing them with fresh candles each night. Dispose of the wax afterward.

CHANT *Power of the Light, come to my call!*
Release (name) from bondage of this curse.
Return it tenfold to the sender.
Fill (name) with the holy power of Light!

Protect Someone from Abuse

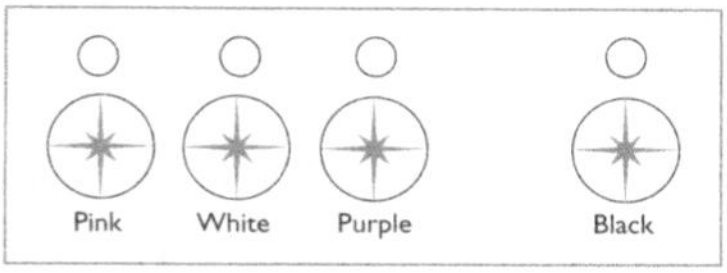

CANDLES Straight or votive candles in the following colors: one white (confidence, mental clarity, spiritual healing), one purple (protection, break bad luck, break influence of others), one black (creates confusion for enemies, unsticks stagnant situations, removes negative energies), and one pink (affection, banish depression).

OIL Frankincense.

HERBS Bay laurel or frankincense.

INCENSE Dragon's blood, frankincense, or patchouli.

STONES Jasper, lapis lazuli, smoky quartz, and black obsidian.

OTHER SUPPLIES Small nail.

TIMING On the new moon or the waning moon cycle.

DAY Tuesday.

ADVICE Although this spell will help protect the victim, she/he must eventually make a decision to move out of the situation.

SPELLWORK Light the altar candles and the incense. Using the nail, carve the name or initials of the abuser into the black candle and the name or initials of the victim into the white candle. Anoint the black candle from wick to the end, the other candles from the end to the wick. Arrange the candles in a straight line on your altar, with the pink on the left, white next, followed by the purple candle. Set the black candle to the far right, away from the other candles. Place the jasper behind the pink candle, the lapis lazuli behind the white, and the smoky quartz crystal behind to the purple. The black obsidian goes behind the distant black candle. Light the three candles to the left, then the black one. Say the chant. Visualize the black candle moving farther and farther away until its flame is only a tiny spot of light. Leave the candles to burn out completely. Dispose of the wax afterward.

CHANT *Change anger to calmness, darkness to light,*
Turn (abuser's name) to love, his/her path to what's right.
Protect those around him/her. Fill all with peace.
Fill all with healing. Let all violence cease.

Spirituality

Communicate with Spirit

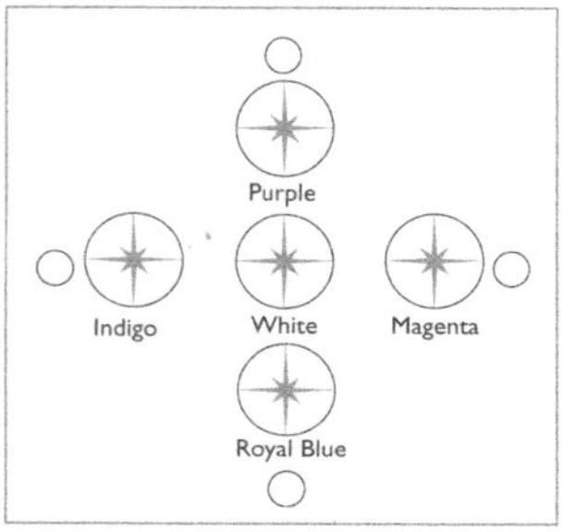

CANDLES Straight or votive candles in the following colors: one royal blue (occult power, expansion), one indigo (meditation, balances out karma), one magenta (spiritual healing), one purple (higher psychic ability, spirit contact), and one white (purity, contact spirit helpers).

OIL Yarrow or frankincense and myrrh.

HERBS Lavender.

INCENSE Frankincense or lotus.

STONES Amethyst, emerald, labradorite, moonstone, and sugilite.

OTHER SUPPLIES None.

TIMING On the full moon or the waxing moon cycle.

DAY Monday.

ADVICE The most perfect communications with Spirit come through meditation and prayer. If you call upon the Light before you do each meditation, and open yourself to what is right, not merely what you want to hear, you will have no problem making a firm and truthful contact with the spiritual realm.

SPELLWORK Light the altar candles and the incense. Anoint all of the candles from the wick to the end. Place the white candle in the center of the altar. Behind it, set the purple candle, with the magenta to the right, the royal blue in front of it, and the indigo to the left. Put the labradorite behind the purple candle, the moonstone to the right of the magenta, the sugilite in front of the royal blue, and the amethyst to the left of the indigo one. Light the white candle first, then the surrounding ones. Say the chant. Leave the candles to burn out completely. Dispose of the wax afterward. Watch your dreams for spiritual communications.

CHANT *Open the doors to Spirit wide.*
Take my hand and guide me inside.
Let me know the great wisdom, the strength, and the love,
That comes from sweet blending with Spirit above.

Meet Your Spirit Guide

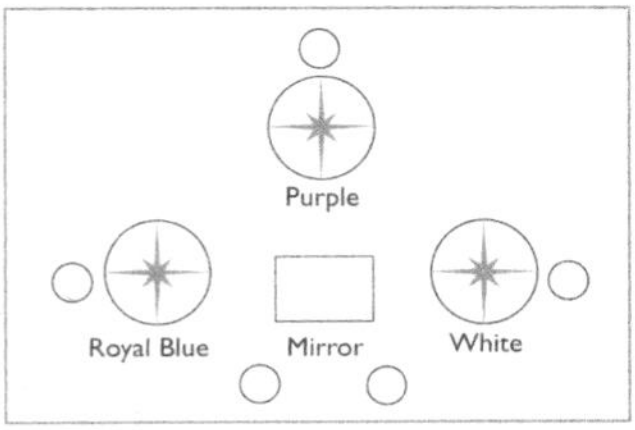

CANDLES Straight or votive candles in the following colors: one royal blue (occult power), one purple (higher influences, intuition), and one white (contact spirit helpers, raise the vibrations).

OIL Honeysuckle.

HERBS Mugwort.

INCENSE Sandalwood or lotus.

STONES Moss agate, lapis lazuli, moonstone, sugilite, and tourmaline.

OTHER SUPPLIES Small mirror large enough to reflect most of your face.

TIMING On the full moon or the waxing moon cycle.

DAY Monday.

ADVICE The mistake most people make when contacting spirit guides is to assume that they will get some great magician or high teacher. The majority of people on the earth are the common people. They are the ones who actually make things run right, not the big officials in some decorated office. If you want true wisdom and aid, ask for some knowledgeable, striving teacher who can help you with everyday problems. Commonsense, grassroots wisdom can beat out an over-puffed ego every time.

SPELLWORK Light the altar candles and the incense. Set the mirror upright in the center of your altar. Anoint all the candles from the wick to the end. Set the purple candle with the sugilite behind it behind the mirror. Place the white candle with the lapis lazuli outside to the right, and the royal blue one with the tourmaline outside to the left. To finish, put the moonstone by the left corner of the mirror and the agate by the right corner. Light the candles and look into the mirror as you say the chant. Watch for subtle changes in your appearance or flickers of movement in the mirror. These are signs that a teacher or teachers are present. Leave the candles to burn out completely. Dispose of the wax afterward.

CHANT *I knock upon the spiritual door*
In search of guidance, knowledge, more.
I seek to know who walks with me.
This I will do. So shall it be.

Enhance Spiritual Growth

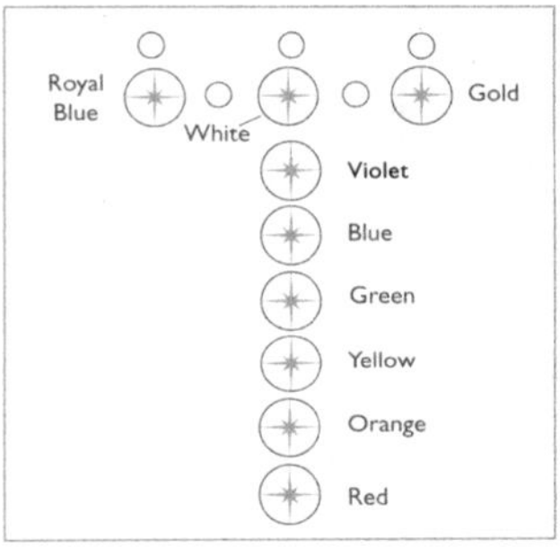

CANDLES Straight or votive candles in the following colors: white (purity, balance the aura), royal blue (expansion, occult power), and gold (intuition, higher influences). Six votive candles to represent the chakras: red, orange, yellow, green, blue, and violet.

OIL Lotus.

HERBS Frankincense.

INCENSE Lotus or sandalwood.

STONES Amber, citrine, lapis lazuli, ruby, and sapphire.

OTHER SUPPLIES None.

TIMING On the full moon or the waxing moon cycle.

DAY Monday.

ADVICE To enhance spiritual growth, all your chakras must be working in a proper manner. The six colored votive candles plus the larger white candle represent the seven chakras each person has in her/his astrological body. This candle spell will help to correct any imbalances in the chakras, thus making a firmer connection with the spiritual.

SPELLWORK Light the altar candles and the incense. Anoint all the candles from the wick to the end. To the back center of your altar, set the white candle with the lapis lazuli behind it. Place the gold candle with the amber behind it to the right, and the royal blue candle with the sapphire behind it to the left. Place the citrine between the blue and white candles, and the ruby between the white and gold ones. Arrange the votive candles in a vertical line in this order leading up to the white candle, red the closest to you, followed by orange, yellow, green, blue, and violet. Light the three larger upper candles first. Then light the chakra candles, beginning with the red and ending with the violet. Say the chant. Leave the candles to burn out completely. Dispose of the wax afterward.

CHANT *I seek only the Light.*

May it fill my life and soul with goodness.

May it bless me in all ways, leading me only in paths of Light.

I sincerely ask the Goddess (God) to open my heart to spiritual growth.

Gain Spiritual Blessings

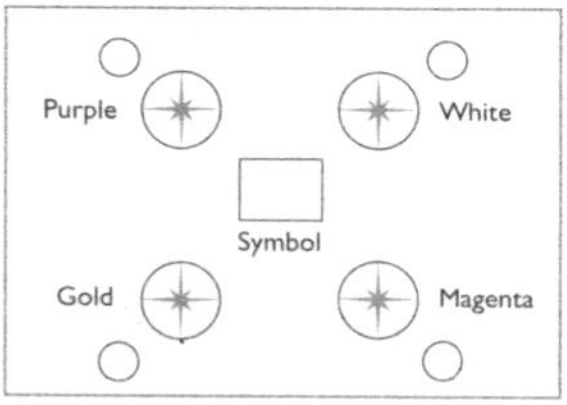

CANDLES Straight or votive candles in the following colors: one white (balance the aura, wholeness), gold (higher influences, healing, happiness), magenta (balance out karma), and one purple (spiritual protection and healing).

OIL Frankincense.

HERBS Frankincense.

INCENSE Frankincense or lotus.

STONES Amethyst, lapis lazuli, moldavite, and black tourmaline.

OTHER SUPPLIES A spiritual symbol that has meaning for you.

TIMING On the full moon or the waxing moon cycle.

DAY Monday.

ADVICE This spell not only creates an inflow of spiritual blessings, but it will also aid you in completing any karmic ties you have with others. Although this is desirable, it can be difficult, especially when relationships fall apart or your whole life undergoes a change. Be very certain you are willing to undergo any of this before you do this spell.

SPELLWORK Light the altar candles and the incense. Place the spiritual symbol in the center of your altar. Anoint all the candles from the wick to the end. Arrange the purple candle to the upper left of the symbol with the moldavite above it. Set the white candle at the upper right with the lapis lazuli above it. Place the gold candle at the lower left of the symbol with the amethyst below it, and the magenta candle at the lower right with the black tourmaline below it. Say the chant. Leave the candles to burn out completely. Dispose of the wax afterward. Place the symbol where you can see it every day.

CHANT *Blessings I seek to better my life,*
To chase away darkness, diminish the strife,
To heal me in body, my mind, and my soul.
This I request. This is my goal.

Strengthen Your Psychic Abilities

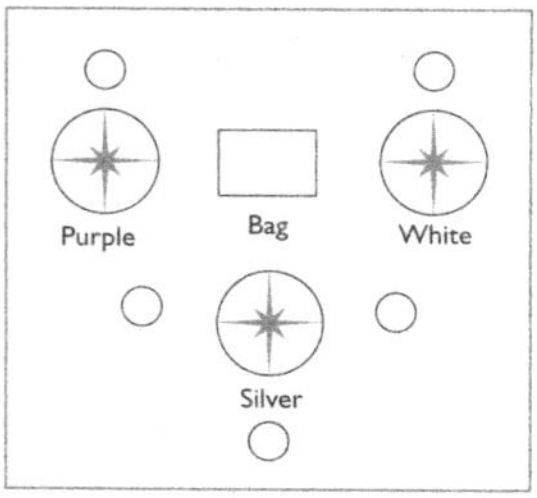

CANDLES Straight or votive candles in the following colors: one purple (higher psychic ability), one white (purity, wholeness, balance the aura), and one silver (develop psychic abilities).

OIL Jasmine.

HERBS Wormwood or jasmine flowers.

INCENSE Honeysuckle, mimosa, or lotus.

STONES Moss agate, moonstone, jet, blue topaz, and purple tourmaline.

OTHER SUPPLIES Small bag that can be tightly closed.

TIMING On the full moon or the waxing moon cycle.

DAY Monday.

ADVICE There are a wide variety of psychic abilities. Do not get caught up in the idea that you have to do something flashy or go out and do readings for other people. Using the psychic to read for others is a very physically and emotionally draining experience. Instead, you should desire to cultivate your psychic abilities to make a better life for yourself.

SPELLWORK Light the altar candles and the incense. Anoint all the candles from the wick to the end. Place the bag in the center of your altar. Set the purple candle to the left of the bag with the purple tourmaline above it. Put the white candle to the right of the bag with the moonstone above it. Place the silver candle below the bag with the jet in front of it. The agate is placed between the silver and purple candles, while the topaz goes between the silver and white candles. Say the chant. Place the stones into the bag. Carry the bag with you, or sleep with it under your pillow. Leave the candles to burn out completely. Dispose of the wax afterward.

CHANT *Open my soul's eye that sees all beyond*
This earthly plane and into the Light.
Teach me to listen, to reach out with my intuition.
This is my spiritual heritage. Help me to use it wisely.

Prepare for Divination

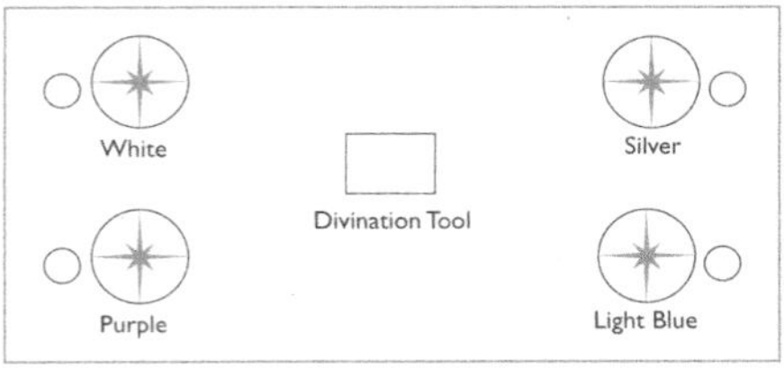

CANDLES Straight or votive candles in the following colors: one purple (spirit contact, divination), one white (purity, balance the aura, raise the vibrations), one silver (develop psychic abilities, raise the vibrations), and one light blue (wisdom, harmony, contacting the Higher Self).

OIL Honeysuckle or myrrh.

HERBS Orris root.

INCENSE Wisteria or lavender.

STONES Amethyst, fluorite, moonstone, and clear quartz crystal.

OTHER SUPPLIES Whatever divination tools, such as tarot cards or runes, you plan to use.

TIMING On the full moon or the waxing moon cycle.

DAY Wednesday or Monday.

ADVICE Skill in any form of divination takes practice. This spell will help you open more easily to spiritual aid.

SPELLWORK Light the altar candles and the incense. Arrange the divination tool in the center of your altar. Anoint all of the candles from the wick to the end. Place the white candle at the upper left of the altar with the moonstone to the left. Put the silver candle at the upper right of the altar with the clear quartz crystal to its right. The purple candle goes below the white candle with the amethyst to its left, while the light blue candle goes below the silver candle with the fluorite to its right. By situating the candles in this manner, you can safely practice your divination in the center without disturbing the candles. Say the chant. Then do whatever divination method you planned. Leave the candles to burn out completely. Dispose of the wax afterward.

CHANT *Unlock the secret inner door. Give to me the key*
That reveals the aged secrets. Let me the future see.
Grant wisdom for enlightenment, understanding, more.
Sweet Spirit, lead me inward to the hidden sacred door.

Enhance Your Dreams and Find Guidance

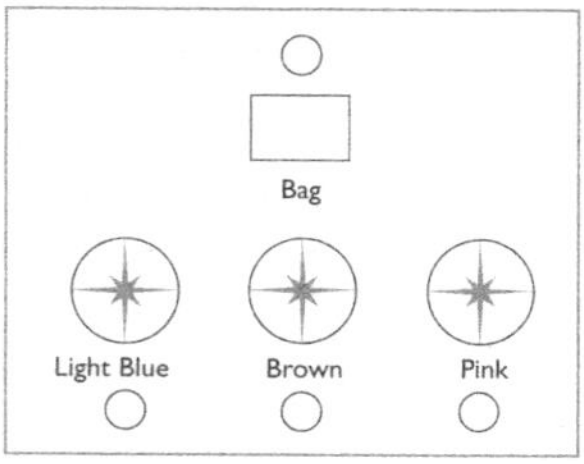

CANDLES Straight or votive candles in the following colors: one light blue (truth, inspiration, wisdom), one brown (ESP, balance, intuition), and one pink (spiritual awakening and healing).

OIL Jasmine or sage.

HERBS Marigold.

INCENSE Frankincense or jasmine.

STONES Agate, amethyst, jade, and clear quartz crystal.

OTHER SUPPLIES Small bag with a secure closure.

TIMING On the full moon or the waxing moon cycle.

DAY Monday.

ADVICE Learning to interpret dreams is difficult, since no dream book will actually help much. What a cat means to one person may not mean the same to another. You need to use a notebook to record your dreams. Study these dreams and what occurs in life after you have them. Only in this way can you figure out what your subconscious mind is telling you in the symbols it uses, for symbols are the only language that the subconscious mind knows.

SPELLWORK Light the altar candles and the incense. Anoint the candles from the wick to the end. Place the bag to the center back of your altar with the amethyst behind it. Arrange the remaining candles in a straight horizontal line in front of the bag with the stones in front of them: the light blue candle and agate on the left, the brown candle and clear quartz crystal in the middle, and the pink candle and jade on the right. Say the chant. Place the stones in the little bag and sleep with it under your pillow each night. Leave the candles to burn out completely. Dispose of the wax afterward.

CHANT *Dreams of mystery, dreams of light,*
Come to me softly, sweetly, tonight.
Give to me guidance to help find my way
Through the problems of life that surface each day.

Strengthen Your Psychic Shield

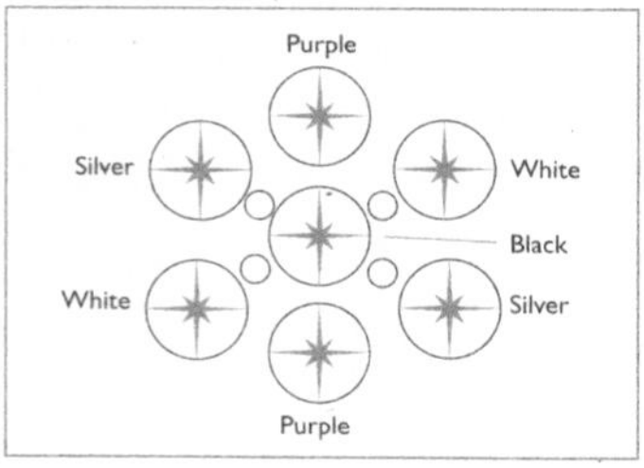

CANDLES Straight or votive candles in the following colors: one black (absorbs and removes negatives, creates confusion in enemies), two purple (drive away evil, spiritual protection), two white (purity, truth, wholeness), and two silver (develop psychic abilities, remove negative powers).

OIL Yarrow, sage, or lotus.

HERBS Peppermint.

INCENSE Lotus, patchouli, or sandalwood.

STONES Two tektite or meteorite, and two tourmaline.

OTHER SUPPLIES None.

TIMING On the full moon or the waxing moon cycle.

DAY Sunday.

ADVICE A strong psychic shield over your astral body will keep you from inadvertently picking up negative thoughtforms from others with whom you come in contact. If you work around many people, it is a good idea to repeat this ritual once a month during the waxing moon.

SPELLWORK Light the altar candles and the incense. Place the black candle in the center of your altar with one piece of tourmaline to the upper left of it, the other piece to the lower right. Place one tektite or meteorite to the upper right of the black candle, the other piece to the lower left. Arrange one purple candle behind the black one, with the other purple candle before it. Place the white candles, one to the upper right, the other on the lower left. Put one silver candle to the upper left of the black candle, the other on the lower right. Say the chant. Spend a minimum of five minutes visualizing yourself covered with a shining silver-blue suit of armor. Leave the candles to burn out completely. Dispose of the wax afterward.

CHANT *By full moon in blackened sky,*
I am not alone. My help is nigh.
Strong armor shields me. I am free,
Of all evil and harm that threatens me.
My shield is of Light, my song is of love.
My protection is strong for it comes from above.
My strength never falters. My faith sets me free.
So I do say, and so shall it be!

Once you begin the practice of candle magick and see its results for yourself, you will find that you use this simple magickal method quite often. Candle burning aids in releasing tension and stress over situations you find difficult to resolve through ordinary actions. It gives you a sense of empowerment and control, which in turn will help you feel better about yourself. When you are more confident, life runs more smoothly.

You need not limit yourself to the chants or spells given in this book. Write your own chants to express what you want. Create the spells that are needed in your life. And realize that there are no boundaries to what you can achieve with candle-burning magick.

PART III

A LITTLE BOOK OF Pendulum Magick

The History of Pendulums

Dowsing, or divining, for everything from water to precious metals to future events has an extremely long history of use by humankind. The words *dowsing* and *divining* have exactly the same meaning: to use a rod or pendulum to find something. The art of dowsing may have begun with the ancient shamans who needed to provide water for their clans. Later, this talent passed to the more structured religious classes who used it for finding water or metals, discovering the causes of illness, or divining the future.

The oldest record of dowsing being used by humans may be the pictographs on the walls of the Tassili Caves in south Algeria. Dating from about 6,000 BCE, these paintings show stylized human figures holding forked sticks.

The wand, or rod, is probably the most ancient of all divining instruments. Some writers of dowsing history cite the biblical reference of Moses finding water within a rock with his wand or staff. Today, however, the wand is not as popular as pendulums, L-rods, or forked twigs for divination or finding underground water or other objects.

Pendulums of all kinds are mentioned in the very oldest written records or divination and the occult arts. Ancient Chinese records tell of a ring suspended on a silk thread that was used to predict the future and warn of danger. The Chinese emperor Yu, who lived around 2,000 BCE, was said to be a dowser.

Predicting the future was often perilous to the health of the diviner. Although ancient Rome used divination of all kinds, usually the bloody entrails type, there are records before 400 BCE of Roman diviners being executed for using a pendulum for this purpose, usually in an attempt to use the information against the Roman government.

One of these types of cases, recorded by Ammianus Marcellinus (c. 352–392 CE), explains the condemnation and execution that occurred because the diviners were using the information gained in just such a matter. Marcellinus was a noble Greek by birth and also a Roman historian. He told of a group of Roman conspirators during the first century CE who plotted the assassination of a man who would succeed the Roman emperor. In order to know who this next emperor would be, they suspended a ring on a thread from a tripod over a circle with alphabet letters around the edge. Using the pendulum like a Ouija board, the conspirators learned the man's name. Before they could carry out the assassination, they were arrested and condemned.

Another account from ancient Rome tells us of a pendulum being used in another manner similar to the Ouija board. In this case, a round pendulum was held inside a glass. The user slowly recited the alphabet letters. When the correct letter was said, the pendulum tapped against the side of the glass.

The use of various tools for dowsing continued through the centuries without much negative comment or repercussions until the Middle Ages. Then it came under attack by the Christian Church.

Pope John XXII issued a bull in 1326 CE that directly attacked the use of the pendulum or any other dowsing tool used for any purpose whatsoever. The pope and the Vatican claimed that the pendulum-wielding diviner got the answers straight from the Devil. This edict led to other restrictions, which brought about the persecutions and burnings of so-called Witches during the Burning Times of the Inquisition in the Middle Ages and the Renaissance. Some figures for these murders estimate that nine million people were killed. Since many of the victims were the village midwives, healers, and dowsers, the Church termed them all Witches and Pagans and executed them. The last Witch was killed in Calvinist Scotland in 1728 CE.

Martine de Bertereau, a Frenchman who lived during the mid-1600s, was a highly successful dowser for coal mines. In fact, he found one hundred fifty such mines before he was condemned by the Church and imprisoned for life. However, good dowsers for water, coal, and metal were so important to the existence of communities that it was impossible for the Church to suppress them all. The townspeople were not about to turn any dowser over for execution and lose their economic edge.

After the persecutions topped, pendulums and other dowsing tools were used more openly. However, for a long time they doubled as tools of a guild trade, which curtailed suspicion. An example of this, which still survives today, is the carpenter's plumb bob. There is a science museum in South Kensington, London, that has a unique collection of tools used by the guilds in the seventeenth and early eighteenth centuries. Among these items is an engraving of two men holding dowsing rods and a third man with a large pendulum.

Scientific investigations of the pendulum were carefully conducted as far back as the late 1700s. One such investigator was Johann Wilhelm Ritter, known as the father of electrochemistry. He performed many tests with the pendulum and was soundly ridiculed by his colleagues for dabbling in "superstitious nonsense." However, Ritter proved through his experiments that the pendulum could provide answers to anything by connecting with the collective unconscious (superconscious or universal mind), as Carl Jung called it. Ritter's detailed studies interested other noted researchers including Professor Antoine Gerboin at the University of Strasbourg, who went so far as to publish a book of 253 tests for using the pendulum.

This book, in turn, influenced Michel-Eugene Chevreul, who gave twenty years of his life to studying the pendulum. Chevreul was a director at the Natural History Museum in Paris in 1830. Chevreul, like Ritter before him, determined that there was a direct connection between the subconscious and superconscious minds of the user and the movement of the pendulum. Today, the pendulum is still sometimes called Chevreul's pendulum.

In the mid-1920s, a Major Pogson of Britain was dowsing for water for the Bombay government, under British rule. He was greatly successful at this, even when more orthodox methods had turned up nothing. He became the official Water Diviner and visited all the districts of Bombay seeking underground water. One official report on his work states that Major Pogson found water in 220 of the 577 sites he dowsed and never failed when he predicted water at a certain depth.

Evelyn Penrose, who was born in Cornwall, was hired by the government of British Columbia in 1931 to find water and minerals. Having an astounding success rate of 90 percent, Penrose was considered to be a valuable employee.

During the 1930s and early 1940s, a clergyman by the name of Abbé Alexis Mermet helped many people in France and Switzerland by finding water and healing people. He also helped the police find missing people. He had a very high success rate. Mermet believed that his clairvoyant powers, combined with a pendulum and a map, enabled him to trace a missing person. He frequently used map dowsing to locate those lost people, but he also came up with accurate details that had nothing to do with maps.

A woman asked him to help locate her missing brother. The police had gotten nowhere. She provided Abbé Mermet with a photo of the young man that he held in one hand while using the pendulum with the other. Keeping his questions to ones that could be answered yes or no, the Abbé determined that the brother was dead. He described where that body could be found, how he had been killed, a general description of the man who did it, and why. The police found the body exactly where the Abbé said it would be, with a knife wound in the heart. His empty purse was discovered nearby in the River Sarine. The brother had obviously been a victim of a robbery.

After World War I, Abbé Mermet used his map dowsing to help the French government locate unexploded German shells. Although a few hundred years earlier Abbé Mermet would have been burned at the stake by the Church, the Vatican recognized him for his work in May, 1935. He invented a special type of pendulum made of several different metals, the top of which could be unscrewed and tiny samples of the sought material placed inside. This is still known as the Mermet pendulum and can be purchased at many New Age bookstores.

Dowsers and diviners are still working today in various areas of the world. Bill Lewis from Wales has worked with Paul Devereux on the Dragon Project, where he found radioactivity at the Rollright Stone Circle. Another dowser, Fran Farrelly from Florida, has worked with Stanford Research International in Menlo Park, California.

Today, the pendulum is once more becoming a popular tool for dowsing, healing, and gaining insight into future events. The pendulum is the most versatile and popular of all divining instruments. However, it is also the one most misused and misunderstood. Its simplicity easily lends itself to use by those who have no self-discipline to learn the craft correctly. Although not everyone will become as proficient as Major Pogson or Abbé Mermet with a pendulum, with practice, patience, and persistence, anyone can learn to use this divining tool.

Making and Using a Pendulum

Pendulums have become very popular in the last few years. There appears to be an inborn human fascination with this divination and dowsing tool that spans cultural backgrounds and ethnic origins. However, many people give up using a pendulum when they don't get immediate results or seem to get ambiguous answers.

Pendulums do work if used properly, but it takes practice, patience, persistence, and experience before one can distinguish between nonsense answers and the truth. After all, you are creating a link with your subconscious mind, which only speaks and understands symbols and symbolic reasoning. If you get the signals wrong, the subconscious mind will not know how to answer other questions. It will become confused. It is up to the pendulum user to develop the skills needed to correctly interpret the coded language of her/his subconscious mind.

The world today is basically geared to the left-brain or analytical and linear thinking. In fact, this "rational" side of our brain and lives is overfed. Schools and businesses rarely try to emphasize the right-brain or creative, intuitive abilities. We are taught to analyze everything, but follow orders without question. It is almost like walking around all the time with one closed eye and one deaf ear. Our subjective, intuitive, right-brain is starving. In order for pendulum divining to work properly, you have to learn to let go with the left-brain and allow the right-brain the freedom to bring up answers.

One of the easiest ways to learn to access the right-brain is through the practice of meditation. This quiet activity allows the creative side of the brain to get exercised, especially if one does not practice the Eastern idea of "no thought," but instead lets the mind cast up whatever mental pictures and expressions it wishes. Meditation is a backdoor method of strengthening the intuitive side of the brain and thus the intuition itself. Other easy methods of right-brain stimulation are the use of the pendulum, tarot cards, runes, or other divination tools. By presenting the left-brain with a physical object to consider, one can create an unobstructed avenue for the right-brain to cast up intuitive messages.

Intuition and dowsing are so closely connected that they may be one and the same thing. One thing is certain, however, the practice of dowsing will exercise your intuitive thinking, thereby causing you to become more aware of nudges from the psychic areas of your mind.

Herbert Weaver, in his book *Divining, the Primary Sense,* did experiments that led him to believe that the dowser or diviner responds to electromagnetic fields given off by the object sought. This definition of electromagnetic fields is a scientific way of describing what psychic people call vibrations. Everything has an energy field that forms an aura around the person, animal, or object. These auras or energy fields vibrate, even in inanimate objects. It is this vibration that is felt and "read" by psychics and dowsers.

Dowsing, like everything else in this world, is not 100 percent accurate. We are dealing with intuition and the collective unconscious sending messages through a human mind. No matter how highly skilled in whatever profession, no human is correct all the time. This fact is even more pertinent when working with intuitive, subconscious messages. Every impression and subconscious message has the possibility of being analyzed, interpreted, and censored by the left-brain. Beginners in anything make a lot of mistakes, and pendulum divining is no exception. However, anyone who is sensitive, and this includes a large percentage of people, can get a reaction from and learn to use a pendulum or dowsing rods.

Dowsers rarely do well in scientific tests of any kind. Perhaps this is because those critical of the practice remove everything intuitive and insist that only the linear be used. Scientists are notorious for disbelieving anything that cannot be seen, touched, cut up, or made to move a dial. So it is best not to engage in any test with a disbeliever. The only person you need to prove anything to is yourself.

Since you cannot learn to dowse or divine with a pendulum by reading about it I suggest you make or buy a pendulum before you go any further in this book. Then practice each exercise as you read through the book. Although the exercises require more than a cursory attempt if you want to become proficient and get reliable answers to your questions, you can learn to get movement results from a pendulum almost immediately.

Make Your Pendulum

Technically, a pendulum is any balanced weight hung on a thread or string. This can be a cork with a darning needle run through the exact center, a hexagonal nut on a string, a carpenter's plumb bob, or, according to folk tradition, a wedding ring suspended on a hair. Although these makeshift pendulums will work if you have nothing else to use, only the carpenter's plumb bob is very effective. The others are either too light in weight or their shape is not conducive to good movement. Although traditionally it is possible to make a pendulum out of rings, buttons, corks, or pencils, these do not prove to be very accurate pendulums. They are far too light and unbalanced. A pencil with a needle stuck in the eraser may be heavier and more balanced, but its long, thin shape is not the best for a pendulum, particularly for beginners.

One of the easiest pendulums to make uses a natural quartz crystal point. Glue a bail to the top and thread a string through the bail. The pendulum is ready to use as soon as it is dry. The crystal point, however, must not have any rough debris on the sides or it will not hang properly.

Another quickly made pendulum is a man-made crystal drop found in many stores. Although you can thread a string directly through the hole in the top of the drop, it makes a better pendulum if you attach a large jump-ring first, then thread the string through the ring. Thread attached directly to the top of the pendulum has a tendency to slip one way or the other, thus throwing the pendulum off balance.

Another inexpensive type of homemade pendulum is a lead fishing weight. Purchase a lead sinker weighing from $^1/_2$ ounce to 2 ounces. Tie about 10 inches of lightweight nylon fishing line to the top of the weight. Begin with about 3 inches of line hanging between the lead weight and your fingers. Gently swing the line, increasing the hanging length as necessary, until you find the point where the weight swings easily and freely. This is the proper length for using the lead sinker as a pendulum.

Some people prefer the bullet-type pendulum, which is a 1-inch steel weight about the thickness of a pencil and pointed at one end. This shape vaguely mimics the many natural crystal points offered in many New Age shops. Although some purists try to dissuade people from buying pendulums shaped by craftsmen in this fashion or man-made crystals, I have not found any difficulty using either type.

Other shapes for pendulums are the fat, little, round ones with a point, or those shaped entirely like a ball. The round pendulums with a shaped point at the bottom are usually made of brass bronze, or a combination of metals, such as the Mermet pendulum mentioned on page 219. Other ball pendulums are frequently made of wood, plastic, man-made crystal, or various types of shaped natural stone. Many dowsers do not like round, ball-shaped pendulums. However, one of my most responsive pendulums is a round, plastic one on a cheap chain.

Whatever you decide to use as a pendulum, do not use one that is so light it has no weight to swing or so heavy that your hand quickly becomes tired. Although any shape of pendulum that is properly balanced will work for most questions, a pointed pendulum is best to use for map dowsing, particularly if you are using the pendulum itself instead of a pointer to indicate specific areas on the map.

You can tell if the pendulum weight and shape is appropriate for you by the length of time it takes the pendulum to swing or move. If it moves very slowly or not at all, try varying the length of the string. Then check to see if the pendulum is balanced exactly at the center. If these changes do not correct the problem, try a pendulum that is heavier, lighter, or differently shaped. The least effective type of pendulum shape for most people, particularly for beginners, is one that is long and thin, like a pencil.

Pendulums are readily available in rock shops and New Age stores, or from any Pagan supplier. When purchasing a pendulum, always choose one that feels good to you. Everyone is familiar with the unexplainable feeling that something is not quite right about a car, a house, a computer, or a piece of jewelry. This feeling frequently manifests by an uncomfortable feeling in the pit of your stomach. It is your psychic sensing or gut feeling warning you that the object in question is not right for you. You can better sense this feeling from a pendulum if you hold it cupped between your hands. The negative vibrations of a pendulum may range from prickly to slimy. No matter how good the price or how much you want a pendulum made of a certain stone, it is not to your benefit to purchase one that makes you the slightest uneasy.

The first thing you should do after purchasing a pendulum is clean it of the vibrations left by anyone who handled it. You can easily do this by holding it under cool, running water if it is made of stone, gemstone, glass, or metal. If it is a wooden or cork pendulum, rub it gently between your hands until it warms with your vibrations. You can embed more of your vibrations into your pendulum by using it regularly.

Test Your Pendulum

When a pendulum is good for you, it will make you feel comfortable with it. Its vibrations may be cold, hot, tingly, or pulsating, depending upon the material from which it is made.

Next, test the way the pendulum is balanced and weighted by dangling it from its string. Is the weight heavy enough to be felt through the string or chain? If it is too light, the pendulum will be affected by the slightest movements, whether of your hand or the air. You need to select a pendulum that weighs from $^1/_2$ ounce to 2 ounces. Each person's requirements will be different.

Is the pendulum bail or hole centered, and is the pendulum shaped properly? If the bail or hole is off-center, the pendulum will not respond properly. If a string is tied directly to the pendulum, I suggest that you attach a small jump-ring through the hole in the top of the ring and retie the string to the jump-ring. If the pendulum does not have a hole through the top, which would be unusual, you need to purchase a bail and glue it on. String directly tied to the pendulum has the habit of slipping to one side or the other and throwing off the hanging balance of your device.

Some pendulums, particularly those carved out of stone, may not be shaped symmetrically. The shape may be heavier or thicker on one side than on the other, or the hole at the top may be off-center. If the pendulum shape is good but the hole is not centered, you can correct this by gluing a bail to replace the hole. However, there is nothing you can do about a badly shaped pendulum.

Eventually you may acquire a collection of pendulums of different shapes, materials, and sizes. It is best not to become dependent upon only one pendulum. You may find that some of your pendulums will not work properly or at all on certain types of questions. I have one pendulum made of lapis lazuli that refused to answer questions unless they are of a spiritual nature. I did not choose this pendulum for that kind of questions and at first could not understand why it sometimes refused to move. When I began to pay attention, it became obvious that it was attuned to spiritual problems, not material ones.

A short list of stones and their traditional meanings is at the end of this section to help if you are planning to use stone energy in pendulum divining.

Purists also quibble over whether the pendulum should be suspended on a thread, string, or thin chain. Folk tradition states that it should be hung on human hair, which actually does not make a good suspending thread at all. It is difficult to get a hair long enough, or strong enough, or flexible enough to tie the hair to the pendulum bail. Hair also frequently breaks. Thread is usually thin and strong, and is easily acquired. If you use string, it must not be too thick and should be strong and very flexible; a cheap string that breaks or frays easily is not a good choice. A very fine, short, silver neck chain makes a good suspending thread if it is flexible. A chain with heavy links will not allow the pendulum to move freely. Try each kind until you find what works best with your pendulum. Also, what works well on one pendulum may not work smoothly on another one.

You will not need any great length of thread or chain for your pendulum, although it should be long enough so that you can adjust it if necessary. Hanging lengths of 6 to 8 inches usually work best. A pendulum that hangs down too far when you hold it will only get in your way. Each pendulum, depending upon its weight, will require a different length of thread.

Use Your Pendulum

The proper method for holding a pendulum is to grasp the suspending thread between your thumb and forefinger. Some people hold the string over the first joint of the forefinger, but this makes the string length keep changing and the finger is frequently in the way of the pendulum swing. The fingertips are very sensitive. Through them you can tell what the pendulum is doing without looking at it. Greater ease of movement is attained by holding the string between the thumb and forefinger.

The proper body position for working with a pendulum is important. Rest your elbow on a table and hold your grasping fingers so that they point downward. Do not cross your feet. Take several deep, slow, calming breaths. Most important, do not use the pendulum when you are tired or when you are ill at ease with another person or the questions she/he wants answered.

When you first begin using the pendulum for answering questions, start with only about 2 inches of thread hanging down between your fingers and the pendulum. Do not hold the pendulum thread too tight. If you do, this tension will keep the pendulum from moving freely. Gradually extend the length of string until the pendulum swings freely and easily for its weight. Some pendulum users recommend putting a knot in the string at this point, but I do not. The length needed for a good pendulum swing may vary from time to time, so a knot would only cause confusion. I have noticed that barometer changes and moon phases sometimes alter the length of thread needed.

When first working with a pendulum, or when you return to pendulum divining after a period of time, you need to practice on movements only. Leave the asking of questions until you become more proficient and confident with the pendulum. When you find yourself without your pendulum in times of emergency, you can substitute a large button or metal nut on a string, or a needle with thread stuck in the eraser end of a short pencil. However, these are more difficult to use and can be far less accurate for a novice diviner.

To become good with a pendulum you need to practice a series of exercises for three to six weeks. Practice each of the exercises in this book in their order for the best results. This is to ensure that you understand each area of pendulum dowsing.

The first set of exercises consists of learning to make the pendulum move without any questions or motives behind it. By practicing these exercises you will learn that you can use the power of your subconscious mind to move your pendulum. This exercise helps you learn the difference in feeling between a true subconscious answer and an answer that is what you want. This also is the first step in communicating with the right-brain for dowsing.

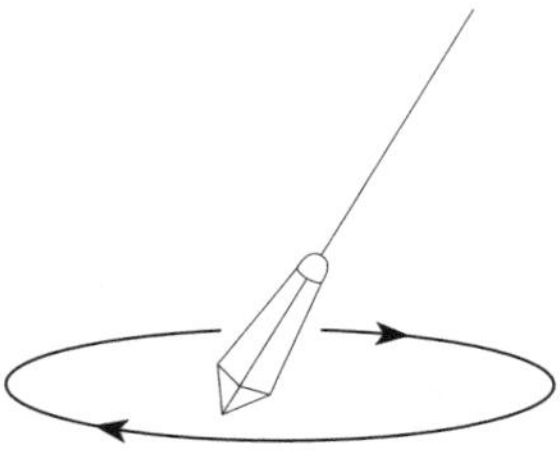

Clockwise Circles

Holding your pendulum in the above-described position, mentally tell the pendulum to make clockwise circles. Continue thinking this command at the pendulum until it circles in a clockwise direction. If the pendulum does not move, and your choice of a pendulum seems to be right for you, physically and gently cause the pendulum to move in the direction you wish it to go. Stop the pendulum and again give it the mental command to circle clockwise. When you are successful in this, command the pendulum to stop. Repeat this exercise as many times as you need.

When you can control the pendulum through the circle and stop movements, work until you can command the pendulum to make first bigger, then smaller clockwise circles.

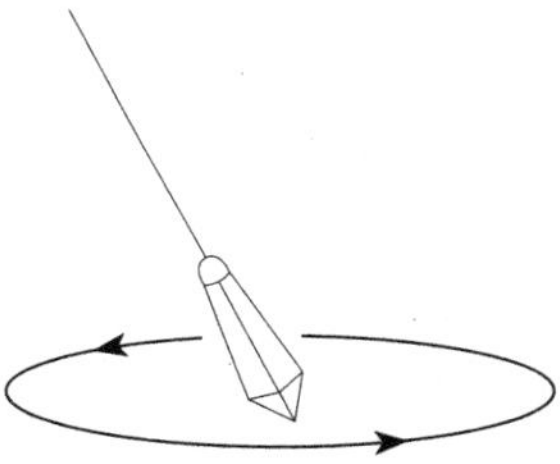

Counterclockwise Circles

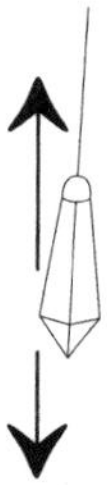

Forward and Backward Movements

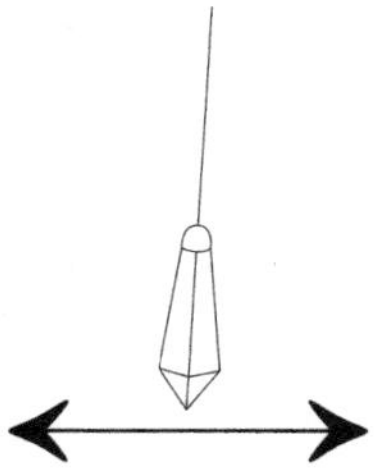

Side-to-Side Movements

When you have mastered this exercise, practice counterclockwise circles. Tell the pendulum to stop. Proceed to making bigger and smaller counterclockwise circles. When you are successful with this, move on to forward and backward movements, then side-to-side movements, ending each motion with the command to stop.

Commanding the pendulum to make specific movements may seem rather silly at first. However, these exercises make you aware of the difference in the feel of "commanded" movement and the motion that is spontaneous and will give a true answer. When you are commanding the pendulum, you have a pushy sensation just under your ribs, as you do when moving to swing higher and higher in a swing. When you aren't mentally commanding the pendulum, you get a "floaty" or noncaring feeling. This is the best description I can give for the two different sensations.

When asking a question, you want your pendulum to give you a strong answer so there is no way you can wonder whether it is answering the question or simply being in the Neutral/Search mode. A friend gave me a statement given to her by her aunt: "Answers should be statements, not whispers or apologies." A true answer will not be a halfhearted pendulum movement, but a motion with strength.

Learning to command the pendulum is also essential as you must learn to stop the pendulum after one answer, before you go on to another question. Your subconscious mind needs to learn that when you issue a command to stop, the pendulum must stop, or when you mentally phrase a question, it must give the pendulum the correct answer.

If you experience difficulties in getting movement out of your pendulum, you may be too tense and trying too hard. Relax for a few moments before returning to the exercises. If this does not solve the problem, become aware of your body to see if you are too tired to be using the pendulum at that time. Also check the question itself, for you may not want to know the answer.

There is no one set of correct movements from a pendulum to indicate an answer. Pendulums react differently to different people. The first position or movement of the pendulum you must identify is what is called the Neutral or Search position. This position should appear when the pendulum is merely hanging there waiting for you to give it a question. The pendulum may react in one of three different motions. It may hang still with no movement. It may show that it is in the Neutral/Search position by making very small clockwise circles. Or, it may gently swing side to side or forward and backward in short, tiny, straight movements. In order for the pendulum to establish a Neutral/Search position, you must tell it to stop. With a little practice, the pendulum will obey this command by hanging dead still or making a small movement. You need to know what movement your pendulum makes for a Neutral/Search answer so you can distinguish between a Neutral and a definite No or Yes answer.

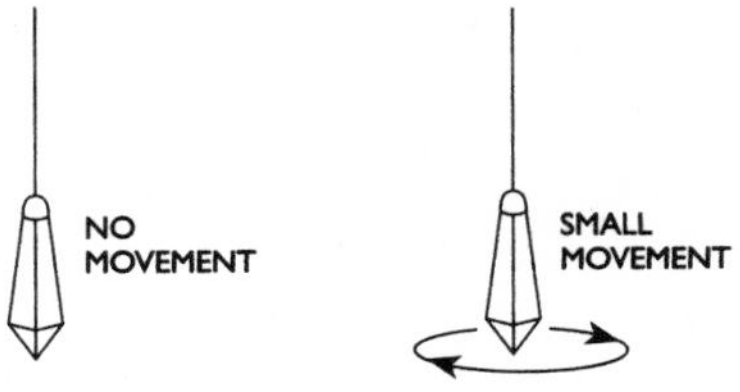

Neutral/Search Position

Next, you must establish the Yes movement of your pendulum. Hold the pendulum in the proper position and ask it to show you a Yes movement. It will do this by either swinging sharply forward and backward or in a clockwise circle. After it has shown you the Yes movement, again ask it to stop.

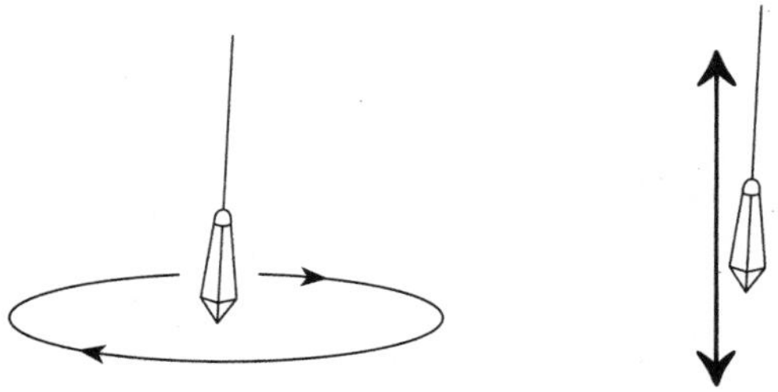

Yes Movements

Now you need to establish a No movement. When asked to show this, the pendulum will move either in a sharp side-to-side motion or a counterclockwise circle. After it has established the No movement, ask it to stop.

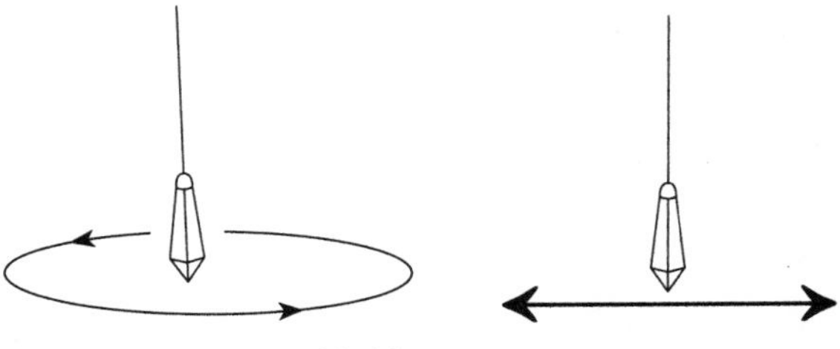

No Movements

The Confusion or Wrong Question movement is either a left or right diagonal movement. This movement can also mean, "I don't know what to answer" or "This question cannot be answered." It is important to know this movement, as it will occur whenever your question is not clear, you are confused about the question yourself, or you are approaching the situation with the wrong question.

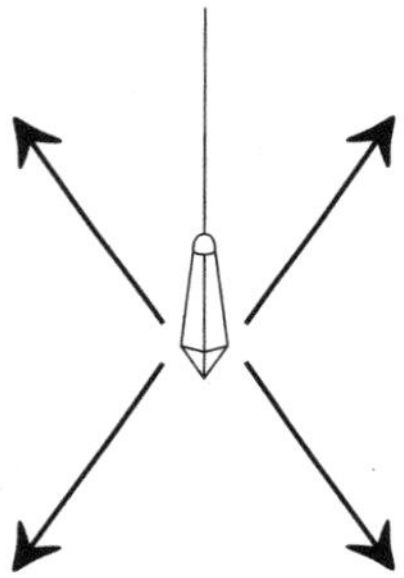

Confusion/Wrong Question Movements

If your Yes movement is forward and backward and your No movement side-to-side, the pendulum may divide the Confusion response by using a clockwise circle for a Maybe answer and a counterclockwise circle for a "This question cannot be answered response."

You need to practice the Yes, No, Confusion, and Neutral movements with your pendulum once or twice a day for a minimum of three weeks before you begin to ask questions. This practice is necessary for setting up a symbolic code with your subconscious mind. Without this set symbolic code, you cannot get trustworthy answers. In fact, the pendulum may refuse to move at all or will give you nonsense answers.

Generally, the movements will be the same for all your pendulums, but on occasion you will find a pendulum that will not respond in the usual manner. Therefore, it is very important that you discover which movements mean what before you begin working.

Sometimes the code appears to become embedded in the pendulum itself by the person who uses it. In cases such as this, if another person uses the pendulum, it will not respond if the expected movements are different from the new user's code.

When you do move on to asking questions, keep in mind that you should never concentrate on the answer you want the pendulum to give because you will not get a truthful answer if you do. Instead, try to keep an expectant attitude, such as "I wonder what the answer will be?" The question must be phrased in such a way that the only answers will be Yes or No. You cannot ask a pendulum "either-or" questions.

You should respect very standard ethics. Do not lower yourself to using the pendulum to snoop on another person or harm her/him in any way. The private lives of others are none of your business. You should not use your pendulum to pry into the affairs of others, no more than you would open their mail or tap their telephone lines. The same ethics apply if another person wants you to ask your pendulum such questions.

With Yes or No answers to questions, it is easy to work your way through a series of questions until you get the proper and sometimes unforeseen answers to the questions you wish answered. Never expect a particular answer, or you will not get the truth. By asking a series of questions, you can determine whether it is the right question to ask, the correct solution you are seeking, or whether your goal is something you should abandon. Timing also plays an important part in pendulum divining, just as it does in the use of any foretelling method. Things, people, and events may not all be in place to give you the answer about a future event at that time.

Also being aware of the strength with which the pendulum answers questions will aid you in determining the validity of a question. A wide swing for Yes is unquestionable, while a half-hearted, weak swing means you could push the issue for which you ask, but it may not be worth the effort and you may not get a truthful answer. Dowsers must keep in touch with reality at all times or things will go wrong, and we will get the results we want instead of the truth. Therefore, you must be aware all the time and word questions very carefully.

Yes and No swings of a pendulum can also be used to answer such polarity questions as masculine and feminine, up and down, or hot and cold. The masculine/feminine polarity can be used to divine the sex of an unborn child or the sex of a person in a future event. For example, if you are considering a change in jobs, you might wish to ask if your new boss will be a man or a woman. The up and down description will help you when dowsing for lost objects. The hot and cold polarity is also useful when searching for something. Hot will mean you are closer to the object, while cold means you are going the wrong way.

Every dowser or diviner has periods when she/he seems to get nothing but idiot answers from her/his device. This frequently shows up when you are showing off instead of taking the pendulum and its powers seriously. This also may happen if the user is tired or uncomfortable asking the question. It may occur at other times for no known reason. This infrequent reaction seems to fall under the universal law that we can never have anything under control 100 percent of the time. When this happens, try another pendulum. If you still get idiot answers, it may be wise not to use the pendulum for a few days, until whatever universal energy affecting your pendulum has passed.

Easy exercises to try out your pendulum involve two and three coins. These simple exercises will help you gain confidence, satisfy your need to work with your pendulum, and aid you in gaining skill and understanding of pendulum movements.

First, take two coins of the same date and denomination. Place them on a table about your hand's length apart. Hold the pendulum in the correct position between these coins. Ask the pendulum to point out the similar coins. Asking this sounds rather dim, I know, but you need the experience of seeing how your pendulum reacts. The pendulum either will swing back and forth between the two coins, or will oscillate in a clockwise circle over both coins.

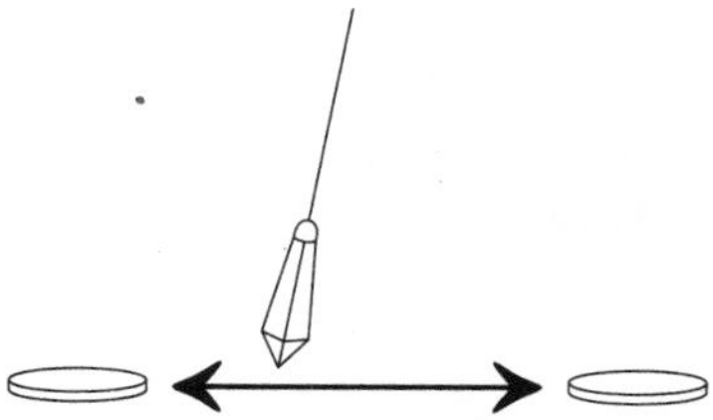

Two Coins Exercise

Next, take three coins, two with the same date and denomination, the third one different. This may mean two coins of the same date, with a third of a different date, or two coins of the same denomination and a third of a different denomination. Place them on a table in a triangular pattern with about a hand's length between all the coins. Now ask the pendulum to show which coins are the same. The pendulum will swing between the two identical coins.

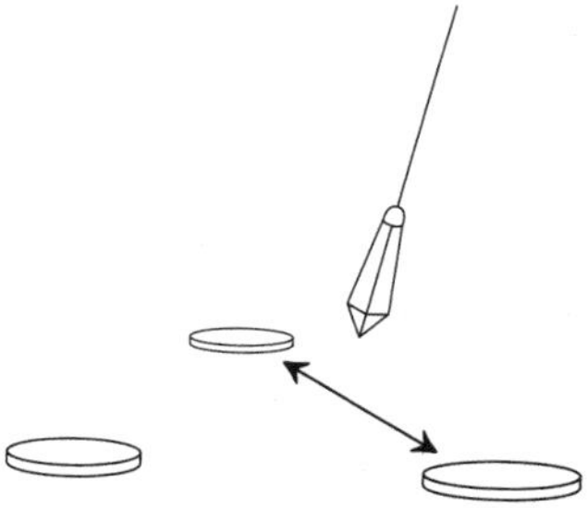

Three Coins Exercise

Since working with a pendulum enhances your psychic senses, you should use the pendulum only for serious reasons, such as for the well-being of other people and yourself, or genuinely to seek knowledge and truth in a situation. Never use a pendulum to show off or because you want others to think you are wonderful and talented. Life has a way of deflating one's ego in crushing and often embarrassing events.

When a pendulum ceases to be a curiosity or a toy, you can use it as a valuable tool in your everyday life. You can test the quality of water or food, search out the basis for an allergy or illness, discover the right car for you before purchasing a vehicle, and locate lost objects or people. It can even lead you to diagnose elusive problems in car engines or other mechanical devices, locate the studs in a house wall, and trace underground pipes of various kinds.

You can use a pendulum to answer any question as long as the answer can be Yes or No. You can test foods, vitamins, herbs, or medicines to see if they will be good for you. To do this, hold a sample of the material being tested in one hand while you operate the pendulum with the other (see page 227). However, never second-guess a prescribed medication. Always discuss such questions with your doctor.

After working with a pendulum for a period of time, you will notice that it frequently works better on some days than others. Do not be discouraged by this. The pendulum is reacting to your physical and emotional energy levels. These energy levels fluctuate during each day and from day to day. If the pendulum persists in not operating properly after several tries during a day, put it away until another time. Also check to see if you are too tense, as this will interfere with your success. It is never wise to practice more than fifteen minutes on any day. The percentage of people who absolutely cannot operate a pendulum is low, less than 1 percent.

You can only learn to use a pendulum by practicing with it regularly. As with any divination tool, it takes a lot of practice to become proficient and reliable with the pendulum. However, pendulum divining is the easiest and fastest of all divining methods to learn.

Stones for Pendulums

The following list includes only those stones that are not too costly and that one may find carved into pendulum shapes. Sometimes you can find an appropriately shaped stone for a pendulum that was made to wear as a pendant.

AGATE Balance on all levels; victory; protection against danger.

AGATE, EYE Connection with the guardian spirit.

AGATE, MOSS Good for finding a new house, job, or relocation site.

AMAZONITE Self-confidence; creativity; communication.

AMBER Past lives.

AMETHYST Develop psychic abilities; increase spirituality; healing.

AQUAMARINE Banish fears; balance emotions; calmness; protection.

AVENTURINE Good health; centering; good luck.

BERYL Innovative thoughts; increase psychic awareness; find hidden things.

BLOODSTONE Protection from deception; good health; prosperity.

CARNELIAN Balancing; self-confidence; drives away evil.

CHALCEDONY Protection during travel; cleanses the aura.

CHRYSOCOLLA Protection; releases tension; enhances communication.

CHRYSOPRASE Reveals the truth; balances actions and attitudes.

CITRINE Raises self-esteem; working with karma; prosperity.

FLUORITE Grounds energy; heals; cleanses the aura; past lives.

HEMATITE Grounds; builds courage; dissolves stress.

JADE, BLUE Neutralizes karmic influences; relaxation.

JADE, GREEN Banishes evil; calms.

JASPER, BROWN Grounds; stabilizes.

JASPER, GREEN Heals; balance.

JASPER, RED Eliminates negative energies.

LABRADORITE Connects with universal energies.

LAPIS LAZULI Releases anxiety; increases creativity and psychic abilities.

MALACHITE Repels evil; removes subconscious blockages; heals.

OBSIDIAN, BLACK Eliminates negatives.

OBSIDIAN, SNOWFLAKE Balances; prosperity; protection.

ONYX, BLACK Deflects and destroys negative energies.

QUARTZ CRYSTAL, CLEAR Protects; enhances communication with the spirit world.

QUARTZ CRYSTAL, ROSE Balances emotions; brings love; heals.

QUARTZ CRYSTAL, SMOKY Grounds and centers; breaks up subconscious blocks; strengthens the psychic.

TIGER'S EYE Gives clear insight into problems; brings good luck; past lives.

TOURMALINE, BLUE Calms; gives clarity of insight.

TOURMALINE, DARK GREEN Attracts money and success.

TOURMALINE, RED Releases buried emotions and past sorrows.

TOURMALINE, WATERMELON Removes imbalances; solves problems.

TURQUOISE Protects, balances, enhances communication; strengthens the psychic.

Divination with Pendulums

One of the most popular reasons for working with a pendulum is to use it to divine the future. Almost everyone is concerned about what the future will bring, particularly in the areas of health, love, and prosperity. What one needs to learn about this facet of pendulum divining, or any divining tool or system, is that the answers are only about possible outcomes, not a rock-solid future. The greater the number of people involved in the events surrounding an outcome, the more possibility there is for change. All it takes is one or more of the people involved to change their minds on even the smallest of decisions, and the future path of the event or question changes.

These possibilities are covered by the law of free will, something for which we should be thankful. I do not believe that our lives are predestined, with no opportunities to forge our own futures through personal decisions. There is always free will, which is a powerful force for change and diverting the life path. If you receive a divination prediction that you consider negative or not to your liking, you can change the course of your life and reactions to events, thus creating changes in the outcome itself. Granted, the outcome still may not be what you want, but it will be different than the divination predicted. Continued and numerous changes in the life path are required in order to create major changes in the outcome.

Be very careful, however, that you are not trying to control another person in any way when you set your goals or try to change a divination outcome. No one has a right to control another person or her/his future. Think how you would feel if someone did this to you against your wishes.

Pendulum Exercises

To prepare yourself for using the pendulum as a prediction tool, you must work long and hard to acquire the necessary skills and experience. A pendulum will react to your thoughts and instructions much faster the more you use it. Its movements will also become stronger. However, no one is infallible, so never assume that you won't ever make mistakes.

You are most apt to run into trouble predicting with a pendulum if you are asking questions for yourself or someone emotionally close to you. The more emotionally involved you allow yourself to be, the less likely you will get a truthful answer from your pendulum. The test of an experienced pendulum diviner is that she/he can separate her/his emotions from the questions, thus entering a neutral emotional state while working with the pendulum. This is very difficult to do.

There are a number of exercises you can do with the pendulum to increase your proficiency and the pendulum's reliability. It is best to begin with simple exercises that reinforce your communication skills with your subconscious mind. Since even predictions with a pendulum require that you ask a series of appropriate questions, the following little exercises will build your confidence and ability in selecting questions.

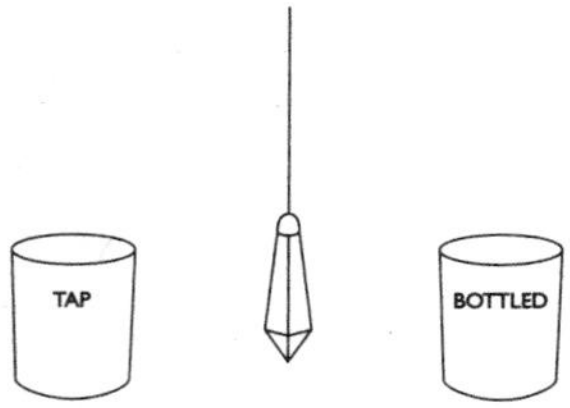

Two Glasses Exercise

Fill one glass with tap water and another glass with bottled water. Set them about two hand lengths apart on a table. Hold the pendulum between them while asking whether the contents in both glasses are water. The pendulum should say Yes. Then ask whether the glasses both contain the same kind of water. You should get a No answer. Ask the pendulum to indicate the glass containing the tap water. It should swing directly at the appropriate glass. Finish by asking it to show you the glass of bottled water, and it will swing toward that glass. Repeat the same exercises with two glasses of tap water. Ask again if the glasses contain the same kind of water. This time the answer should be a Yes.

You have worked your way through a series of questions to discover the truth about the glasses of water. Although both glasses contain water, there are subtle differences in the composition of that water. This is the same procedure you need to adopt whenever you ask the pendulum a question. One question and its answer will not cover all the possible facets of a problem or event. By carefully wording your series of questions, you can cover all areas of an initial question and give a broader, more comprehensive answer. You may also discover that what you thought was an answer is something different when all facets of the problem are exposed.

Using a regular deck of playing cards, remove all the Jokers from the deck. Select six black cards and one red card. Shuffle these cards and lay them out face down in a line on the table. Do not look at the cards. The object is to discover which cards are black and which one is red. Hold the pendulum over each card as you ask whether the card is black. The pendulum should respond to one card with a No, for it will be red. Keep track of how many you get right.

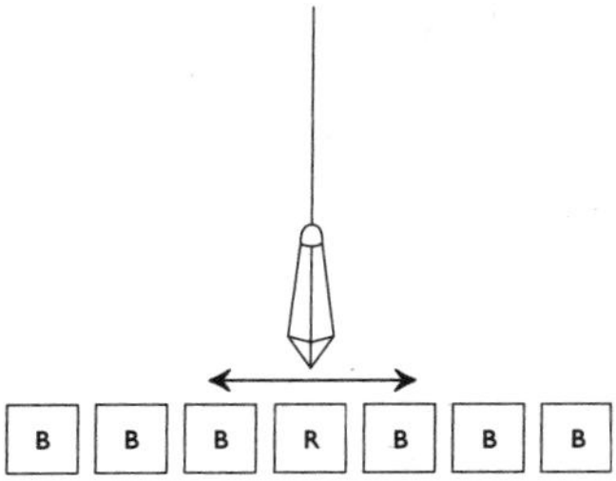

Red and Black Cards

When you score more correct finds than wrong ones in the last exercise, select five red cards and one black card. Shuffle these, laying them face down in a line on the table without looking at them. See if you can find the black card.

The next step is to shuffle the entire deck minus the Joker and lay out seven cards in a line on the table. This will be more difficult, as you are not selecting a certain number of red or black cards. Keep track of your score as you hold the pendulum over one card at a time and ask about the color. Since the card will be either red or black, it does not matter which color you name when asking the question.

When you reach a high success rate at this, separate the face cards (Kings, Queens, Jacks, and Jokers) from the desk. Shuffle these cards and lay them face down on the table without looking at the cards. Now use the pendulum to search out certain cards, such as the Kings. Since this exercise is more involved than the previous ones, you will need to work your way through a series of questions until the pendulum gives you a Yes. For example, you may ask the pendulum if the card is a King. If it answers No, you must work your way through the lot of possibilities until the pendulum gives you a Yes.

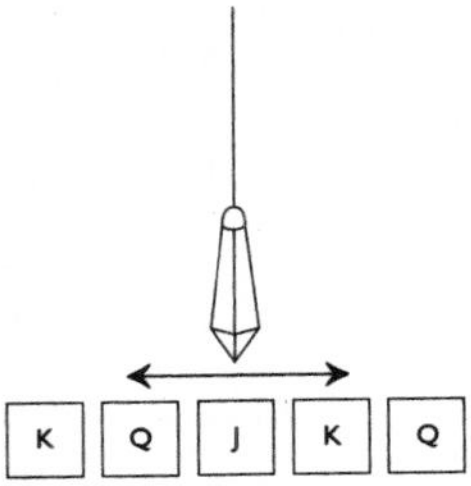

Face Cards

Practice the exercises with the cards until you feel confident enough to move on to the more difficult exercises that follow.

The next exercises require the help of a friend. Choose three different small objects, or coins of three different denominations. Look at the objects or coins so you will know what they are. Have a friend hide them under three opaque cups while you are not watching. Since you know what the objects are, ask the pendulum what is under each cup. For example, the friend has put a nickel, dine, and quarter under the cups. If you ask the pendulum if the coin under the cup is a dime, and it says No, work your way through the list of possibilities.

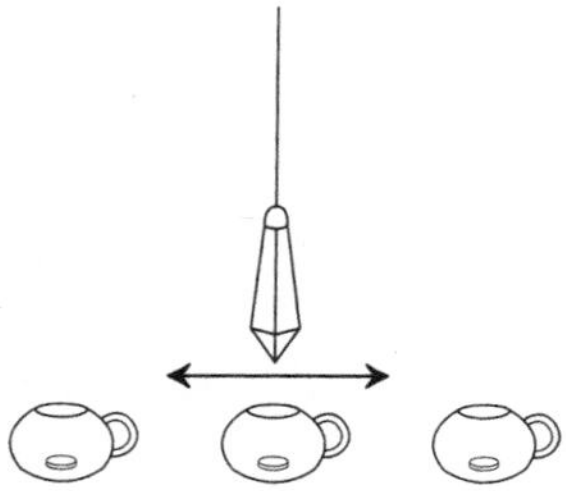

Three Objects

You may find that you have difficulty divining an object if it is hidden under a cup of a certain type of material. This may vary from pendulum to pendulum or from person to person. One dowser I know has difficulty divining anything under a particular brand of margarine container. I do not know the reason for this, but I suspect it may have to do with the material of which the pendulum or the container is made. Perhaps the vibrations of the pendulum are such that they do not mesh well with the vibrations of the cup or container.

The next exercise is more difficult than the last one as you must now divine physical human vibrations left on an object. Have someone hold one of three coins for about twenty seconds before putting the three coins under the cups. Use the pendulum to determine which coin the person held. This practice is similar to psychometry, which is reading the vibrations of an object. However, you are doing the psychometry without seeing or touching the object in question. Practice by having different people hold a coin, then finding it. In rare occasions, a person will be able to block her/his vibrations from reaching the coin. In this case, you will have difficulty finding the proper coin. However, it is very unlikely that this will happen.

Have someone hide one coin under a cup in a line of three cups while you are not watching. Find the coin with the pendulum. You can do this by holding the pendulum over each cup as you ask the question, or by asking the pendulum to indicate which cup in the line holds the coin. This exercise is preparing you for learning map dowsing or property dowsing. If you have trouble finding the coin, hold a coin of similar denomination in one hand while using the pendulum with the other. This practice is identical to the method used by dowsers for finding missing people, water, oil, or minerals.

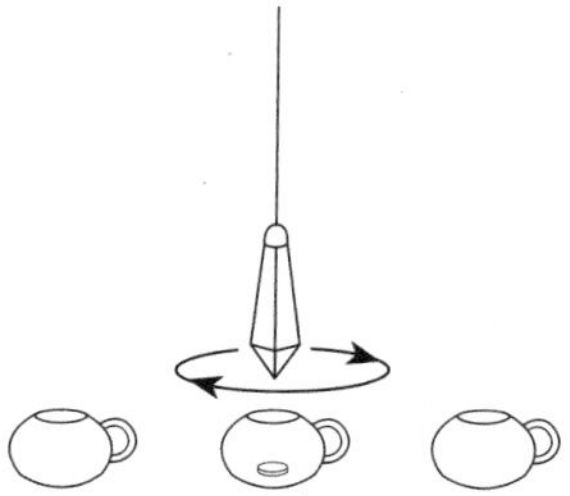

Three Cups and One Coin

The following exercise is very similar to the old parlor game of Hide the Thimble; a thimble was hidden somewhere in a room and everyone tried to discover where it was by a series of questions that were answered by Hot or Cold. Have a friend choose an object in a room but not tell you what the object is. Use the pendulum to discover what the object is. For example, the friend has chosen a small statue. Begin by asking the pendulum to indicate the direction in the room in which the object lies. By a series of questions, slowly work your way through the objects in that area of the room until you discover the chosen statue. Or you can hold the pendulum over each object in that area while asking whether this is the chosen object.

Next, sketch out a floor plan of your home. Then have the friend choose an object in your house in any of the rooms, again not telling you the choice of either the object or the room. Begin your search by holding the pendulum over the house sketch and asking which room the object is in. When you decide which room you need to search, go to that room. Ask the pendulum which area of the room contains the object you are to find. When it indicates a specific area, work your way through the objects in that area until you discover what the object is.

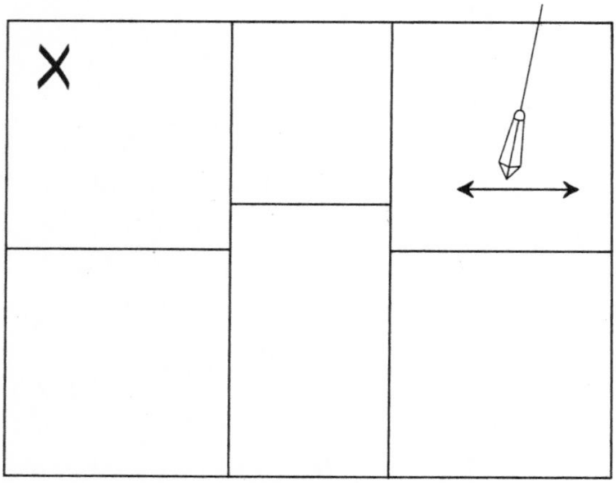

Finding an Object in a House

Divining the Future

You have now hopefully worked your way through the preceding exercises until you are more confident of your abilities and your pendulum. If you think carefully about these exercises, you will see the important connection to divining the future or prediction methods with the pendulum. The exercises have been teaching you to explore all possible facets of a question. One question should lead to another, until you reach a definite answer. Now you are ready to take the first step into the psychic area of future predicting.

Before asking the pendulum to answer any question of a predictive nature, or any question for that matter, you must formulate that question as clearly as possible, the shorter the better. Be very certain you do not combine two questions or ask a question that cannot be answered with a Yes or a No.

Avoid asking questions out of curiosity or those that pry into the lives of others. These types of questions are an invasion of privacy and basically are immoral in intent. The same applies to questions whose answers might harm the interests of other people.

Each time before you ask the pendulum to answer the question, you should have it show you the Yes, No, Confusion/Wrong Question and Neutral/Search movements. This reestablishes the code with your subconscious mind.

After doing this, and before asking a question, you need to ask the pendulum to clarify some other important points. Ask "Am I ready to know the answer?" You might think you want an answer because your left-brain is pushing to have something resolved. The left-brain is good at deluding us and pushing issues so they can be gotten out of the way. However, your subconscious mind and right-brain might know that you cannot handle or understand a truthful answer at this time, or that this is not the right time for the action, event, or goal you are asking about. The same applies if you are asking a question for another person. If the pendulum says No, either do not ask the question or try rephrasing the question. If the pendulum still says No, leave the question for a time before asking again.

The next question is just as important. Ask, "May I ask this question?" You have no idea sometimes if you are asking about a karmic issue that is best left alone at this time. If the pendulum says No and you ask the question anyway, you will not be able to rely on a truthful answer. If you are asking a question for another person, you have no idea whether she/he is telling the entire truthful situation behind the question.

Never answer a question about a third person for anyone. This is prying into a private area that is not any of your business or the business of the person asking. The only exception to this rule is if a mother with young children asks about them. If a spouse or lover asks about the fidelity of a partner, she/he already guesses at the answer and does not need you to confirm or deny anything. She/he must take the responsibility of making a decision on her/his own. Occasionally you may get a partner asking this question out of paranoia. In these cases, it is best to avoid divining for the person at all. Nothing you say will be heard as you say it, but as she/he wants it to be.

The third question also can be vital in getting an accurate answer from your pendulum. Ask, "Do I have enough skills with divining to find the correct answer?" Sometimes a question must turn into a long series of questions, all carefully phrased, before the situation is fully explored. This question is vitally important if you plan to attempt to find an object or missing person. Finding an object in a house with a pendulum is an entirely different set of circumstances than trying to find an object lost elsewhere or a missing, and possibly deceased, person. Every time a person is missing, the police are flooded with calls from would-be psychics who think they know where the person is, and who would love the publicity if the person were found. However, accurate, useful information of this kind is extremely rare. Using a pendulum to search in this manner requires a lot of practice and experience. Even then, most people do not have the intuitive connection to accurately find anyone.

Getting correct answers from a pendulum is not by chance, but a matter of practice and experience. Now that you are aware of all the necessary steps to future divining, you are ready to ask your pendulum a question pertaining to your own future. Always practice on yourself before you jump into trying to answer questions for others.

Think very carefully about a question you want answered about your future. Word the question so that it can be answered with a Yes or a No. Shuffle a tarot deck and choose nine cards at random. If you do not have tarot cards, you can use rune cards or rune stones. Hold the pendulum over each card and ask if that particular card is important to the question you have in mind. If you are not familiar with the meanings of the tarot cards or runes, look up each card in its accompanying book and see how it pertains to your question. Think about the pendulum answers, for the cards may point out new options or challenges that you had not considered.

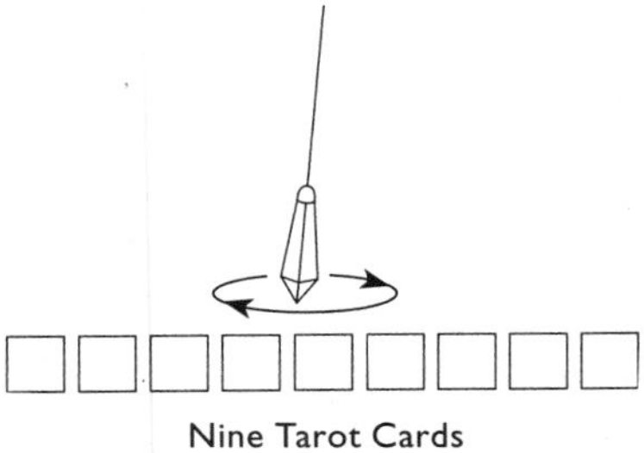

Nine Tarot Cards

Do not think about the answer you want or any answer at all, for that matter. Doing this will interfere with a truthful reply from the pendulum. Instead, think, "I wonder what the answer will be." Since the left-brain always requires something to occupy its attention and keep it from interfering with the answer from the right-brain, thinking of such a statement will occupy your left-brain's time and let the real answer slip through unimpeded.

Perhaps you have so many questions about your future you cannot decide where to begin. The chart shown here is a fan chart that can help you choose the most important aspect of your life to inquire about with your pendulum. Often the area we think is the most important to a positive future is not, under the surface, the correct one at all. If you are elsewhere when asking this question and do not have access to this book, you can draw out a circle on a piece of paper and divide it into four quarters. Label the quarters as physical, mental, social, and spiritual. Circle dowsing is more difficult, however, unless you have years of practice.

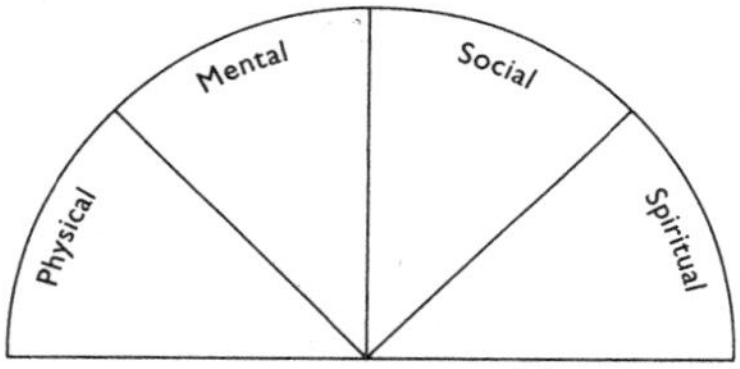

Realms of Life Chart

Most pendulum charts are designed on either the circle or the fan layout. The circle layout is self-explanatory: a circle with marked segments that meets in the center. When using this layout, hold the pendulum over the center of the chart. However, dowsing on a circle chart can be confusing as to which segment the pendulum is indicating. For this reason I have chose to use only fan charts in this book.

The fan chart is shaped like an Oriental fan with one flat edge at the bottom. The marked segments all converge in the center of the flat edge. To work with this layout, hold the pendulum over the center of the bottom edge where all the lines converge when you ask as question.

Now, ask the pendulum to indicate the area of your future that is most important to you at this time and to the goals you wish to accomplish. Or, you can ask which area you should be most concerned with. When your pendulum has answered, think seriously about the area indicated, for you may have missed the possibility of future trouble in that part of your life. This will make you more aware of problems before they get out of hand. It also will help you to eliminate problems by making changes.

Sometimes the areas of this chart are not specific enough for your needs. The fan chart below is divided to better clarify life areas. It is divided into seven parts or segments, labeled career, finances, love, health, mental, family, and spiritual. Hold the pendulum over the point where all the lines come together at the bottom. Ask the question, "Which part of my life needs work?" Again, seriously consider the answer the pendulum gives you. In creating the best future for yourself, you cannot afford to overlook even the smallest hints.

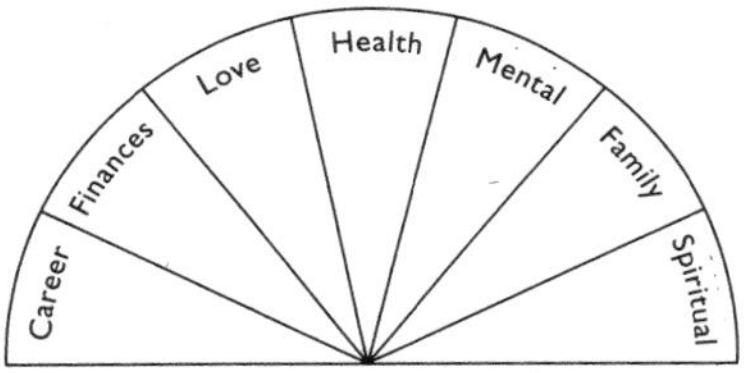

Life Areas Chart

If you dread getting an answer about one area of your life, your emotions will interfere with an accurate pendulum reading. Separation of personal emotions from your pendulum work is the only way to reach the truth. The area you most dread to hear about may be the very one the pendulum will help you in solving. Remember not to think of the answer you want or even an answer you dread. Keep as much of a neutral emotional state as possible by concentrating on "I wonder what the answer will be."

You now have all of the basics of pendulum divining that are necessary to divine the future for yourself or anyone else. Please use these methods with integrity, ethics, and morals, keeping your ego and sense of self-importance out of it.

On page 250 is a fan chart for Yes/No/Maybe Yes/Maybe No. I did not mention this chart before as I feel it is important for a pendulum user to learn the basics without relying on a chart. I have included this particular chart to help those beginners who may feel they do not have what it takes to work with a pendulum. Such people can start with this chart as an aid, but I encourage all dowsers to become self-sufficient and dispense with the use of this particular chart as soon as possible.

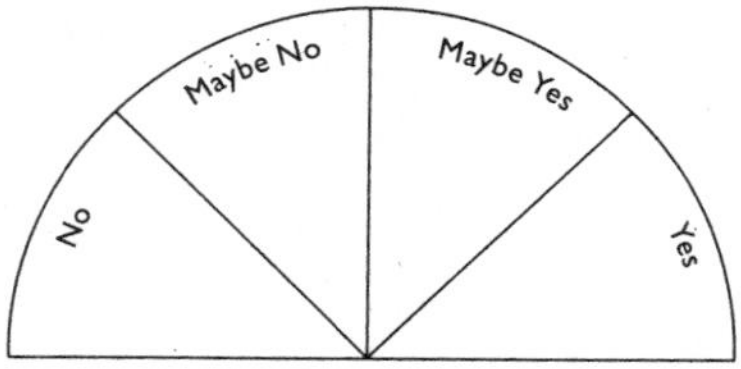

Yes/No/Maybe Chart

To work with the Yes/No/Maybe Yes/Maybe No chart, hold the pendulum over the center of the flat edge where all the lines converge. Dowsers call this point the "hinge." Make certain your question is formulated to have only one answer. The pendulum then will move toward the marked segment that it sees as correct.

Sometimes the pendulum will swing in a line between two segments. If this happens, you must decide if the question has been formulated properly. If the answer is questionable, or if you wish further confirmation, ask the pendulum whether this question can be answered at all. If it answers Yes, reformulate the question and try again. If you still get an idiot answer, do not ask again for a period of time. Remember, do not think of the answer you want.

Pendulum divining or dowsing can be very helpful in choosing the right path in your life, whether the issue at stake is small or large. However, you should never become so dependent on any divination tool that you fear to make a move without consulting it. Use your pendulum responsibly. It is not a toy, nor is it the supreme answer to every single problem. However, the pendulum can be a wonderful tool for opening your subconscious mind and letting the needed, correct answers surface.

Balancing and Healing with Pendulums

Few dowsers or diviners are good at all uses of the pendulum. Some are very good at dowsing in health matters, but cannot find water underground. Some are excellent in witching for water or oil, but have no luck whatsoever in using a pendulum to answer other questions. You should try all methods of using the pendulum before you decide that some application of dowsing will or will not work for you. It is also probable that with practice, patience, and experience you can learn to use the pendulum in any area of dowsing you wish to explore.

Personal health and the health of your family are of prime importance to all people. With the cost of insurance and medical care skyrocketing, each person must be as well informed as possible. Giving your doctor polite suggestions to help with diagnosis and knowing something about an illness can cut medical costs and give you a greater chance for a quick recovery. This makes learning how to heal and balance the four main bodies of humans well worth the effort (see also page 257).

Although a pendulum can be very useful in diagnosing illnesses, you should never make medical recommendations for others. This can get you into serious trouble with the police and the American Medical Association. Also, you should never diagnose for another person unless she/he specifically asks you to do so.

In asking about health matters, perhaps more than with any other questions, the dowser must take great care to detach the emotions from the question. You have to work at not thinking about an answer while waiting for the pendulum to move. Keep telling yourself, "I wonder what it will be" or keep repeating the question to block out expectant thoughts. Otherwise, your pendulum will give you the answer you want, not necessarily the truthful one.

The best place to begin learning the healing techniques with a pendulum is to learn how to diagnose and balance your own seven main chakras of your astral body. The chakras are part of the Hindu tradition, and are frequently called "light centers" or "wheels of light." The chakras are called "wheels" because they appear to spin. The seven chakras can be diagnosed with a pendulum for imbalance in much the same manner as the physical body can be. All diseases of the physical will appear first in the astral body, via the chakras and the aura.

The Seven Chakras

Although there are more than seven chakras in the astral body, I will talk about only the seven most commonly known ones. The first (red) lies at the base of the spine, the second (orange) midway between the navel and pelvic region, the third (yellow) near the navel, the fourth (green) at the center of the chest, the fifth (blue) at the base of the throat, the sixth (purple) between the eyebrows, and the seventh (violet or white) at the top of the head. There are also powerful chakras in the palm of each hand and the sole of each foot, plus a number of lesser chakras in various places over the body. Although I will not discuss these last-mentioned chakras, it is important that you know they exist. Below is a fan chart for dowsing the chakras as well as a figure indicating the traditional chakra placement of the seven main chakras.

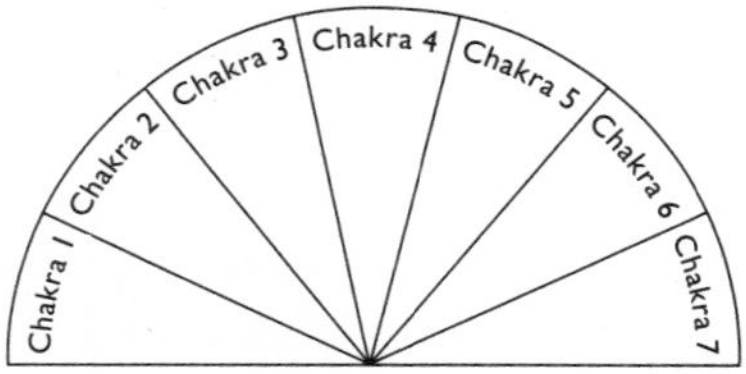

The Chakras Chart

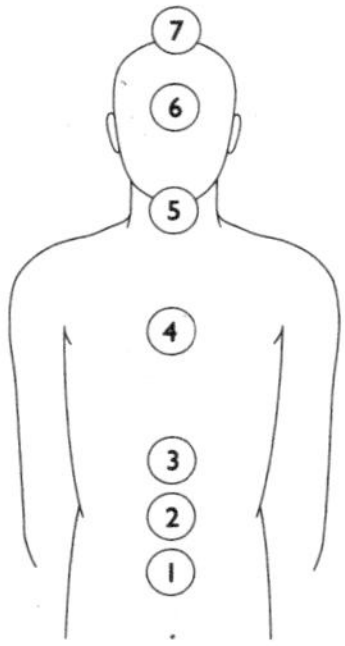

Chakra Positions

Chakras can become blocked, over- or understimulated, or out of balance because of approaching diseases, negative emotions, or stressful events. You can use your pendulum to recharge and rebalance them.

Since holding your pendulum over each of your own chakras, as you would another person, would be difficult, there is another technique you can use. Purchase film sheets of the appropriate chakra colors from a photographic store. These film sheets are commonly used over a camera lens to change the color. If you cannot find film sheets, you can use squares of colored paper. From these sheets, cut a 1 to $1^1/_2$-inch square of each color. Put these squares in the correct order, beginning with red for the first chakra and ending with violet for the seventh one.

The chakras in the palms of the hands are associated with giving and receiving; you will use them to properly input energy to any imbalanced chakras. By using the pendulum and the colored squares in the palm of your hand, you can avoid overcharging these "light" centers.

Begin by placing the red square in the palm of one hand. Hold the pendulum over this colored square with your other hand. If any of your chakras do not need balancing, the pendulum will not move or will move very little. If the chakra does need balancing, the pendulum will circle clockwise until the adjustment has been made. Then it will stop. When the pendulum stops, lay aside the red square and place the next color (orange) in your palm. Repeat with the pendulum over it. Keep changing colored squares and checking with the pendulum until you have gone through all the colors, ending with violet.

If working on another person, have her/him lie on the back while you hold the pendulum over each chakra area. You can have the person lie on her/his stomach if you wish, but most healers seem to work more efficiently on the front of the body instead of the back. Hindu tradition says that the chakras radiate outward from the spine toward the front of the body. Hold the pendulum over each chakra, beginning at the base of the spine and ending at the top of the head. The pendulum will indicate a Yes or forward and backward motion if the chakra is balanced, a No or side-to-side movement if it is out of balance. Occasionally, a balanced, unblocked chakra will cause the pendulum to move in a clockwise direction, while imbalance will make the pendulum move counterclockwise.

When you discover an out-of-balance chakra, place the appropriate colored square on that chakra. The pendulum will swing in a clockwise direction until the adjustment is complete.

If you prefer to work on a more impersonal level when divining the chakras, or the person requesting the healing is absent, use the chakra chart and a photo of the person involved. Touch the position of each chakra on the chakra chart or photo while asking the pendulum to show you if it is balanced. If the pendulum indicates No, place the appropriate colored square on the chart or photo. Hold the pendulum over the square until its clockwise motion has finished.

Although there are more chakras than the seven listed, the imbalance or blockage of these seven is more apt to cause physical disease or distress. To diagnose with the pendulum for disease, instead of searching for imbalanced chakras, you need to know what imbalance in each chakra can mean in the way of diseases. The following suggestions will differ somewhat from other chakra discussions, for each healer will approach chakra healing a little differently.

In this case, the first chakra represents the spine, bones, rectum, legs, intestinal tract, the circulatory system, and the blood itself. The second chakra is for the reproductive system and sex organs, the kidneys, urinary tract, and digestion. The third chakra symbolizes the liver, gallbladder, pancreas, and the entire nervous system. The fourth chakra represents the heart, the skin, the lower portion of the lungs, and the hands. The fifth chakra is for the throat, the top portion of the lungs and the bronchia, the thyroid gland, and the voice. The sixth chakra regulates the face along with the ears, eyes, and nose; it also affects the cerebellum portion of the brain. The seventh chakra represents the skull and the rest of the brain. Some healers also list the seventh chakra as an indicator of the health of the soul.

For example, you find that the pendulum indicates that the second chakra of the person you are testing has something wrong. The pendulum is swinging in a counterclockwise or side-to-side direction, indicating a No. You ask if the problem is in the reproductive system. The pendulum says No. You proceed down the list of possible diseases, asking about the sex organs, the kidneys, and digestion, receiving a No each time. When you ask about the urinary track, the pendulum says Yes.

You now place the orange square over the appropriate area of the second chakra, then hold the pendulum about 6 inches above the square. The pendulum will swing in a clockwise direction until it has fed in as much chakra energy as it can. Although this procedure will help the patient with the disease, you should instruct the person to see her/his physician as soon as possible for a checkup. Do not diagnose or prescribe treatments. A urinary track problem can range from an infection to kidney stones.

Frequently, a health problem associated with a chakra is more difficult to pinpoint, or does not seem to be entirely related to a specific chakra. The pendulum user then must go beyond diagnosis through the chakras, and use the pendulum over the entire body in a slightly different manner. In this case, the pendulum will respond with a clockwise or forward and backward motion (a Yes) for good health and a counterclockwise or side-to-side motion (a No) for ill health, damage, or disease.

Healing with Pendulums

When determining what part of a human body is in need of treatment, have the patient lie on her/his back while you slowly move the pendulum about 6 inches above the body. Begin at the head and work down to the feet. Remember to take your time, as the pendulum must be given an opportunity to respond. Cover the entire front of the body, then have the patient lie on her/his stomach and repeat the procedure with the pendulum.

The pendulum will give a Yes or positive movement over areas in good health. It will give a No or negative movement over areas in which there is disease, imbalance, or pending health problems.

If the person to be diagnosed cannot be present, you can work with a full photo of the person by using a pointer to touch each area while holding the pendulum in the other hand. After you have gained much experience in this form of problem diagnosis, you can work on a person even if no photo is available. You do this by holding the person in mind while you use the pendulum over pictures in an anatomy book. However, it is much easier to work from a photo.

This method of pendulum dowsing will reveal not only present problems, but also past injuries and even surgeries. It will be common for irregularities to appear in the neck and shoulders where stress and tension accumulate. Past injuries also will show up in this examination, particular to the back and joints. Before you state that the patient has a problem in any area indicated by the pendulum, be certain to ask her/him of there was a past disease, injury, or surgery in that area.

A simple exercise will show you that the pendulum does indeed pick up injuries, however slight. Sit in a chair and hold you pendulum over one of your thighs. Ask about the health of your thigh, and observe what motion the pendulum over that particular leg. Then slap your other hand sharply against the same thigh. Observed what the pendulum now does. You will get two entirely different readings from your pendulum.

A pendulum will not only tell you what part of the body is ill, it also can help you determine the cause behind the bodily sickness. The whole person consists of four bodies: physical, mental, emotional, and spiritual. An imbalance in any one of these bodies will affect the other three, and open the immune system to the possibility of disease. It is very rare that all four of these bodies are in perfect alignment at any one time. It is considered to be average if two out of the four bodies are in balance.

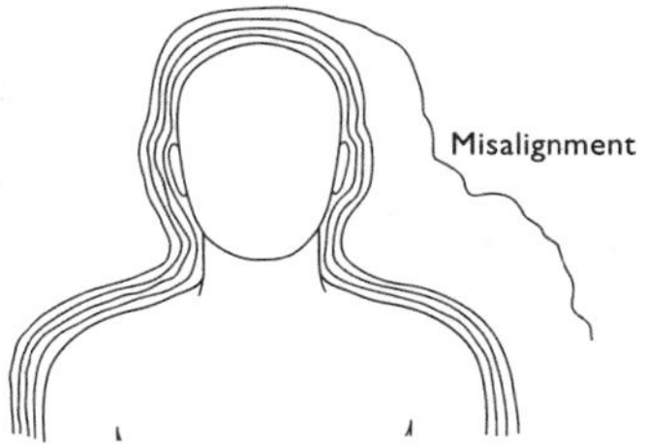

The Four Bodies

The chart for physical cause of a disease (see below) will help the diviner in pinpointing any specific physical source that is detrimental to the inquirer. If nothing is pertinent on this chart, or you suspect that there may be more than one cause, try the chart for psychic causes of a disease (see page 258). This chart deals with emotional and mental causes. However, the segment "psychic attack" should not be taken to mean "black magick" or "spellworking." It is more likely that the psychic attack will be a build-up of jealousy, hatred, or a deep desire for control or punishment that comes from another person or persons, rather than a deliberate effort to use magick against someone. This same build-up within a person often can be the cause of disease inflicted upon herself/himself.

Animals can also be diagnosed in the same way with a pendulum to see if they are ill and may need a veterinarian. Pets are dependent upon their owners to be observant and get them health care when they

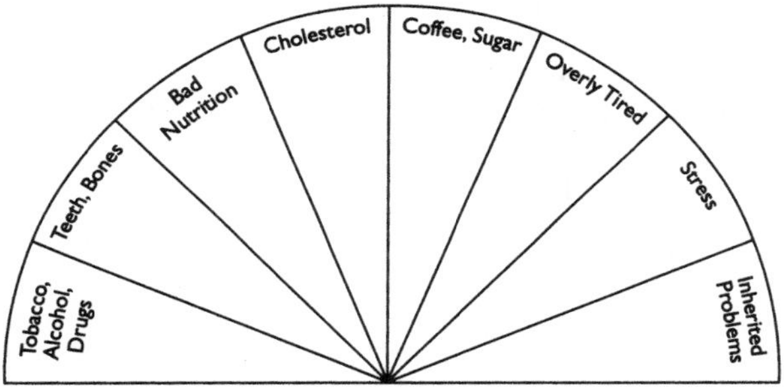

Physical Cause of Disease Chart

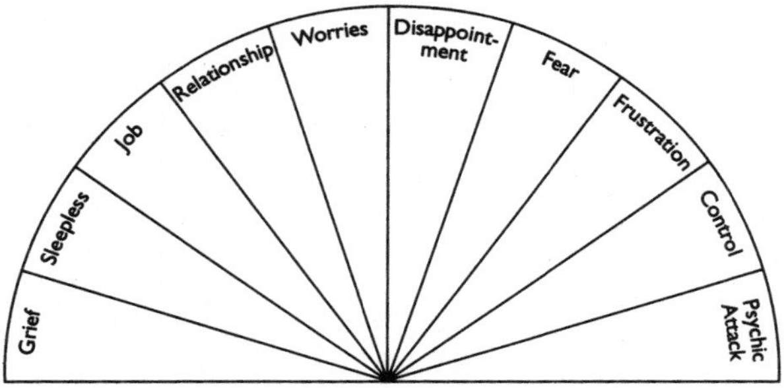

Psychic Cause of Disease Chart

need it. Although many pets develop a psychic or telepathic bond with the owner, they cannot always tell us exactly what the problem is, no more than we often can tell our physician the exactness of a disease. The only problem you may have in dowsing a pet for health is that it might consider the swinging pendulum a fascinating toy.

There is also much discussion on whether animals have the same number of chakras as humans, and whether these chakras are in the same positions. I believe animals do have the same number of chakras and surrounding astral bodies as humans do. Those who do not believe this base their theories on the idea that animals are less evolved. Having observed animals and humans for many years, I cannot subscribe to these theories. I have seen animals that have more common sense, compassion, and spirituality than quite a few humans.

Pendulums and Auras

Another interesting and useful area of pendulum dowsing is that of finding and reading the human aura. Although there actually is more than one human aura surrounding us, it is best to skip this esoteric information and concentrate on the one main body aura. Before trying to read the aura, you should learn to use your pendulum simply to find the aura on another person and determine how far out it extends from the human body.

Have the test person sit in a chair while you slowly move the pendulum around her/his body. For beginners, it is easiest to find the aura around the head and shoulders. Begin by holding the pendulum about 4 to 6 inches away from the top of the head. Ask the pendulum to show you where the person's aura is. It will respond with a Yes movement if it is within the aura field. Move the pendulum out an inch or so more, and ask the same question again. Repeat this until you have reached the outer limits of the aura, when the pendulum will answer with a No motion. You also can do this with plants, animals, and inanimate objects, such as rocks.

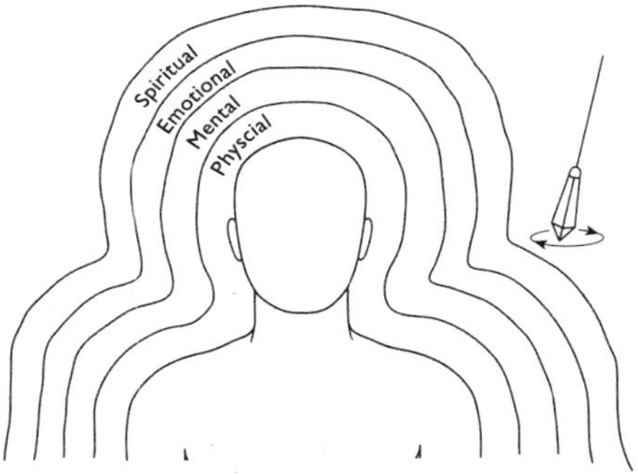

Auras

You may find that certain areas of a person's aura may be closer to the body or much farther out than the average range of the aura. This is an indication of a disease or potential illness. When you discover such a depression or flare, you then must use your pendulum to determine if the problem is physical, mental, emotional, or spiritual. You do this by asking whether the problem is of a physical nature. If the pendulum answers with a No, work your way through the other three categories. Sometimes, the pendulum will indicate that none of these are responsible for the depression or flare. If this happens, you need to ask whether the reason is a karmic one. If the answer is Yes, see Dowsing in the Field of Past Lives, Karma, and Reincarnation on page 270.

Pendulums and Your Diet

Pendulum dowsing can also be used to help in personal health and diet. However, you should only use this aspect of dowsing on yourself and your immediate family. Do not make recommendations or take action to eliminate or add something to your diet and lifestyle without exploring more deeply the fields of herbalism and vitamins.

Using a pendulum, you can test whether certain vitamins and foods are good for you and which will cause problems. A good example is to set out a cup of tea or coffee. See what the pendulum says about your reaction to the drink. Then ask whether you should add any cream or sugar. Use the pendulum over another beverage, such as a soda. Is it good for you? Before deciding to take action one way or another, carefully think about how you feel when you ingest these beverages. Did you experience digestive problems, or a nervous reaction? If you answer Yes, consider eliminating the beverage in question for a few days and see what happens. The beverage itself may not be to blame. It may cause negative reactions only when combined with certain other foods.

If you suspect that a new food may give you digestive problems, use your pendulum to find out for certain. Then sample the food in question in very small quantities to see what the reaction will be.

You can also use the pendulum to test your physical reactions to food additives, sweets, or foods you ordinarily eat. Some of us eat certain foods all our lives and wonder why we suffer digestive problems. Often, it is not the food itself, but whatever is added to it or on it. In determining the negative or positive reaction of your body to a food, phrase your questions carefully, and be certain that you cover all possibilities, from additives and sprays to how the food is cooked and in what.

If you suffer an unpleasant reaction such as bloating after an ordinary meal, use your pendulum to discover which food caused the problem. It may even be a combination of foods. Since the body changes over time, what you could eat without distress at one time may not be good for you at a later date or as you age. For example, you may eat raw onions with impunity until you reach middle age. Then you might find that you only can tolerate cooked onions in small amounts.

The pendulum can be a valuable tool in discovering which vitamins you may need or should eliminate from your daily health routine. The same divining process can be used to test herbs.

While you are using the pendulum to test food, vitamins, or herbs, you should avoid thinking about any specific theory or health report. This can result in an incorrect answer. If the mind wanders while dowsing, it overrides the link you must create with all your senses and awareness. It divides your focus and breaks the contact with the subconscious mind.

Hold the vitamin or herb in one hand while holding your pendulum in the other. Ask if the vitamin or herb is helpful to you. If the pendulum answers with a firm No, you should reconsider keeping the vitamin or herb as part of your daily regime. If the answer is a Confusion movement, you need to question further if the substance reacts negatively when combined with other vitamins or herbs, or whether it is a supplement that you should not use on a daily basis, but is fine to use once a week or so.

Even if the pendulum gives you a firm Yes answer, you need to go a step further and ask if the substances is one you can take every day, or whether you should skip days. Never rely on a single answer. You must explore the full parameters of the product. Also, what your body needs during one phase of your life may not be appropriate at another time.

Map and Ground Dowsing

A pendulum is a very versatile tool, good for purposes beyond divination and healing. It also can be used to trace underground water lines, storage tanks, earth energy lines, power spots, or ancient sites. Dowsing for underground pipes or tanks is nothing new. Although not highly publicized, this technique was taught to soldiers in the Vietnam War to help them find underground bunkers. Since the soldiers did not have pendulums, they were taught to make L-rods out of bent coat hangers.

Dowsing for earth energy, water, oil, or minerals is a process of listening to your intuition. Intuition cannot be proved in a lab or in a test atmosphere because "knowing" something intuitively is not provable. The dowser seems to pick up signals from the earth subconsciously, such as moving streams of water, a certain feeling for oil and coal, or a subconscious reaction to certain minerals. One theory that makes the most sense is that all humans are part of the universe and can be sensitive to whatever else is part of the universe. When you open your subconscious mind and listen to your intuition, you are using a kind of radar to search for the vibrations of something you want to find.

Dowsing or divining is usually connected by the human mind with finding water or oil. These are very specialized fields and require a lot of practice and the asking of very specific questions. Dowsing is often called witching, as in a water witch who looks for water. A water witch who is really good at dowsing will be accurate between 85 and 90 percent of the time. Although most water, oil, and mineral dowsing is done with L-rods or forked sticks, there is no reason one cannot use a pendulum. Since a pendulum is more affected by body movements than L-rods or forked sticks, however, the dowser will have to walk very slowly, frequently coming to a full stop to see how the pendulum reacts.

Dowsing for Water

The best way to learn dowsing for water is to dowse for underground water lines. Pendulum reaction to moving water in lines can be in two ways. The pendulum may respond with a Yes or positive movement when you slowly walk over the pipe's position. Or, it may swing in the direction in which the pipe lies. When you stand directly above the pipe, the pendulum may go into the Search or Neutral movement, or may circle wildly in a clockwise manner.

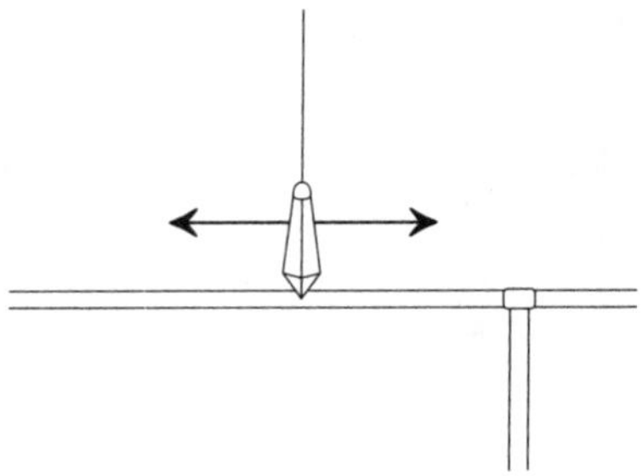

Finding Underground Lines

Beginners in dowsing need to be aware that it is only running or flowing underground water that makes the pendulum react. This action can be affected by water or sewer lines that have running water in them at the time of the dowsing. This is helpful if you are seeking the whereabouts of water or sewer lines, but not if you are seeking a new source of water. If you dowse a piece of land for water, be sure that you mark out any known sources of water before you begin.

Many dowsers who use the pendulum to locate underground pipes use what is known as the Bishop's Rule. This rule will aid you in determining how deep in the ground the pipe lies. First, find the pipe and mark the location. Then ignore the pipe and ask the pendulum to show you its depth. Slowly walk outward from the pipe's location until the pendulum responds with a Yes or positive movement. You must move slowly, as the pipe can be anywhere from a few inches to a few feet down. The distance from the pipe should match its depth. The same principle applies to new and untapped underground sources of water.

Because each dowser is different, the pendulum may respond by giving you the depth in a different manner. Some dowsers find that their device will measure the distance of the depth at half or twice the length walked. Experience is the only way to judge which works for you. Personally, I have little luck in determining depth.

Dowsing for Objects and Other Substances

Dowsing for other substances, such as oil or minerals, is much the same as dowsing for water. The pendulum will react with a firm, sometimes very rapid, clockwise circling when the dowser walks over an area that contains the sought substance. To aid in the search, some dowsers use the metal pendulum that has a twist-off top and interior cavity. They will put a small amount of the sought substance into the pendulum cavity, thus working on the theory that like substances attract. Others merely will hold a tiny glass vial of the substance in their other hand.

There also is another method that can be used for finding a substance. You may ask the pendulum, "Show me the direction in which _______ is." This question can save you time, as the pendulum's method of movement will help you determine whether you are moving in the correct direction. You must watch the outer edge of the pendulum swing for clues. This outer edge of the swing is called the leading edge by dowsers. If the pendulum swings forward and backward, you are facing in the right direction to search for the object. If it swings clockwise or counterclockwise, turn in the direction of the swing and try again. Any time you are directly facing the object sought, the pendulum will swing forward and backward. A clockwise or counterclockwise swing will turn you full circle in about fifteen tries.

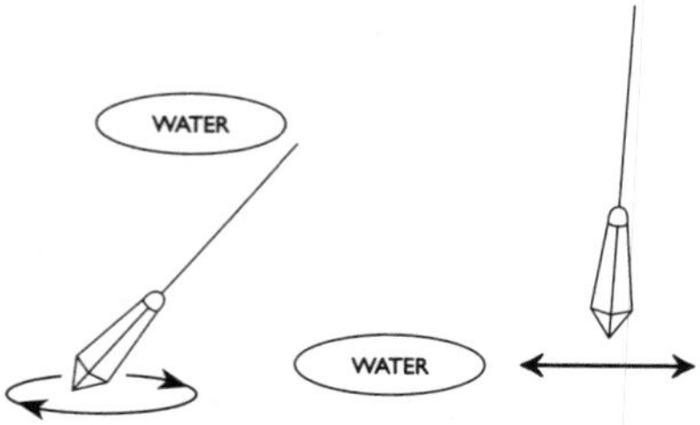

The Leading Edge Swing

You can use triangulation to further pinpoint an object. When you have a forward and backward swing of the pendulum, move to another point and repeat the question. Do this until you get another forward and backward swing of the pendulum. Then mentally draw a line from where you stood in both places. Where the lines intersect, you will find the object you seek.

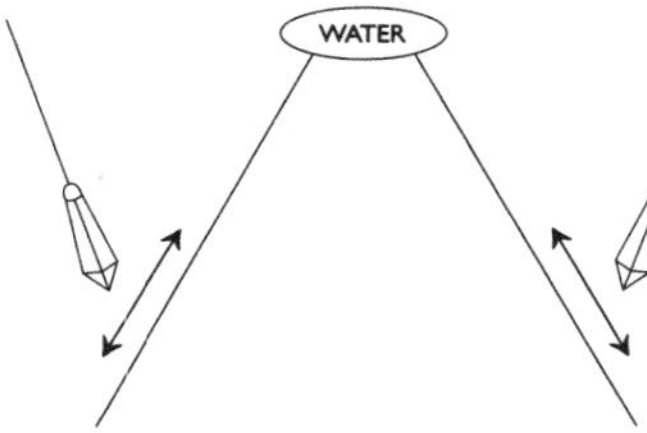

Triangulation

Trying to find an object or substance on a sketched map of a house or property with a pendulum is more difficult and requires that you ask a series of appropriate questions. The questions must be phrased for Yes or No answers, as in "Am I facing the right direction to find _______?" This question requires that you move only slightly to face a new direction.

Another method, if you know the general area in which you lost something, is to do a triangulation first. Then walk slowly in the direction indicated, holding the pendulum before you. The pendulum will swing in an oval path, with the leading edge pointing in the correct direction. When you are directly over the object, the pendulum swing will change to a circle motion. If you pass beyond the object, the pendulum will once more swing in an oval. Some people use this method to find studs in interior walls or the part of a machine that is not working properly.

If something is lost within your house, draw a floor plan of all the rooms. Then use the pendulum over each room until you find the room containing the lost object. As with map dowsing, you can point to a room or area of a room with one finger or a pencil while asking the pendulum questions. Then go to the chosen room and ask the pendulum to show you the direction in which the object lies. Remember to move only a little at a time as you work your way around a room.

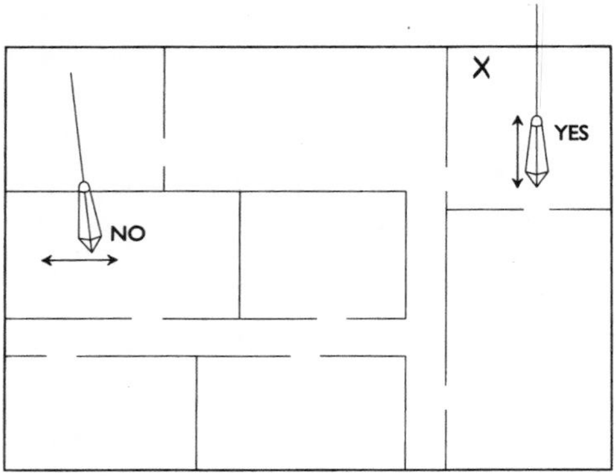

Floor Plan Dowsing

Map dowsing requires much the same technique as finding an object within a house. Map dowsing can be used to find underground water, minerals, or missing persons. It also can be used to find the general location of an appropriate house or apartment, if you are searching for somewhere to move. To begin, you need a regular map of an area. Using your finger or pencil, slowly point to various areas on the map until you get a positive response from the pendulum. You may find that the pendulum responds to more than one area. After you have discovered a general area in which you may find what you are seeking, you need a larger scale map that has more details. Again, slowly point out various spots in the larger scale map until the pendulum swings in a positive or Yes motion. You can work the information down to a specific block or street. However, it is easier to go to the area and look for yourself at this point. For example, if you are seeking a house, have a real estate agent run a check for available houses in that area.

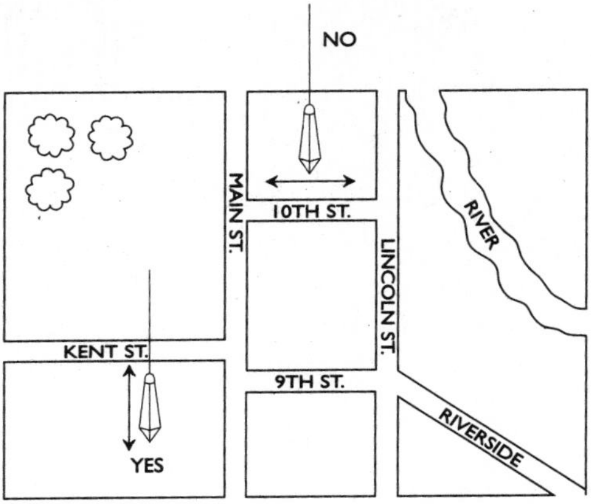

Map Dowsing

An experienced map dowser can find anything she/he sets the mind on. Ordinary maps are useful only for a wide area dowsing. To find anything in a very specific place, you will need the largest scale map you can get. Begin by asking the pendulum if what you seek is on the map at all. Sometimes what the conscious mind perceives as the correct area for the object sought is totally incorrect. A map featuring every road, city block, or other details is needed to pinpoint the exact locations. Hold the pendulum over the map with your dowsing hand while slowly pointing to one small area after another with a pointer or pen in your other hand. Each time you move the pen, ask the pendulum again if this area contains what you seek. When you touch the correct area, the pendulum will respond with a Yes.

Many people are familiar with the dowsing done along the ley-lines in England, but are unaware that these energy lines exist everywhere, encircling the entire earth. It is quite common for underground streams of water to flow along or very close to these lines. When a vein of water reaches the surface along one of these energy lines, it is sometimes called a holy well. Dowsers call this water "juvenile water," meaning that it does not go through the evaporation and rain cycle, but bubbles up from deep within the earth and frequently has high mineral content.

You can dowse for energy lines by walking slowly over an area and watching the pendulum movement. Just keep asking the pendulum to show you where the energy lines are. Until you gain experience with energy line dowsing, you should stay away from areas with underground water or sewage pipes. These can cause you to misread the pendulum movements. When you are directly over an earth energy line, the pendulum will move in a perfect circle.

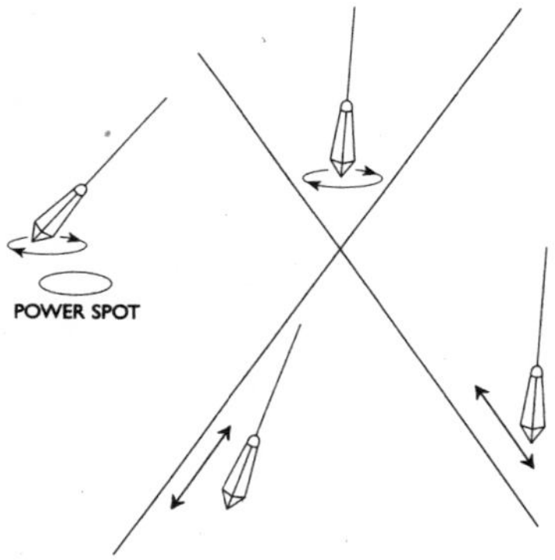

Dowsing Energy Lines

If you discover a sacred place (power spot) where two or more lines meet, the pendulum will circle so fast that it will be nearly parallel to the earth. The stronger the energies in such a place, the faster the pendulum will circle. Sometimes a power spot or sacred place will appear where there are no energy lines to cross. The energy of these spots seems to reach the earth's surface directly from some central reservoir of power.

Some dowsers can discover the timing of events by pointing to calendar dates and even the numbers on a clock face. However, this type of pendulum dowsing is very untrustworthy, and you easily can be misled by your thoughts or the thoughts of another person.

To dowse for a specific ingredient, such as minerals, water, or certain stones, hold a small sample of the material in the other hand. To practice for this, have someone prepare three glasses of water: one plain, one with a little sugar, and one with a little salt. You may find that you have to increase or decrease the length of the string in order to find certain substances.

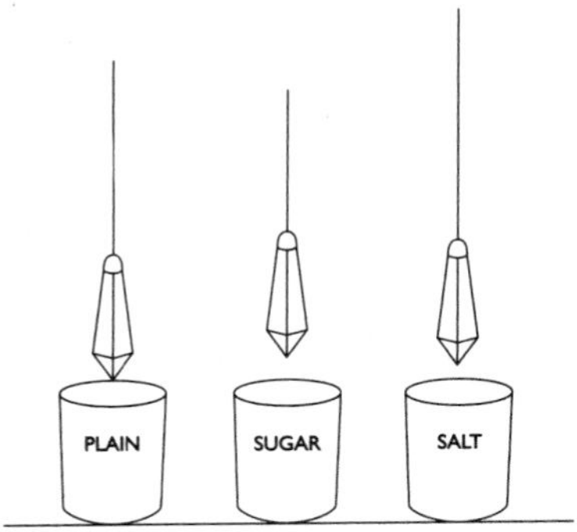

Three Glasses

If you are interested in weather forecasting, dowsing can be a fun way to pit your skills against those of the National Weather Bureau. The National Weather Bureau's accurate prediction rate is actually quite low, about thirty percent. Get a list of the forecasts for a number of cities around the country or even around the world. Then write out a list of the cities you want to cover. You can dowse for such things as sun, rain, clouds, or temperatures. Later, you can check your accuracy.

Dowsing in the Field of Past Lives, Karma, and Reincarnation

Most major events and relationships in life have a karmic background. Karma is not all negative, or having to pay for past mistakes, whether in this life or other lives. Karma can also be the reaping of just and positive rewards. Sometimes we return to a relationship believing that we can help other people pay back karma or make positive changes in their lives. Too often we find ourselves in a repetitive situation in which the other person has no intention of paying back or changing. If that person's behavior and intent make it clear that she/he has no plans to repay to you the debts owed, you must face reality and take steps to remove yourself from the negative relationship.

Using your pendulum to dowse in the field of karma and reincarnations will aid you in pinpointing the cause of problems, whether with yourself and your past lives, or with others and their past lives. None of us are blameless when we find ourselves in a negative situation, based in either this life or a past one. We all contribute something to every such situation, whether this contribution is deliberate or passive. We can turn these events into positive energy only when we take responsibility to look truthfully at things and do something to better ourselves.

Often we need to look at our own past lives and worry less about others' influence on us. Every life is composed of what went before, just as what occurred in childhood may be the basis for the way we act later. Frequently, these past lives influence us subconsciously as to the manner in which we react to certain people or experiences, the importance or unimportance that we assign to ourselves, and many of our personality quirks.

You can use your pendulum to open doors to past lives if you are careful in how you word your questions and keep your desires and emotions out of it. Never dowse for past lives with a particular destination in mind. This mental frame of mind will be certain to give you false answers. Also, do not fall into the trap of thinking you were someone famous or important in past lives. The vast majority of people were those who subtly influenced history by their common, everyday lives and decisions, not the people recorded by history as famous.

The chart of past lives dates will help you to determine where the present influences are coming from in your past, if you ask, "What time period is the biggest influence in my present life?" These dates are divided into two charts to make it easier for the inquirer to use. Alternatively, you may use the charts to answer such questions as "When did I live my last life?" or "When did I live a past life with (name)?"

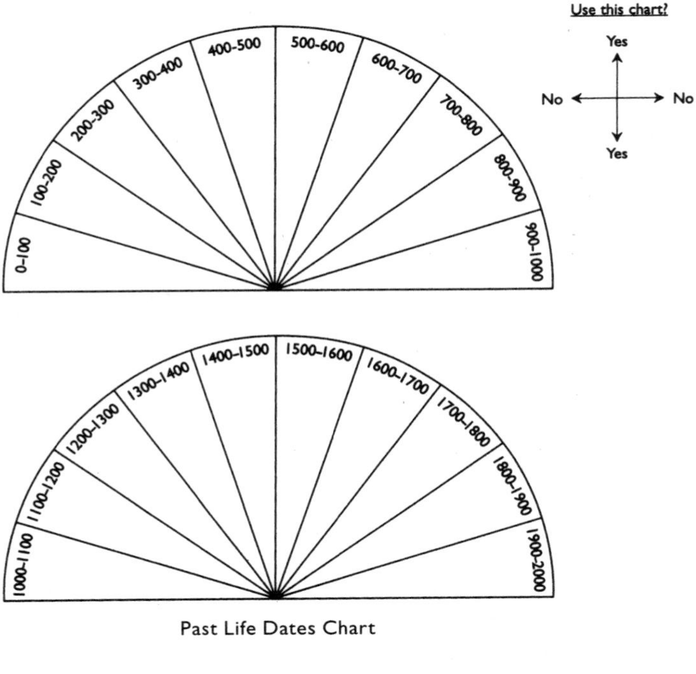

Past Life Dates Chart

The next charts are for locating where in the time period you lived a past life. There are two charts for location to make it easier for the inquirer to use. Frequently, the past life location indicated by the pendulum will explain why you have a deep interest in certain cultures or areas of the world.

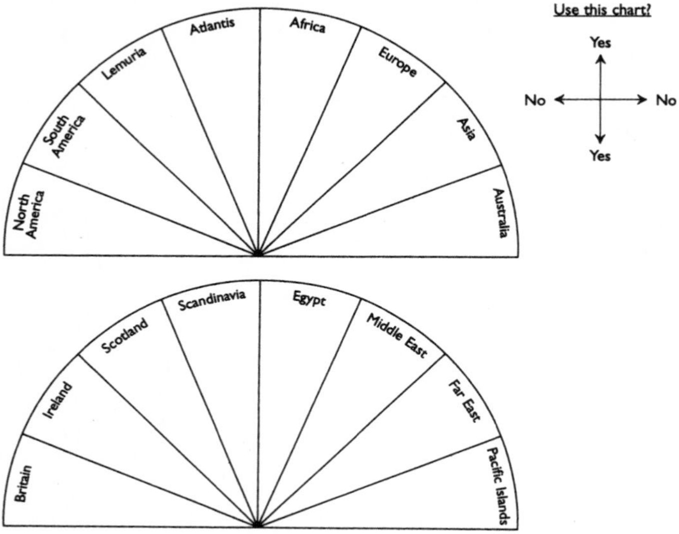

Past Life Location Periods Chart

The past life gender graph is located on the corner of the chart for the past life social background chart (see page 273). The gender graph will help you in determining if you were male or female. Gender often changes as we go from one life to another, so that we can experience the different social restrictions and benefits of a particular time period and culture.

The past life social background chart will aid you in discovering what role you played in society and what experiences you were likely to have had. Were you in a social position that did not allow you to become all you could have been? Did you resent the unbreakable social barriers? Do you still harbor these resentments today? These questions and more must be asked if you want to know a past life in depth.

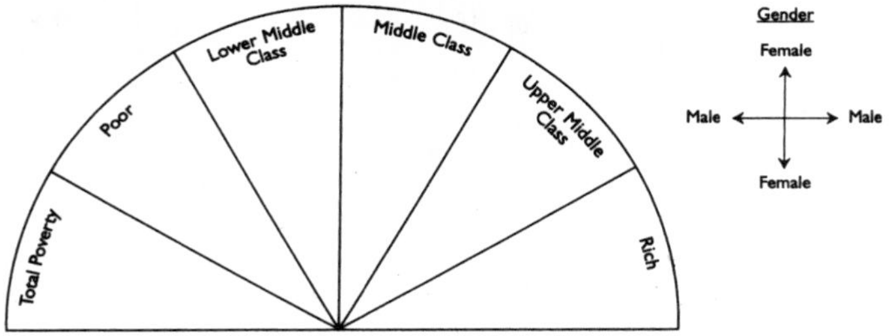

Past Life Social Background Chart

The past life occupation charts help to uncover the method by which you made your way in a given past life. What we once learned as a farmer may influence our present interest in gardening, what we learned as a merchant may influence how ethically or unethically we do business today. If you wish to delve further into the occupation of a past life, you must formulate a series of carefully worded questions that will reveal what you learned from that lifetime.

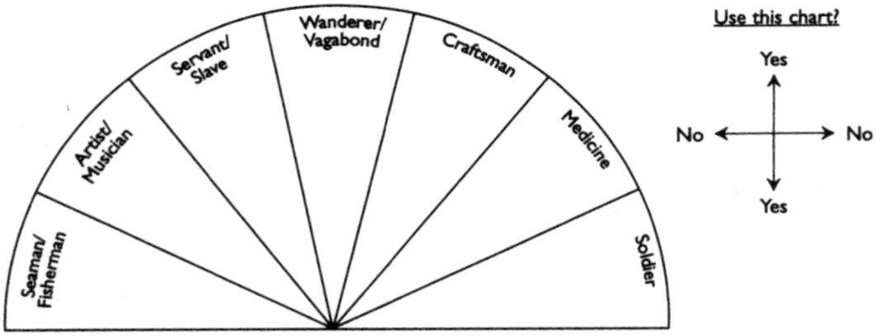

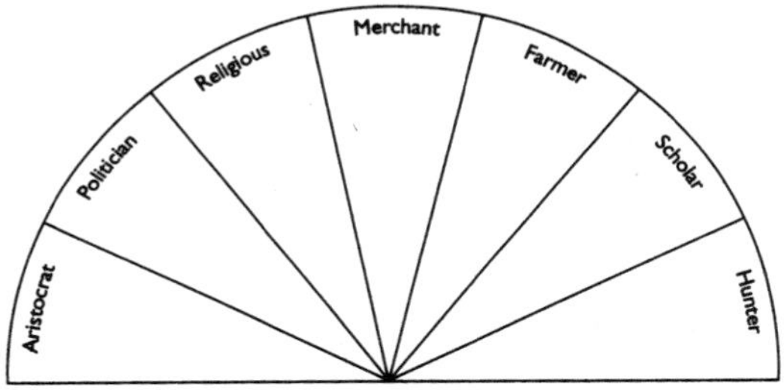

Past Life Occupation Chart

For example, if your pendulum indicates that you were of a religious order, you might ask:

"Did I like what I did?"

"Did I learn compassion for others?"

"Was I influenced by corruption within the religious order?"

"Did I join the order because I was forced to do so?"

"Did I rebel against the rules of the order?"

To learn the truth, you must not be afraid to cover all aspects of that life, both positive and negative.

Frequently, people who are interested in karma and past lives want to know what their relationship with family or a specific person was in that life. The chart of karmic relationship will aid in getting such an answer. Often this answer helps a person understand why there are difficulties or unpleasantness in dealing with certain people in her/his life. Just because the pendulum indicates that a specific person was a spouse in a prior life does not mean she/he is the perfect spouse this time. The person may have been cruel, unfaithful, or had addictions, some or all of which may surface in this life. Also, a perfect and loving relationship in one life may not be so perfect and loving this time. People change, that is the nature and meaning of karma. That is why I do not believe that "soul mates" are particularly associated with past relationships. What worked in a relationship long ago may well not work at all now.

A "soul mate" is a person who is the perfect complement to you in any given lifetime. Sometimes she/he does appear out of a past rela-

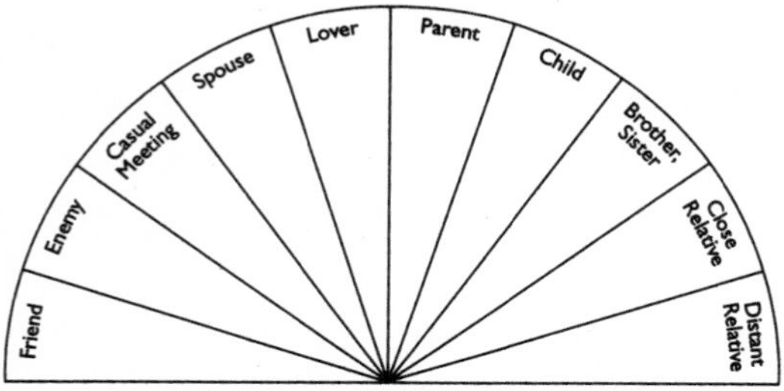

Past Life Karmic Relationships Chart

tionship, but more often she/he has changed and evolved into that perfect niche through lifetimes of casual acquaintance and life trials. It also is possible for there to be more than one "soul mate" available in a lifetime.

Sometimes we are blinded by the intuitive recognition of a past love with a person and do not see the unsatisfactory changes for a time—changes that have made the love no longer viable or acceptable. This frequently occurs when two people experience an immediate, strong physical attraction, or love at first sight.

Any time you delve into the arena of past lives, you must be extremely careful to keep your emotions, desires, and prior thoughts on the matter out of your mind while dowsing with the pendulum. Your thoughts on this subject are even more apt to influence the pendulum than in the area of health and healing. However, learning about your past lives and their influence on this life can be very liberating and insightful if you take the matter seriously. Knowing where certain habits or urges originated can help you to create positive changes in yourself. Discovering the background to an uncomfortable or negative familial or sexual relationship can give you the courage to break away and build your life anew. The entire purpose of delving into past lives should be to make positive personal changes and revive past talents.

Obstacles, Destiny, Astrology, and Other Subjects

Now that you have learned a great many things about yourself and your pendulum, it is time to tackle the much more complex areas of pendulum dowsing. These areas definitely require that you keep a separation of your emotions and desires from your mind while dowsing or the results will be untrustworthy.

The accuracy chart (see page 276) is self-explanatory. It is very important to use this chart each time before you begin dowsing on past lives, astrology, or the planets, as you must be assured that the pendulum's accuracy is high enough to give you the true and potentially valuable answer you seek. This chart will give you the accuracy rating of a particular pendulum at any given time. Since your emotional state and physical vitality will change from day to day or from one part of a day to another, you may wish to check the accuracy of your pendulum at that time. Any time the accuracy rate falls below 60 percent, it is best not to use that particular pendulum at that time, or not do any pendulum divining at that time.

The inaccuracy chart (below) will help you pinpoint why the pendulum is not working at peak efficiency. If you dowse on the accuracy chart and get a low figure, this chart can help you pinpoint the reason. All of the segment names are easily understood, except perhaps for the "Other People" category. People who are skeptical or who really do not want you to reveal an answer to their question can influence the pendulum's accuracy. It is also possible that your own subconscious

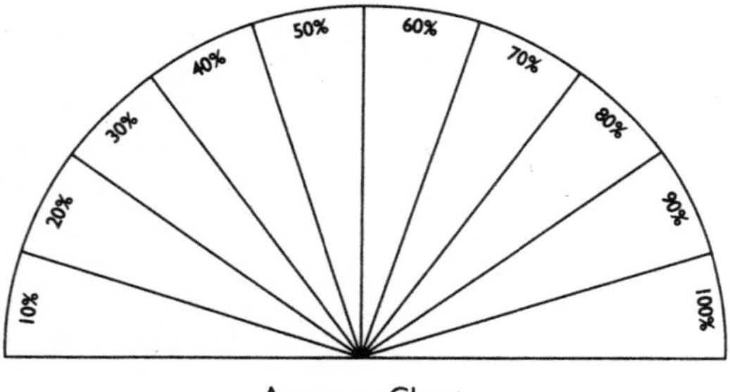

Accuracy Chart

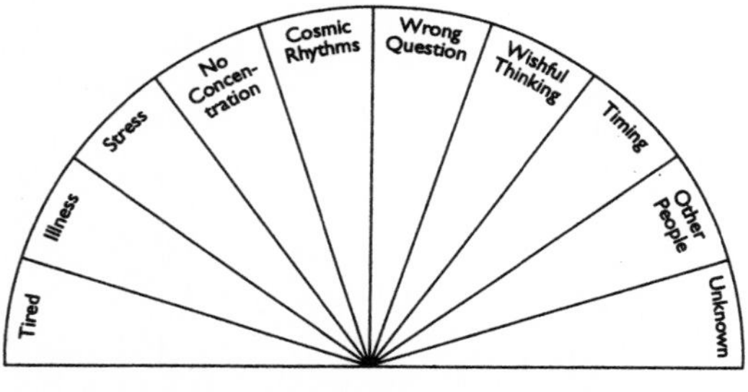

Inaccuracy Cause Chart

mind is afraid to reveal the answer you say you are seeking. This negative influence also extends to people who are jealous of your abilities and wish you to fail. Remember that some pendulums simply are not useful for dowsing on certain types of questions. If a certain pendulum consistently rates a low percentage of accuracy in preparation for asking particular questions, you will need to use another pendulum.

You will notice that on one corner of some of the charts (particularly those charts that are continued on another chart) is a sample Yes/No indicator. To save time, hold your pendulum over the this Yes/No and ask, "Is this the chart I need?" if the pendulum answers No, go to the next chart.

The first chart of obstacles (below) is used to reveal possible trouble ahead in events and situations. When using this chart, you should ask, "What are the obstacles ahead in this situation (name the situation)?" This chart is useful in uncovering what internal, subconscious attributes should be changed or modified to bring success.

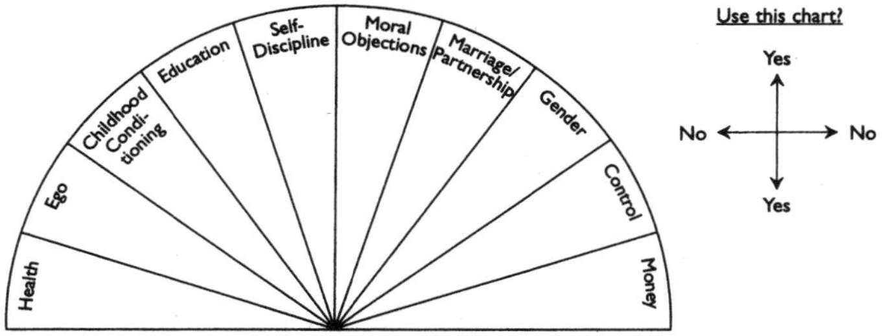

Obstacles (1) Chart

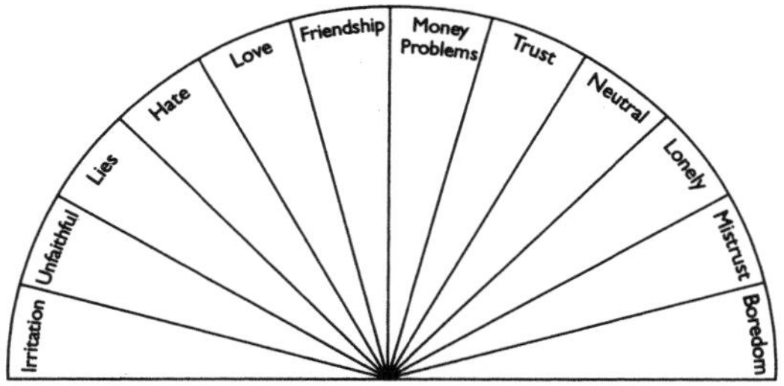

Obstacles (2) Chart

The second chart (see page 277) of obstacles should be used for relationship questions, such as "What obstacles are ahead in the relationship with (name)?" Some relationships, either as friends or lovers, can create unwanted emotions if the parties involved do not look at all the little signals in complete honesty. The outcome can be totally different from what was expected.

The destiny chart (below) can be used in conjunction with either or both of the obstacles charts. It can be applied to personal or business affairs to give the inquirer clues to the outcome of an event or relationship if all things remain on the present path. Any answer indicated by the pendulum on this chart will be much more difficult to change, as it will require major changes in all aspects of your life and/or goals.

The chart for blockages (below) can help you understand what is impeding your progress toward a goal. If the pendulum indicates a particular blockage, be certain to ask more specific questions to give you a wider view of the trouble.

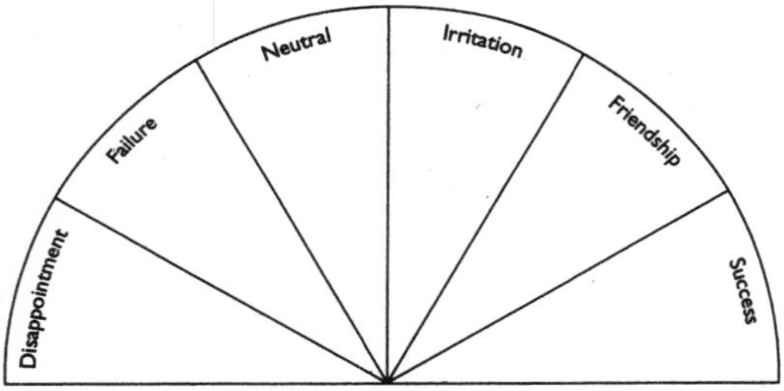

Destiny Chart

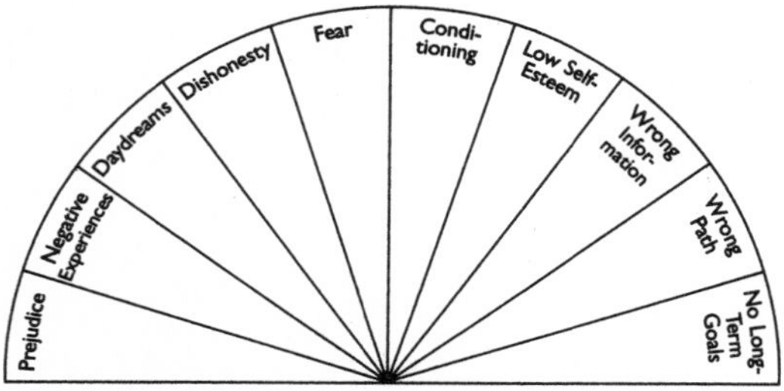

Blockages Chart

In using the charts of astrological house (below), you need to ask questions that have their basis in everyday life, such as family, business, social, or personal problems or goals. These two charts, which together make up the traditional astrological wheel, are even more specific than the charts of obstacles, blockages, or destiny. If you use these charts, you must be prepared to think long and hard about the indicated segment in order to determine the reason for it being chosen by the pendulum. The more personal the house and characters indicated, the more closely you must be willing to look. As humans, we tend to gloss over personal indications, preferring to believe that others are the source of our troubles, not ourselves.

FIRST HOUSE This house rules the physical self and the personality; in other words, the way the world sees you. It also describes influences and molding of early childhood; mannerisms; disposition and temperament; likes and dislikes; what you want in life and how you achieve it.

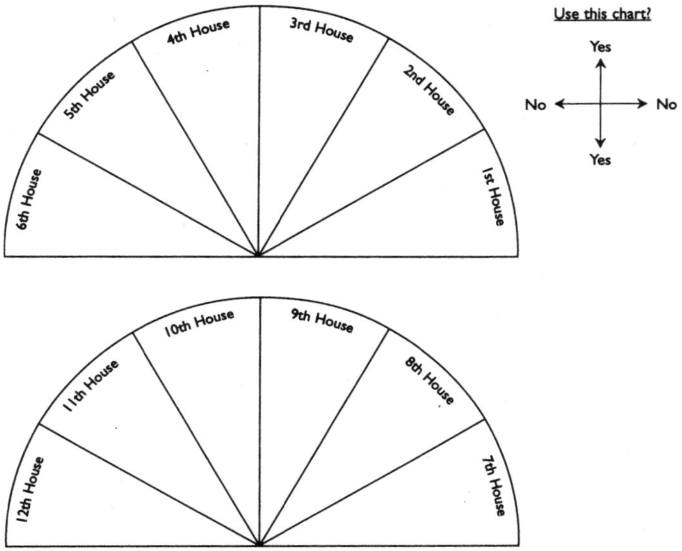

Astrological Houses Chart

SECOND HOUSE This house has to do with money; movable possessions; earning abilities and the way you handle money; self-esteem.

THIRD HOUSE This house refers to your siblings and relatives and the family ties you do or do not have. It also influences your knowledge; environment; short trips; communications; the way you think, speak, and write; logic; memory; manual skill; early education and the ability to learn.

FOURTH HOUSE This is the house of the home and immediate family; the foundation of your present life. It also points to the father's character and influence; your background and roots; what you keep protected and secluded from the world.

FIFTH HOUSE This area symbolizes the heart, romance, love affairs, and your sexual nature in general. It also points to children; entertainment; creativity; new undertakings; gambling; pets and playmates.

SIXTH HOUSE This house is for personal responsibilities, and the way you do or do not handle them. It also shows the influences of colleagues and employees; work; service to others; health; illnesses brought on by worry or emotional upsets.

SEVENTH HOUSE An area of primary relationships and partnerships, this house reveals marriage; divorce; remarriage; business and legal affairs; contracts; open enemies; adversaries in the business world; the public.

EIGHTH HOUSE This house points to joint resources; investments; taxes; inheritances; debts of partner; death and rebirth or regeneration; spiritual transformation; surgeries; psychic powers or knowledge; occult studies.

NINTH HOUSE This is the house of social areas; higher education; philosophy; religion; law, long-distance travel; foreign places and peoples; your public expression of ideas; publishing.

TENTH HOUSE This is the area of reputation; career; social responsibilities; ambition; attainment; outward expression of talents. It also reveals the mother's influence and character on your life.

ELEVENTH HOUSE This house governs your goals; friends; social values; teamwork; long-term dreams and wishes; involvement with groups and organizations; idealism and visions.

TWELFTH HOUSE This last astrological house is concerned with the subconscious; past karma; privacy; retreat or confinement; prisons; hospitals; secret enemies; self-defeat or self-undoing; troubles; secrets; sorrows; disappointments and troubles; accidents; psychic powers.

The chart of the planets (below) shows the different ways we relate to life. It is best used for questions such as "What planetary energy do I need in my life?" or "What planet causes me stress?" Other good questions are "What is the best planetary energy for me?" or "Which is the most challenging planetary energy for me?"

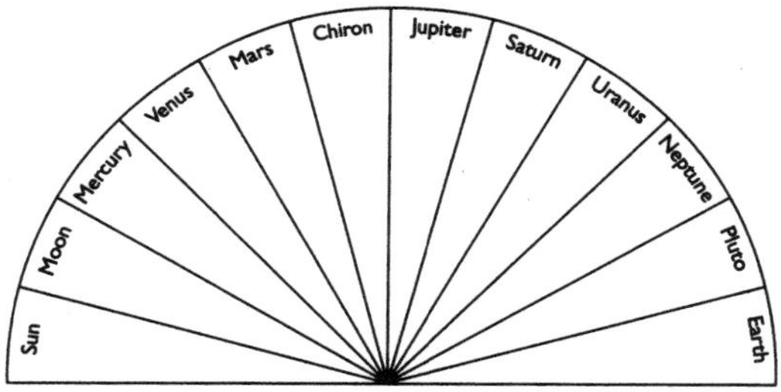

Planets Chart

This chart is composed of the five inner visible planets and the two luminaries that most strongly affect our lives, the three outer invisible planets, and Chiron, which is now being used more and more by astrologers. The five inner visible planets are Mercury, Venus, Mars, Jupiter, and Saturn, while the two luminaries are the Sun and the Moon. These seven "planets" were known and used by ancient astrologers long before there were telescopes to prove their existence.

The three outer invisible planets are Uranus, Neptune, and Pluto. The three outer planets are fairly new to astrology, for Uranus was only discovered in 1781, Neptune in 1846, and Pluto in 1930.

Chiron (pronounced Kyron) has an orbit between Saturn and Uranus, but which also allows it sometimes to wander between Jupiter and Saturn. Charles T. Kowal of the Hale Observatories in Pasadena, California, discovered it in 1977. Chiron is larger than any asteroid, yet smaller than a planet. Not certain how Chiron should be classified, astronomers coined the name "planetoid," which means "like a planet." Its orbit is elliptical and takes fifty years to complete. This planetoid is named after the Greek centaur Chiron.

The inner planets and luminaries directly affect the way we live our lives—our personalities, our thoughts and feelings, our energies, our relationships, and the way we react to happenings around us. The outer planets affect less tangible aspects of life—our willingness and resolution to break from the past and create new paths, our awareness and sensitivity to the psychic and spiritual, and our ability to ride through transformations and begin renewals.

The chart of the planets is best used for certain kinds of questions such as:

"How can I deal with my parents?"

"What will occur if I make a specific change?"

"How should I handle a problem (name it)?"

Because it is possible for you to respond to any given situation in more than one way, it is best to dowse the chart at least twice, if not more times. This will show you all the possible ways you can use your individual energies and personality.

SUN Your outer personality; the individuality you show to the world; your active, energetic side; the conscious mind; will.

MOON Your inner personality; the side you rarely show to the world; the reflective, more emotional side; past conditioning that affects all your thoughts; the subconscious mind; the emotions; sensitivity; spontaneity; hidden personality.

MERCURY The mind and conscious thought; messages or messenger; the way you communicate; intelligence; perception; speech; memory; sarcasm; deceit; coldness.

VENUS The energy you give or demand in love; creative ability; your ability to love at all; happiness; indulgence; the arts; harmony; sensuality.

MARS Your assertiveness or lack of it; the willpower and drive you possess; your energy in general; wants and desires; drive; initiative; courage; violence; selfishness; aggression.

JUPITER Good fortune, expansion; abundance; wisdom; success; over-confidence; extravagance; ethics; opportunity; faith; understanding; higher education; philosophy; overbearing; luck; morals; optimism.

SATURN Restrictions and self-limitations; the way you handle responsibility; your commitment to any person or goal; tests and lessons; fear; force of circumstances; discipline; limitations; order; obstacles; authority conflicts; time; ambition; material status; work; doubt; repression; responsibility; pessimism.

CHIRON The Wounded Healer; ancestral heritage; the black sheep or outsider; release and expansion; healing in a personal and universal sense; self-discovery; the inner teacher; our contributions to life; finding one's purpose in life.

URANUS Radical and sudden changes; the intuition; the degree to which you may or may not separate yourself from others; change; originality; upheaval; revolution; inventive; independence; unconventional turn of mind; disruption; unique; groups; unexpected; erratic; truth; reform; science; metaphysics; astrology; chaos; outsiders.

NEPTUNE Spiritual; mysterious; mystical; psychic; delusions; sensitivity; escape; victim; compassion; suffering; healing; drugs; alcohol; fantasy; dissolving; confusing; imagination; artistic; visionary; clairvoyant.

PLUTO Transformation; illumination; confrontation; regenerative forces; destruction; destiny; obsession; hidden things; birth and rebirth; insight; empowering; inner truth.

Burning incense many times will change the vibrations and atmosphere of a room or house. In many ways this is similar to the art of aromatherapy. Use the incense fan charts (below) to determine which incense will be best for you at any given time and for any given problem. Often the immediate personal environment becomes contaminated with negative vibrations, whether from interaction of the people living there or by negative-minded people who visit. After dowsing with the pendulum for an incense, read the following descriptions to further clarify what may be happening and why this incense would help. Remember to use the Yes/No indicator to help you get through the charts more quickly.

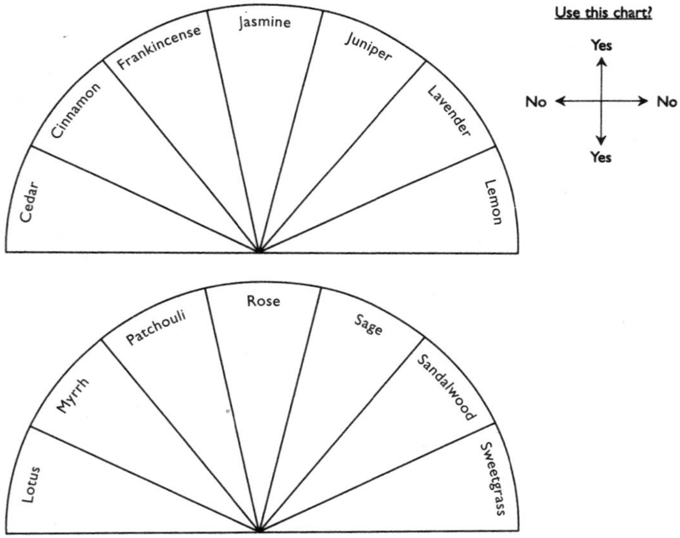

Incense and Aromatherapy Chart

CEDAR Purification of an environment; repels evil spirits; associated with the summer solstice.

CINNAMON Protection; healing; prosperity; stimulates; clairvoyance.

FRANKINCENSE Protection; purification; exorcism; raises vibrations.

JASMINE Love; prosperity.

JUNIPER Protection; especially from accidents; repels thieves; attracts a lover.

LAVENDER Purification; protection; love; helps to reveal ghosts; aids in sleep.

LEMON Purification; aids in prophecy and divination.

LOTUS Fertility; visions; helps with magick.

MYRRH Protection; purification; blesses an environment; helps with exorcisms.

PATCHOULI Attracts love and passion; protection; aids in clairvoyance and divination.

ROSE Attracts love; fertility; clairvoyance; aids sleep.

SAGE Purification; healing; prosperity.

SANDALWOOD Removes fears; protection; purification of an atmosphere; healing.

SWEETGRASS Purification; brings blessings.

The gemstone chart (see pages 286–87) is divided into seven charts for greater ease in divining. Use these charts when you need to know what gemstones to wear or carry with you on an occasion. Wearing or carrying certain stones will add their vibration to your own vibrations, either strengthening what you need to face an event or adding a vibration in which you may be temporarily deficient. Remember to use Yes/No indicators to help you get through the charts more quickly.

AGATE Grounding; strengthening the mind and body; discovering the truth; protection.

AMAZONITE Soothes the nerves; aligns the mental and spiritual bodies; creative inspiration.

AMBER Discovering past lives; calms fears; clears mental confusion.

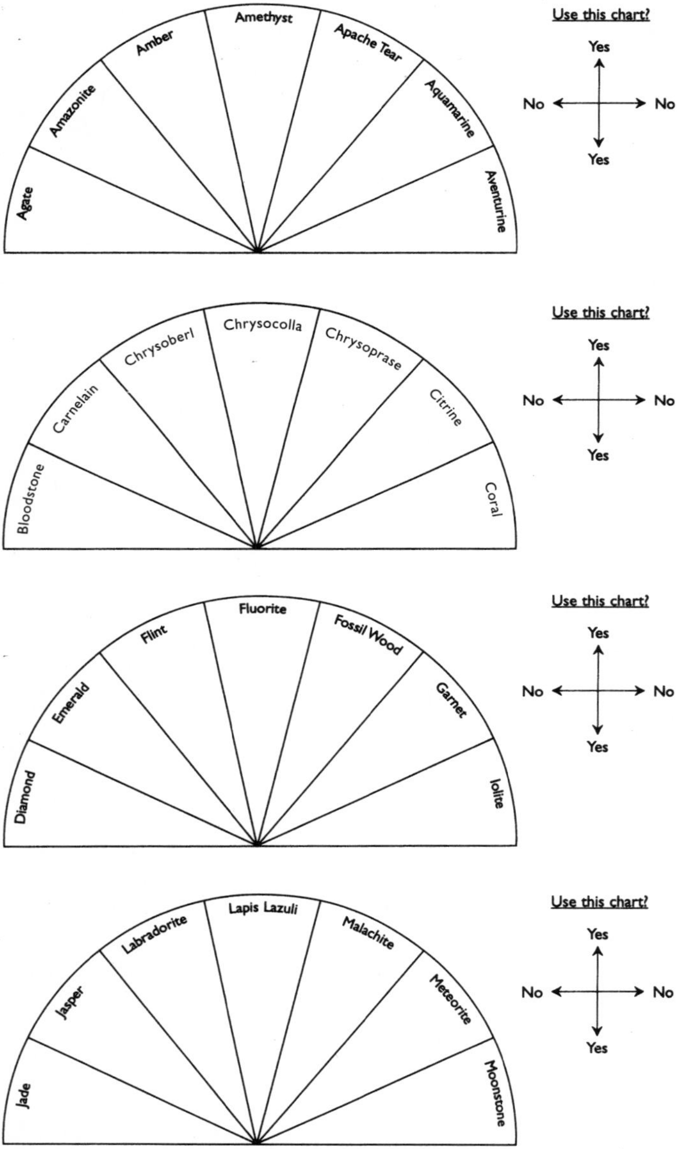

Gemstones Chart

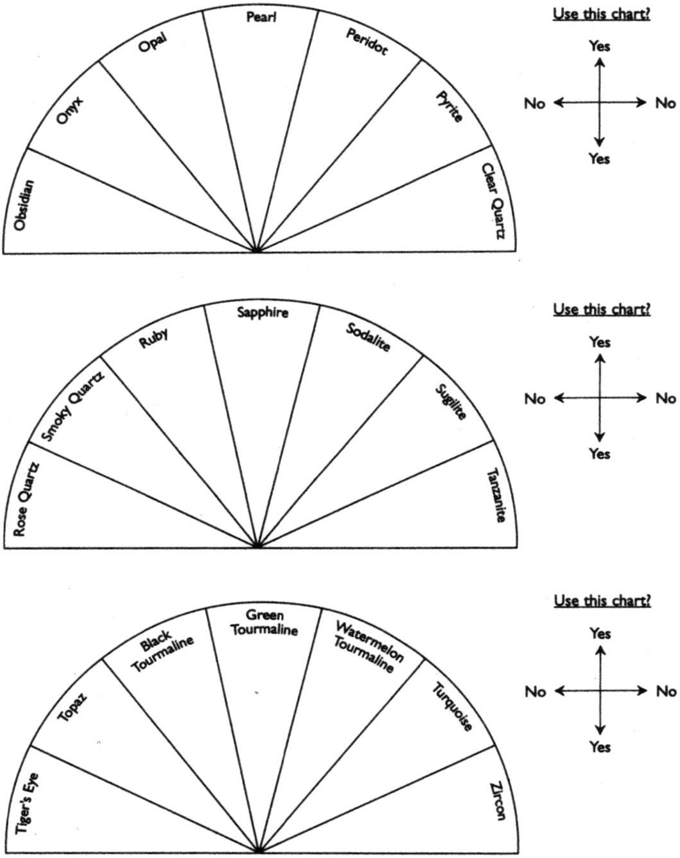

Gemstones Chart

AMETHYST Promotes dreams; attracts good fortune; brings justice in court cases.

APACHE TEAR Channels higher beings and spirit guides.

AQUAMARINE Clears the mind; promotes creativity; banishes fear; balances the emotions and brings calmness.

AVENTURINE Releases anxieties; balances and calms; protection.

BLOODSTONE Guards against deceptions and cheating; prosperity; self-confidence.

CARNELIAN Speeds manifestation of desires; aligns the physical, mental, emotional, and spiritual bodies.

CHRYSOBERL Increases psychic awareness; strengthens the memory; prevents psychic manipulation by others.

CHRYSOCOLLA Clears away fears, guilt, and tensions; helps in dealing with anger connected with abuse; enhances creativity.

CITRINE Raises the self-esteem; protects the aura from negative influences; helps in dealing with karmic events.

CORAL Calms the emotions; repels negative thoughts from others.

DIAMOND Helps to align the thoughts with the Higher Self; courage; victory.

EMERALD Attracts prosperity; wards off negatives; enhances dreams and meditations.

FLINT Helps survivors recover from abuse.

FLUORITE Increases concentration; cleanses the aura; transformation.

FOSSIL WOOD Attracts good luck; screens out negatives; eases stress.

GARNET Lifts depression; brings business opportunities; prevents nightmares.

IOLITE Strengthens self-confidence; attracts friends.

JADE Increases fertility in all areas; balances the emotions; calms.

JASPER Protects and grounds; use for long-term changes.

LABRADORITE Stimulates physical energy and activity; protects and balances.

LAPIS LAZULI Releases tension and anxiety; balances all the chakras; attracts a better job.

MALACHITE Repels evil spirits and accidents; helps with sleep; balances and heals all the chakras.

METEORITE Reveals past lives; expands the awareness.

MOONSTONE Helps to contact spiritual teachers; opens the psychic abilities.

OBSIDIAN Grounds spiritual energy; protects; clears subconscious blockages.

ONYX Balances the emotions; self-control; helps in resolving past life problems.

OPAL Enhances the intuition; balances the emotions; connects with the higher realms.

PEARL Balances and heals all the chakras; helps in the search for higher wisdom and truth; absorbs negatives.

PERIDOT Reduces stress; stimulates the mind; opens doors to opportunities.

PYRITE Increases self-esteem; harmonizes relationships; strengthens the will.

CLEAR QUARTZ Stimulates thinking; balances and harmonizes; repels negatives; enhances communications with the spirit world; helps with psychic powers.

ROSE QUARTZ Heals emotional wounds; releases negative emotions; breaks up blockages; brings love.

SMOKY QUARTZ Grounds and centers; breaks up subconscious blockages; strengthens dream messages; absorbs negatives.

RUBY Removes limitations; spiritual love; wisdom; stabilizes.

SAPPHIRE Wards off poverty; breaks up confusion and blockages; aids in developing psychic powers.

SODALITE Calms and clears the mind; cuts through illusions; creates inner harmony.

SUGILITE Balances and heals all the chakras; opens the mind to higher influences.

TANZANITE Mellows out extremes in a personality; calms and balances emotions.

TIGER'S EYE Strengthens personal power; brings good luck; balances the emotions.

TOPAZ Dispels nightmares; repels depression and negative influences; prevents accidents.

TOURMALINE, BLACK Processes information from past lives; releases deeply buried negative emotions.

TOURMALINE, GREEN Regenerates; attracts prosperity; inspires creative ideas.

TOURMALINE, WATERMELON Removes imbalances and guilt; helps to solve problems.

TURQUOISE A master healer stone; enhances meditation; brings emotional balance; protects; helps to discover answers to life problems.

ZIRCON Brings peace with oneself; creates unity with spiritual teachers.

Many people have become familiar with the Native American concept of totem animals and want to know how to use them in their daily life. Others are aware that the Celts practiced a form of shamanism that incorporated animal allies. The charts for animal allies and totem animals, of which there are six (see pages 291–92), can help you determine which animals you should focus on in order to attract certain animal characteristics. These characteristics are blended into the human aura for a brief period of time to help one cope with a troublesome situation or to aid in bringing the auric vibrations back into balance. Remember to use the Yes/No indicators to help you get through the charts more quickly.

ANT Orderliness; diligent work; planning; stamina; determination.

ANTELOPE Learning to be aware when faced with new circumstances; recognizing and listening to your survival instincts.

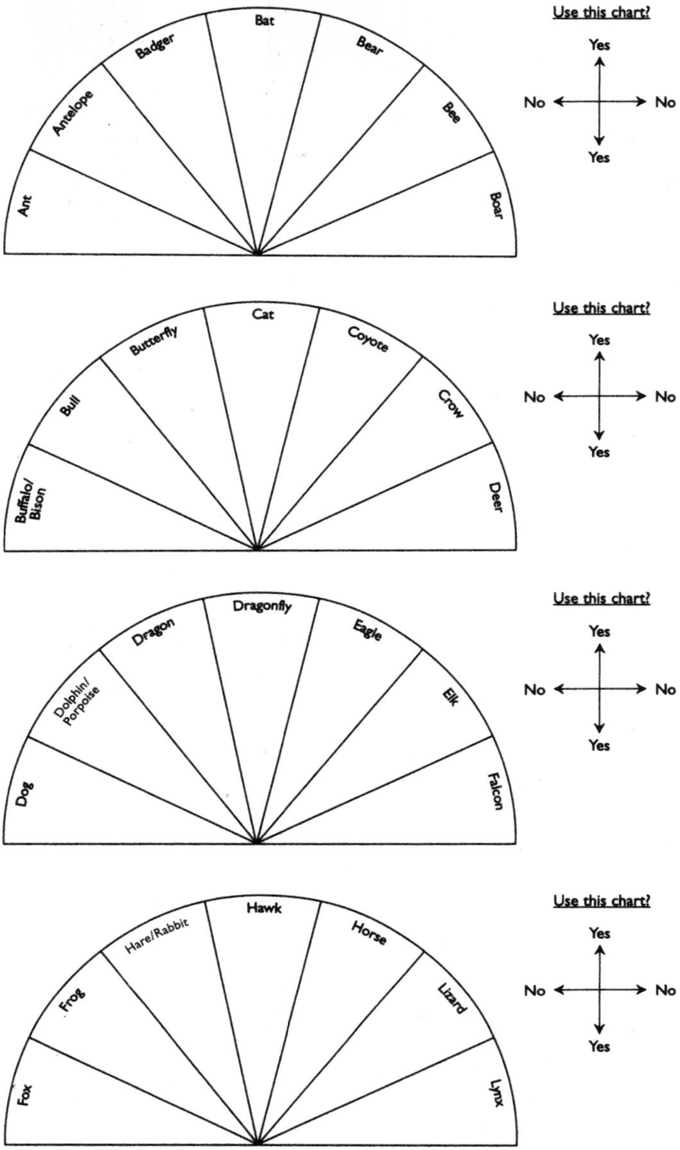

Animal Allies or Totems Chart

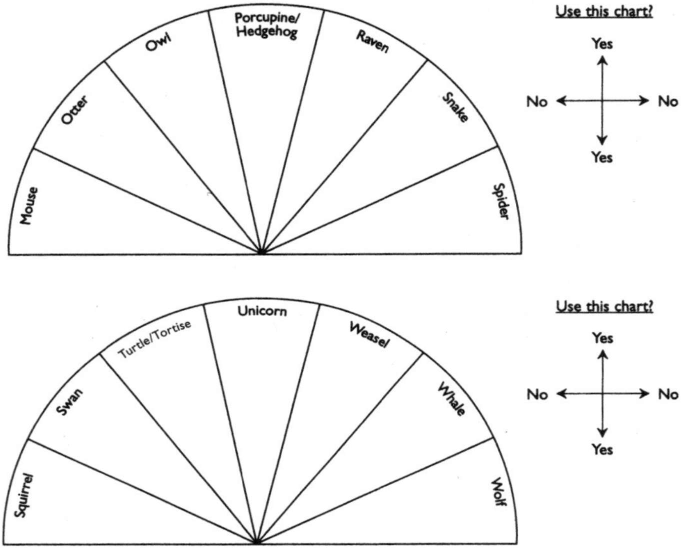

Animal Allies or Totems Chart

BADGER Standing up for your rights; learning when to release and when to control anger.

BAT Avoiding obstacles and negative people; leaping barriers; seeing the patterns in your past lives that influence this life.

BEAR Strength; stamina; harmony in the family and life; listening to dreams.

BEE Planning for the future; prosperity; understanding reincarnation.

BUFFALO/BISON Working with spirit forces to accomplish goals; establishing a family; abundance; courage.

BULL Fertility; strength; abundance; protection.

BUTTERFLY Transformation within this life.

CAT Recognizing when to fight and when to retreat; developing independence.

COYOTE Recognizing and grasping opportunities; unveiling tricksters.

CROW Boldness and cunning when faced with enemies; keeping your eyes on your goal; releases painful past memories.

DEER Being alert to danger; developing poise and grace; abundance; learning from dreams; psychic abilities.

DOG Breaking through illusions to the truth; finding companionship; protection.

DOLPHIN/PORPOISE Freedom; eloquence; changes; discover the truth; learning to communicate; harmony; creating balance in your life.

DRAGON Protection; transformation of your life; spiritual knowledge.

DRAGONFLY Visions; mystical messages through dreams; breaking down illusions so the truth may be seen.

EAGLE Strength; courage; wisdom; fearlessness in the face of great odds; discovering the overall pattern of your life and spiritual growth.

ELK Strength; stamina; learning to pace yourself in a job.

FALCON Healing; coming to terms with death; learning magick.

FOX Stealth; wisdom; cunning; masking your intentions when dealing with troublesome people.

FROG Initiations and transformations; dispelling negative vibrations; a new cycle in life.

HARE/RABBIT Transformation; quick thinking; learning to stop worrying.

HAWK Recalling past lives; being observant; overcoming problems; making decisions.

HORSE Freedom; friendship and cooperation; taking journeys.

LIZARD Facing and defeating your fears; learning spiritual knowledge from dreams and astral travel; handling difficult situations.

LYNX Developing divination skills and the psychic senses; understanding mystical secrets; looking within yourself and facing the truth.

MOUSE Developing the ability to remain inconspicuous when necessary; watching for small details when signing contracts.

OTTER Recovering from a crisis; enjoying life; learning to trust.

OWL Seeing through illusion; guidance in matters of dreams and astral travel; discovering hidden truth and secrets.

PORCUPINE/HEDGEHOG Building protective barriers that discourage enemies.

RAVEN Learning divination techniques; transformation; wisdom; creating or dealing with a change in consciousness.

SNAKE Facing your fears; connecting with psychic energy and spiritual initiation.

SPIDER Creativity; new life; industrious; patiently awaiting for opportunities; beginning a new project.

SQUIRREL Preparing for the future; moving to a higher level of consciousness.

SWAN Understanding dream symbols; spiritual evolvement; development of the intuition; keeping a serene exterior while dealing with private turmoil.

TURTLE/TORTOISE Developing patience and perseverance; giving yourself permission to slow down and enjoy life.

UNICORN Building individual power; gaining wisdom that will lead to success.

WEASEL Using cunning; stealth, and ingenuity to overcome enemies.

WHALE Developing positive relationships with your family and friends; learning psychic abilities.

WOLF Escaping dangerous enemies; outwitting enemies; learning from dreams; transformation.

Learning to use the pendulum in an effective manner can take you years, but these years will be filled with the excitement of learning more about yourself, your subconscious mind, your intuition, and the subtle effects of all these on your everyday life. Pendulum dowsing will open inner doors to greater psychic abilities, frequently enabling you to recall and use talents out of past lives. The truthfulness of your pendulum will depend upon your determination to see the truth, no matter how painful it may be at that moment. There is no greater experience than truth, for it sets us free of past and present shackles that hinder our spiritual growth. The pendulum can help you to become all you should have been and still can be.

PART IV

A LITTLE BOOK OF Healing Magick

What Is Healing Magick?

Healing magick. These two words describe a method of using spiritual connection, physical means, and magickal spells to heal the body, mind, and spirit, not only of humans, but also of animals. For tens of thousands of years, this method was the only technique used. And it was used successfully. Then "modern" medicine took over and decreed that only physicians trained in a certain way could heal and that the spiritual and magick did nothing. This viewpoint still exists.

The Origins of Magick

Originally, the word *magick,* which may come from the word magi, described the learning that was taught to the priests and the sages of the Medes and Persians. These healers were famed for their skill in working enchantments, which also included incantations, divinations, and astrology.

Many people get upset whenever the word magick is mentioned. However, magick is only supernatural until science explains it. An example is alchemy, which was a skill practiced in secret until chemistry was validated. Astrology was the foundation upon which astronomy was built. The use of magick wouldn't continue if it didn't get results, even if we don't understand exactly how it works.

However, today people are beginning to question this attitude. According to a number of recent surveys (not by physicians or hospitals), more than 60 percent of people believe in using alternative medicine, prayer, and/or magick along with orthodox medicine. Whenever the general populace questions enough about methods of healing, accepted techniques begin to change. Fortunately, more doctors and medical centers are becoming open to alternative healing methods.

The connection between healing and magick was a valid and successful concept from the beginning of the human race. The separation began when the healers of later cultures condemned magick as an invalid practice and separated it from healing.

The original definition of magick was not the same as the corrupted meaning attached to the word today. Don't bother to look up the word in any dictionary, as they only give the meaning attached to stage magicians. The true meaning of magick is to draw universal, spiritual energy from the Otherworld, mold it by concentrated thought into a specific desire, and release that energy-thought into this world to manifest. This definition applies to strong prayer as well as to magickal spells.

Many people who apply healing prayers to illnesses call the positive results miracles. Miracles have nothing to do with scientific reason or what a person supposedly does or doesn't deserve. This places miraculous events in the same category as the results that magick produces. In magick, the healer should never question whether the recipient is worthy of healing, but work on the belief that all humans are worthy of healing. The condition of each person's soul and what they do or don't deserve is between each individual and the Goddess/God. Miracles, whether by prayer or magick, don't have to make sense to us or the scientific world. If they did, they wouldn't be miracles.

You do not need to be a shaman to practice the healing in this book, nor do you have to be knowledgeable about magick or psychic healing. This book is for laypeople who are concerned about a loved one's illness or perhaps their own illnesses, and desire alternative ways to work for healing.

Magickal Healing in Practice

This book is not slanted toward any one religious group or idea. Goddess/God is known by hundreds of different names that all strive to define an unknowable force in the universe. There is no difference between the prayers to saints and the prayers to ancient deities. The same energy is attached to burning a candle at church as to burning a candle at home. The only difference may lie in the amount of concentration, determination, and desire put out by the healer and the patient.

For any healing to take place, healing magick requires total cooperation between the healer and the patient. The patient must take an active part. In other words, the patient must be responsible for their illness and do everything they can to facilitate the healing. Otherwise, the healing will not be permanent, if it occurs at all.

You should be aware that some patients, consciously or subconsciously, do not want to be healed. Some patients like the attention they get from their illness or the control they can exert over family members and friends because they are sick. No matter what you do, you will not be able to heal these people. All the time, effort, and energy you pour into trying to heal such a person will be wasted.

The same applies to the roles of family and friends in healing. If there is a persistent negative, pessimistic, or hateful attitude or atmosphere around a patient, it can harm instead of heal. At the very least, negative attitudes can interfere with healing. If this type of attitude exists in only one person, or in a small number of family and friends, the patient is best advised to sever communications with these people. However, that must be the patient's decision. This action will be of little use if the patient does not have other positive-minded friends and family left, unless the patient has a strong will and is willing to form new friendships. Positive support systems are vitally important to getting well.

Sometimes you will encounter a patient with a serious illness who truly wants to be healed, but the process doesn't seem to work no matter what you do. In these cases, it may be that the patient's lifespan is at its end. The patient may not consciously know this, but their subconscious does. When this happens, work for peace, spiritual harmony, and freedom from pain and fear.

Some of the methods presented in this book may not seem magickal at first, but they are. Remember, all magick requires that you draw upon universal energy for healing, that you mold it into a specific desire in your mind, and then release it to manifest in the here and now. It doesn't matter if the magickal process is prayer or spells, for the same rules apply to all magickal healing. The same rules apply whether you are a healer working on another person or a patient working on yourself.

You do not need to use all the methods mentioned here, but I do ask that you read the book in its entirety before choosing a method with which you feel comfortable. You may use any of the methods in any combination. In fact, using more than one method seems to raise more healing energy.

The practices in this book may also be used by the patient, either with or without a healer. The best healer is you, anyway. No healing, even if aided by the most proficient of psychic healers, will occur unless the patient cooperates and takes an active part.

A Few Words of Caution

Although the ideas and practices of alternative healing in connection with magick discussed in this book can be used by anyone at any time, they are meant to be used along with orthodox medicine, not to supplant it. I do not recommend that you stop orthodox treatment for any disease. And as a healer yourself, you should never recommend that any person stop orthodox treatment or medication in favor of something you think is better. Erroneous recommendations lead to legal problems.

Although this book does not address herbal medicine, I feel a word of warning on their use is needed. If you delve into the use of herbs for healing, be certain that you understand exactly how they will interact with any orthodox medicine before taking them. And never assume that the healing will be faster if you take more than the recommended amount of herbs. Herbal medicine acts slowly, so be patient.

Also take extreme care that you know the toxicity of certain herbs, regardless of what some books advise. For example, I know of one book on cancer that recommends toxic quantities of wormwood. Herbal medicine is an exact science and is best understood and practiced only if you train in the field or have the benefit of a person certified in herbal medicine.

A History of Healing Magick

Healers have been in demand from the beginning of humankind, for accidents and illnesses of the body, mind, and spirit have always been with us. These early spiritual healers were shamans; shamanism is the world's oldest spiritual healing profession. The traceable roots of shamanism date from the Stone Age, at least forty thousand years. However, common sense tells us that the profession of shamanism must go back even further, before humans felt any need to record their activities in cave paintings.

Although the descriptive word used to designate a shaman was different from culture to culture, the training and practices of a shaman were remarkably similar everywhere in the world, even today. In this book, the word *shaman* is used to simplify the description, although the word *shaman* comes only from the Tunguso-Manchurian dialect and means "to know."

People generally connect shamanism with the Eskimo, African, and Native American cultures. However, a branch called Celtic shamanism existed for centuries, finally dying out in Scotland and Ireland as the cultures succumbed to the power of implanted religions.

Out of necessity, the early shamans (both men and women) were a combination of healer, magician, and priest. Early peoples knew that healing, magick, and the spiritual were inexplicably intertwined and should not be separated. The primary purposes of shamans were, and still are, to travel to the Otherworld in their spiritual bodies, to work positive magick, and to mediate and communicate with spirits and deities in the Otherworld. In this way, they are able to retrieve information that is unknown on the ordinary levels of consciousness. This especially applied to healing of the body, mind, and spirit. Shamans needed their spiritual abilities (altered state of consciousness) to contact the Otherworld to determine the cause of any illness and what herbs or practices were necessary to treat the disease.

When tribes or clans became too large for the shaman to do all the work alone, this responsibility was frequently divided into two separate categories: priest-magician and healer. However, people in both categories were instructed in the same practices. For example, although healers focused on the healing arts, they also understood that a strong connection with spirit or the Otherworld and the magickal energy of that world were necessary for any healing to take place.

Throughout history, cultures continued to have their priest-healers who were required to know magick themselves or work closely with those who did. The ancient cultures of Sumer, Babylonia, Ur, and Egypt had groups of priests, healers, and magicians who were trained in certain temples and expected to work together. We know this because of the surviving clay tablets and papyri. Even the ancient Greeks had their shamanistic equivalents, particularly those who worked in the sacred asklepieia, or temples of the healing god Aesculapius. The patients in these Greek temples were treated by physical methods, magickally induced dream therapy, and communication with Aesculapius.

This treatment of the whole person by spiritual connection, physical methods, and magickal spells continued in the Middle East and Mediterranean areas until the end of the fifth century BCE, when Hippocrates of Cos appeared. His admonitions that only the body was involved in physical illness and that spiritual and magickal techniques were unnecessary and useless challenged the ancient premise that body, mind, and spirit were vitally connected. He declared that only physical methods could cure illness, an unfortunate attitude that has persisted in today's medicine. He did mention healing hands, but he did not mean healing with the hands. His limited definition of healing is still taught by every Western medical school.

Fortunately, many of the alternative healing practices of the Eastern cultures have survived and are in sharp contrast to Western medicine. In Western medicine, only dysfunction and disease are treated. Eastern healing treats the whole person. Western medicine views the patient as only a body. Eastern medicine views the patient as an inseparable combination of body, mind, and spirit, all of which interact constantly. This Eastern idea is known as holistic health.

In ancient China, the physician was paid only as long as the patient stayed healthy. As soon as the patient became sick, the payments stopped. Thus, physicians were motivated to help people heal quickly and keep them well. In Western medicine, some physicians view healing in terms of how many treatments and how much money they will receive for their services. Common sense will tell you that the ancient principles and ideas behind Eastern holistic medicine are more valuable to healing than those of a traditional Western physician. Unfortunately, Western ideas have corrupted some of the orthodox Eastern physicians. However, many of the ancient ideas of alternative healing practices behind Eastern healing have been kept alive and are still practiced.

We are fortunate today that the old knowledge of magickal healing is being reclaimed and presented to the reading public. The old methods have been refined and modernized to fit our present society and needs, a process that is vital in all healing methods. This makes it possible for anyone to combine magickal healing with orthodox treatment.

If your religious background makes you uncomfortable with certain healing methods in this book, skip them or convert them into an acceptable practice. Magick isn't static and is open to change. The magick doesn't occur because a certain spell is done in an exact manner, although doing such a spell will help you concentrate the healing energy. The magick lies in your finding a way to an altered state of consciousness in which you can mold universal energy and manifest it in this physical world.

The healing profession looks as if it may be coming full circle, and that is good. Sick people should be able to use every method at their disposal to get well again.

The Aura and the Chakras

Before you can effectively use any healing technique, you need to understand a few ancient and basic ideas. These ideas will help you work better, be more confident in what you are doing, and concentrate the healing energies in the correct places, which will make a huge difference in whether your healing efforts don't work, work a little, or work well.

Energy creates everything in the cosmos. Einstein's theory of relativity and his formula, $E = mc^2$, is based on that concept. However, Einstein was only rediscovering a very ancient truth known to many cultures. This universal, spiritual energy was called *mana* by the Polynesians, *prana* by the Hindus, and *ch'i* by the Chinese. Because everything is composed of energy, then everything, without exception, can be affected and influenced by energy. This definitely includes deliberately directed energy, whether positive or negative. This is the foundation of truth behind the workings of magick, which is the directing of energy for a specific purpose and the affecting of an idea, object, event, or person by this energy.

Auras

Every living body, whether human or animal, is surrounded by what is called an aura (also see page 258). Many cultures also believe that every object, whether animate or inanimate, has an aura, which is why we speak of a crystal or an area in nature as having vibrations.

The aura we will study here is the human aura. This aura consists of layers of various types of energy that surround the physical body. The aura's energy is affected by the universal energy that is everywhere in the cosmos. These layers are also affected by the energy molded by individual thought and action. The aura can be powerfully affected when that energy is gathered and directed by willpower.

The aura is a kind of electromagnetic field, and can be compared to the field that surrounds the earth. We can't ordinarily see the earth's electromagnetic field, but scientists know it exists because of gravity, the air it traps around the planet, and the way it makes a compass point to the north. This electromagnetic field around the earth gets denser as one moves closer to the planet from space. Without this field or atmosphere, the earth would have no life and would not be a living entity itself.

The same applies to the human aura. We are surrounded by an electromagnetic atmosphere, which allows us to exist. When this atmosphere becomes fatally contaminated or destroyed, the body dies. The inner layers of the aura, the ones closest to the physical body, are denser than the outer layers. This denseness also makes the inner layers of the aura easier to detect with the hands or a pendulum.

Many scientists have studied the existence of the aura within the last one hundred years or so. Mesmer called it magnetism, Jussieu the electric fluid, Reichenbach the odylic flames, de Rochas the exteriorized sensibility, and Dr. Baraduc the vital rays. The only two scientists, however, to discover a way to show the aura in scientific experiments were Dr. Walter Kilner and Dr. Semyon Kirlian.

Just after the turn of the twentieth century, Dr. Kilner, a British physician and not a psychic, created chemical dye screens using dicyanin dyes. These screens revealed the human aura to untrained eyes. He used these screens to diagnose various physical illnesses and mental conditions. He was extremely accurate and in 1911 wrote a book on the subject, *The Human Atmosphere*. This book is still in print under the title *The Aura*. Because what he learned was so unorthodox, Dr. Kilner was attacked by the medical profession and the hospital where he worked, and his medical license was revoked.

A weak version of his invention is found today in aura glasses. Actually, these glasses are nothing more than dark violet plastic held in a cardboard frame. You can get the same results with a piece of dark violet photographic lens plastic held over your eyes. The color helps to open the Third Eye or brow chakra and makes you more sensitive to seeing the aura. Aura glasses are fun to use but don't become dependent on them.

You can train yourself to see at least the two inner layers of the aura by using a simple technique. Stand in front of a mirror in a darkened bathroom. The only light should come from a half-open door or a dim nightlight. If you wear glasses or contact lenses, remove them; in this case, perfect sight is not beneficial. Look at yourself in the mirror. Focus your gaze slightly beyond your image and let your eyes go out of focus. You may find that squinting your eyes slightly will help. Take your time and don't try too hard. In a moment or so you will see a thin light around your body. This is your aura. In some cases, you may also see what appears to be another face overlaying your face. If this happens, you are seeing yourself in a past life.

If you have people to work with, you can use another technique. Have one person stand a few feet away from a blank dark wall or in the doorway to a darkened room. Place either a small candle at a safe distance behind them, or have a dim nightlight there. Everyone else should stand about four to eight feet away from this person, viewing their form against the dark background. Use the same eye instructions given above. Take turns looking at each other. In this way, you can see the differences in people's auras.

In 1939 a Russian couple, Valentina and Semyon Kirlian, developed high-frequency photography that revealed the aura on film. The Russians called this bioplasmic energy. Although Kirlian photography can record on film the state of health, mental conditions through means of energy moving around the body, and whether the emotions present at the time were positive or negative, the scientific world outside of Russia refused to accept this physical proof.

The most recent aura energy researcher is a Japanese physician named Hiroshi Motoyama. He has developed an electronic instrument that can measure the effect of acupuncture and chart the meridian lines in the body. The meridians are rivers of energy that run along specific pathways in the physical body. His findings have elicited little interest in the scientific community outside of Japan.

Knowing about the aura, universal energy and how it affects the aura, and how to use this energy to heal the aura is a vitally important part of magickal healing. If the inner layers of the aura are sick, the physical body will have disease. If the outer layers have problems, it is possible to prevent this trouble from moving closer and affecting the body. All disease works from the outer layers of the aura inward, until it manifests in the physical form.

Some people are born able to see the auras of others, while most others can train themselves to see it. And with just a little training anyone can feel the aura. We all feel it subconsciously and react to certain people getting too close to us. This reaction occurs because a person's aura may not feel comfortable when it comes in contact with ours.

As a beginner, don't have unrealistic expectations of what you will see or how it will feel when working with the aura. If you have expectations of some flashy or really spectacular occurrence, you will be disappointed. Most psychics don't receive flashy impressions. Good psychics never gush on about violent colors, reciprocating movements (whatever that is), or dissociate harmonics. They are more likely to feel hot, cold, prickly, or a flare of energy within an aura. Some don't ever see colors but see only light. Some don't see either of these, but flashes of colors or symbols in their mind. Remember, your experiences will likely be different from those of other aura readers and workers, so don't judge yourself by them. Also, your experiences may change as you practice aura healing and become more comfortable with it.

I have found that the aura itself is composed of nine layers. Not all writers will agree with me about the composition of these layers, their numbers, or what they reflect. I base my information on personal experience. The best way to learn about the aura is to start with simple exercises to find your own energy field.

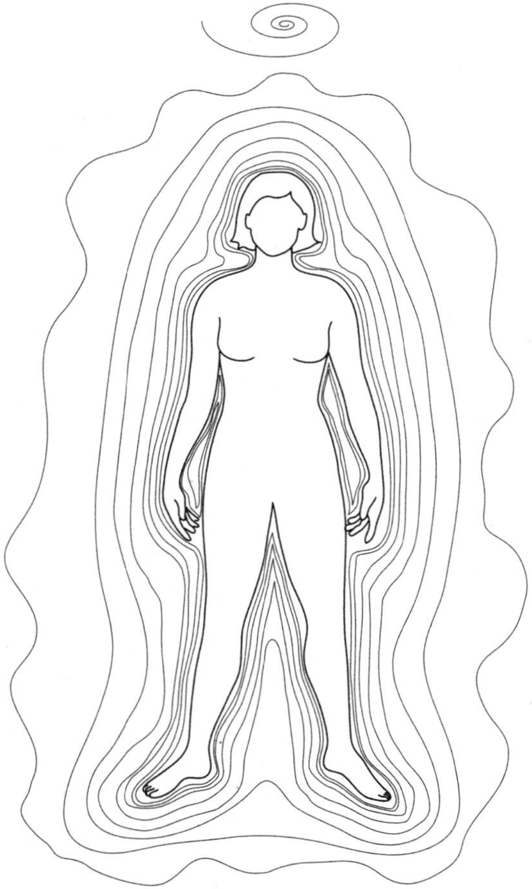

Nine Layers of Aura

The Nine Layers of the Aura

The **etheric body**, the first aura layer, is very close to the physical body, sometimes only a matter of a half-inch or less away from it. It reinforces the shape of the physical form so that the soul or spirit will be contained. It corresponds to the root chakra.

The **physical body,** the second layer, is tightly connected to the first layer. This layer reflects exactly what is going on in the body at any time and is associated with the belly chakra.

The **emotional body** is the third layer. Our emotions and our feelings shape this layer and it corresponds to the solar plexus chakra.

The **mental body** is the fourth layer. It is directly affected and impacted by our thoughts and how strongly we think them. It is associated with the heart chakra.

The **astral body** is the fifth layer, the essence that links us to the astral plane. The astral plane is where many guiding spirits, guardian angels, and ancestral beings live, as well as where deceased people continue their existence. We travel in the astral body when we sleep at night, when we do shamanic journeys, sometimes during deep meditations, or whenever we have a near-death experience. This layer is associated with the throat chakra. The first five layers of the aura are the ones most commonly seen with the physical eyes.

The sixth layer links us to **parallel universes**, other dimensions, and cross-time travel. It is also deeply linked to psychic phenomena. It is associated with the brow chakra.

The seventh layer is associated with the **past, present, and future**. It will often hold clues to past life experiences that are influencing the present life. It is associated with the seventh, or crown chakra. However, layers six through nine are difficult to find and read, particularly for healers without a lot of experience.

The eighth layer is an iridescent egg-shaped layer that can extend as much as four feet beyond the physical body and often has waves of energy rippling through it. This layer reflects the **spiritual growth and**

connection, or lack of it, in the patient. It is connected with the eighth, or transpersonal chakra, that lies above the head.

The ninth layer, sometimes called the **ketheric layer**, is the only layer that does not completely surround the physical body. Instead, it exists as a small whirling vortex above all the other layers. Because it is associated with the ninth chakra, or universal chakra, it connects all the other layers with the world and energies of spirit.

As a beginner, do not expect to detect all the layers. It is uncommon for healers to feel more than the first three or four layers until they have practiced for a very long time.

Energy Flowing between Hands

Aura Healing Exercises

The first exercise is simple. Work in a positive, relaxed atmosphere where you won't feel self-conscious about what you are doing. Rub your hands briskly together for a few seconds. Then hold your hands, palms facing. You will feel a warm, tingling ball of invisible energy between the palms. Slowly move your hands away from each other until you feel the tingling and warmth begin to dissipate. Move your hands back toward each other until you can feel the sensation again. You have just felt the extent of your own aura between your hands.

Practice this exercise until you are comfortable doing it. You will discover that the extent of your aura will change according to your physical condition and mental attitude. If you are tired or depressed, the aura draws in upon itself and appears to become smaller. When you are elated and feeling refreshed, the aura will expand.

Many healers will rub their hands together just before working on a healing. This sensitizes the minor chakra centers in the palms of the hands and makes them open up for the drawing in and giving out of universal energy. This action will also make the hands more sensitive to the aura of the person on whom they are working.

The next exercise requires a partner. If you don't have a human partner, you can work with a pet. Rub your hands briskly together as before. Then, keeping your hands about two to four inches from the partner's body, move your hands up and down and around their body. You will feel the same warm, tingling feeling emanating from them. This is their aura. You are feeling the dense inner layers of the electromagnetic field that surrounds them.

If you discover a place that seems hotter or colder than the rest of the aura, you have discovered a possible trouble spot. You can pour universal energy into this spot by holding your hand there and visualizing white light pouring into it. Visualization requires that you trust your instincts to make the connection with universal energy and pour it freely through your own aura and body into the patient. Without visualizing, you will pour personal energy into the patient, not universal energy. This will cause you to leave yourself depleted and possibly vulnerable to illnesses. If done properly, you should feel exhilarated because of the influx of universal energy, some of which will remain within your own aura.

If the patient is extremely ill, you may not be able to pour in universal energy fast enough. In this case, it is possible for the patient to drain off your own aura's energy as well. This psychic draining happened to me when my husband was unconscious with cancer. He was drawing off energy faster than I could channel it. I allowed it to happen so he could be healed, but most people may not be able to stand the exhaustion that follows. I chose to put myself in a precarious position because I was determined that he would not die. Many healers cannot stand up under such an onslaught, so think carefully before you allow this to happen.

Unfortunately, you may also experience this psychic draining from people who are not ill. Sometimes they are referred to as the psychic vampires because they feed on the energies of other people. Most people guilty of this don't realize on a conscious level what they are doing. They can be the friends who show up feeling depressed and miserable but who leave full of energy. Then you feel depressed and tired. The only way to defend yourself from such people is to throw up a blue psychic shield around you and hope for the best. Or avoid these vampires entirely. To construct a psychic shield, visualize yourself surrounded by brilliant blue light, or see yourself wearing shining blue armor. Pour more energy into this shield if you feel it weakening.

If you are a novice at aura healing, or if you don't feel comfortable with the draining that can happen during a healing, break the connection at once. Immediately wash your hands or at least wipe them several times against your legs or sides to make certain the connection is broken. This is a good method to practice whenever you have completed an aura healing, as it makes certain the auras' ties are broken.

Sometimes, you will discover what is known as a flare in an aura. In this case, the field abnormally jumps out from the person's aura in a long flare. These flares are usually caused by emotional distress of some kind. Left unattended, they can burn a hole in the aura's layers and let in diseases. Touching a flare may bring with it mental images or feelings of the emotion that caused the problem. If you suddenly feel anger, sadness, or depression in a flare, that is a good indication that the patient is either going through or just passed through intense events that triggered such feelings.

Again, try to seal the hole with universal energy. You may have to smooth over this flare several times before it will stay in its proper place. However, unless the emotional distress is remedied, the flare will soon pop out in the aura again. As in all healings, the patient must actively take a part in their own healing and be responsible enough to correct what needs correcting on a physical level.

Every time you touch an aura in healing, even for a brief moment, you may make a significant change, so be certain you are in a positive frame of mind. Otherwise, you may transfer negative energy even though you don't mean to. Always finish an aura reading or healing by swiftly moving your hands from the top to the bottom of the aura, thus sealing it again.

You need to practice touching auras as much as you can with a variety of people. For this reason, it is nice to work with a group of people studying aura healing. In this way you can acquaint yourself with different auras and broaden your own understanding of the subject. Also, you will notice that an aura will change from one time to the next, depending upon what health or life conditions the person is experiencing.

Chakras

The aura is closely connected with what are called chakras (also see page 252). *Chakra* is a Hindu word that means "wheel of fire." Traditionally, there are seven major chakras, although there are many minor chakras also. The chakras are whirling vortexes of energy in the aura and etheric body that suck in universal energy when they are working properly. If partially or completely blocked, a chakra will cause a breakdown in physical, mental, emotional, or spiritual health. This results in illness.

In Hindu belief, the *prana*, which is universe energy, comes in seven colors that match the seven major chakras of the human body. These colored universal rays constantly move into and out of well-balanced chakras, keeping the body healthy and vital. If you want to do complete magickal healing, you need to acquaint yourself with these chakras, where they are, what they do, and learn how to put them into balance.

There are eleven important chakras of the etheric body, and a gemstone is associated with each chakra. Some writers believe there are thirty-two major and minor chakras, but these eleven are the most important in healing.

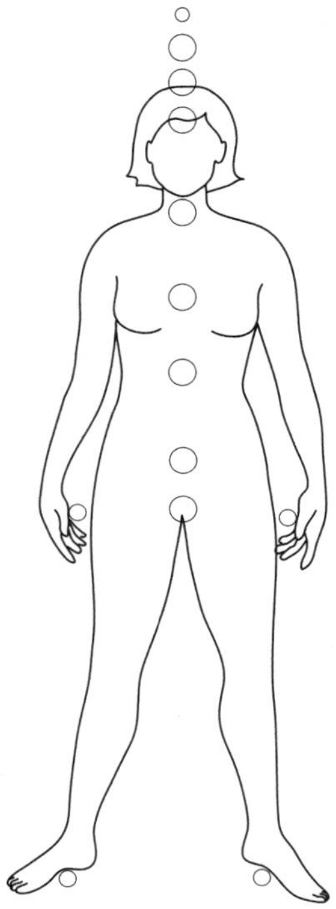

The Chakras

The chakras radiate out from the spinal column to the front of the body and connect with the etheric body, or that portion of the aura that is closest to the physical body. Healthy chakra colors are pure, not dark or muddy. Impure colors signal a disease or possible problem. The size, shape, and intensity of the colors reveal the development and health of each person. Partially blocked chakras are common, because we live in an imperfect physical world and are not perfect beings.

As with the aura, not all healers will see the chakras. However, they can be felt with the hands and imbalances will respond to a pendulum. Sometimes the chakras will create a feeling of color or condition in your mind. Learn to trust your instincts when working with the chakras for healing. Your first impression will likely be correct.

Never work on just one chakra, particularly the root chakra. Overstimulating one chakra will cause major imbalance in all of them. You can do major harm by working on a single chakra. Instead, work on all seven major chakras during a healing, beginning with the root chakra and working up to the crown chakra.

You will notice in reading the descriptions of the chakras that diseases can be related to more than one chakra. This happens because the chakras are all connected.

The Eleven Chakras

The first chakra is the **root chakra**. This is found at the base of the spinal column. The traditional color is red, and the associated glands are the ovaries and testes. This is the survival center and corresponds to physical needs and survival instincts, procreative urges, willpower, and the establishment of success or failure. Imbalance in this chakra can cause circulation problems, depression, infertility because of slow ovulation rates or low sperm count, low energy, irritable bowel syndrome, colitis, spastic colon, Crohn's disease, chronic constipation, adrenal dysfunction, Addison's disease, depression, chronic fatigue, allergies, anxiety, premature aging, anemia, frostbite, neuralgia, paralysis, or troubles with the menses. Stones: Garnet, black obsidian, smoky quartz, hematite, black onyx.

The second chakra is the **belly chakra**, sometimes known as the spleen chakra. It lies just below the navel in the center of the abdomen. Its color is orange and the associated glands are the adrenal glands that lie atop each kidney. This chakra is vital because it transforms lower energy into higher. Blockage is common because many diseases occur from mental or emotional patterns of thought or emotional traumas. Work on this chakra for many types of nervousness, eczema, difficult skin diseases, coughs, exhaustion, menstrual cramps, arthritis, sexual disorders, the kidneys, worry, defensiveness, hatred, menopausal problems, mood changes, hormonal decline, urological problems, impotence, prostate and testicular problems, trouble with the lower back, and uterine, cervical, and other general sex organ difficulties. Stones: Carnelian, Mexican fire opal.

The **solar plexus chakra** lies just above the navel in the center of the abdomen. Its traditional color is yellow; it is associated with the islands of Langerhans located on the pancreas. These glands regulate the amount of insulin released into the body. Clear this chakra when working on stomach and duodenal ulcers, diabetes, insomnia, flu, fear, exhaustion, indigestion, constipation, irritable bowel syndrome, malabsorption syndrome, hepatitis, gallbladder trouble, cirrhosis of the liver, pancreatitis, diabetes, swelling of the spleen, all types of abdominal cancers, emotional frustration, deep emotional pain, bitterness, and deep fear. Stones: Golden amber, tiger's eye, citrine, green fluorite, malachite.

These three lower chakras are the most earthy and are connected with earthly emotions and needs as well as energies. The next four upper chakras are more closely connected with a mixture of earthly and spiritual energies.

The **heart chakra** is located in the center of the upper chest. Its color is green, and the associated gland is the thymus. Unblock this chakra when working on diseases of the heart and lungs, high blood pressure, coronary artery disease, arteriosclerosis, asthma, chronic obstructive lung disease, the stomach, intestinal trouble and ulcers, the eyes, sunburn, headaches, infections, difficulty with the blood and bones (particularly with cancer in these areas), repressed emotional pain, insecurity, deep loneliness or love loss, autoimmune disorders such as lupus, rheumatoid arthritis, and polymyositis. Stones: Green jade, aventurine, rose quartz, watermelon tourmaline, chrysoprase, malachite.

The **throat chakra** is in the front area of the throat just above the points of the collarbone. Its color is electric blue or turquoise and it is associated with the thyroid glands. Use healing on this chakra for pain, burns, sleep, calming of emotions, headaches, inflammations, infections, swellings, fever, menstrual cramps, laryngitis, colds, flu, tonsillitis, mastoiditis, poor thyroid function, chronic laryngitis, parathyroid gland lesions, esophageal cancer, laryngeal cancer, and irritations of the throat, sinuses, and the nose. Stones: Azurite, lapis lazuli, chrysocolla, turquoise, blue lace agate.

The **brow chakra** is located in the center of the forehead, between and just above the eyes. This is also the area of the psychic Third Eye. Its color is indigo or a bluish purple; its gland is the pineal. Clear this chakra for headaches, muscle spasms in the neck and shoulders, deafness, mental and nervous disorders, pneumonia, eye and nose disease, hypothyroidism, hyperthyroidism, anxiety, depression, insomnia, Alzheimer's disease, migraines, strokes, multiple sclerosis, chronic pain, and lingering negativity of thought. Stones: Sodalite, sugilite, amethyst, purple fluorite, lapis lazuli.

The **crown chakra** is located at the top of the head. Its gland is the pituitary, and its color is violet or white. Rarely you will see gold in this chakra. Spiritual awakening in this area will connect the person to the eighth and ninth chakras, which are associated with realms of high spiritual growth. Unblock this chakra for stress, sleep problems, stress diseases, nervousness, low melatonin secretion, low immunity, diseases of the physical brain, spiritual imbalances, cataracts, mental disorders, and tumors and diseases of the scalp, skull, and brain. Stones: Amethyst, clear quartz; blue, white, or gold fluorite.

The eighth chakra is the **transpersonal chakra**, which lies about eighteen inches above the crown of the head and is not directly connected with the physical body. It is a transitional chakra that mediates between the physical and the spiritual. Its color is pure white or a flashing of rainbow colors, as seen in a crystal when exposed to sunlight. No physical diseases are directly associated with this chakra. However, on rare occasions you may see a deep spiritual disease here, one that has lingered or continued through several lifetimes. Stone: Clear quartz crystal.

The ninth chakra, or **universal chakra**, lies about six inches above the transpersonal chakra. This chakra is totally disconnected from the physical and has only connections with the pure spiritual part of a human. It is a direct pipeline for each person with the Goddess/God or Supreme Universal Force. No diseases are ever found in this chakra, although it may be almost completely closed due to lack of spiritual growth. Stone: Clear quartz crystal or rutilated crystal.

The eighth and ninth chakras rarely need to be worked on during a healing, as their energies and purposes are so esoteric that it is difficult for a healer to manage them. The patient, however, can clear these with prayer and meditation.

The **minor chakras in the palm of each hand** are very sensitive; they can send out universal energy, as well as gather and direct it toward a physical person or a mental goal. It is frequently helpful during a healing for the patient to hold a crystal in each hand. Stones: Clear quartz crystal, amber, amethyst.

The other **minor chakras in the sole of each foot** are useful for drawing earth energy upward into a patient. Because we are beings of the earth, we use a lot of earth energy as well as universal, spiritual energy. This earth energy helps us maintain our connection with the planet earth and deal with everyday life. These chakras are also important in that they allow us to discharge negative energy back into the earth where it is transformed into positive energy. They also ground us and siphon off excess energy. It is beneficial for people to walk barefoot whenever possible for these reasons. Stones: Clear quartz crystal, smoky quartz, black obsidian, black onyx.

Chakra Healing

There are three methods for working on the chakras, all of them simple to learn and use. In the first, the patient lies on their back in a comfortable position. Now simply lay the appropriate stones over the areas for each chakra. Put the stone for the crown chakra leaning against the top of the head. Place a clear quartz crystal in each hand and near the sole of each foot, with a larger clear quartz crystal just above the crown chakra stone. Beginning at the root chakra and ending with the universal chakra, hold your dominant or power hand over each stone as you tone "Om." If you can't bring yourself to tone "Om," instead say "Amen." When you finish, sweep your hand from the universal chakra down to the root chakra. This draws down high spiritual energy to flood each chakra and break loose any obstructions.

The second method requires the use of a pendulum (see page 252) and one-inch squares of correctly colored paper to match each chakra. Lens plastic is especially good and can be purchased at photography stores. Again, you work from red (root chakra) to violet (crown chakra). Before beginning this pendulum-chakra work, determine which is your power hand. Ordinarily, the power hand is the one you use most of the time. However, in a few individuals, they may find that the power hand is the opposite of the one they use. Go with the hand you feel most comfortable using.

If you are working on yourself, hold the pendulum in your power hand and an appropriately colored square in the palm of the other hand. Hold the pendulum over the paper while you visualize the chakra on which you will be working. If there is a blockage, and thus a decreased amount of energy in that chakra, the pendulum will circle clockwise or counterclockwise until the correction is made. If the chakra doesn't need work, the pendulum will not swing. When finished with one chakra, take up the next colored square in order, and repeat the process. Continue to do this until you have treated all the chakras.

If you are working on a patient, have them lie on the back in a comfortable position. Hold the pendulum in your power hand and the appropriately colored paper square in the other. Hold the pendulum over the patient's corresponding chakra and visualize the color. Again, the pendulum will swing clockwise or counterclockwise until the correction is complete. Continue up to the seventh chakra at the crown of the head.

Some pendulum users disagree about the counterclockwise swing. However, this assumes that all people react in the same manner when detecting chakra energy. Pendulum swings and energy detection differ

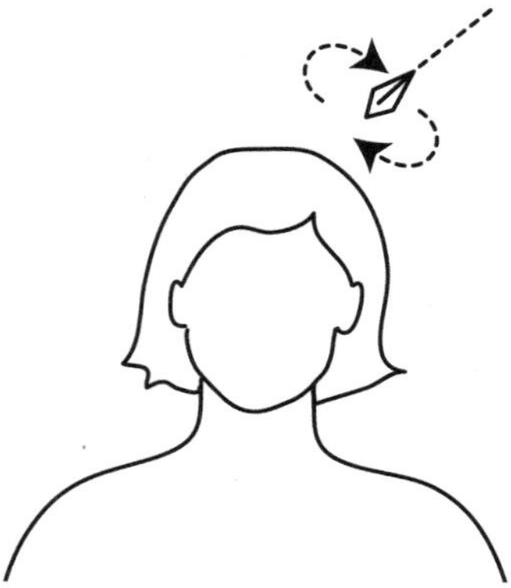

Using a Pendulum for the Aura and Chakras

from person to person. With practice, you can determine which is the correct swing for you when using a pendulum. When using a pendulum for chakra correction, there doesn't appear to be a specific reason why the pendulum swings one way or the other. For most healers, a clockwise swing will be normal.

The third method of chakra cleansing again requires the patient to lie on their back. Hold the palm of your power hand above the area of the root chakra and your other palm above the area of the second chakra. Tone "Om" or "Amen." Move the power hand to the second chakra and your other hand to the third chakra, and tone again. Repeat this process, moving up one chakra each time until you reach the crown chakra. While you hold your power hand above the crown chakra, hold your other hand above the root chakra. This links all the chakras and causes energy to run in a continuous loop through these light centers.

Chakra and aura healing are simple magickal healing methods. They are easy to use and very effective.

The Healing Touch

For thousands of years, many ancient peoples were healed by touch and magick. In the temples at Malta and Gozo, the sick slept in huge stone chambers, while priestesses there communed with the Gods and did their healing magick. Egyptian healing books dating as far back as 1,800 BCE combined healing and spells. In the early Irish Celtic society, healers at a royal hospital, called the Bearg, or House of Sorrows, at Tara used special magickal stones, water from sacred wells, charms, and magick, as well as herbs and surgery. The Irish medical schools were so highly esteemed that students came from all parts of Europe to learn the techniques. All ancient healers were connected with the spiritual in some manner.

Ancient Eastern healing methods describe meridians and nadis (pronounced *naw-dees*) running through the body. There are twelve major channels for the ch'i, or universal energy, to flow through, with many other branching channels. These all end in the fingers and toes. Think of meridians as rivers, streams, and tributaries for universal energy that flow in specific channels and do not change. They are all connected to nerve endings in the physical and etheric bodies. Both the meridians and chakras take in cosmic energy and distribute it to every body organ. The aura holds this energy in place unless the aura is damaged.

The Chinese use these meridians or streams of energy during acupuncture treatments. If there is a blockage in the meridian, the acupuncture treatments release it. Some of these meridians are also used in reflexology and acupressure for the same results. If you decide to use any of the points known in acupressure or reflexology, take great care when working on the very young, the elderly, or the very sick. Sudden breakage of blocks of negative energy can overload the body and the aura, thus making the patient even sicker. In Japanese shiatsu massage, the therapist uses both acupressure and a special kind of massage to break blockages in the meridians.

I do not recommend using acupressure or reflexology unless you study these subjects in depth. It is too easy to think you know all about acupressure and reflexology after reading a book, but both subjects require training to be used correctly and successfully.

Healers must have some spiritual path in their lives, even if it is only the belief in a supreme creative force, a power without a name. Having a spiritual path is not the same as belonging to a church or group. Technically you don't have to believe in a superior force to heal, but I've yet to see a nonbeliever be able to accept the fact of spiritual healing. The healer and the patient need not believe in the same spiritual path to create a healing. It is not the healer's place, either, to discuss religion with any patient.

Healing by touch involves not only the accepted tradition of laying on of hands, but also aura massage, aura cleaning, and aura sealing. It requires patience, dedication, and practice to learn. You don't have to be psychic, nor do you have to practice a certain religion. As long as you have a spiritually motivated desire to help someone who is ill, you can get results.

Find Your Power Hand

Before you begin using your healing touch, you must decide which is your power hand and which is your removal hand. Ordinarily, your power hand is the one you use most often. If you are right-handed, this would be your right hand, and your left hand would be the removal hand. If you are left-handed, it would be the reverse. Hereafter, when the power hand is mentioned, you should use the hand you determined was your power hand.

The power hand draws in universal energy and directs it to the aura or body when healing someone. The removal hand draws off negative or excess aura energy and returns it to the earth or the cosmos, where it is automatically recycled into positive energy. In other words, you put in with your power hand and take out with your removal hand.

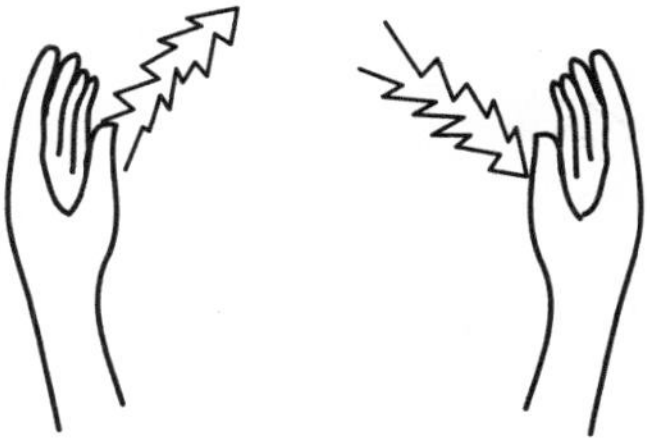

The Power Hand and the Removal Hand, with Energy Flowing In and Out

Healing Methods

Before undertaking any healing methods on a patient, you should first systematically check the patient's aura and chakras with your hands. Check and rebalance the chakras with your pendulum (see page 252). Then run your hands through the outer layers of the aura. Look for hot or cold spots, places that seem to leak energy, hard and inflexible areas, and the long flares that shoot out from the aura. A badly diseased site may make your hands feel burned or frozen because of the intensity of the blockage or the violent release of energy.

A person may be able to hide their true character when interacting with others, but it always shows in the aura. The aura will always reflect a person's habits, tendencies, emotional moods, and physical condition, as well as any potential or existing diseases.

Until you have practiced for many years and become proficient in handling cosmic energy, I do not recommend touching a patient's body during a healing. Until you learn how to regulate the flow of energy through your hands, touching patients' bodies may transfer the energy too quickly and cause greater disruption of their aura. Keep your hands two to four inches away from the body at all times.

Also remember that everything in the universe, even a single thought, is composed of energy. Therefore, wherever you place your attention, the cosmic energy you pull into your hands will follow your thoughts to that place. This is especially important to know when working with the aura, for you must direct the universal energy both with your hands and your thoughts.

There are five main aura disturbances that may cause health problems: 1) slow leaks, lesions, and tears; 2) more toxic or negative energy than the aura can process; 3) flares; 4) stagnation of energy in any one place; 5) collapse of aura areas. All of these disturbances must be healed and sealed before the patient can recover.

Slow leaks and tears will emit small seepages of energy. These will feel like moving tingles on the palm of your power hand. They are usually caused by minor emotional difficulties or life problems. People may have many of these little tears during the course of a day, and most of them seal themselves. However, if a person is dealing with a major problem or an attitude that may attract a disease, these unhealed leaks and tears can allow greater damage to occur.

A lesion feels like a small rough spot in the aura. It is the site of a past damage that didn't make it completely through the aura's layers. This is like a scar on the physical body and is a potential area for future problems unless softened and sealed by cosmic energy.

A flare can be caused by two things: too much unprocessed energy in an aura or a huge disastrous break in an aura. Having too much energy is similar to hyperventilation. The aura and chakras become clogged with excess energy brought in by the subconscious during a time of stress. This energy will churn purposelessly until it sours and changes into negative energy. In this case, a flare is an aura's attempt to rid itself of this "infection." To correct this, the healer must use their removal hand to help draw out the negative energy. Then using the power hand, the healer must seal the break. This type of flare will feel either very cold or very hot.

The flare caused by a huge break may feel like energy rushing out, rather like a hole in a dam. The patient will likely feel extremely tired all the time. Such flares are always caused by large emotional traumas or extremely serious diseases. You should begin by massaging and cleaning the aura, as explained later in this section. Then balance the chakras. Follow this by holding the power hand over the flare for some time and doing the usual aura smoothing.

Stagnation of energy in one place will create hot or cold spots in the aura. This can be either a site for an undetected disease or a potential one.

A collapsed aura is usually found in patients who are extremely ill or close to death. You may also find a collapsed aura in someone contemplating suicide. A collapse can manifest in two ways: 1) the aura is so close to the body that it appears to be almost nonexistent; or 2) the aura has deep indentations. The indentations will feel like large inward dips in the patient's aura, as if a chunk of aura has been removed. The deeper the pit, the more aura layers are involved. This indicates a disease that has reached the spiritual levels or that began there. In cases of collapse, the healer must work on the seventh and eighth aura layers first, because no input of cosmic energy or chakra rebalancing will hold until these levels are repaired.

Disease or illness is primarily a disruption and imbalance of a body's chakras and aura. Negative energy works its way inward through the aura's layers until it affects the chakras and meridian lines in the etheric body, thus causing blockages. Blockages are congested pools of negative energy that break down the physical body's resistance and often provide food for bacteria and viruses or mental or spiritual collapse. This condition creates openings and opportunities for a disease to manifest itself in the physical body. Because all disease is considered an imbalance, it is possible that epidemics may be caused by imbalances in an entire group of people.

It is extremely difficult, if not impossible, to detect exactly what caused a disease. To cure a disease is impossible without full cooperation of the patient. Diseases can arise for a number of different reasons. Past or present emotional traumas and constant stress, which weaken the aura, may be to blame. So may severe and persistent character flaws, such as extreme, constant impatience, revengeful attitudes, compulsive behavior, or constantly dwelling on the negative. Other culprits can be an inherited family tendency or a past life tendency toward a specific disease. A healer can heal the visible physical symptoms by repairing the aura and rebalancing the chakras. However, unless the patient does much introspection and makes conscious changes in spiritual outlook, lifestyle, habits, and diet, the healing will not hold.

Other accidents and diseases may have more of a physical cause, such as man-made substances like chemicals. In the case of accidents, something in the lifestyle or life path plan weakened a portion of the aura, which then allowed the accident to happen. Man-made substances may weaken the aura and then damage the physical body. Everything works from the outer layers of the aura inward to the physical body.

Instead of searching for the root problem or passing judgment, you should concentrate on healing the aura and chakras. If you receive mental pictures of symbols or inwardly hear a message about a cause of disease, you must determine if the patient is open to these before passing along the impressions or messages. It is a patient's responsibility to make changes that will aid the healing. Always suggest ways for patients to self-heal, never demand that they do it. And always ask patients if they wish to be healed before you begin.

Preparing to Heal

When you prepare for a healing, have the patient sit in a straight chair or lie on their back. I prefer the chair method, because the patient does not have to turn over during the healing and the healer can move easily around the patient to check all sections of the aura.

Before you begin a healing, and between healings of more than one patient, you should always calm your mind by taking several slow, deep breaths and saying a prayer. In fact, it is very beneficial if the healer takes time to meditate briefly before doing a healing.

Visualize yourself surrounded by a brilliant white light, as if the sun were directly over your head and shining straight into your crown chakra. Feel any negative energy in your body and aura pouring out through your feet into the earth. When the negative energy flow ceases, feel the earth energy flow up through your feet and mingle with the sun energy. This visualization connects you to both the spiritual cosmic energy and the grounding earth energy of this planet.

Those who are ill can also use this exercise to help heal themselves. Drawing in the white fire of the sun also helps treat cancer, while the softer, gentler earth energy is useful for soothing all illnesses.

Next, briskly rub your hands together. Then cup them about 6 to 8 inches apart so you feel the energy ball between them. If your energy isn't strong enough, do more deep breathing and repeat the sun fire visualization. Then rub your hands again to check your energy. A weak healer always runs the risk of inadvertently drawing off energy instead of putting it into the patient's aura. A weak healer can also pick up disease symptoms from a patient.

To begin an aura massage, balance the patient's chakras (see page 320). This will move the blocked energy of the chakras either out of the etheric body entirely or deposit it into the aura, as in a difficult case of illness. To remove this transferred negative energy or any previously residing negative energy from the aura, you need to break it up by massage and scrape it away.

For the best results in aura massage, you need to work through the aura in a definite pattern. Begin in the aura around the head. With your power hand, work the aura with your fingers in a downward scratching motion. Work over the head and down the neck first. Use the side of your removal hand to rake or brush the aura in a downward movement. This scrapes the negative residue off the massaged portion. Flick your removal hand frequently when doing this. Continue the massage and raking motions over the left shoulder and down the left arm to the fingertips. When you reach the fingers, scrape the residue off the hand with a flicking movement of your removal hand. Go back to the right shoulder and repeat this massaging and scraping until the right arm is cleared. Do the same over the back and chest to the waist, then massage and rake over each leg to the feet. Always flick off the residue when you reach the fingers and toes.

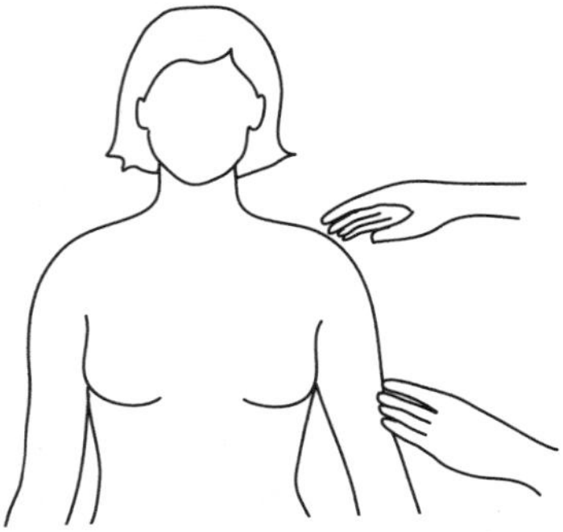

Raking Off Negative Energy

When massaging and cleaning the aura in this manner, you may discover hard or resistant spots. This area can feel like a callous or a hard scab. Negative energy has been in this area so long it has solidified and will take extra work, perhaps even extra healing sessions before you can break it loose.

After washing your hands or rubbing them briskly against your legs, go back and smooth the entire aura from head to feet. Check for any flares, tears, or leaks in the aura that you may have missed in the initial work. If you find any, seal them by creating balls of energy between your hands and applying this directly to the troubled area with your power hand. Hold the energy there with your hand until it attaches. If the problem area is a flare, remember to pull out the excess energy with your removal hand before attaching the energy ball. Until you get the excess energy under control, you will not be able to successfully seal the aura.

Repeat the chakra balancing with your pendulum and then seal the entire aura again. Ground the patient by placing your power hand in the outer aura layers while you visualize all excess energy flowing into the earth through your removal hand.

While some believe a healer can't pick up negative energy from a patient's aura, I have found that this transfer of negative energy is possible, particularly if the healer's body or mind has problems that resonate with the patient's. If you suddenly find yourself dealing with anger, sadness, depression, or vindictiveness after giving a healing, you probably picked up negative vibrations from the patient. In this case, quickly run your hands through your aura from the head to the feet and wipe away these energies while they are still on the outer layers.

Try not to do too many healings in a day or a week. You can become too tired if you stretch your efforts and time too much. A properly done healing requires more time than a beginner would think. Only healers who have practiced for many years should do more than one or two healings per day.

If you have no healer to work on you, you can do the aura massage and cleaning by yourself. However, it is more difficult to find trouble areas in your own aura.

Meditation and Visualization

Meditation is a vital part of healing for the physical, emotional, mental, and spiritual bodies. Unfortunately, many people still think of meditation as sitting in a full lotus pose with a blank mind. Unless you are adept at yoga, you will have to force your body into the full lotus pose, and all you will be able to think about is pain. Fortunately, this isn't the only way to meditate. In Western meditation methods, it doesn't even require that you keep a blank mind.

Meditation is simply a method that helps quiet scattered and racing thoughts. By doing this, it reduces stress and heals the body, mind, and spirit.

Meditation in its many versions has been around for centuries, and is part of many religions in one form or another. The word meditation is derived from the Indian Sanskrit word *medha,* which means "doing the wisdom." It can also be traced back to the Latin root word *meditari,* which means "to muse or ponder."

Most religions recognize some form of meditation, whether it is simply prayer and contemplation or saying a rosary. Using prayer beads during a meditation is an Eastern—and Western—practice. But meditation can be practiced by anyone of any religion or anyone without a religion. It is a method to calm your emotional and physical bodies and relieve stress. Since 50 to 80 percent of all illnesses are stress-related in some manner, meditation is a valuable tool for healing.

Caregivers are frequently forgotten partners in treating a sick person. The stress on a caregiver increases dramatically when the illness is extremely serious or long-term. This stress increases if the caregiver has no one to help. This places the caregiver at risk for illness. Meditation is an inexpensive therapy the caregiver can practice without leaving home.

Scientists have discovered that meditation has a direct beneficial effect on the physical body. It can lower blood pressure, control pain, speed healing time, calm heart palpitations, lower body temperature, relax the breathing, and help build the immune system. Meditation calms, relaxes, and can even make you drowsy by raising serotonin levels. Serotonin is a natural brain chemical involved in the sleep process.

In 1987, Dr. David Orme-Johnson of the Maharishi International University, surveyed people who meditated. In the nineteen to thirty-nine-year-old age group, he discovered that people who meditated were 54.7 percent less likely to require visits to a doctor. In the over forty group, this percentage rose dramatically to 73.7 percent. And the percentage of meditators in all age levels who were admitted to the hospital for heart disease or tumors was extremely low.

With these figures in mind, sick people, caregivers, and healers should make meditation part of their weekly routine. Meditation doesn't have to be practiced every day to work its wonders but should be done at least three times a week. All meditation requires is you, a comfortable straight chair (or a pillow so you can sit on the floor), soft nonvocal music, and five to twenty minutes. I include the soft music because it masks many distracting sounds.

Meditation also produces what is known as an altered state of consciousness. Shamans know that an altered state of consciousness is necessary to heal yourself or another person. You can't force yourself to achieve this. Shamans frequently produce this trancelike state through drums and dancing. Modern meditation allows you to ease gently into an altered state of consciousness in which the physical body is so relaxed that the meditator is no longer aware of it. The consciousness is raised to the level of the eighth and ninth chakras, a place where communication with the Divine is possible and secret universal healing knowledge is available. When you reach this state, you can mold universal energy into any healing form you choose, and the healing will be complete.

Some people like to burn candles or incense while meditating. If you do this, be certain that the candle or incense is in a fireproof container in a safe place well away from anything that could catch fire. Lavender is a good relaxing scent. If you use lavender in an aromatherapy burner, make sure that there is enough water in the container so that the hot oil won't pop out and make a mess or crack the container. If you use incense, don't set it close to you or use it in a small room. The smoke can make you cough or choke. If you don't like incense smoke, place a few drops of lavender oil on a cotton ball in a small dish.

If you feel more comfortable following a guided meditation tape, you can purchase these or make them yourself. Then you can replay the tape whenever you meditate.

I have learned over the years that people in Western cultures find it difficult to practice the Eastern idea of meditation with a blank mind. Paramahansa Yogananda, who started the Self Realization Fellowship years ago, understood this when he tailored the techniques from India to the Western mind. This is why my meditations in this book and others have guided imagery and suggestions.

Visualization techniques entice your subconscious mind to heal the body. The subconscious mind understands only symbols and pictures, so visualization connects you with it. As the saying goes, change your mind and you change your life. Healing visualizations are also essential if a healer is working on a sick person some distance away (see page 371).

Choose a meditation spot where you will not be disturbed. Play your meditation tape or a soft, nonvocal tape of music. To begin a meditation, sit in a straight-backed chair with your feet flat on the floor and your hands in your lap. If you prefer, you can sit cross-legged on the floor with a pillow under the back portion of your buttocks. This will tip you slightly forward so that you rest on a portion of your knees. If you are ill and in bed, lie flat on your back with a pillow under your knees and another under your head. I don't recommend lying down unless you can't sit because the prone posture is conducive to sleep. If you really want to try a yogic pose for meditation, most people can safely do the half-lotus. Sit cross-legged with one foot on the opposite thigh but the other foot on the floor. Don't use this position if it causes you pain. Meditation isn't about enduring pain but about relaxing and connecting with the flow of universal energy and information.

Half-Lotus Pose

You will never be in any spiritual danger while meditating. You can end the meditation simply by opening your eyes. Your body and soul won't be possessed by evil spirits, either.

A Healing Meditation

Close your eyes and take a slow, deep breath. When you exhale, purse your lips, tighten your body muscles, and blow slowly. This expels any stale air that is in the bottom of your lungs. This exhalation method is also helpful to people who hyperventilate or have asthma. Now relax again and take another slow, deep breath. As you inhale, visualize a bright white light or the sun over your head. See this light filling your body as the breath fills your lungs. When you exhale slowly and normally, this light will wash out all negative energy and emotions within you.

Breathing normally, begin to mentally tell your body to relax, beginning with the feet and legs and ending with the shoulders, neck, and head muscles. Take your time but don't dwell too long on this part of the exercise. If you try too hard to relax, you will defeat your purpose.

After a short time, visualize yourself standing beside a small stream of running water. Take all of your negative emotions and events (including troublesome people) and throw them into the stream. This action tells the subconscious mind that these people and events should be resolved or removed from your life.

You turn away from the stream and see a wall with a door. You go to the door and open it. Inside is an empty room with a chair. On the wall in front of the chair is a huge screen, like a movie screen. You sit in the chair and look at the screen. You will use this screen and the power within this room to build yourself an Otherworld healing temple where you can go to heal yourself or work on healing for others.

Begin building this temple by visualizing on the screen what setting you wish it to be in: on top of a mountain, beside the sea or a lake, in the forest, out on a desert, even on the moon or in the clouds. The setting can be anything you wish. Now, mentally construct the temple in any shape, of any size, and of any material you wish. You may want it to look like a castle or perhaps like a giant seashell. The choice is yours. Create any windows and doors you want.

Now, go inside your healing temple and decorate the interior in any manner you want. You may wish to have your main healing room within a place of worship, or it may look like a modern house furnished with soft beds for patients or yourself to lie upon. You can come to this Otherworld place anytime you are in meditation, either to be healed, to relax, or to work on healing for another. This is your refuge from stress and your spot to connect with universal energy.

Take as much time as you need to create this sacred space. It will remain intact in the ethereal realms, waiting for you whenever you enter meditation.

When you are ready to return to this time and place, open your eyes and move slowly until you are reoriented.

You can return to your healing temple at any time. Just be certain that you dump the negatives before you go there so you don't contaminate your healing space.

To do healing work in your temple, mentally call the name of the sick person. Their astral body will appear in the temple, and you can begin your work. See Absent Healing on page 371 for more suggestions about healing techniques using meditation. To heal yourself, lie down on one of your healing beds in the temple and call for your spiritual guides, guardian angels, or a deity to help you.

If you experience painful memories while in meditation, acknowledge their existence, but tell yourself that you will not let them control or influence your life. You may need to drop them into the stream several times before your subconscious mind gets the message that you don't need to relive these any longer.

Sometimes, you will get visions of unfamiliar events. These are images from past lives, images that contain clues to present problems and health trouble. If you are healing another person, these unbidden images belong to them. Look closely at these fragmentary events for clues to present life troubles. These past life memories are dealt with the same as those from your past in this life.

At some time during a meditation, you may become aware of something attached to you that you didn't know was there. If healing another person, you may see something attached to them. These are called "cordings." Cordings are attachments between people. These cordings may arise in this lifetime or in past lives. Although they appear positive between good friends, lovers, and close family members, they are frequently negative connections that you don't want or need. You may see these in meditation as a rope-like attachment to one or all of your, or the patient's, first three chakras. They are usually dull and muddy in color, although active ones can appear fire-red. You can sever and eliminate these unwanted energy drainers and controllers by visualizing a bright sword or a flaming torch in your power hand. Simply cut or burn the cordings in two. It may take several attempts to completely sever strong cordings.

Your own silver (sometimes a light blue) cord that attaches your astral body (soul) to the physical body is always with you and is not the same as a negative cording. The silver cord can't be suddenly attacked by evil astral entities and severed. It detaches itself when your life is finished, and only then.

It is possible that you will meet spiritual guides, guardian angels, or deceased loved ones while meditating. They want to help you. If they make you uncomfortable, ask them to leave.

If you are working on healing another person while in meditation, be aware of the patient's body language as soon as you make mental contact with them. Some people do not want to be healed but wish to leave the earth plane for a more pain-free existence in the Otherworld. I had this forcefully brought home one time when I was working on the father of a friend. During my meditation, when I contacted with the comatose elderly gentleman, who was in the hospital, I immediately saw two images of the man. One was lying quietly on the hospital bed, but the other was actively wielding a kitchen broom, batting away all the healing energy. I had never met the father and was amazed that his spirit body was so active in resistance. When I described the man to my friend, thinking I might have contacted the wrong person, he assured me the description fit his father, who used a kitchen broom to oust both unwanted Texas critters and salesmen. His father had once remarked that if he ever got too sick to live life as he wanted, he didn't want to continue living. So, instead of a healing, I worked for a pain-free, peaceful passage from this life.

Mantras and Mudras

Sometimes you may wish to meditate on a more spiritual level without using a guided journey. In this case, you can use mantras and mudras. Mudras, however, can be used in either type of meditation, guided or silent.

A *mantra* is a single word or a series of words that center and calm the user through their vibrational qualities (see page 353). This word or series of words is chanted with each exhalation of breath while you meditate.

A *mudra* is a hand gesture that has held a certain meaning for thousands of years. A few of these are explained below. In the ancient Hindu tradition these mudras, or hand gestures, are considered very powerful. Some mudras are also quite elaborate. The ones I list here are simple and can be used easily by anyone during meditation to increase their contact with the spiritual and to amplify healing energy. The Chalice and Gomukha mudras are inconspicuous enough that you can use them at almost any time.

The **Om mudra** is usually made when chanting the mantra "Om (ohm)." In this gesture, you bring the tips of the thumb and index finger of each hand together to form a circle. The hands are rested palms up on the knees.

The **Namaste mudra** is done by holding the palms of the hands flat together, fingers pointing upward, at heart level, as if in prayer. This gesture honors God/Goddess and the spiritual flame within every other person.

The powerful **Chalice mudra** is usually made while sitting in the half-lotus pose. It represents the receiving of spiritual blessings and healing energy from the Divine. Hold your hands together, slightly cupped. Let the tips of the thumbs touch. If your right foot is on the opposite thigh in the half-lotus, put the right hand inside the left. If your left foot is on the opposite thigh, place the left hand inside the right. Hold your hands just below your navel.

Om

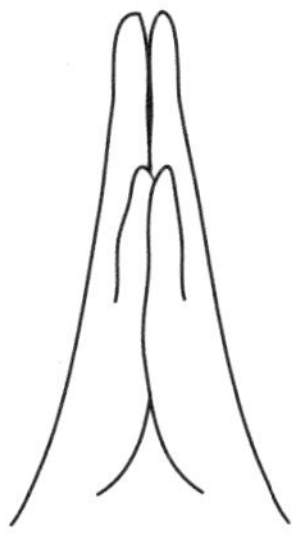
Namaste

Chalice

Gomukah

The **Gomukha mudra** is a powerful gesture to use when your energy feels scattered and you are having difficulty concentrating. Interlace the fingers of both hands while holding one thumb on top of the other. Hold your hands in your lap.

Combine the mudras with chants and affirmations, and you will greatly enhance both your meditations and their results.

Often, physical visual effects are helpful during a meditation. The person meditating can look at certain symbols before and after a meditation to help produce an altered state of consciousness. Some healers make healing altars and have candles and clear quartz crystals placed around a photo or paper bearing the patient's name. See page 410 for more on healing altars. The same technique can be used in absent healing.

If you want to intensify and strengthen your meditations, place certain tarot cards and stones where you can see them before and after a healing meditation. If you have a photo of the sick person, place this in the center of your cards and stones. If you don't have a photo, write the patient's full name on a piece of paper instead.

If you use one tarot card, place a stone on each side of it or surround it with stones. If you use several tarot cards, alternate the cards and stones around the photo or name of the sick person. The following lists of cards and stones give their healing meanings so you can determine which you want to use. The stones are all inexpensive and easily found.

Tarot Cards

THE CHARIOT Self-discipline, willpower, forging ahead.

THE EMPRESS The Goddess or Mary, compassion, emotional order, good luck.

FOUR OF SWORDS Rest, recuperation, quiet contemplation, regrouping of energy.

THE HERMIT Peace in solitude, hidden knowledge brought to light.

NINE OF CUPS Wishes granted.

SIX OF SWORDS Journeying away from problems, improved situation.

SIX OF WANDS Victory.

THE STAR Balance and harmony, peace, spiritual enlightenment.

STRENGTH Inner control of emotions and problems, harnessing inner strength.

THE SUN Good health, enlightenment, healing.

TEMPERANCE Brings harmony, balance, and tranquility.

TEN OF CUPS Joy and contentment, complete happiness, permanent success.

Healing Stones

AGATE, RED This stone brings peace and calmness, and aids in healing blood diseases.

AMBER This stone soothes and heals. It increases the strength of your healing spells and meditations.

AMETHYST This stone helps strengthen your communication with your spiritual teachers and guardians. It also aids in achieving the altered state of consciousness.

CARNELIAN This stone strengthens and energizes the blood and internal organs. It also aids in regenerating damaged tissue.

HEMATITE This stone releases stress and brings in optimism, will, and courage.

LAPIS LAZULI This stone is one of the greatest healers and purifiers. It helps reduce tension and stress, as well as balance the chakras.

MALACHITE This stone heals the heart and circulatory system, revitalizes the body and mind, and regenerates tissue. It also stabilizes the energy and heals the chakras.

ONYX, BLACK This stone deflects and destroys negative energy, particularly the kind sent by others. It aids with spiritual inspiration, balancing karmic debt, and helps when facing transformational events.

QUARTZ CRYSTAL, CLEAR This stone is a great healer and also amplifies all healing energy.

QUARTZ, ROSE This stone helps heal emotional wounds and release negative emotions. It attracts universal love and healing energies.

A good healer is always searching for new methods of healing. If you are interested in making your own healing weapons, for example, I suggest you read Michael Smith's books *Crystal Power, Crystal Spirit,* and *Crystal Warrior*. He gives full details for healing wands and other useful items.

Never give up hope and never stop your healing work for yourself or a patient. When it seems the darkest, a change is often right around the corner. Willpower directed through a healing meditation is very powerful. It can also be a spiritually uplifting experience for the patient, the caregiver, and the healer.

Affirmations and Chants

Healers of all ages, past and present, have known that the patient's will to recover and the will to live are essential for a healing. Sick people can die quickly of a nonfatal disease if they give up hope and believe they will die. We see this combination of illness and despair more and more, because modern medicine has separated the body from the mind and spirit in healing. You would think we would learn to reinforce modern medicine with ancient alternative practices that will heal the entire person, on all levels. Without healing a patient on all levels, there can be no complete healing.

There are physicians who believe in the connection between irresponsible or negative thinking and illnesses. One physician I know insists that his patients become responsible for their diseases. Although his definition of being responsible and mine are not quite the same, we have definitely established a way of understanding each other.

Affirmations

It is the responsibility of patients and their families to take active roles in healing. The easiest method is to use positive affirmations, which are short sentences, without negative words. For example, don't say, "George doesn't have cancer." Instead, say, "George is completely healed." And hold a mental picture of George happy and healthy. If a negative thought does arise, immediately counter it by saying, "I don't accept that!"

Never speak of a disease as a reality unless this is counteracted by positive words, for this sets into motion disintegrating forces within the body, mind, and spirit. Instead of claiming a disease, speak of it as the disease, not my cold, or George's cancer.

Negative thoughts, words, and attitudes have become so much a part of human life that they arise without our being aware of them. However, the subconscious mind recognizes these and acts upon them. The subconscious reaction to negatives appears first in the aura, then in the body in the form of diseases. If you say something negative about an illness or disease, or someone says something negative to you, immediately and mentally say, "No, I don't accept that." Then replace it with "I (or the patient's name) am getting well."

The ancient Egyptians and the Brahmins of India knew the power of negative words and thoughts. They deliberately used certain healing words to set up vibratory actions that could help heal broken bones and depleted internal organs. They used prolonged sessions of healing chants to stimulate the glands and nerve centers. The healers of India believed that spoken or sung words were 80 percent more powerful than the same words spoken only in the mind. Hindu scriptures say that words are all-powerful. The ancient Babylonians taught that every word is a command or a promise that must come true. The Greeks believed that words contained power and cosmic energy to build up or tear down. Oriental cultures have long taught that the spoken word has tremendous power, and that certain arrangements of words (as in healing affirmations and chants) can profoundly affect physical substance.

These ideas were not used in Europe after the terror of the witch hunts, for the wise men and women who knew these secrets were killed or had gone into deep hiding and no longer served the people. However, spiritual healing secrets never stay hidden forever. Eventually, people begin to rediscover and use them.

Around the turn of the nineteenth century, a French pharmacist named Emile Coué had a free clinic where he taught patients to use positive affirmations. One of these affirmations has survived and is still used today: "Every day in every way, I am getting better and better." His patients who repeated this twenty times when they awoke each morning did get better. He chose morning because affirmations work best when the patient is relaxed and calm.

In 1964, Norman Cousins, author of *Anatomy of an Illness*, learned he had a deadly form of arthritis that attacks the body's connective tissues. His chances of surviving more than a few months were not good. Determined not to give up, he began to fill his life with a positive attitude, positive speech, and lots of humor. In four months, he was back to work full-time, although his complete cure took several years. Mr. Cousins had instinctively used the ancient healing technique of positive affirmations and thinking, and proved that it works.

Mental thoughts also affect the body, mind, and spirit. Repeated imagining of negative thoughts produces a powerful astral thoughtform that the subconscious mind takes as a literal wish. Robert Monroe, author of *Ultimate Journey*, did research on this in the 1970s. He coined the term "H-Band" noise to describe the thought pollution of negative thoughts created by undisciplined human mental imagining and negative speech. This pollution surrounds us constantly. And this, combined with negative words and thoughts can have an extremely detrimental affect on a sick person's health.

Negative-speaking and -thinking people are detrimental to your health. Avoid them, when possible. This includes people who are always complaining, making excuses, blaming others for their actions, and finding fault with others. Life is difficult enough without added problems, so choose your companions carefully.

You need to rid yourself of secret resentment, anger, or despair over past injustices. Begin by using affirming statements that tell your subconscious mind to solve these problems and kick out the negative debris. Even if you can't bring yourself to be around someone who harmed you in some manner, at least heal yourself by changing your thinking. For example, say aloud in private: "I forgive (name) for what she/he did (or said), but I have no need for (name) in my life. He/she is free to pay whatever karmic debts are owed in some other way, but not to me." From experience I know this will take time, sometimes a long time, but it can be done. The release of this negative debris will improve your life and health. It is the first step to true healing. You must do this yourself, for no one else can do it for you.

Cancer is a difficult disease for orthodox modern medicine to cure. It is also a difficult disease for psychic healers and may require many treatments over a long period of time. With cancer, more than any other disease, patients must truthfully look at their life and thoughts, and make changes. Many cancer patients refuse to discuss their feelings. However, they may be seething inwardly with anger, power, control, betrayal, or other emotional traumas. The aura's layers may hold the beginnings of this disease for years before the problem reaches the physical body.

When cancer is still in the aura's layers, healers may find intense hot spots that will burn their hands with flares of excess energy or see it as a black area with coruscating red dots flashing in it. This black spot will be perpendicular to the body where it will eventually manifest unless rooted out. The closer to the body the spot is in the aura, the more compacted the disease is and the sooner it may manifest. All cancers already in the body will show this dark area and the aura will feel extremely hot there. Although the healer may work on the aura, the patient must perform self-healing by affirmations and positive visualizations to attack and eradicate this disease.

Ancient healers knew about cancer, but not to the extent we know of it today. They were also aware that people can become predisposed to the disease through bottled-up negative emotions.

Dr. Masaharu Taniguchi, a Japanese metaphysician and successful cancer healer, believed that pessimism, resentments, fault-finding, and criticism were detrimental to good health. Many psychic healers and metaphysicians believe that cancer may be caused by holding onto some secret resentment, anger, or bitterness.

The first time I saw clearly the connection between cancer and bitterness/resentment was in the case of a woman in her late thirties. Lucille had little love in her childhood. She had been deliberately pushed aside for her two younger siblings. She married young to a cruel, manipulative man who abused her physically and mentally. He was also an alcoholic womanizer who sexually abused his daughter. His son was a copy of his father. Through all of this, Lucille presented a sweet, loving face to the world, rarely criticizing and stoutly defending her family. In actuality, she was afraid to have her husband arrested because he threatened to kill her, and the daughter was using the incestuous relationship to gain material objects she wanted. Lucille kept her resentment and rage bottled up inside. At age thirty-four she was diagnosed with breast cancer and had a mastectomy. Three years later, she had a small lump and cancer recurred at the mastectomy site; these were treated with radiation therapy. A year later, she was diagnosed with advanced bone cancer in the skull and hips. When her exhausted body and spirit finally gave up, she died at age thirty-nine. The irony of the entire situation was the husband jokingly spoke of long-term anger producing cancer, but he completely absolved himself of any wrongdoing and blamed it on his wife's parents.

If you hold on to a negative past and injustices done to you, you are poisoning your aura and body. This type of attitude attracts more such negative experiences your way, adding to the debris piling up within your aura until a disease will at last erupt in the physical body.

Anyone, regardless of their religious background, can use affirmations, which are about health, not religion. If you want a religious-based practice, however, you can use prayer. Prayer is simply a form of spiritual affirmation that can bring about healing changes.

Repeat a healing affirmation over and over, even if you don't believe at first. This will raise your subconscious thinking and change your body. By repeating a verbal affirmation over and over, the subconscious mind gets the message and acts upon it. This produces a profound effect on the auras, the physical body, and the mind. If you can picture the healing within your mind, you can hold it in your hand. However, patients must picture this healing for themselves. No healer can, or should, try to force a healing on a patient who will not cooperate and take part in getting well.

In magick, a chant or spell repeated three times is considered more powerful. Repeating affirmations at least three times will amplify the desire you are sending out. The more often you say an affirmation, the stronger it gets. If you will speak an affirmation forty-nine times and hold the desired image in your mind with each affirmation, you can gain the result.

For those people who don't feel comfortable making up their own affirmations, the following list may help.

I forgive all who have done me harm and step forward into a new and better life.

Every day in every way, I am getting better and better.

I am completely healed of all disease on all levels of my body.

I am well. I am whole. I am happy.

My body, mind, and spirit are filled with healing light and energy.

I am one with God/Goddess and healed of all afflictions.

I claim complete healing and believe that it will be so.

Chants and Mantras

Chanting has been a vital part of religion and healing sessions for thousands of years in almost every culture. Frequently, chanting was combined with music, as with the Gregorian chants of the early Christian churches and monasteries. Today, the Gregorian chants are available on CD. The Gregorian chant, although Christian in origin, can transcend religious barriers and bring peace and harmony to any listener. Chants are capable of bridging the sacred and the secular, and thus help you to attain an altered state of consciousness. This altered state of consciousness brings both the chanter and the listener closer to the Otherworld realms and healing power.

Ancient deities of music were often associated with healing as well. An example is the god Apollo, who was a deity of both music and healing. The Greek god Aesculapius was Apollo's son and considered to be a great healer.

Words are simply a blend of vowels and consonants. These vowels and consonants have long been considered words that have a universal meaning. The sounds are a bridge between languages and cultures. The priest-magicians and healers of many ancient cultures, such as the Egyptians, Babylonians, Hindus, Orientals, and Greeks, studied the power and effect of certain sounds, particularly when chanted with intent. They discovered that, without directed intent, words and sounds would accomplish nothing. Only toning or chanting with intent will balance and heal.

The healers and magicians of the past knew that these sounds had vast reservoirs of power for magick and healing. At first, this knowledge was the sole property of the temples. However, the priest-magicians and healers later taught this information to the people through the use of chants and mantras. Frequently, the chants and mantras were only a special combination of sounds that had no literal meaning, but were chosen for their healing effects.

Scientists have not completely explored the power of sound. We know that certain sounds have a visible effect on objects. A high-pitched sound will shatter glass, and certain levels of sound will rearrange fine sand into subtle patterns. We also know that noises measuring ninety decibels or more can double the heart rate. Still, modern medicine does not accept that chanting and the use of mantras can help heal.

When mantras are mentioned, people immediately think of the Hindu religion. However, both the Buddhists and Hindus have used mantras in meditation for centuries. They believe that the sounds of certain mantras, when used repeatedly, can heal and positively influence events. Ancient Hindu texts state that the mantra "Om" is the most powerful mystic sound, and when repeated many times can harmonize the body and spirit with the cosmos. This scripture also says that certain *bija* mantras (called seed mantras) correspond to and affect the seven chakras.

Most people are not aware that the Sufi religion has a deep respect for, and uses, the power of sound. The Sufis practice deep breathing, chanting, and mantras as a vital part of their religion. Their word *ghiza-i-rhu*, which translates to music, really means food for the soul. To them, singing increases *prana* or *ch'i*, which is life energy. They also use chanting to achieve an altered state of consciousness, much as shamans do, and say that there is true healing power in the sounds of chanting. The Sufis frequently use the *bija* mantras (discussed later in this section) to focus and calm the mind, just as the Hindus do.

By saying mantras, you can switch on the chakras safely and make them operate at full power. Even if you don't understand what you are saying, these ancient formulas work because mantras are fundamentally about energy rather than meaning. Mantras are a single word or a series of words that were chosen for their vibrational and centering qualities. Mantras help you to reach the eighth and ninth chakras, the doorways to *ch'i*, or cosmic energy. The more you say a mantra, the more power you can tap. When you focus the sound vibration of a mantra with a consciously held intent, you can direct its energy to whatever portion of the body you choose. Mantras can also burn off karma.

Numbers and sounds are also connected in ancient lore. The sixth-century BCE Greek philosopher Pythagoras studied sound and numbers for years, especially the number nine. The number nine had great significance in ancient healing ceremonies, as it was considered a complete number and capable of creation. Any number that was a multiple of nine was also considered powerful.

The Hindus recommend a forty-day repetition of a mantra for maximum benefit. However, few people can set aside forty days for constant mantra repetition. Instead of being overwhelmed by the idea of forty days of chanting, you can choose to say a mantra for a specific number of times.

If you are striving for a set number of repetitions a day, you can keep count by using a *mala*, a rosary-like object that originated in the Far East. It is composed of 108 beads. The Vedic *malas*, later used by the Buddhists, existed for thousands of years before the Catholic rosary was first used. Twenty rosaries equal ten malas, a good number of repetitions to use for a specific prayer or mantra.

Malas can be purchased at specialty shops or through catalogs and are not expensive. The one bead at the end of the mala is called the *meru*. Hindus say that the *meru* contains the accumulated power of all the mantras performed. The Sanskrit word *meru* means mountain of stored energy. Never cross over the *meru* when you go around the mala. To continue chanting the mantra, start the count again by going backward from the *meru*.

Hindu Ayurvedic medicine uses the power of the voice to balance and align chakras through reciting mantras. However, you can also use related vowel sounds.

It is not necessary to sing your chants or mantras unless you wish to do so. You don't have to sing a certain note or in a certain key, either. When chanting either vowels and consonants or mantras, the patient or healer should take a slow, deep breath, and chant while slowly exhaling. The sounds should be in your ordinary, natural voice. When done properly, the sound should vibrate in your head.

Never chant on a full stomach when your body's energy is primarily concentrated on digestion. Wait at least an hour after eating so your body will be more receptive. Also, relax your body as much as possible. This will enable you to breathe naturally and produce vibrating tones. Sit with your back straight, whether you sit in a chair or cross-legged on the floor. This will allow the cosmic energy you are enticing into your body to penetrate all chakras and meridians. If the energy can't penetrate all portions of your aura and all of your chakras, it can't flow unimpeded along the meridians. Thus, the cosmic healing energy won't do the best job.

Certain vowels and consonants historically have been linked to certain results. These vowels and consonants are known to all cultures and are in all languages. If you aren't comfortable with the mantras given later in this section, at least use the vowels and consonants. The following sounds can help with healing.

A The a sound, as in "ahh," can help with depression. It also helps the body assimilate more oxygen, which causes the brain to release endorphins, substances that aid in natural pain control.

LONG E The long e sound, as in "emit" or "feel," stimulates the pineal gland and arouses the body's energies.

SHORT E The short e, as in "echo," affects the thyroid gland, increasing the metabolism and secretion of hormones. This is useful for patients who have lost their appetites and aren't eating properly.

LONG O The long o, as in "ocean," can be used to control sugar cravings, for it stimulates the pancreas. This sound will also help create a connection between the toner and the environment.

DOUBLE O Intone the oo sound, as in "tool," to stimulate the spleen. This stimulation will build the immune system. It also aids in bridging the conscious and subconscious minds.

MMM The mmm sound is connected with the Goddess. Today, Her counterpart in orthodox religion is the Virgin Mary. This sound, when vibrated through the physical body into the astral body, will create balance on all levels.

SHH The shh sound made by mothers the world over can restore harmony and peace.

Using vowel sounds to balance the chakras will not overload or unbalance any of these light centers.

UH The uh sound, as in "huh," works on the root chakra.

OOO The ooo, as in "fool," affects the belly chakra.

OH The oh, as in "low," will clear the solar plexus chakra.

AH The ah, as in "hah," will benefit the heart chakra.

EYE The sound "eye" is for the throat chakra.

LONG A The long a, as in "hay," will help the brow chakra, also known as the Third Eye.

LONG E The long e, as in "feel," will benefit the crown chakra at the top of the head.

Certain combinations of sounds can also be used together to attain specific goals. Spells for love and relationship are affected by "ahh eh," a combination of Mother and Father sonics. "Shoo maa" will help manifest material goals, while "paa maa eye oh" strengthens protective spells. These sample combinations may also be combined with the *bija* mantras and chakra mantras that follow.

If you wish to work primarily on the chakras themselves, the following mantras will aid you. They are easily pronounced one-word mantras. Sit with your back straight. Place your power hand over each chakra and visualize its color as you chant the mantra. Remember to breathe in and then chant while you exhale. Begin with the root chakra and end with the brow chakra. The crown chakra doesn't have a mantra associated with it. When the other six chakras are cleared and balanced, the totality of the sounds of these six resonate in the seventh chakra. Mantras for the chakras are:

LAM (*lahm*)—root chakra

VAM (*vahm*)—belly chakra

RAM (*rahm*)—solar plexus chakra

YAM (*yahm*)—heart chakra

HUM (*hoom*)—throat chakra

OM (*ohm*)—brow chakra

Bija mantras, also called seed mantras, are one-word Hindu mantras that are used for specific purposes. You can combine them with chakra mantras or vowel and consonant sounds. The seed mantras are the simplest of Hindu mantras and the easiest to chant. Work with a seed mantra for at least ten days, repeating it as often as possible. Do the same with the chakra mantras but chant all of them, one after the other in the correct order, each time you say them.

SHRIM (*shreem*) This affects the energy of abundance in all forms and is connected with the goddess Lakshmi. It also helps with spiritual abundance, health, inner peace, financial wealth, friendship, and love of children and family. According to Vedic teaching, if you say *shrim* one hundred times, your experiences of abundance will increase a hundredfold.

EIM (*I'm*) This rules artistic and scientific endeavors, music, education, and spiritual endeavors. It is connected with the goddess Sarasvati.

KLIM (*kleem*) This seed mantra is often combined with other mantras to attract an object of desire.

DUM (*doom*) This invokes the energy of protection.

GUM (*as in chewing gum*) This mantra is connected with the god Ganesha, who removes obstacles and brings success to endeavors.

GLAUM (*glah-own*) This removes obstacles that may exist between the throat and the base of the spine in both the physical and astral bodies. It is connected with Ganesha.

HAUM (*how, with an m added*) Connected with the God Shiva, this mantra greatly affects contact with the transcendental consciousness that is found in the eighth and ninth chakras.

KSHRAUM (*unvocalized k with sh, followed by row [how] and an "m"*) Connected with the God Vishnu, this mantra is used to be rid of the most stubborn evil situations and to release pent-up energies.

HRIM (*hreem*) This helps see through the illusions of everyday life. It can put you in contact with the higher spiritual realms where spiritual teachers, guardian angels, and exalted beings dwell.

Unless a patient is unconscious or totally unable to make a sound, mantras and chants can be used. Even if the patient must whisper, the power of these ancient mantras will draw in healing power from the cosmos.

Tonal and Musical Healing

Ancient cultures fully understood the power within music. They used music to create receptive attitudes during religious worship and healing atmospheres for the sick. We can see the effects of military-type music, which can produce national fervor and a militant attitude. Mothers have used lullabies for centuries to help their children sleep.

In ancient times, musicians were valuable members of society and often combined their talents with healing. We find references to this in writings from ancient Egypt and Greece. Celtic bards were prohibited from creating the wrong attitude in their audiences.

Today, doctors are beginning to accept that certain forms of music are conducive to healing, whether it is patients playing or listening to music. Many people are familiar with Don Campbell's book, *The Mozart Effect,* in which he discusses the modern scientific studies done with music and the results that were found. This book made many parents more watchful about the types of music their children listen to. Gregorian chant was found to be excellent for quiet study and meditation and can reduce stress. Slower baroque music can produce a sense of stability and order; examples are certain compositions by Bach, Handel, and Vivaldi. Classical music, such as that of Haydn and Mozart, can improve concentration and memory. Compositions by the New Age musician Stephen Halpern were specifically written to help bring about positive results.

Beyond creating a harmonious environment for learning and evolving, tone and sound can produce powerful effects on cells and tissue, and even help shrink malignant growths. While there are few modern studies of these effects, ancient healers were adamant about this healing effect.

Healing with Tuning Forks

One of the newest methods of using musical tones to heal involves tuning forks. You may buy tuning forks in a special set of eight that comes with a protective cloth bag with individual compartments for each fork. The cloth bag can be rolled up and tied to protect them (see the Resources for product suppliers).

In tone, these tuning forks go from middle C up an octave to C. Basically, these forks correspond to each of the eight chakras, beginning with middle C and the root chakra, and working up to the transpersonal chakra and the next C. The sounds produced by the tuning forks work in two ways. First, the auditory senses transfer the sound to the body, aura, and chakras through the ears. Second, the sound waves produced by the vibrating forks can directly transfer moving energy to the chakras, aura, or parts of the body. To use the tuning forks, hold one gently by the stem. Tap it lightly against the block provided with the set. Don't hit a tuning fork against a hard surface or ever strike them with great force.

You can use tuning forks to cleanse the chakras and aura in several ways. If you discover a flare, depression, or any other anomaly in the patient's aura, you can choose a tuning fork that corresponds to the chakra that controls that area of the body. Strike the fork and hold it near the damaged or diseased area. Then, seal the aura with the hands. If the problem persists, the healer should cleanse the chakras and then go back to the damaged area and try again. Sometimes, holding a tuning fork near the end of a quartz crystal that is pointed at the area will amplify the energy.

To cleanse the chakras, begin with the largest fork, middle C. Strike the fork, hold it over the root chakra, and visualize the color red. When the fork stops vibrating, move to the next fork and the belly chakra. Continue this procedure until you have worked your way up to the transpersonal chakra, which lies just above the head. You may also chant the appropriate vowel/consonant or mantra while doing this. If you wish, you can also sing or hum the tone while working with the tuning forks.

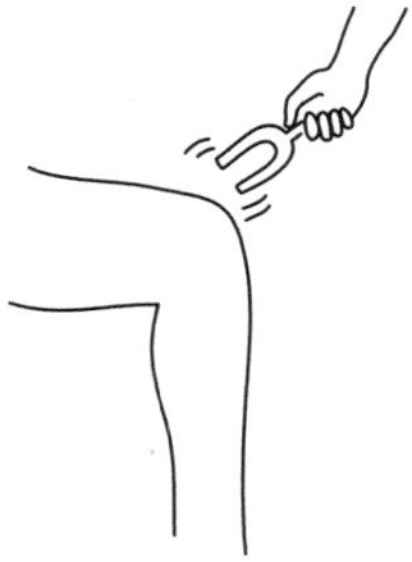

Use of Tuning Forks on the Body

In healing, if you discover that two chakras are connected with an illness, you can choose the appropriate tuning forks for those two chakras and strike both at the same time. Holding the vibrating forks in the aura should aid in attacking stubborn, persistent, or severe illness.

If the exact site of an illness is known, the healer can apply the vibrating tones of the tuning fork directly to that area. Be certain that you understand which chakra controls that area and/or disease so that you can use the correct tuning fork.

If two healers are working on a patient at the same time, one healer can work on the aura with the hands, while the other strikes and uses the tuning forks. This is a bit difficult if you are applying this technique to your own body, but with a little practice, it can be done in most areas.

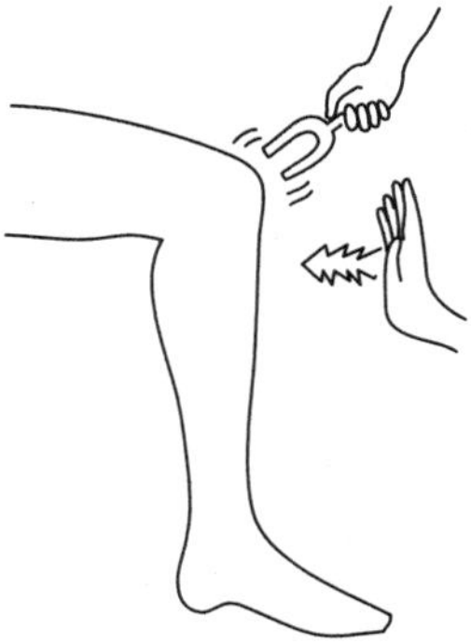

Toning and Using of Hands

Tuning forks are also useful to create an altered state of consciousness in some healers and patients. When doing this, two tuning forks are used at the same time. Middle C and D will project an outer calming vibration that is soothing to the atmosphere and the patient. Middle C and B affect the mind and nervous system for an inner calming. Middle C and E produce an atmosphere of outer energy, while middle C and A produce an inner energy. This last set of forks should be used with great care so that neither the patient nor the healer becomes uncomfortably energized. Middle C and G vibrate mental activity and inspiration into the surrounding atmosphere, while middle C and F provide personal and inner inspiration. Middle C and the higher C affect the etheric levels and often aid in deep meditations and spiritual enlightenment. Some psychics claim that middle C and A are conducive to mystical inspiration. However, I have found that middle C and the higher C work much better for this.

One can also use the tones of tuning forks during magickal spells, such as candle burning, making healing poppets, making colored elixirs, creating talismans, and such. This will increase the spell energy, often giving a boost that the healer-magician needs to heal successfully.

Tones for Healing

The following list may be helpful. You can also experiment to see if different tones work better for you on specific spells.

MIDDLE C This tone strengthens the willpower and the desire to survive. It helps increase physical energy, love, conception, brings success in any desire or project. It also is good for any diseases affected by the root chakra.

D This tone can change your luck. It helps you accept responsibility and get rid of negative situations. It is good for any diseases affected by the belly chakra.

E This tone helps you protect yourself from emotional events, understand upsetting life events, remove unrealistic fears, get your life in order. It is good for any diseases affected by the solar plexus chakra.

F This tone helps you learn to accept life and move gently through it, establish a connection with nature spirits and other ethereal beings, determine your place and purpose in this lifetime. It is good for any diseases affected by the heart chakra.

G This tone helps you gain confidence for public appearances or duties, learn to stand up for yourself, expand your knowledge, and gain proficiency in your chosen career or in magickal endeavors. It is good for any diseases affected by the throat chakra.

A This tone helps you open the Third Eye, expand your knowledge and use of the psychic, learn to heal yourself and others, seek the right spiritual path. It is good for any diseases affected by the brow chakra.

B This tone helps you expand your spiritual growth, make contact with your spiritual teachers, guardian spirits, and Goddess/God. It is good for any diseases affected by the crown chakra.

HIGHER C This tone helps you seek the ultimate source of spiritual knowledge and power, and establish a universal connection with all things spiritual. There are no diseases, except deep spiritual diseases, associated with the eighth chakra.

Music in all its forms is healing for both the patient and the healer, indeed, for everyone. Choose your music wisely and avoid negative forms of this art, forms that have detrimental effects on the body, mind, and spirit.

Color Healing

We have ancient records detailing how priests in Egypt, Babylonia, and China used colored light in their healing practices. Healing through sunlight therapy was a common medical practice for relief of skin disorders, such as psoriasis, in Greece, China, and Rome. In the late 1890s, Nobel prizewinner Dr. Neils Finsen expanded upon this ancient knowledge and learned how to heal skin lesions using red and infrared light treatments. In 1920, Dinshah Ghadiali from India developed a color healing system that he called Spectro-Chrome. Through experience he determined what colors were most effective in treating a variety of diseases. Today, dermatologists frequently use ultraviolet phototherapy for certain skin disorders.

However, not more than fifty years ago, the Food and Drug Administration banned the use of colored light in healing, saying it was quackery. Now, the government has approved a device, developed by Dr. John Downing, called the Lumatron which uses colors and light frequencies for therapy. Dr. Jacob Liberman, another pioneering light therapist, called light the medicine of the future because it directly affects the cells.

Today it is possible to buy special light projectors for use in healing, but these machines are expensive. You can make your own projector by using a snap-clip on the end of a small metal rod and fastening this rod so that it extends in front of an ordinary lamp. Make certain the rod is long enough so the plastic is not too close to the heat of the lamp. This device enables you to change colors easily when treating yourself or a patient. Cut out adequately sized squares of colored photo lens plastic and clip whatever color you want to use in front of the lamp. The patient sits at a comfortable distance from the lamp and relaxes for five to ten minutes while soaking up the rays. You don't have to look at the light to benefit from it.

Another method of color light projection requires a small penlight flashlight and squares of colored photo lens plastic. You can use the same colored squares mentioned on page 253 for balancing the chakras. Place the appropriate color in the palm of the patient's power hand and shine the light onto the plastic for two minutes at a time. The receiving chakra in the palm of the hand will transfer the power of the color directly into the aura and the chakras.

The color technique can also be used in various visualization techniques. The healer mentally creates balls of energy of specified colors with the hands and then applies these balls of energy directly to the patient's body and aura. Chanting while visualizing will strengthen the power of the colors. If you are doing absent healing (see page 371) you can create balls of colored light-energy in meditation. You can then apply these balls of light to yourself or send them to a patient.

Healing with Colored Water

Another ancient color technique is becoming more popular today—color-infused water. Water charged with color is sold on the market under the following names: rubio for red; ambero for orange and yellow; verdio for green; ceruleo for blue; and purpuro for indigo and purple. Or you can make your own color-charged water.

To color-charge water, fill a clean, sterilized jar with pure water that contains no additives such as fluoride. Tape a sheet of photo lens plastic of a specific color to a window with the jar of clear water behind it. Another method is to tape the sheet of lens plastic directly to the jar and make certain that the sun strikes the colored plastic. The sun shines through the window and the film onto the jar of water. Let the jar of water stand for one to four hours and then refrigerate. Without refrigeration, it loses its charge in three or four days. Read the color descriptions that follow to determine how to use color-charged water. For example, take a few sips of orange-charged water before meals for constipation.

The water can be sipped in small amounts, such as a quarter of a cup at a time, two or three times a day. It may also be added to bath water.

Making Color-Infused Water

To make stronger elixirs, set the jar of water out on a specific planetary day. Sunday is the Sun's day, or yellow, orange, or gold. Monday is the Moon's day, or white or light blue. Tuesday is Mars's day, and is good for red or magenta. Wednesday is Mercury's day, or orange, lemon, or yellow. Thursday is Jupiter's day, or violet, purple, turquoise, or dark blue. Friday is Venus's day, or green or pink. Saturday is Saturn's day, or dark purple or indigo.

You can charge your elixirs with greater power by using tuning forks (see page 355). When the elixir is finished, and you have poured it into the properly labeled bottle for storage, strike the appropriate tuning fork and hold it close to the bottle.

The following list will help you decide which tuning fork to use.

MIDDLE C Red, magenta

D Orange

E Yellow, lemon, gold

F Green, pink

G Blue

A Indigo, turquoise

B Violet, purple

HIGHER C White and clear quartz crystal elixirs only (see Gem Elixirs on pages 366–70)

Color Healing

The following list of colors will help you determine which colors you should use for certain diseases or illnesses. Frequently, more than one color can be used for healing a specific disease. In this case, choose the color that your intuition says is best or treat the patient with several different colors. If you decide to use more than one color, allow at least an hour between treatment with one color and treatment with another color. Never combine the light colors for one treatment. If you are using color-infused water, have the patient take the doses separately, half an hour apart.

You will notice that some of the colors state that they should be followed by treatment with another specific color for certain diseases. This is to strengthen the treatment or to minimize side effects from the first color.

You will also notice that some colors are not recommended for specific diseases because they have a negative effect on those diseases.

BLUE A calming color for the nervous system, blue reduces fear and rapid heartbeat, and cures insomnia. It can also be used for burns, itching, painful skin abrasions, apoplexy, biliousness, cataracts, glaucoma, chicken pox, colic, diarrhea, fever, laryngitis, sore throat, dysentery, eye inflammation, gastrointestinal diseases, hysteria, painful menstruation, heart palpitations, goiter, headache, acute rheumatism, shock, toothache, tonsillitis, duodenal ulcers, vomiting, and jaundice. It is particularly useful in localizing and limiting the destructive effects in the areas around tumors. Because of its sedative qualities, blue also helps with pain. When using blue to treat gastric and duodenal ulcers, asthma, pleurisy, cystic mastitis, diarrhea, and prostate enlargement, follow this color with orange. Do not use blue on colds, constriction of muscles, hypertension, or paralysis.

GOLD A combination of orange and yellow, this color can revitalize the entire nervous system, as well as increase vitality and energy.

GREEN This color stimulates the pituitary gland and is useful in treating dysfunction of that gland. It also helps rebuild damaged muscles and body tissues, disinfect, detoxify, and dissolve growths. Use green for ulcers, cancer, asthma, back disorders, head colds, colic, hay fever, high blood pressure, irritability, laryngitis, malaria, malignancies, nervous diseases, neuralgia, and sleeplessness. However, there is a difference of opinion on using this color to treat heart disease, some saying it is not advisable. Personally, I find it works fine for heart problems. If in doubt, use pink and pale violet instead. Use green followed by magenta when treating toxicity caused by problems in the colon, liver, or kidneys. Use with orange to loosen up and remove diseased etheric matter in the aura.

INDIGO This combination of blue and violet light will increase white blood cell counts, stimulate the pituitary gland, and help with blood purification. It also helps with cataracts, appendicitis, asthma, bronchitis, hearing loss, cataracts, convulsions, dyspepsia, hyperthyroidism, all lung problems, nervous ailments, nasal trouble, nosebleed, tonsillitis, and various types of pain. Follow it with gold when treating sinus infections, spine and lower back pain, angina, headaches, hepatitis, and inflammation of the small intestine.

LEMON This combination of yellow and green is helpful in treating persistent or chronic medical disorders that have not responded to other forms of alternative healing. It also aids in strengthening bones, coughing, dissolving blood clots, and stimulating the immune system.

MAGENTA A combination of red and violet, this color helps with many emotional problems. Follow it with green when treating tumors of the pituitary, lungs, breast, stomach, colon, kidneys, uterus, and testicles. Also use it with green for breast cysts, detached retina, tinnitus or ringing in the ears, and water retention.

ORANGE This color helps with regeneration of lung tissue and stimulates the thyroid gland. It benefits the entire respiratory system, helps muscle spasms and abdominal cramps, and is useful in treating ovarian cysts, uterine fibroids, and prostate diseases. It is also a good color for gallstones, emphysema, and bronchitis. This color helps with the elimination of waste, toxins, and germs from the body and diseased ethereal matter from the aura. Use orange for asthma, bronchitis, rheumatism, colds, epilepsy, gallstones, malignant and benign growths (particularly in the precancerous stages), hyperthyroidism, hypothyroidism, the lungs, mental exhaustion, and kidney ailments.

PINK This color is good for emotional healing and to promote self-nurturing.

PURPLE This dark, potent color will induce relaxation and promote sleep, as well as lower the body temperature, decrease the blood pressure, and slow the heart rate. It is also useful in treating the kidneys, lungs, and stomach.

RED This color stimulates the sensory nervous system and the liver and causes regeneration, increases the red blood cell production, and helps with circulation. Red causes rapid tissue and cellular repair and helps with all types of wounds and broken bones. Use for anemia, blood ailments, colds (if no fever), constipation, weight loss, the endocrine system, melancholia, pneumonia, and tuberculosis. Red stimulates the elimination of toxins from the body through the skin, so never treat the patient for more than five minutes at a time. Because red can induce anger in susceptible people, you should take great care when using it. Watch the patient closely for any signs of agitation. In most cases, red is most beneficial when followed by blue or white. Do not use red for nervousness, mentally disturbed people, hypertension, inflammatory conditions, neuritis, asthma, high blood pressure, heart disease, or epilepsy.

TURQUOISE This color is obtained by combining green and blue filters in a projection lamp. It affects the thymus gland, which is the major immune center of the body. It is helpful for burns, chronic fatigue syndrome, AIDS, and inflammatory problems. When followed by red, it aids in treating acute sore throat, ear infections, nephritis, and bladder infections.

VIOLET An extremely potent color, violet (as well as purple) can be used on severe health problems and diseases, because it promotes rapid healing of damaged internal organs. This color stimulates the spleen and immune systems and will depress the activity of heart muscle, the lymph glands, and the pancreas. It is also useful for painful sciatica, bladder trouble, bone growth, cerebrospinal meningitis, concussion, cramps, kidneys, epilepsy, mental disorders, neuralgia, rheumatism, and tumors. It can increase the white blood cell count and help tranquilize the nervous system. This color is useful in treating any spiritual disease, as well as helping with headaches and mental disorders.

WHITE This color actually contains all other colors and is milder than the colors themselves. Therefore, it is very useful in treating infants, young children, the elderly, and extremely ill patients. You can also use it for any disease or at any time to charge the aura's field.

YELLOW A stimulant of the motor nervous system (the neuromuscular system), this color helps regenerate damaged nerves, stimulates the lymphatic system and intestinal tract, and breaks down deposits in arthritis. It is also useful in treating skin wounds and broken bones, soothing stomach and liver problems, and in increasing positive cellular growth. Use yellow for constipation, diabetes, digestive problems, eczema, flatulence, kidney trouble, indigestion, the liver, mental depression, rheumatism, and the spleen. For paralysis or dysfunction of the nervous system, use yellow followed by violet on the soles of the feet, where there are spinal-reflex points. Do not use yellow for acute inflammation, delirium, diarrhea, fever, neuralgia, or heart palpitations.

Gem Elixirs

Healing with gem elixirs or tinctures partly uses the science of color healing and partly uses the science of gem power. Gem elixirs are easy to make and can be an important part of a healer's weapons against disease.

A. K. Bhattacharya successfully treated patients for years in India with gem elixirs. In his practice, he used the seven principal gems given in ancient Sanskrit writings plus three other gems. The seven gems are said to match the seven cosmic rays, light rays that make up the universe. *The Kurma Purana* of the Hindus says that even the seven planets known to the ancients are condensations of these seven rays of light. These seven rays also match the colors of the seven major chakras in the astral body.

The best gems are authentic, with synthetic gems, manmade to weigh and refract light in the same way as genuine gemstones, next in value. Do not use simulated or glass look-alikes. When creating gem elixirs, choose stones of the purest color, not mixed with any other stone or colors. Ideally, the stone should be tumbled or faceted and have no particles that might come loose in the liquid. Jewels set in silver or gold mountings can be used if they are clean. In Hindu gem therapy, gems are not chosen for the color seen by the physical eye, but by the color seen through a prism or microscope.

A complete list of stones and their uses for diseases follows the procedures for preparing gem elixirs. Pearl and coral are in this list of Hindu healing stones, although technically they are not true stones. Also, it is not necessary to have large gemstones to make elixirs. A small tumbled or faceted stone of good color works well and is easily inserted and removed from the bottles.

There are two kinds of cat's eye stones. The chrysoberyl cat's eye is extremely expensive; a small cabochon the diameter of the tip of your little finger can cost as much as $7,000. The quartz cat's eye, or crocidolite, is far less expensive and, in my experience, works just as well as the chrysoberyl cat's eye.

The Hindus add to their list of single-gem elixirs what are known as Seven-Gem Elixir and Nine-Gem Elixir. The Seven-Gem Elixir uses emerald, diamond, ruby, sapphire, topaz or moonstone, cat's eye, and pearl. The Nine-Gem Elixir adds coral and onyx to the Seven-Gem Elixir.

The gems used to make elixirs will readily discharge their power into water or alcohol. However, the pearl should never be placed in alcohol; alcohol will damage it.

To prepare elixirs for a vast array of diseases, you need at least nine of the gems in the above list, several one- or two-ounce glass bottles with screw caps (preferably bottles colored blue or green), and vodka or pure water. Pure water is best, as it doesn't react adversely with any gemstone. You can use vodka, if you wish, but it isn't necessary. Not only will alcohol damage some stones, but some patients may have negative reactions to alcohol in a gem elixir. Never use medicinal or rubbing alcohol.

Making Gem Elixirs

First, wash and sterilize the bottles. Fill a bottle with water, then drop in the required gem. Seal the bottle with the cap and store in a dark place for seven days and nights. The best time to begin this is after the new moon so you are finished by the next full moon. At the end of this time, shake the bottle gently, and then transfer the liquid into another labeled bottle. The water will not look any different after it is made into gem elixir. Store out of the sunlight.

Wash the gemstone thoroughly and store until you need it again. Always give your stones time to rest between making batches of elixir. A small stone is capable of charging an ounce of water at a time.

The Seven-Gem Elixir is made by placing all seven gems in the bottle at one time. With the Nine-Gem Elixir, place the nine gemstones in the bottle. The rest of the procedure is the same as for a single-gem elixir.

Unless patients are very ill, have them take six to twelve drops of the elixir, three or four times a day. For all single-gem elixirs, give the more seriously ill patient four to six doses each day. Nine-Gem Elixir is stronger and is only given once or twice a day. The Seven-Gem Elixir is given only two or three times a day. In all chronic cases, one dose per day of Seven- or Nine-Gem Elixir is useful, along with single-gem elixirs. It takes time to see any tangible results. (The elixirs may also be added to bath water or massage oils.)

Use the following list of gemstones to determine which ones to give a patient. Sometimes more than one stone will be useful in treating a disease.

AGATE, BROWN Excessive menstrual bleeding, fever, epilepsy, water retention.

AMBER Colds, ulcers, malignant and benign growths, soreness, hay fever, asthma, goiter, and respiratory diseases.

AMETHYST Gout, nightmares, eye diseases.

CARNELIAN OR BLOODSTONE Hemorrhages, ulcers.

CAT'S EYE Skin diseases, acne, headaches, indigestion, cancer, paralysis, uterine diseases.

CORAL Liver diseases, impure blood, high blood pressure, skin ailments, hemorrhoids, sexual diseases, gallstones, hemorrhoids, hepatitis, liver trouble.

DIAMOND Gastritis, problems of the heart and circulatory system, eye diseases, various forms of paralysis, enlarged spleen, epilepsy, diabetes, infected glands, itchy skin, menopause, nephritis, sterility.

EMERALD Insomnia, throbbing, tension, headache pain, weak digestion, colic, cancer, skin problems, hypertension, heart trouble, ulcers, colitis, diarrhea, duodenal ulcer, gastric ulcer, gastritis, heartburn, indigestion, vomiting.

GARNET Eczema, psoriasis, skin eruptions.

HEMATITE Eye diseases, hemorrhages of the lungs or uterus, sunstroke, headache.

JADE Heart palpitations, difficult childbirth.

LAPIS LAZULI Prevent miscarriage.

MOONSTONE Fever, epilepsy, mental illness.

ONYX Bacterial or virus infections, hyperacidity, insomnia, brain disorders, glandular diseases.

OPAL Clears the brain and revives the memory.

PEARL Mental problems, diabetes, asthma, gallstones, diarrhea, menopausal difficulties, Bright's disease, bronchitis, edema, fevers, persistent low fever, hemorrhages, high blood pressure, influenza, insomnia, kidney stones, melancholia, pneumonia, rhinitis, tonsillitis, urinary tract disease. Never soak pearls in alcohol. Use only pure water.

QUARTZ CRYSTAL, CLEAR Glandular swellings, glaucoma, conjunctivitis, fevers, abdominal pains, strengthening the heart.

RUBY Benefits the liver, spleen, gallbladder, and pancreas. Helps with heart diseases, circulatory problems, anemia, loss of vitality, eye diseases, arthritis, circulatory system, constipation, irregular heartbeat, low blood pressure, heart palpitations, rheumatism, and various mental disturbances.

SAPPHIRE Backache, eczema, headache, heart trouble, laryngitis, migraines, neuralgia, neuritis, pericarditis, psoriasis, vertigo.

TURQUOISE Weak eyesight, inflammation of the eyes, headaches, fever, problems with urine retention.

TOPAZ Female problems, colds, lung conditions, sinus and nose problems, throat diseases, asthma, insomnia, epilepsy, laryngitis, childhood infectious diseases, shock, coughs, swollen glands, obesity, pancreas problems.

SEVEN OR NINE GEMS Anemia, arthritis, asthma, backache, Bright's disease, bronchitis, cancer, constipation, diabetes, duodenal ulcer, eczema, gallstones, gastric ulcer, swollen glands, heart trouble, irregular heartbeat, hemorrhages, high and low blood pressure, hepatitis, insomnia, kidney stones, liver trouble, melancholia, menopause, nephritis, obesity, heart palpitations, pancreas trouble, pericarditis, pneumonia, psoriasis, rheumatism, sterility, tonsillitis, vomiting.

You should be open to using a variety of treatments in your efforts to promote healing in a patient. However, make certain the patient will accept the technique before using it. Some people will not be open to color light therapy or gemstone elixirs.

Absent Healing

Absent or distant healing is a mental and spiritual process a healer uses when working with patients who aren't present. It is accomplished through mental imagery and an altered state of consciousness, much like the work of shamans. A photo is helpful but isn't necessary. All a healer needs is a name, what town the patient lives in, and a general description of the disease. After much practice, some healers don't even need to know the illness. They can determine this by making contact with the patient's etheric body. Absent or distant healing takes place when a healer contacts the subconscious mind of a patient and sends visualized symbols or pictures that influence the patient's mind to heal the body.

This type of healing will use the Otherworld healing temple built during the meditation on page 335. Enter a meditative state, direct your thoughts toward your temple, and you will be there. Then you can call the patient by name. The etheric body of that person will appear in your temple for healing. All of your study on the aura and chakras, meditation, and building your Otherworld healing temple will now bear fruit.

Most doctors will admit that patients are primarily responsible for healing themselves. Patients can't pray and then do nothing else, expecting a healing to fall into their laps. Patients can participate in the healing by using every alternative noninvasive method in this book that seems to work.

By entering an altered state of consciousness in your Otherworld healing temple, you contact the patient, see the disease or damage, and sometimes its cause. Then you trigger a healing through imaged treatment. Some healers may see a patient through a type of X-ray vision, especially when working on broken bones. This type of vision work rarely comes without a lot of practice by a healer, and never by trying to force it. Just relax and let your intuition guide you.

The healer must concentrate on the patient at all times during the healing and not think about the healing itself. Don't dwell on the healing after it is finished because that will siphon off healing energy.

The healer must use mental pictures to convince the patient's subconscious mind to heal the body. The subconscious mind is able to do wonderful things, most of them considered impossible by the conscious mind. The subconscious mind regulates all the body activities, so healing a disease is a relatively insignificant task. Mental pictures will show the patient's subconscious mind how to correct the problem, thus opening up a connection with universal healing energy.

Guided imagery in meditation or absent healing is important in the healing arts. Imagery can increase the natural killer cell activity, increase the production of immunoglobulin, and increase the activity and numbers of disease-fighting lymphocytes.

A good book on anatomy can be helpful. In this way, the healer gets a better idea of where internal organs are.

Understanding the endocrine glands is another vital part of healing. If these are working properly, many illnesses will correct themselves. To understand better how these glands work, a brief description of each follows.

The pituitary gland is in the center of the head, in back of and between the eyes, at the root of the nose. It hangs from the hypothalamus gland, which is attached to the brain. The pituitary gland is really the master gland and controls all the endocrine glands in the body.

The hypothalamus gland is about the size of a sugar cube and is located in the brain. It connects the chemical and neural systems. The thalamus gland is slightly above and to the rear of the hypothalamus. It is the reception area for touch, pain, heat, cold, and muscle sensations.

The pineal gland is behind the thalamus and lies almost in the center of the head. It is only about a half-inch long and it's believed to stimulate the action of the other glands.

The thyroid gland is butterfly-shaped and lies on each side of the throat just above the points of the collarbone. It controls metabolism and the calcium content of the blood. The button-like parathyroid glands are imbedded in the thyroid, two on each side. They help to control blood calcium and the phosphate in the kidneys and pancreas.

The thymus gland lies in the front of the chest and just below the thyroid gland. It governs the actions of the lymph glands for fighting infection.

One adrenal gland sits atop each kidney. These glands produce adrenalin for the sympathetic nervous system. They also release other hormones to regulate the amount of salt and water in the body.

Absent healers work with images and send certain colors of healing energy during an absent healing treatment. In general, red healing energy produces energy for physical body maintenance; it is a stimulus that speeds up sluggish organs. Green energy aids the subconscious mind in replacing or rebuilding damaged areas. Blue energy will support the interaction of body functions, calm pain, relax the body, and soothe the nervous system. Pink energy calms intense nervous conditions. Use white energy for general healing, disinfecting, energizing, stimulating, and normalizing any physical problem.

There are a number of ways to interpret diseases that appear during a healing, but you must find the one that helps you the most. Images of diseases usually appear as symbolic impressions. For example, if you are working on a patient with diabetes, this disease may appear to you as a pipe with a thick, syrupy, reddish brown liquid flowing through it or as large white specks in the blood stream. The white specks could be interpreted as sugar crystals, just as the thick, syrupy liquid would be the blood stream clogged with sugar particles. Broken bones often look like snapped sticks. Painful muscles may appear as long red streaks giving off a fiery heat. Arthritic joints might look like ball bearings coated with pebbles and sand. With practice, you will understand what your intuition is trying to explain.

Symbolic Healing

Several general visualization techniques work well for all healers. These are symbolic techniques only and have nothing to do with physical reality. The subconscious mind deals only with symbols and must be presented with such to understand what you want it to do. If your instincts come up with symbolic techniques other than the ones in this book, use them.

One important fact to remember in all absent, imaged healing is that you must destroy all removed and infected tissue in a psychic, spiritual fire. You might wish to install a large bowl or cauldron in your Otherworld healing temple for this purpose.

- Use skin tape to fix cuts and tears in the skin.
- Clean out clogged blood vessels with a long wire brush.
- Zap tumors, growths, or cancer cells with a laser light.
- Cover wounds and bruises with skin putty.
- Drain poisons from kidneys with a suction faucet.
- Pick out gallstones and kidney stones with long tweezers, then fill the space with blue healing putty.
- Lessen pain by saturating the painful area or the entire body with green, blue, or white pain-removal light.
- Place blue or green ice packs on swollen injuries.
- Use sandpaper, fine files, or a small grinder to smooth off rough arthritic joints.
- For broken bones, zap the break with healing light, then tape it together with bone tape, and pack it with bone putty. Or you can

use psychic glue for broken bones, torn muscles, and a number of other problems.

- Tie together a torn muscle or ligament with elastic tape.
- Stop bleeding by cauterizing the cut with a healing laser.
- Cover scrapes or sores with large pieces of new skin tape.
- Use a small suction machine and hose to remove tiny pieces of glass, splinters, bone fragments, small growths, or poisonous crystals in the blood that can become arthritis or other diseases.
- Paint blue healing gel on painful joints or the entire body to remove pain.
- Inject lubricating oil into stiff joints.
- Remove any red threads from the body as these symbolize lines of pain. Do the same with any black threads that may be disease tendrils. Destroy these threads or any removed material in your cauldron of universal flames.
- Use sponges to soak up fluid in the lungs, throat, and sinuses. For the hard-to-reach sinuses in the forehead, use a small suction machine.
- Infections are carried by the blood once they establish a hold in body tissues. When this occurs, install a mental germicidal filter in the blood stream to trap and kill all germs and foreign matter.

Let your subconscious mind come up with new ideas that fit your needs. The only way to explain how to do absent healing through correct visualization is to give examples. Then you can explore further on your own, discovering what symbols and impressions work. Stories from my healing classes illustrate the many valuable uses of visualization used in healing.

Healing Sessions

In one session, we worked on Al, a diabetic. Al had let his diet and medication slide until he was in serious difficulties. We mentally installed filters in several of the main arteries to filter out the sugar crystals. Then we washed out the liver and pancreas in a green healing solution to dissolve any harmful residue. After checking for any viral infection that might be lurking undetected, we reset the pituitary, pineal, and adrenal glands so that they properly controlled the insulin. We finished by bathing the patient in blue and green healing lights. Al's blood levels evened out, and by following his diet and medication schedule as he should, he was soon able to dispense with insulin shots.

Leukemia is an insidious and potentially deadly disease. When Jim requested a healing, he was in the middle stage of the disease. We began by injecting blue healing energy into the long bones of his legs and arms, and into the pelvic bone, to normalize the production of white blood cells. Then we sent streams of red energy into those same areas to increase the production of red blood cells. We injected green energy into the liver, spleen, and lymph glands to destroy any remaining cancer cells, and finished by bathing his body in white and gold light. Jim improved greatly but refused to return for another healing treatment, believing that one session should do it. One healing session is never enough for any disease. Jim's disease eventually gained ground again.

When treating a respiratory infection, first you need to get rid of the congestion. Soak it up with sponges or install a suction faucet. Then eliminate the cause of the inflammation. You may need to spray germicidal spray through the lungs and sinuses.

In pneumonia, you need to remove as much of the lung fluid as you can. Next, pour blue gel into the lungs to remove pain. Finish by filling both lungs with white healing light. You may need to also install germicidal filters in the bloodstream to help remove viruses and bacteria.

For asthma, check the lungs, nose, sinuses, throat, and bronchial tubes for infection and irritation. Drain off any accumulated fluid, and spray these areas with blue liquid to minimize any further irritation.

In dealing with emphysema, you will notice that the lungs will look distended and stiff, with the inside walls dry and likely covered in what looks like blisters. Using your Otherworld tweezers, remove the blisters and any damaged air sacs. Disinfect the lungs with blue or green light. Fill any holes left by removal of tissue with body putty. Then flood the lungs with a softening healing oil that will give them elasticity. Finish by flooding the entire chest area with gentle white light.

Frequently children suffer painful earaches, although adults may get them on occasion. First drain off the infection in the inner ear. Check the eustachian tubes; if they are blocked, gently run a small, long brush through to open them. Then flood the entire ear and the tube with soothing blue gel to remove the pain.

When working on head colds and sinus infections, drain off the infection, making sure that you get into all the sinus cavities. Open any blockages. Spray all the infected areas with blue healing liquid to kill the germs and flood the head with white light.

A patient with a sore throat will often have several connected areas infected at the same time. Check the throat, sinuses, and lungs. Suction out any infection and open any blockages. Paint the infected areas with green healing gel. Install a germicidal filter in the blood stream and inject a universal antibiotic.

Skin problems such as rashes, moles, or warts can be treated in a similar way. First check the blood for impurities and install a germicidal filter to handle that problem. Spray a disinfectant over the diseased area. Paint a violet-colored skin peeler on the affected skin and then peel off the mole, wart, or rash. Recover the area with new skin tape.

When dealing with a breast tumor or cancer, check for any tiny black threads issuing from the main site. Remove these and burn them. Check the lymph glands for contamination. Shrink the tumor with a violet laser light and remove any remaining portion with the tweezers. Install filters in the lymph glands to catch any floating cancer cells and destroy them. Flood the entire body with brilliant white healing light.

When healing internal growths or tumors, be certain to remove all the immediately surrounding tissue and blood vessels when you remove the tumor or growth itself. Burn these. Pack green gel into the site of removal and hold it in place with body tape. Flood the entire area with blue light to remove the pain, followed by white light for healing.

When working to eradicate any cancer or tumor, always make certain you destroy any removed tissue in your cauldron of spiritual fire. You don't want the vibrations of such deadly diseases floating around in the atmosphere.

Cancer requires long-term healing sessions. Use the above-mentioned healing techniques, and expand upon them as necessary. You may need to install cancer-killing filters in the bloodstream if no tumors are found. This ensures that any floating malignant cells are trapped and destroyed.

Chronic or recurring headaches can be debilitating and frequently involve more than blood vessels. Check first for any aneurysms; if you find one, reinforce it with flexible body tape. If there are no aneurysms, check that the pituitary, pineal, thalamus, hypothalamus, thyroid, and thymus glands are working properly. Reset them if necessary. The endocrine glands are reset by visualizing them with a dial with settings for low, medium, and high. You will then be able to see if the gland is working overtime (high) or not enough (low). Set the dial at medium for proper operating. Find any expanded or contracted blood vessels (usually at the base of the skull and in the neck). If expanded, cool them with blue gel packs. If contracted, pack them with red gel packs until they expand to the proper size. Bathe the entire head in blue and white light to ease the pain and tension.

Nervous headaches are usually caused by nervous tension and a depletion of energy. Send red energy into the nervous system to recharge the body's energy. Bathe the entire body in blue gel to relieve tension and pain. Finish by shooting gold light throughout all the aura levels. Since nervous headaches frequently cause the shoulder muscles to tighten, you will need to massage blue gel into these areas to relieve the pain and loosen the tension.

Heart and artery problems require a slightly different approach because you must stop time while working on these. This does not harm the patient or stop the heart. Picture a clock beside the patient and order it to stop. Check out the entire heart—valves, muscles, and arteries. Replace any bad valves by picking out the old ones and installing new ones. Inject red energy into damaged muscles. Clean out any clogged arteries with a long brush. Flood the entire chest with blue light to relieve pain and then gold light to continue healing indefinitely. Return to the clock and order it to resume time.

When working with the liver and gallbladder, remove any stones or growths; fill the cavities with body putty. Wash out the organs with a green liquid and drain off this waste. Spray the inside with blue energy until the liver or gallbladder attains a healthy color. Flood the entire area with blue light to relieve pain. If the patient has cirrhosis or hepatitis, the cleaning may take some time. Be certain that you drain off all the waste you wash from the liver. Raise the body's healing rate by 25 percent. You can do this by again visualizing a dial set in the organ involved. The face of the dial will be marked in easy-to-read degrees. Simply set the dial 25 percent higher than it was.

For kidney or bladder infections, examine the complete urinary tract for areas of infection and spray it with green liquid to kill gems. Wash the entire tract with green germicide and drain off the waste. Remove any stones or growths. Flush the entire system with blue energy to relieve pain.

Intestinal and stomach ulcers need immediate pain relief, so flood the entire intestinal tract from one end to the other with blue energy for pain. Using a green laser light, destroy the ulcer. Fill the cavity with blue body putty and seal with body tape. Coat the entire intestinal tract and stomach, inside and out, with white healing paint. Finish by installing a germicidal filter in the blood stream, as many ulcers are caused by a bacteria.

When healing the spinal column for whatever reason, check it from top to bottom for broken or chipped vertebrae, herniated disks, and bone spurs. Put broken or chipped vertebrae back together with bone glue and patch with bone putty. Grind off any bone spurs. Be sure to check the inside of the vertebrae for spurs often lurk on the inside. Pack blue gel around herniated disks to shrink them and cushion between the vertebrae. Bathe the entire spine, nerves, and adjacent muscles with blue healing light to relieve pain.

This type of healing imagery can be used whenever you are in meditation, even if the patient lives near you. Sometimes the subconscious mind will be more open to symbolic images if the patient is asleep while you are working.

Healing Images

The use of a poppet in healing is known as sympathetic magick, meaning that the healer performs a healing ceremony with a created image in an effort to affect the patient's subconscious mind. As in absent healing, the magick follows the thought to the patient whom you have in mind and produces the results. This magickal art can be misused, as when making dolls to harm another person, but that was never its primary use. No healer will indulge in negative magick.

Sympathetic magick has a long history in the healing arts of the ancient cultures. For example, in ancient Egypt, physicians made images out of wax or clay and red substances to symbolize blood. They then added a great variety of minerals and plants to these images, all in an effort to persuade the patient's subconscious mind to help with the healing.

In 1869, J. E. Quibell excavated several sites in Egypt. One of these was the house of a medical magician who lived at Thebes. In the ruins of this house, he found four small wax figures that represented the sons of Horus (the four sons of Horus were used to represent the four directions during magickal rituals; modern magicians frequently use four different-colored candles to represent these directions), two clay *ushabtis* (or *shawabtis*), and a wooden box with an image of the Goddess Isis, mistress of magick, on the lid. This box contained a number of small magickal papyrus scrolls. However, the scrolls were so delicate that they could not be completely unrolled. The box also contained four ivory curved wands with mythical creatures painted on them. These magickal wands were used for making gestures when the magician made such items as talismans and amulets. Also inside were small human figures (poppets) made of clay, red and black inks, reed pens, and stone beads and amulets.

Today these little human-shaped images can be made of cloth, wood, clay, or, in an emergency, even paper. Each one is made to represent a specific person. The power doesn't lie within the poppet, but within the will and intent of the healer-magician.

Making a Poppet

A poppet usually looks something like a gingerbread cookie. It does not have to be very large, just big enough to hold some herbs and perhaps a stone or two. You don't have to be a seamstress or even handy with a needle to make a poppet. In fact, you can use fabric glue to hold the two pieces of cloth together.

The supplies you will need are few: a small amount of light blue, light green, or white material; fabric glue or thread; a black pen; a small amount of herbs; whatever stones you choose; a long piece of white yarn; two light blue or light green candles; a red candle; sticks or cones of frankincense; and a small basket or box lined with a piece of white material. Choose your herbs and stones from the lists later in this section.

Tradition holds that something belonging to the person whom the poppet represents should be put inside it, even if this is only a piece of paper with their handwriting. However, you can make a useful poppet without this.

The poppet is best made out of cloth instead of other substances so that you can draw on features that represent the man or woman for whom it is being made. It is also useful to write the person's name across the body of the doll. This enables you to know which doll represents what person, especially if you are working on more than one patient at a time. If you know the patient's sun sign, draw that astrological symbol on the poppet also.

Poppet Image

Enlarge the pattern in the following illustration to the size you want. While you are cutting out two pieces of the material for each poppet, visualize the sick person whom you wish to help by making the healing doll. It is best to finish one poppet before you start on another. You can use either fabric glue (available in fabric shops) to attach the two pieces of material together, or you can sew the pieces together about one-quarter of an inch from the edges. Leave an opening along one side of the poppet. You will use this opening to stuff the doll with herbs and stones. When the poppet is completely stuffed, sew or glue this opening shut.

When choosing the herbs, be sure to include herbs for body, mind, and spirit, as well as for healing. You want to bring the patient back to a balanced life, for healing will not last without balance in all areas and on all levels.

You can also put in certain small gemstones. Try to put one gemstone in the diseased area. You can also include other small stones that will aid in healing.

If the patient has any wounds or visible marks from an illness, draw these onto the poppet in the proper places. During your healing ceremony, cover these marks with wax dripped from a red candle. This symbolizes the healing that will occur in the patient.

After making the outer portion of the poppet, lay it in a basket or small box lined with white cloth. You will finish the healing doll at the full moon. Check an astrological calendar for the correct date, as some ordinary calendars are off by a day.

Have all your needed materials on hand when you begin the final part of assembling the poppet. For the best results, a poppet should be cleansed and empowered on a full moon. You will work on the poppet from one full moon until the next.

At the full moon, place the poppet between two blue or green candles on your altar. Light the candles and burn frankincense incense.

Have your chosen herbs ready. You should use at least three or five different herbs in each poppet. Three and five are magickal numbers and are important in spells of all kinds. You do not need to have an even amount of each herb. If you don't have enough herbs on hand to completely fill the poppet, stuff it with cotton batting, leaving enough space for the herbs. The herbs should be dried, not fresh, which may mildew.

Choose your herbs from the following list or consult books on magickal herbalism to make correct choices.

ALLSPICE Good health, happiness, banishing negativity, spiritual wisdom.

BASIL Healing, banishing fear, calming.

BAY LEAVES Good health, reducing stress, spiritual blessings.

CARNATION PETALS Healing, success, peace.

CHAMOMILE FLOWERS Good health, calmness, peace.

CINNAMON Healing, confidence, grounding.

GARDENIA PETALS Good health, confidence, happiness, cleansing of the spirit.

JUNIPER BERRIES Healing, happiness, spiritual blessings.

LAVENDER FLOWERS Good health, calmness, banishing negativity.

MUGWORT Good health, healing of the mind and emotions, connecting with spiritual teachers.

PEPPERMINT Healing, eliminating anger, connecting with spiritual teachers.

PINE NEEDLES Grounding, calming the mind, banishing negativity, reducing stress.

ROSE PETALS Good health, eliminating anger, spiritual blessings.

ROSEMARY Grounding, pain relief, banishing negativity, spiritual cleansing.

VERBENA OR VERVAIN Good health, reducing stress, peace, connecting with spiritual teachers.

YARROW FLOWERS Healing, gaining confidence, cleansing the environment.

Before stuffing the herbs into the poppet, you must empower them. Place the chosen herbs in a small bowl. Hold the bowl in one hand, while placing your power hand over the herbs. Visualize healing energy pouring into the herbs. Say an incantation, such as this:

> *I bless these herbs with healing power, to heal the body, mind, and soul, of (patient's name) in this hour, that she/he may once again be whole.*

Stuff the herbs carefully into the poppet. Choose your stone or stones from the following list or consult a good book on magickal uses of stones. General stones for health and healing can be any green, blue, or pink stone. Or you may choose from the following stones.

AGATE, MOSS A powerful rapid healer.

AMBER Heals chest problems and digestive diseases, will cleanse the entire system.

AMETHYST Calms mental problems, purifies the blood, strengthens the immune system, balances all chakras.

AVENTURINE Strong healing powers through the pituitary gland.

BLOODSTONE Cleanses the blood, detoxifies the body.

CARNELIAN Helps regenerate tissue, cleanses the blood, shrinks tumors.

GARNET Purifies and regenerates all body systems.

JADE Purifies the blood, strengthens the immune system, calms.

LAPIS LAZULI A great healer and purifier.

MALACHITE Regenerates tissue, strengthens the heart.

MOONSTONE Unblocks the lymphatic system, reduces swelling.

QUARTZ CRYSTAL, CLEAR An extremely powerful all-purpose healer.

QUARTZ, ROSE Heals mental, emotional, and spiritual distresses.

TOURMALINE, WATERMELON Soothes the nervous system and the aura field.

TURQUOISE A master healer, strengthens and regenerates the entire body.

If you can't afford to buy a variety of stones, you can use clear quartz crystal alone. However, it is more effective to have more than one kind of stone. Hold your chosen stones in one hand with your power hand over them. Empower them by saying:

O, stones of star and earth and sea, heal (patient's name).
So must it be.

Place the stones inside the poppet. If you have a personal object from the patient, put that inside also. Sew or glue the poppet closed. Take up your red candle and dribble wax over any wounds, cuts, or blemishes you have drawn onto the poppet. While you do this, say:

Red as the blood of life, I mark the wounds of (patient's name).
I seal them. I bind them. I heal them.

Tie a long piece of white yarn around the middle of the poppet to symbolize the doll's connection with spirit and with the patient. Leave one long end hanging loose. Say:

This cord connects (patient's name) and this healing doll.
When the healing is complete, at my word the tie will be broken.

Snuff out the candles and return the poppet to the basket. Every day, light the candles and incense, and say the following chant three times while holding the poppet in both hands. Do this until the next full moon. Concentrate on the patient being totally well while saying the chant. This builds a psychic link with the patient. You can also pray however you wish.

(Patient's name) is restored and whole. This is my wish; this is
my goal. Disease, be gone! All illness flee! This is my will.
So mote it be.

Each time you finish the ritual, place the poppet back into the basket or box and cover it with the white cloth. Tradition says that a poppet should never be destroyed but given to the person it represents.

However, this is not always a good idea, as most people connect poppets with voodoo dolls and would be shocked to know a healer made a doll of them. That is why each poppet should have a white thread or piece of yarn tied around its waist with one long end of the thread hanging loose. When the poppet has done its work and needs to be dismantled, the healer-magician should hold the doll and chant:

The tie between (patient's name) and this doll is now broken.
All healing energy left within this doll flies to (patient's name).
Only good shall come of this action.

Then the white yarn is cut free, the poppet opened, and the herbs sprinkled on the earth. Any personal object from the sick person that was enclosed in the poppet is buried in the earth. Any gemstones that were included can be cleansed and reused. The remaining parts of the poppet can then be safely burned or buried.

Never save a poppet to use again. That is tantamount to saying you don't believe in your healing work. If a patient does become ill a second time, make a new poppet.

Talismans and Amulets

From the beginning of civilization, people have worn or carried amulets and talismans to which they attributed certain powers. Amulets are some of the most common objects found in archaeological sites. They date back to prehistoric times and are not confined to any one place or historical period or culture.

The modern equivalents of these ancient magickal objects are rosaries, saints' medals, crosses, crystal pendants, a rabbit's foot, a lucky coin, the Egyptian ankh, and the charm bracelet. In the Punjab area of India, people wear copper bracelets, rings, and earrings to protect against arthritis and sciatica. In Oriental cultures, jade bracelets and anklets symbolize protection against misfortune.

The dictionary defines an amulet as "a charm often inscribed with a magickal incantation or symbol to protect and aid the wearer." Talisman means "a charm to avert evil and bring good fortune."

Ordinarily, amulets are naturally formed substances like herbs, stones, or animal claws. They are chosen for their unusual forms or colors. Some, however, are man-made representations of these objects. People believe they will safeguard the owner from trouble and attract happiness and good luck. A natural amulet is said to be full of universal and earth energy, while the man-made amulet is empowered by magick or faith.

Some believe that the word *amulet* is derived from an Arabic root, which means "to bear, to carry." Others hold that the word is derived from the Latin *amuletum*, which is an object that protects a person from trouble.

The ancient Egyptians had several names for amulet. One early Egyptian name for amulet was *hekau*, which is a form of the word for magick. Another was *udjaou*; the literal translation is "the thing that keeps safe." Other times the word *mekti*, or "protector," was used.

Talismans are similar to amulets, except that a talisman is a man-made object and is charged through ritual to do one specific duty for a specific person, while amulets are general in nature. Talisman is derived from the Greek root *teleo*, which means, "to consecrate."

Charms can be symbols or written words and combine the functions of both talismans and amulets. The modern charm bracelet is very old in origin. Examples of charm bracelets and anklets have been found in early Roman ruins.

Amulets were very popular among the Egyptians and were frequently part of the grave goods in tombs, where they were inserted into the mummy wrappings. Most amulets had small holes in them so that they could be hung on a neck chain, pectoral, or bracelet (like the modern charm bracelets), or fastened to a ring. A pectoral is a wide collarlike piece of Egyptian jewelry that laid flat around the neck and hung down onto the chest.

Amulets were made according to strict magickal rules and traditions. It is possible that certain priests oversaw their production. An ancient document known as the MacGregor Papyrus listed seventy-five different amulets, the names by which they were known, and their uses. This information is verified by a list carved on the walls of the temple at Dendera. This list gives the materials from which the amulets should be made. The ancient Egyptians used amulets in specific shapes for certain results. The following figures illustrate a few of the talismans and amulets with which you may not be familiar. Today, most people are familiar with certain reproductions of ancient Egyptian amulets.

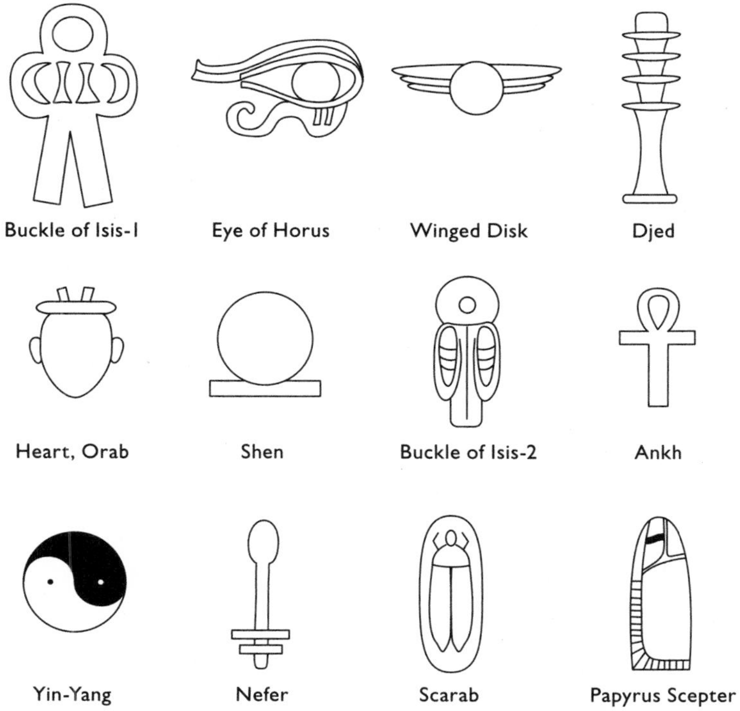

Various Talismans and Amulets

Although Egyptian amulets were made of every known material, the finest ones were carved out of stone, such as lapis lazuli, carnelian, turquoise, feldspar, serpentine, and steatite. Sometimes metals such as gold, copper, bronze, and iron were used. However, the largest number of amulets found in excavations were made of faience. Faience is a paste made out of ground quartz crystal, molded, covered with an opaque colored glaze, and then fired. Today, copies of Egyptian amulets are frequently made of clay, ceramic, or silver. In this section, I will use the amulet to describe all of these magickal objects, whether they are amulets, talismans, or charms.

Types of Amulets

There are actually two kinds of amulets. One type is inscribed with magickal words, and the other type is not. For example, Egyptian amulets such as the scarab were inscribed on the reverse side of the amulet, while those made by medieval ceremonial magicians often consisted only of magickal words engraved on metal or written on paper.

You can make many of the amulets out of clay, thin wood, thin pieces of metal, or draw them out on paper (see the illustrations on page 389). Paper amulets are usually carried in a small cloth or leather bag. Each amulet is activated by chanting prayers or certain words over it. You can do the blessing yourself. If you purchase an amulet, you still need to activate it by chanting.

Amulets can be a valuable healing tool, for the visible images work on the patient's subconscious mind and reinforce any other healing methods you are using.

A typical ritual for activating the powers within an amulet is simple to do with a minimum of material. Light two white candles and lay the amulet between them. Light frankincense incense. Fill a small bowl with a little water and place a pinch of salt on a saucer. Hold the amulet in one hand, with your power hand over it. Chant:

Fire, Water, Earth, and Air, I call upon your powers fair.
Empower this amulet for me. For so I will. So shall it be.

If you make this amulet for another person, be certain to state: "I bless this amulet for [patient's name]" before you do the actual blessing.

Quickly pass the amulet in the heat above the candle flames, then through the incense smoke. Sprinkle a few grains of salt on the amulet; tip the salt back onto the saucer. Sprinkle a few drops of water onto the amulet from the bowl. The amulet is now ready to wear.

The following list of amulets will help you decide which ones a sick person may wish to wear or carry.

ACORN This represents good luck, protection, and long life. It also symbolizes the accomplishment of a difficult task, usually one that takes time.

APPLE This represents healing and long life.

ANKH This is also called the looped cross or *crux ansata*. It meant life or everlasting life. All Egyptian deities are portrayed holding an ankh. It is a very powerful protective symbol and the oldest of Egyptian amulets.

BATS In the Chinese culture, the image of two bats gave good fortune.

BELLS This amulet frightens away evil.

BIRDS The Chinese believed that images of the stork and crane brought good health and long life.

THE BUCKLE OF ISIS This amulet is also called the *tjet* or *tjed*. Some writers believe this object represents the buckle on the girdle of the goddess Isis, while others think it represents female genitalia. Also called the knot of Isis, this amulet was always carved out of red stone, such as jasper or carnelian, or other red substances, for the blood of Isis was said to contain great magickal powers. On rare occasions, archaeologists have discovered the buckle made of gold or substances covered with gold. It was the all-powerful symbol of the Goddess Isis, who was a powerful magician and healer. It is used for protection and the removal of blockages.

BULL This represents strength and virility.

BUTTERFLY This represents eternal life and reincarnation, or a transformation within this life.

CAT This protective amulet was connected with the Egyptian Goddess Bast or Bastet, who gave aid to those who called upon her. To the Egyptians, the black cat was an extremely powerful healing symbol.

CLOVER The four-leaf clover represents hope, good luck, love, and faith. The typical three-leaf Irish shamrock symbolizes good luck, love, and prosperity. The three-leaf clover was also used as a magickal emblem by the Greeks, Romans, and Egyptians, who believed it gave immortality, riches, and protection from evil.

CONCH SHELL This represents protection against evil.

CRICKET This represents good luck.

CROSS The equal-armed cross is an ancient sun symbol of protection.

DJED This amulet was connected with the power of the Egyptian God Osiris, and was worn only by the dead to assure stability of the afterlife. Although sometimes this object is said to be a symbol of the tree in which the body of Osiris was hidden, it is more likely that this represents the backbone of the God Osiris. The four crossbars represent the four cardinal directions. In modern terms, the *djed* can be used to give strength to the backbone or spine.

DOG This amulet is a warning image against evil.

EAGLE This ancient symbol of the Sun God gives vitality and strength. The eagle was also considered to be a messenger from the gods to humans.

ELEPHANT To the Hindus, this emblem represented the elephant-headed God Ganesha, who removed all obstacles and difficulties.

EYE OF HORUS The ancient word for this amulet was *utchat* or *udjat*. It symbolized the all-seeing eyes of the god Horus and ensured good health. The eyes of Horus were considered to be the sun and the moon. It was made of silver, gold, hematite, carnelian, or lapis lazuli. The *udjat* can give the wearer good health and physical protection.

FAIRY This represents unexpected help from the Otherworld.

FISH This image has long been an important symbol used in many cultures. To the Egyptians, it meant abundance, prosperity, happiness, and wealth. To the Hindus, it meant protection, fertility, and wealth. Two fish mean fertility.

FROG This amulet was associated with the Egyptian Goddess Hekat and symbolized fertility, fruitfulness, resurrection, inspiration, and a new life. The Burmese use the frog image for protection, especially for children.

HAND The Hand of Fatima is an Arabic symbol of protection and good fortune. However, the hand symbol goes back to Stone Age cultures. The Egyptians used the hand as protection against evil arising from envy. The Etruscans used it as a symbol of justice and victory. The image of a life-sized hand guards against evil and brings good luck. It is more powerful if you use the outline of the hand belonging to the person who will receive this amulet.

HEART This was thought to be the source of the power of life and also the source of individual good or evil. The Egyptian word for heart was *ab*, and the image was always made in a red color. The *ab* brought love, protected against hatred, and symbolized the power of the subconscious mind, vital power, and the seat of the soul.

HOLLY This ancient emblem is for good luck, friendship, and goodwill.

HORSE, WHITE This amulet represents long life and determination to gain what you desire.

HORSESHOE This is for good luck and protection from evil.

IVY This represents faithful friendship.

KEY This was an ancient symbol in many cultures. It represents knowledge and the opening of doors to the unknown. It was sacred to the Roman deities Apollo and Diana. It was also an emblem of the God Janus and represented prudence, memory of the past, and perception of the future. The Japanese said that three keys brought happiness, riches, and love. In many other countries, three keys represented love, wealth, and good health.

LADYBUG A protection against poverty, this image attracts wealth and is also said to remove illness. The Norse believed that ladybugs came to earth by means of lightning strikes.

LION'S HEAD This amulet represents strength.

MOON When a crescent moon, with the horns pointing to the left, is worn, it symbolizes protection against bad luck and the gaining of incoming prosperity.

MONKEY To the Hindus, this emblem represented the God Hanuman, who brought great good fortune.

NEFER Worn as a pendant on necklaces, this object may be a stylized musical instrument. It was usually made of carnelian, red stone, or red porcelain and worn on necklaces. It represented joy, strength, happiness, and good luck.

PAPYRUS SCEPTER The Egyptian word for this image was *uadj*. It was made of light green or blue substances. This amulet represented the power of the Goddess Isis over abundant harvest. It also symbolizes vitality, renewed youth, and constant growth.

PIG This is a symbol of fertility, good fortune, and protection.

PYRAMID A version of the sacred triangle, the pyramid means protection and indicates that helpful knowledge will be discovered.

RABBIT'S FOOT Hopefully, you will not buy a real one but will settle for a man-made one instead. It represented great good luck and protection.

SCARAB The most popular amulet in ancient Egypt was the scarab, or *kheper*. The use of this amulet predates the pyramids. Connected with the God Kheper, the scarab amulets often had hieroglyphic messages carved on the underside. This image of the dung beetle represents new life, resurrection, strength, immortality, and good luck.

SHEN This Egyptian symbol represents the sun in its orbit and means eternity and long life.

SNAKE OR SERPENT This image represents wisdom and drawing power from the earth.

SPIDER The Etruscans believed that spider images gave wisdom, foresight, and riches. Other cultures credited the spider with great ancient wisdom, inspiration, and protection.

STARS This image represents hope and the fulfillment of wishes.

TORTOISE The Chinese used an image of the tortoise for protection against black magick and to attract good health and long life.

TUSK Usually a boar's tusk, this is a symbol of good fortune, success, and protection.

UNICORN Many cultures believed in the existence of the unicorn and credited it with the ability to grant good luck, fierceness, purity, and protection.

WINGED DISK An ancient symbol of the Sun God, this image grants the wearer protection from accidents and all serious threats to life. The circle portion of the winged disk represents total protection from all evil.

WISHBONE This symbolizes that wishes will be granted.

YIN AND YANG SYMBOL Known in the Orient, this is a circle divided into a white section (yang) and a black section (yin) by a wavy line. It represents perfect balance.

Amulets can be carried in the pocket or purse, hung on chains as pendants, or several of them worn on a charm bracelet. They may also be put into in healing boxes, as described on page 408.

Healing Plaques

Another way to use the amulet symbols is to make a healing plaque for a specific person and carve healing symbols onto that plaque. Write out the patient's name in runes in the center of the plaque. Writing in another alphabet is more powerful because it requires more concentration. Or you may simply draw appropriate runes that represent the qualities you want to empower in the plaque. Sketch out symbols from the above list around this name. See the illustration on page 399 for examples of healing plaques.

The following list of Nordic runes will help you write out the name and also determine what each rune means. This list is in alphabetical order according to the spelling of the rune. I have chosen the Nordic runes because they are easy to draw or paint.

ANSUZ Alphabet letter A; transformation, new goals, information that changes your life.

BERKANO Alphabet letter B; new beginnings.

DAGAZ Alphabet letter D; enlightenment.

EHWO Alphabet letter E; new attitude, steady progress.

EIHWAZ Alphabet letters EI, I, Y; end of a matter, situation, or problem.

ELHAZ Alphabet letter Z; blockages removed.

FEHU Alphabet letter F; money, fulfillment, good luck, goals reached.

GEBO Alphabet letter G; great good fortune.

HAGALAZ Alphabet letter H; delays while waiting for the right time.

INGWAZ Alphabet letters NG; benefits from family.

Runes

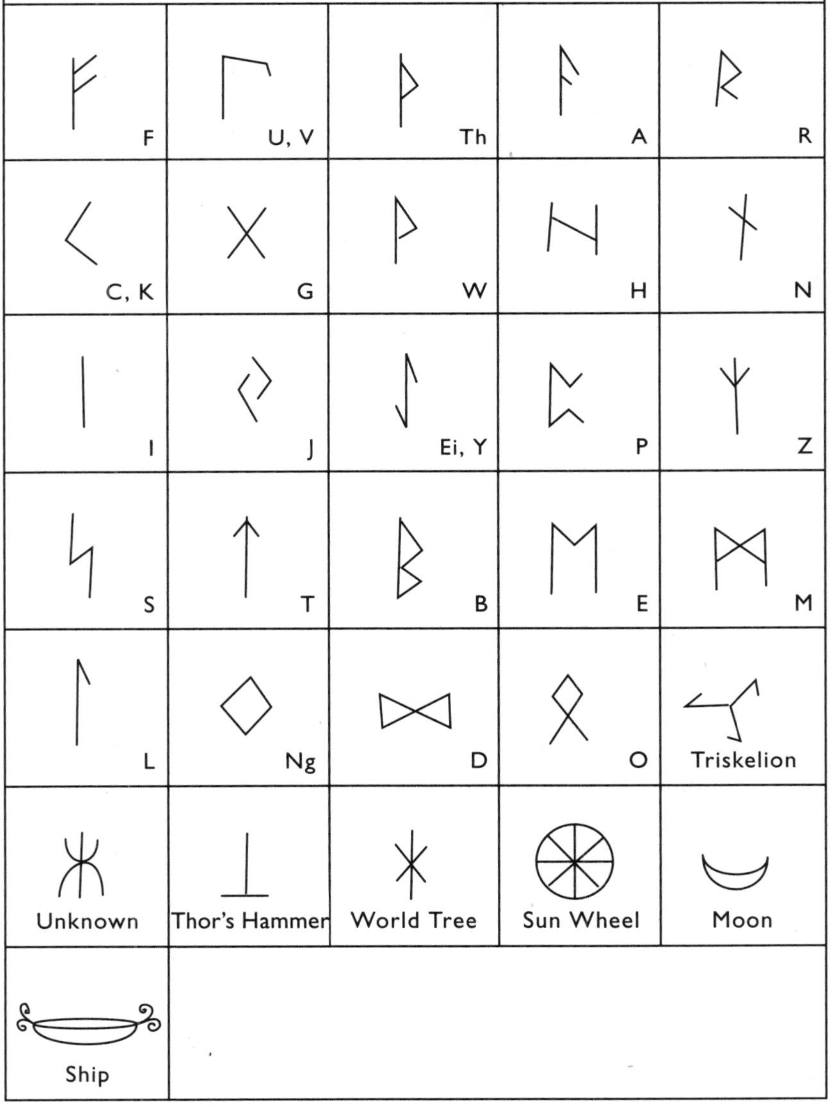

ᚠ F	ᚢ U, V	ᚦ Th	ᚨ A	ᚱ R
ᚲ C, K	ᚷ G	ᚹ W	ᚺ H	ᚾ N
ᛁ I	ᛃ J	ᛇ Ei, Y	ᛈ P	ᛉ Z
ᛋ S	ᛏ T	ᛒ B	ᛖ E	ᛗ M
ᛚ L	ᛜ Ng	ᛞ D	ᛟ O	Triskelion
Unknown	Thor's Hammer	World Tree	Sun Wheel	Moon
Ship				

ISA Alphabet letter I; no movement seen.

JERA Alphabet letter J; no quick results.

KENAZ Alphabet letters C, K; determination.

LAGUZ Alphabet letter L; hidden movement below the surface.

MANNAZ Alphabet letter M; positive link with the Gods.

NAUDHIZ Alphabet letter N; caution needed to succeed.

OTHALAZ Alphabet letter O; inherited genes or property.

PERDHRO Alphabet letter P; unexpected changes.

RAIDHO Alphabet letter R; getting to the truth.

SOWILO Alphabet letter S; time of renewal, advancement of plans.

THURISAZ Alphabet letters TH; news from a distance, inner strength to pass a time of waiting.

TIWAZ Alphabet letter T; victory.

URUZ Alphabet letters U, V; advancement, good fortune, manifestation.

WUNJO Alphabet letter W; security, comfort, happiness.

The last seven symbols on the chart are not actual runes but mystical pictograms used by the Norse. They are powerful when used for magickal purposes.

MOON An orderly change, a transformation.

SHIP Movement, transforming problems into positive solutions.

SUN WHEEL Inner guidance, seeking spiritual truths and answers.

THOR'S HAMMER Increase, protection, willpower, protection from all negatives.

TRISKELION A form of the sun wheel. Movement, advancement of plans.

UNKNOWN SYMBOL Wealth, material success, material gain.

WORLD TREE Divine guidance, total protection, overpowers all negatives.

To make a healing plaque for yourself or another person, use colored clay (that can be air- or oven-dried), and an awl, thin knife, or toothpick for drawing designs on the clay. Work on a flat, smooth surface. Work a ball of clay until it clings together, visualizing good health for the patient. Flatten it into a circle. Roll it smooth with a rolling pin and then cut out the circle with a sharp knife. Etch onto this circle any healing runes you have chosen, plus the name of the person for whom the plaque is made. If the clay can be air-dried, place it in a warm place where it will not be disturbed. If it must be baked, bake the clay on a metal cookie sheet according to directions on the box the clay came in. Baked clay may have a strong odor while in the oven, so you may need to open a window for ventilation. Remove from the oven at the recommended length of time, and cool the clay on the cookie sheet.

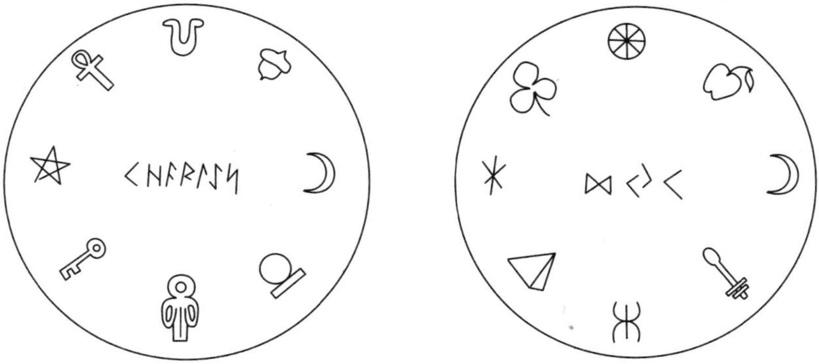

Healing Plaques

The ancient Babylonians used what is called a devil-trap to keep evil out of a house. These devil-traps consisted of a bowl with a magickal spell written in spiral fashion, with the beginning of the spell on the outer edge and the ending in the center of the bowl. These bowls were buried under the foundation of a house, or under or near the threshold.

Today, these bowls can be made to trap all negative thoughts, words, and deeds before they enter the house of a sick person.

The bowl or saucer should be fairly flat, as this will make it easier to write upon. Write the following spell in black paint in a spiral fashion on the bowl or saucer. "No evil or negativity may enter this house. It is trapped inside this bowl and returned to the earth for purification." Then bury the bowl near the threshold of the main door if possible. If it isn't possible to bury the bowl, place it under the porch or in the crawl space under the house. If you live in an apartment and have no way to bury the bowl, you can write the spell on a circle of paper and tuck it under the doormat.

Healing Charms and Spells

Healers have made and used healing charms and spells for thousands of years. The original healers were also priest/priestess-magicians who knew that magick, medicine, and religion needed to be combined to heal.

Every ancient culture had deities who specialized in healing. For example, the Sumerians called the God Ea the founder of healing and the patron of herbalists and physicians. They considered that all water had healing properties; therefore, all patients were washed thoroughly. Their God Ninazu was called the Master Physician, and the Goddess Ninhursag was also connected with healing.

We know more about the ancient Egyptian culture than many others because of the surviving scrolls and papyri. The Egyptian Goddess Sekhmet was the most important of healing deities and was directly associated with medical doctors. However, Isis was also known as the

Goddess of magick and healing. The Gods Horus and Thoth were also associated with the magickal healing arts. The physicians, or *wabus*, were priests of these deities and primarily worked in the healing temples, where they treated patients with a combination of medicine, religion, and magick.

Two ancient Egyptian temples were known for miraculous cures. One was the Temple of Dendera, where the physicians used magickal water in their cures, followed by magickally induced sleep for the patients. The other temple was the mortuary temple of Queen Hatshepsut at Deir el Bahari. The upper terrace of this temple was specifically dedicated to Imhotep and Amenhotep, both of whom were regarded as great physicians.

However, there was another minor branch of physicians, who likely worked among the common people. These were the *sunu*, or lay-physicians, who were not directly attached to a temple. The *sunu* used all the techniques known to the *wabu* priests but used more magick in their healings than their counterparts did. Frequently, they wrote out little protective spells on slips of papyrus that were put into small leather pouches to hang around the neck of a patient.

Ancient Irish medicine included charms and incantations, many of which have survived in folklore and folk medicine. Folk charms can soothe the patient's nerves while acting as a remedial agent.

Folk Remedies

An example of a folk remedy is Four Thieves Vinegar. During the years of the Black Plague in Europe, a band of thieves came up with a recipe for four thieves vinegar. They swore that this vinegar and herb combination protected them from catching the plague while they plundered the bodies and houses of dead plague victims. The thieves would bathe their hands, arms, necks, and heads with this vinegar. Today we know that vinegar is a type of antiseptic, and some doctors use a vinegar and water spray to disinfect their examination rooms.

Four Thieves Vinegar

To make Four Thieves Vinegar, put a quarter ounce of each of the following herbs into a glass container: calamus root, cinnamon, ground cloves, ground nutmeg, lavender blossoms, mint leaves, thyme, hyssop, rosemary needles, rue, sage, and wormwood. Slice two garlic cloves into the herbs. Add one quart of apple cider vinegar. If you wish, you can heat the vinegar to boiling before adding it to the herbs. Cover the container with a tight lid. Let sit in a warm room for five days. Strain the mixture through a fine sieve or cloth. Add a quarter ounce of powdered camphor if you wish. Then pour into a labeled bottle.

This mixture smells more like a salad dressing than a disinfectant, so you can use it in sick rooms and around the house without offending anyone. In its time, this recipe was considered to be magick, because no one could explain why it worked.

Like many other types of alternative healing and magick, herbal charms and spells aren't instantaneous. Nor will a magickal spell work if you only do it one time or with a skeptical attitude. The healer-magician's attitude is very important. Negative thinking has no place in magick. A healer must visualize the patient at all times as healed and free of disease.

There is a standard rule in magick pertaining to the phases of the moon. To decrease anything, work from the day after the full moon until the next new moon; this is called the waning moon. To increase anything, work from the day after the new moon until the next full moon; this is called the waxing moon. Growths and such should be worked on during the waning moon, while wounds and sores should be worked on during the waxing moon. Diseases like pneumonia, lung diseases, and heart problems should be worked on during the waning moon to draw out infection or damage and on the waxing moon to strengthen the organs and muscles.

There are many magickal healing recipes, some of which have come down to us in folklore and folk medicine from hundreds of years ago.

Healing Oil

Healing oil heals the spirit more than the body. To make healing oil, clean and sterilize a small glass jar, preferably green or blue in color. It must have a tight lid. Some healers will paint the outside of several small jars with translucent paint in the colors they want and save them especially for magickal use. Measure out equal portions of rose petals, rosemary leaves, and hyssop, as much as it will take to fill the jar of your choice. Put these into the jar and cover with cold-pressed almond oil. Set the jar where it can get sunlight and moonlight for seven days. Do this beginning on the day after the new moon. At the end of the seven days, strain the herbs and oil through several layers of cheesecloth or through a very fine sieve. Return the oil to the colored jar and cap tightly. Use this oil sparingly to anoint the patient's brow, over the heart chakra, and on the palms of the hands and the soles of the feet.

Healing Incense

If you like to use incense that is burned on incense charcoal, you can make your own healing incense. In a mortar and pestle grind together one tablespoon of dried rose petals, one-fourth teaspoon of dried dragon's blood resin, one tablespoon of juniper berries, and one teaspoon of yarrow flowers. Store this mixture in a small sealed jar. Burn a small amount of it on incense charcoal in a censer during healing rituals.

Healing Water

Healing water is similar to Four Thieves Vinegar, although it is primarily used as a psychic cleanser. Do not drink this. It is used to wash the hands before and after a healing. Bring to a boil one pint of pure water—no additives—in a pan. Fluoridated tap water isn't a good choice. Add one teaspoon of saffron, one-half cup of dried rose petals, one-half cup of lavender flowers, and one tablespoon of ground orrisroot. Remove immediately from heat and cover with a tight lid. Let stand three to four minutes. Strain through a fine strainer or cloth. Store in a blue or crystal clear bottle that can be tightly capped.

Herbal Charm Bag

A healing pillow or small herbal charm bag can be helpful to a sick person. Not only is it a constant reminder that someone cares and is working for their healing, the scents of the herbs can be soothing and relaxing. See pages 383–84 for a list of appropriate herbs for healing pillows and bags, and pages 363–66 for a list of colors and their magickal uses when choosing material colors. A pillow stuffed with mugwort is traditional for dreams. However, if patients are upset by dreams while using sleep pillows, they should discard it.

A healing pillow or small bag to carry doesn't need to be large. It is simply a square of material that is sewn together on three sides, stuffed with the appropriate stones and herbs, and the fourth side sewn shut. See the following illustration for a pattern for a small herbal bag.

Each healing pillow should contain three types of herbs: one for sleep, one for spiritual growth, and one for healing. This little pillow is put under the regular pillow at night. Be certain that the patient isn't allergic to any of the herbs before you give it to them.

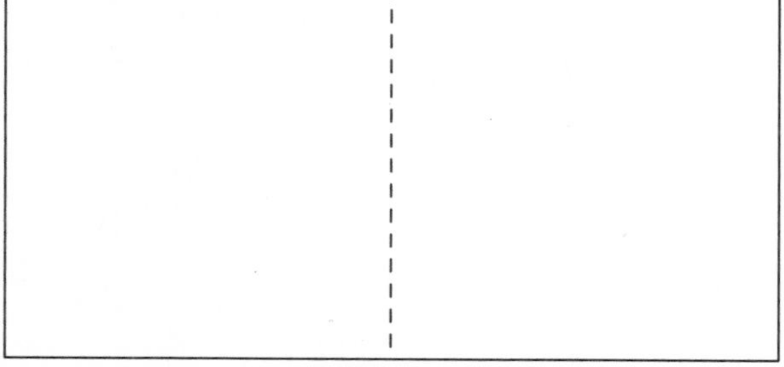

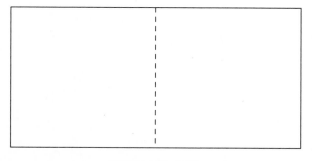

Making an Herbal Bag

Herb bags are meant to be carried in a pocket or purse, or worn on a cord around the neck like a talisman. An herb bag is sometimes called a sachet. In fact, the idea of sweet-smelling sachets may have originated from herb bags. You may embroider, paint, or draw a symbol on this bag that matches the purpose for which it was made.

Healing pillows and bags should be spiritually cleansed and empowered on a full moon. Consecrate the bag by slowly moving it through the smoke of frankincense incense. Visualize the sick person while saying: "Pure and healing shall you be, O herbs of the earth and sun and sea. Comfort, soothe, and all ills bind, of the body, spirit, mind."

Using the pattern, you can make an herbal bag for the patient to carry. Fold the strip of cloth at the dotted line shown in the diagram. Then sew or glue closed two of the sides, leaving the third side open until you have put in the herbal mixture. A pinch is usually what you can hold between your thumb and forefinger. Mix together a pinch of cinnamon, two pinches of sage, two pinches of rose petals, and two pinches of ground frankincense. Anoint the mixture with three to five drops of sandalwood oil. Put this mixture into the little bag. Sew or glue closed the open side. Give it to the patient to carry at all times. If the patient has lung problems, add two pinches of spearmint leaves to the bag. If the troubles are in the head area or the mind, add two pinches of rosemary. The scent of rosemary is good for headaches.

Wind Healing

Other types of healing charms use the powers of the four elements: Earth, Air, Fire, and Water. Many of these have come down to us through folklore from many cultures. One of these is healing with Air through the power of the wind.

The sick person must do this wind healing. It can only be done for another person if that person is too ill to do it. Collect small fresh leaves, one for each illness you or the person has. Take a dead tree branch with several limbs on it. Go to a place where the wind is strong and push the end of the dead branch into the ground. Push each leaf onto the very tip of a dead branch. Chant:

Power of Air, remove all ills. Let [patient's name] be healed and whole.

Then leave without looking back. When the wind removes the leaves, the action will release powerful energy for the healing.

Sick people must do most healing charms using the elements themselves. This is part of the patient's involvement and responsibility for healing.

Water Healing

For a charm that uses the power of Water, get a small piece of wood that will float, like a Popsicle stick. Write on it every illness you have. Hold it in your hands and visualize your sicknesses going into the stick. Chant:

All illnesses float away from me. This is my will. So shall it be.

Place the stick in moving water and let it carry away your illnesses.

Tree Healing

Many cultures believe that trees have magickal power, particularly in curing illnesses. One only has to visit sacred wells in Ireland and other countries to see that people still believe in this. The shrubs and trees around these wells are frequently decorated with colored strings and ribbons, each denoting a supplicant who wishes to be healed.

Here is one sample of a tree healing. Tie a piece of red thread, string, or yarn loosely around the patient's wrist at bedtime. Leave it on all night. The next morning, take the thread and tie it around a tree or tree branch. Tradition says the illness will pass into the tree and then into the earth, where it will be destroyed.

Another ancient tree healing is simple. Find a tree that you can easily stand against without hitting your head on branches. Circle the tree clockwise nine times, chanting:

Round and round this tree I walk, in search of healing old and deep. O tree of healing, cure my body. Take thou my illnesses and them keep.

Then stand with your back against the trunk and visualize your sickness going into the tree.

Cord Magick

Cord or knot magick is another ancient practice. Use a long piece of cord or yarn of natural fibers, if possible. The cord should be green, blue, or white. Assemble small feathers and leaves or twigs of appropriate healing herbs. As you tie nine knots in the cord, chant:

Knot one, I tie the sickness tight. Knot two, I bind all mental woes. Knot three, I tie up the sorrows and fears of my emotions. Knot four, I bind all negative thoughts of others and myself. Knot five, I tie all pain and discomfort so it has no power over me. Knot six, I bind all habits, thoughts, or tendencies that may have led to the illness. Knot seven, I tie up healing power that I may draw upon whenever I have need. Knot eight, I bind forgiveness to be freely given to all who harmed me. Knot nine, I bind myself to Divine Spirit, that my mind, body, and spirit may be healed and made whole again.

As you tie each knot, insert a feather and a piece of herb into it while you visualize binding up the illness. The following list of feather colors will help you decide which colors to use. The feathers can be found or bought. When finished, either hang this cord up in the patient's room, or from a tree branch outside.

BLACK absorbs all negatives.

BLACK AND WHITE Protection.

BLUE Peace and good health.

BROWN Health, stability, and grounding.

BROWN AND WHITE Happiness.

GRAY AND WHITE Hope and balance.

ORANGE Energy and success.

PINK Love.

PURPLE Deep spirituality.

RED Courage, good fortune.

WHITE Purification, spirituality, hope, protection, and peace.

Spell Box

Another type of healing charm is a spell box. Choose a box that appeals to you and then line it with a color that matches your purpose. The meanings of colors in this instance are:

BLACK Banishing and absorbing negativity.

BLUE Healing, peace, and happiness.

GOLD Great healing energy.

GREEN Healing.

ORANGE Energy.

PINK Relaxation.

PURPLE Healing of severe disease and increasing spirituality.

RED Maintaining health, strength, and physical energy.

SILVER Spiritual growth and healing.

WHITE Protection, purification, and all purposes.

YELLOW Confidence.

You can also add feathers, stones, and shells to the boxes. You may wish to put a healing poppet in the box to represent the sick person (see page 381).

Shells have special meanings according to their type. Mark clams with a rune so they will be a potent talisman for wearing, carrying, or in the box (see pages 396–99 for rune meanings). Limpets are for making dramatic positive life changes. Oyster is for good fortune. Sand dollars are for wisdom.

Give the healing box to the ill person and encourage them to add other symbols that have meaning to them. They can open the box whenever they meditate. The symbols will help them connect with spirit and divine healing from the Otherworld.

Coriander seeds can be carried in a small bag to prevent illness. Eucalyptus leaves are put into a sleep pillow for colds. Pinecones mean good health, longevity, and fertility; hang them in the house to attract these qualities. Burn thyme to attract good health. Violets can be sprinkled at the corners of the house for healing vibrations and to protect against disease.

There is no end to the possibilities for making healing charms. If you make anything with the desire for healing in your heart, it will attract divine healing energy. The charm's power comes from your positive thoughts and actions, not from any object. The objects are only symbols of those thoughts.

Healing Altars

An altar makes any place sacred. Creating an altar (also see page 9) opens you to the spiritual dimension of whatever spiritual path you choose. It allows you to express your personal glimpse of the Divine in whatever way you imagine it. Altars are places of centering and rebalancing.

Altars also open a connection between the physical and the spiritual, this world and the Otherworld, which is the source of great healing energy. Healing altars are powerful and valuable in healing the most desperate cases of illness. They are also a way for the family and close friends to participate in healing their loved one.

Altars don't have to be large or elaborate. Begin with what you have. An altar space can be anything: a small shelf, a table, a covered box set in a corner, the top of a dresser, or one corner of a coffee table.

If you wish, place on the altar representations or statues of deities, angels, or saints to symbolize the element of Spirit. Use objects that represent the four elements: a candle for Fire; incense for Air; a stone or flowers for Earth; and a small bowl of water for Water. If you plan to light a candle or burn incense on this altar, make certain there is nothing flammable nearby.

For a healing altar, place on it a photo or something that reminds you of the person for whom the altar is being made. A healing altar attracts people to go there to pray and meditate, to lift their spirits toward the Divine Source. In this way, the family and patient can easily enter an altered state of consciousness, thus aiding any other forms of healing that are being done. These altars bring a state of peace, calmness, and joy that relieves stress in all who sit before them.

If you don't have statues of the deities, angels, or saints for your altar, don't despair. Write the names out carefully on a white card or piece of paper, and place it on the altar. If you want to explore the wide variety of ancient deities and saints before choosing one or more statues, read through the following lists. See the Resources section for a list of product suppliers who sell such statues.

Ancient Healing Deities

ANU Ireland. This Goddess is associated with health and prosperity.

ANUBIS Egypt. Although this God was primarily the deity of death and endings, he also has power over protection, surgery, and hospital stays.

APOLLO Greece. A God of music, Apollo also helps with healing.

ARTEMIS Greece. This Virgin Huntress Goddess has power over mental healing.

ASA Kenya. Known as the God of Mercy, this deity helps one to survive the impossible or insurmountable.

BAST Egypt. Shown as a cat-headed Goddess, she is associated with healing.

BEL Ireland. This Sun deity also aids with healing and success.

BRIGIT/BRIGHID Ireland. A Goddess of divination, she is also powerful with healing.

BUTO Egypt. This cobra Goddess is powerful when called upon for protection.

THE DAGDA Ireland. This God was the High King of the Tuatha Dé Danann, and is known for his healing powers.

DIANCECHT Ireland. This God was a famous ancient physician who still has power over medicine, regeneration, and healing.

FREYJA/FREYA Norse. Called the Mistress of Cats, this Goddess was a powerful shapeshifter. She can help with enchantments, good luck, and protection.

FU-HSI China. This God of happiness helps with success.

FUKUROKUJU Japan. This is the God of happiness and long life.

GAEA/GAIA Greece. Known as an Earth Goddess, this deity helps with healing.

GANESHA/GANESH India. This elephant-headed God is very powerful for removing obstacles.

HECATE Greece. Known in Thrace as the Triple Goddess of the Moon, she has the power to avert evil and cause transformations.

HERMES Greece. Known as the Messenger between the Gods and humans, this God also rules over orthodox medicine and music.

HOTEI OSHO Japan. This rotund little deity is the God of good fortune.

HORUS Egypt. A falcon-headed God, this deity helps with problem solving and success.

IMHOTEP Egypt. This is a God of medicine and healing.

ISHTAR Middle East. Called the Queen of Heaven, this Goddess helps you overcome obstacles.

ISIS Egypt. This Goddess, whose worship lasted long after the collapse of the ancient Egyptian culture, is adept at healing and protection.

JANUS Rome. Originally an Etruscan deity, this God helps with new cycles of life and beginnings and endings.

KUAN YIN China. This compassionate Goddess gives mercy and love.

LAKSHMI India. A Goddess of love and creative energy, she is powerful in granting success and good fortune.

LUGH Ireland, Wales. This famous legendary figure is considered to be a God of healing and magick.

MUKURU West Africa. This God of rain helps with healing and protection.

PAN Greece. A God of the woodlands and wild creatures, he is also associated with medicine.

PERUN Russia, Slavonia. Although a God of storms and oracles, he also provides defense against illness.

SEKHMET Egypt. This fierce lioness-headed Goddess is a patroness of physicians and bone-setters.

SHEN NUNG China. This deity is a God of medicine.

SHIVA India. Known as the Demon-Slayer, this God is portrayed with four arms. He aids with medicine, healing, and long life.

TARA India. You can call upon the White Tara for long life and health. The Green Tara is powerful for growth and protection.

YAO-SHIH China. This God is the master of healing.

Healing Angels

CAMAEL This being helps with courage, purification, and protection.

GABRIEL One of the archangels, he gives mercy and hope, and helps with herbal medicine.

MICHAEL One of the archangels, this being protects and grants guidance in all things.

RAPHAEL One of the archangels, he helps with healing, success, and the curing of all diseases.

TZAPHKIEL This angel aids spiritual development, overcoming grief, and helps with the balancing of karma.

Healing Saints

THE INFANT JESUS OF PRAGUE He aids in health matters, surgery, and guidance.

OUR LADY OF GUADALUPE Although she helps with any situation, she is powerful in overcoming sickness and bringing peace.

OUR LADY OF THE IMMACULATE CONCEPTION She helps with all sicknesses.

OUR LADY OF LOURDES She helps to heal sicknesses and regain health.

SAINT AGNES She is the patroness of nurses and particularly helpful in curing breast diseases.

SAINT ALBINUS He aids in curing gallstones and kidney diseases.

SAINT ALPHONSUS LIGUORI This saint has power over rheumatic fever, arthritis, osteoarthritis, gout, and joint and muscle ailments.

SAINT BARTHOLOMEW He is the patron of surgeons and has power over surgeries.

SAINT CADOC OF WALES He helps with glandular disorders.

SAINTS COSMAS AND DAMIAN This duo are patrons of druggists, physicians, and surgeons. They also help with getting a correct diagnosis of disease.

SAINT ELMO This saint aids with intestinal diseases.

SAINT JAMES THE GREATER He helps in removing obstacles, and treating arthritis and rheumatism.

SAINT JUDE This saint specializes in helping hopeless cases.

SAINT LUKE He is the patron of physicians and surgeons.

SAINT PEREGRINE LAZIOSI He helps with health problems, particularly cancer.

SAINT PETER He aids in achieving success, gaining courage and good luck, and removing obstacles.

SAINT PHILOMENA She helps with any desperate situation.

SAINT RITA She aids those in desperate situations and has the power to stop bleeding.

SAINT RITA OF CASCIA The patroness of hopeless cases, she helps in healing wounds and tumors.

SAINT TERESA OF AVILA This saint helps with headaches and heart attacks.

THE VIRGIN MARY Known as the mother of Jesus, this powerful saint will intercede for any need.

You can also add healing stones (also see pages 43–46, 123–33, and 341–42) to your altar, both for their beauty and for their power. Some of the stones you might choose are moss agate, amazonite, amber, amethyst, aquamarine, beryl, bloodstone, carnelian, chrysocolla, citrine, emerald, fluorite, garnet, hematite, jade, jasper, lapis lazuli, malachite, tourmaline, or turquoise.

Incense (also see pages 120–22) will raise the vibrations in any room or house. Examples of healing incenses are carnation, cedar, cinnamon, gardenia, lavender, lotus, myrrh, orange, rose, and sandalwood. When in doubt, use a blend of frankincense and myrrh, frequently available in stick form. Sticks or cones are fine.

If you choose to burn candles on your altar, you can use either the glass-contained seven-day candles, or six-inch straights in fireproof holders (also see pages 106–10). Seven-day candles usually come in green, blue, or white. These glass-contained candles are meant to be burned steadily for seven days, beginning the day after the new moon. If you can't start a seven-day candle just after the new moon, be certain that you start burning it so it will burn out by the full moon exactly, not a day later. Candles always represent spiritual enlightenment.

The skull candle is another powerful healing candle that some people refuse to use because they don't understand its meaning. Burn one of these for healing serious, deadly, or terminal diseases. It is best burned along with a white candle.

Traditionally, candle colors have specific meanings and uses. To read about the meanings of traditional candle colors, see pages 114–19.

Some cultures add images or pictures of certain animals to their altars to signify specific energies they wish to attract. To read about the meanings associated with particular animals, see pages 14–22.

You can also add any other symbolic object that you connect with healing, willpower, determination, and the spiritual realm. For example, a small table fountain can represent the flow of life force and the receiving of blessings, while keys mean finding a hidden truth or unlocking secrets, perhaps the secret to a cure. Design your healing altar to represent the sick loved one and your hopes and prayers for healing.

It is my hope that all of the alternative healing techniques in this book will help each healer grow spiritually as well as heal the ones you love. Never give up hope. Never lose your connection with the Divine Source and the greatest healing power in the universe. When you least expect it, your work for healing, however inexperienced you may be, could create a miracle.

Resources

The following businesses sell a variety of products and ritual supplies. Most can be found online. If you prefer a catalog, order one at the online site, write, or call the supplier. Usually these catalogs are free. Except for candles of certain unusual colors and image candles, you can purchase your candles at discount stores or shopping centers. These candles should be unscented. You can find pendulums at rock shops, New Age stores, or from Pagan stores. Herbs and spices in local grocery stores are frequently too old for magickal healing use. Instead, check with herb shops, New Age stores, or purchase online from a Pagan supplier.

Aphrodesia
264 Bleecker Street
New York, NY 10014
Phone: 212-989-6440
www.aphrodisiaherbshoppe.com
All varieties of herbs.

Azure Green
PO Box 48
Middlefield, MA 01243
Phone: 413-623-2155
www.azuregreen.net
Jewelry, stones, oils, incense and burners, herbs, books, bottles and jars, mortars and pestles, herbal teas, music, aromatherapy oils and diffusers, candles including image ones, statues and wall sculptures, bells, talisman bags, divination tools, holy water, and more.

Crescent Moon Goddess
PO Box 153
Massapequa Park, NY 11762
Phone: 516-827-4399
www.crescentmoongoddess.com
Incense and burners, oils, wide variety of candles, aromatherapy oils and diffusers, stones, jewelry, music, divination tools, capes, books, crystals, wands, chalices, bath salts, videos, herbs, salves, cauldrons, talisman bags, and more.

Earth Star Connection
1218 31st Street, NW
Washington, DC 20007
Phone: 202-965-2989
Candles, incense, drums, rattles, crystals, and minerals.

Mystic Trader
1334 Pacific Avenue
Forest Grove, OR 97116
Phone: 800-634-9057
www.mystictrader.com
Stones and gems, prayer beads, malas, statues, jewelry including copper and magnetic, tonal music, books, prints including angels, videos, tuning forks, incense, smudge sticks, musical instruments, and many Eastern items.

Nichols Garden Nursery
1190 Old Salem Road NE
Albany, OR 97321
Phone: 800-422-3985
www.nicholsgardennursery.com
High-quality herb seeds and plants, herbal teas, oils and soaps, dry potpourri, dry herbs and spices including sweetgrass, and gardening books and supplies.

Pyramid Collection
Northwoods Trail
PO Box 6529
Chelmsford, MA 01824
Phone: 877-756-1628
www.pyramidcollection.com
Wide range of items, including crystals, stones, musical instruments, and statues.

Sacred Source
PO Box 163 WW
Crozet, VA 22932
Phone: 800-290-6203
www.sacredsource.com
Statues of deities and sacred images from around the world, including archangels. Excellent prices.

Tools for Wellness
638 Lindero Canyon Road
Suite 128
Oak Park, CA 91377
Phone: 800-456-9887
www.toolsforwellness.com
A wide array of products, including colored filters and light projectors for color healing. However, this company's products are expensive.

Two Sisters Trading Company
Phone: 877-878-9474
http://2sisterstrading.stores.yahoo.net
Candles, books, jewelry, music, talisman bags, Goddess/Madonna wall pictures, oils, spell kits, angel bowls, divination tools, incense, incense bowls, pocket stones, soaps, and massage oils.

Bibliography

Altars

Altheim, Franz. *A History of Roman Religion*, translated by Harold Mattingly. New York: no publisher, 1938.

Angus, S. *The Mystery-Religion*. New York: Dover Publications, 1975.

Bachofen, J. J. *Myth, Religion, and Mother Right*, translated by Ralph Mannheim; ed. By Joseph Campbell. Princeton, NJ: Princeton University Press, 1973.

Barber, Elizabeth Wayland. *Women's Work: The First 20,000 Years*. New York: W. W. Norton & Co, 1994.

Baring, Anne, and Jules Cashford. *The Myth of the Goddess: Evolution of an Image*. Middlesex, UK: Viking Arkana, 1991.

Barker, Cicely M. *Flower Fairies: The Meaning of Flowers*. London, UK: Penguin, 1996.

Beck, Renee, and Sydney Barbara Metrick. *The Art of Ritual*. Berkeley, CA: Celestial Arts, 1990.

Bennett, Florence Mary. *Religious Cults Associated with the Amazons*. New York: University Books, 1987. (Originally published 1912.)

Boulding, Elise. *The Underside of History*. Boulder, CO: Westview Press, 1978.

Briffault, Robert. *The Mothers: A Study of the Origins of Sentiments and Institutions*. 3 vols. New York: Macmillan, 1952.

Budge, E. A. Wallis. *Amulets & Superstitions*. New York: Dover Publications, 1978.

——. *The Gods of the Egyptians*. 2 vols. New York: Dover Publications, 1969.

Campbell, Joseph. *The Masks of God: Primitive Mythology.* New York: Penguin Books, 1968.

——. *The Mythic Image.* Princeton, NJ: Princeton University Press, 1974.

——. *The Way of the Animal Powers.* San Francisco, CA: Harper & Row, 1983.

Cavendish, Richard, ed. *Mythology: An Illustrated Encyclopedia.* New York: Rizzoli, 1980.

Cirlot, J. E. *A Dictionary of Symbols,* translated by Jack Sage. New York: Philosophical Library, 1971.

Conway, D. J. *Animal Magick.* St. Paul, MN: Llewellyn Publications, 1997.

——. *By Oak, Ash and Thorn: Modern Celtic Shamanism*. St. Paul, MN: Llewellyn Publications, 1995.

——. *Celtic Magick.* St. Paul, MN: Llewellyn Publications, 1990.

——. *Crystal Enchantments: A Complete Guide to Stones and Their Magickal Properties*. Berkeley, CA: Crossing Press, 1999.

——. *Magick of the Gods and Goddesses.* St. Paul, MN: Llewellyn Publications, 1993. (Originally titled *The Ancient & Shining Ones.*)

——. *Magickal, Mythical, Mystical Beasts.* St. Paul, MN: Llewellyn Publications, 1996.

——. *Maiden, Mother, Crone.* St. Paul, MN: Llewellyn Publications, 1994.

Cotterell, Arthur, ed. *Macmillan Illustrated Encyclopedia of Myths and Legends.* New York: Macmillan, 1989.

D'Alviella, Count Goblet. *Migration of Symbols.* Wellingborough, UK: Aquarian Press, 1979.

Davidson, H. R. Ellis. *Myths and Symbols in Pagan Europe.* Syracuse, New York: Syracuse University Press, 1988.

Diner, Helen. *Mothers and Amazons: The First Feminine History of Culture,* translated and edited by John Philip Lunden. New York: Doubleday/Anchor, 1973.

Frazer, James G. *The Golden Bough.* New York: Macmillan, 1963.

Gimbutas, Marija. *The Civilization of the Goddess.* San Francisco, CA: Harper SanFrancisco, 1991.

——. *The Goddesses and Gods of Old Europe.* Berkeley, CA: University of California Press, 1982.

——. *The Language of the Goddess.* San Francisco, CA: Harper & Row, 1989.

Graves, Robert. *The White Goddess.* New York: Farrar, Straus & Giroux, 1978.

Gray, Louis Herbert, ed. *The Mythology of All Races.* Boston, MA: Marshall Jones Company, 1916.

Greenaway, Kate. *Language of Flowers.* New York: Dover, 1992. (Originally published c. 1866.)

Guirand, Felix, ed. *New Larousse Encyclopedia of Mythology,* translated by Richard Aldington and Delano Ames. London, UK: Hamlyn, 1978.

Hooke, S. H. *Babylonian and Assyrian Religion.* London, UK: Hutchinson, 1953.

James, E. O. *The Cult of the Mother Goddess.* New York: Barnes & Noble Books, 1994.

——. *From Cave to Cathedral: Temples and Shrines of Prehistoric, Classical, and Early Christian Times.* New York: Frederick A. Praeger, 1964.

Jobes, Gertrude. *Dictionary of Mythology, Folklore, and Symbols.* New York: Scarecrow Press, 1962.

Johnson, Buffie. *Lady of the Beasts: Ancient Images of the Goddess and Her Sacred Animals.* San Francisco, CA: Harper & Row, 1988.

Jung, Carl G. *The Archetypes and the Collective Unconscious.* Princeton, NJ: Princeton University Press, 1990.

Kingston, Karen. *Creating Sacred Space with Feng Shui.* New York: Broadway Books, 1997.

Kramer, Samuel N. *The Sumerians: Their History, Culture, and Character.* Chicago, IL: University of Chicago Press, 1963.

Larrington, Carolyne, ed. *The Feminist Companion to Mythology.* London, UK: Pandora Press, 1992.

Linn, Denise. *Sacred Space: Clearing and Enhancing the Energy of Your Home.* New York: Ballantine Books, 1995.

Malbrough, Ray T. *The Magickal Power of the Saints.* St. Paul, MN: Llewellyn Publications, 1998.

Nahmad, Claire. *Garden Spells.* New York: Gramercy, 1998.

Neumann, Erich. *The Great Mother: An Analysis of the Archetype,* translated by Ralph Mannheim. Princeton, NJ: Princeton University Press, 1974.

Rossbach, Sarah. *Feng Shui: The Chinese Art of Placement.* New York: E. P. Dutton, 1983.

Sandoval, Annette. *The Directory of Saints.* New York: Signet/Penguin, 1997.

Scobie, Grechen, and Ann Field. *The Meaning of Flowers.* San Francisco: Chronicle Books, 1998.

Scully, Vincent. *The Earth, the Temple, and the Gods.* New Haven, CT: Yale University Press, 1979.

Seaton, Beverly. *Language of Flowers: A History.* Charlottesville, VA: University Press of Virginia, 1995.

Sjoo, Monica, and Barbara Mor. *The Great Cosmic Mother: Rediscovering the Religion of the Earth.* San Francisco, CA: Harper & Row, 1987.

Stone, Merlin. *Ancient Mirrors of Womanhood: A Treasury of Goddess and Heroine Love from Around the World.* Boston, MA: Beacon Press, 1990.

Streep, Peg. *Altars Made Easy.* San Francisco, CA: HarperSanFrancisco, 1997.

Turville-Petre, E. O. G. *Myth and Religion of the North.* New York: Holt, Rinehart & Winston, 1964.

Vermaseren, Maarten J. *Cybele and Attis: The Myth and the Cult,* translated by A. M. H. Lemmers. London, UK: Thames & Hudson, 1977.

Ward, Marina. *Alone of All Her Sex: The Myth and Cult of the Virgin Mary.* London, UK: Pan Books, 1985.

Wells, Diana. *100 Flowers and How They Got Their Names.* Chapel Hill, NC: Algonquin Books of Chapel Hill, 1997.

Willetts, R. F. *Cretan Cults and Festivals.* London, UK: Routledge & Kegan Paul, 1962.

Candles

Buckland, Raymond. *Advanced Candle Magick*. St. Paul, MN: Llewellyn Publications, 1996.

——. *Practical Candleburning Rituals*. St. Paul, MN: Llewellyn Publications, 1981.

Dunwich, Gerina. *Candlelight Spells*. New York: Citadel Press, 1988.

Ilkes, Judith. *The Element Encyclopedia of 5,000 Spells*. Shaftesbury, UK: Element Books, 2004.

Ketch, Tina. *Candle Lighting Encyclopedia*. Stone Mountain, GA: Ketch Productions, 1991.

——. *Candle Lighting Encyclopedia, Volume II*. Stone Mountain, GA: Ketch Productions, 1993.

MacGregor, Trish. *The Everything Spells & Charms Book*. Avon, MA: Adams Media Corporation, 2001.

Murphy-Hiscock, Arin. *Power Spellcraft for Life*. Avon, MA: Provenance Press, 2005.

Pajeon, Kala & Ketz. *The Candle Magick Workbook*. Secaucus, NJ: Carol Publishing Group, 1996.

Pendulums

Bentov, Itzhak. *Stalking the Wild Pendulum: On the Mechanics of Consciousness*. Rochester, VT: Destiny Books, 1988.

Bird, Christopher. *The Divining Hand*. New York: E. P. Dutton, 1979.

Chandu, Jack F. *The Pendulum Book*, translated by Tony Langham and Plym Peters. London, UK: C. W. Daniel Company, 1990.

Davies, Rodney. *Dowsing*. Wellingborough, UK: The Aquarian Press, 1991.

De France, Le Vicomte Henry. *The Elements of Dowsing*. London, UK: G. Bell and Sons, 1948.

Finch, W. J. *The Pendulum & Possession.* Cottonwood, AZ: Esoteric Publications, 1975.

Graves, Tom. *The Diviner's Handbook.* Wellingborough, UK: The Aquarian Press, 1986.

——. *The Dowser's Workbook: Understanding & Using the Power of Dowsing.* New York: Sterling Publishing, 1990.

——. *Dowsing Techniques and Applications.* Wellingborough, UK: Turnstone Books, 1976.

——. *The Elements of Pendulum Dowsing.* Shaftesbury, UK: Element Books, 1998.

Hitching, Francis. *Pendulum: The Psi Connection.* London, UK: Fontana, 1977.

Jurriaanse, D. *The Practical Pendulum Book.* New York: Samuel Weiser, 1986.

Lethbridge, T. C. *The Power of the Pendulum.* New York: Routledge & Kegan Paul, 1976.

——. *Ghost and Divining Rod.* London, UK: Routledge & Kegan Paul, 1963.

Lonegren, Sig. *Earth Mysteries.* Danville, VT: ASD Book & Supply, 1985.

——. *The Pendulum Kit.* New York: Simon & Schuster, 1990.

——. *Spiritual Dowsing.* Somerset, UK: Gothic Image Publications, 1986.

Nielsen, Greg. *Beyond Pendulum Power.* Reno, NV: Conscious Books, 1988.

——, and Joseph Polansky. *Pendulum Power.* Rochester, VT: Destiny Books, 1987.

Powell, Tag & Judith. *Taming the Wild Pendulum.* Pinellas Park, FL: Top of the Mountain Publishing, 1995.

Schirner, Mark. *Pendulum Workbook.* New York: Sterling Publishing, 1999.

Scott-Elliott, Major General James. *Dowsing—One Man's Way.* London, UK: Neville Spearman, 1977.

Underwood, Guy. *The Pattern of the Past.* New York: Abelard-Schuman, 1973.

Underwood, Peter. *The Complete Book of Dowsing and Divining.* London, UK: Rider & Company, 1980.

Weaver, Herbert. *Divining, the Primary Sense.* London, UK: Routledge & Kegan Paul, 1978.

Webster, Richard. *Dowsing for Beginners.* St. Paul, MN: Llewellyn Publications, 1996.

Healing Magick

Amber, Reuben. *Color Therapy.* Santa Fe, NM: Aurora Press, 1983.

Anderson, Mary. *Colour Healing.* Wellingborough, UK: Aquarian Press, 1981.

Ashley-Farrand, Thomas. *Healing Mantras.* (Compact disc) Boulder, CO: Sounds True, 1999.

——. *Healing Mantras.* New York: Ballantine Wellspring, 1999.

——. *The Power of Mantras.* (Compact disc) Boulder, CO: Sounds True, 1999.

Bernstein, Albert J. *Emotional Vampires: Dealing With People Who Drain You Dry.* New York: McGraw-Hill Companies, 2000.

Beyerl, Paul. *The Master Book of Herbalism.* Custer, WA: Phoenix Publishing, 1984.

Bhattacharya, A. K. *Gem Therapy.* Calcutta, India: Firma KLM Private Ltd., 1992.

Bibb, Benjamin O., and Joseph J. Weed. *Amazing Secrets of Psychic Healing.* West Nyack, NY: Parker Publishing, 1976.

Brennan, Barbara Ann. *Hands of Light: A Guide to Healing Through the Human Energy Field.* New York: Bantam Books, 1988.

Brier, Bob. *Ancient Egyptian Magick.* New York: Quill, 1981.

Bruyere, Rosalyn L. *Wheels of Light: A Study of the Chakras.* Arcadia, CA: Bon Productions, 1989.

Bryan, Cyril P., translator. *Ancient Egyptian Medicine: The Papyrus Ebers.* Chicago, IL: Ares Publishers, 1974.

Bryant, Ina. *Magnetic Electricity a Life Saver.* Kingsport, TN: Kingsport Press, 1978.

Budge, E. A. Wallis. *Amulets & Superstitions*. New York: Dover Publications, 1978.

——. *The Divine Origin of the Craft of the Herbalist*. New York: Dover Publications, 1996. (Originally published 1928.)

——. *Egyptian Magick*. New York: Dover Publications, 1971.

——. *Gods of the Egyptians*. 2 volumes. New York: Dover Publications, 1969.

Budilovsky, Joan, and Eve Adamson. *The Complete Idiot's Guide to Meditation*. New York: Alpha Books, 1999.

Campbell, Don. *The Mozart Effect*. New York: Avon Books, 1997.

Chadwick, Gloria. *Discovering Your Past Lives*. Chicago, IL: Contemporary Books, 1988.

Chopra, Deepak. *Creating Health*. Boston, MA: Houghton Mifflin Co., 1987.

Conway, D. J. *The Ancient & Shining Ones*. St. Paul, MN: Llewellyn Publications, 1993.

——. *Laying on of Stones*. Berkeley, CA: Crossing Press, 1999.

——. *Wicca: The Complete Craft*. Berkeley, CA: Crossing Press, 2001.

Cunningham, Scott. *Cunningham's Encyclopedia of Magickal Herbs*. St. Paul, MN: Llewellyn Publications, 1985.

Davidson, Gustav. *Dictionary of Angels*. New York: The Free Press, 1967.

Dossey, Larry. *Healing Words: The Power of Prayer and the Practice of Medicine*. New York: HarperCollins, 1993.

Eden, Donna. *Energy Medicine*. New York: Jeremy P. Tarcher, 1998.

Farmer, David. *The Oxford Dictionary of Saints*. Oxford, UK: Oxford University Press, 1997.

Gardner, Joy. *Color and Crystals*. Berkeley, CA: Crossing Press, 1988.

Gawain, Shakti. *Creative Visualization*. New York: Bantam Books, 1982.

Gaynor, Mitchell L. *Sounds of Healing*. New York: Broadway Books, 1999.

Georgian, Linda. *Your Guardian Angel*. New York: Simon & Schuster, 1994.

Gerber, Richard. *Vibrational Medicine for the 21st Century.* New York: Eagle Brook, 2000.

Goldman, Jonathan. *Healing Sounds: The Power of Harmonics.* Shaftesbury, UK: Element Books, 1999.

Gonzalez-Wippler, Migene. *The Complete Book of Amulets & Talismans.* St. Paul, MN: Llewellyn Publications, 1991.

Hall, Manley P. *The Secret Teachings of All Ages.* Los Angeles, CA: Philosophical Research Society, 1977.

Hay, Louise. *You Can Heal Your Life.* Carlsbad, CA: Hay House, 1999.

Hirshberg, Caryle, and Marc Ian Barasch. *Remarkable Recovery.* New York: Riverhead Press, 1995.

Howard, Michael. *Finding Your Guardian Angel.* Wellingborough, UK: Thorsons, 1991.

———. *The Runes & Other Magickal Alphabets.* Wellingborough, UK: Aquarian Press, 1981.

Howes, Michael. *Amulets.* New York: St. Martin's Press, 1975.

Hunt, Valerie. *Infinite Mind: The Science of Human Vibrations.* Malibu, CA: Malibu, 1995.

Judith, Anodea. *Wheels of Life: A User's Guide to the Chakra System.* St. Paul, MN: Llewellyn Publications, 1993.

Kamal, Hassan. *Dictionary of Pharaonic Medicine.* Cairo, Egypt: The National Publication House, 1967.

Karagulla, Shafica, and Dora van Gelder Kunz. *The Chakras and the Human Energy Fields.* Wheaton, IL: Quest Books, 1989.

Khalsa, Dharma Singh, and Cameron Stauth. *Meditation as Medicine.* New York: Pocket Books, 2001.

Kilner, W. J. *The Aura.* York Beach, ME: Samuel Weiser, 1984.

Klotsche, Charles. *Color Medicine.* Sedona, AZ: Light Technology Publishing, 1993.

Kriegger, Delores. *The Therapeutic Touch*. Paramus, NJ: Prentice-Hall, 1979.

Krystal, Phyllis. *Cutting the Ties That Bind*. Los Angeles, CA: Aura Books, 1982.

Leadbeater, C. W. *The Chakras*. Wheaton, IL: The Theosophical Publishing House, 1927.

Lewis, James R., and Evelyn Dorothy Oliver. *Angels A to Z*. New York: Visible Ink, 1996.

Lippman, Deborah, and Paul Colin. *How to Make Amulets, Charms, and Talismans*. New York: E. Evans & Co., 1974.

Malbrough, Ray T. *The Magickal Power of the Saints*. St. Paul, MN: Llewellyn Publications, 1998.

McManus, Jason, editor. *Powers of Healing*. Alexandria, VA: Time-Life, 1989.

Meadows, Kenneth. *Rune Power*. Boston, MA: Element Books, 1996.

Mesko, Sabrina. *Healing Mudras: Yoga for Your Hands*. New York: Ballantine Wellspring, 2000.

Morris, Desmond. *Body Guards*. Shaftesbury, UK: Element Books, 1999.

Motoyama, Hiroshi, and R. Brown. *Science and the Evolution of Consciousness: Chakras, Ki, and Psi*. Brookline, MA: Autumn Press, 1978.

Myss, Caroline. *Why People Don't Heal and How They Can*. New York: Three Rivers Press, 1997.

Ostrander, Sheila and Lynn Schroeder. *Psychic Discoveries Behind the Iron Curtain*. Paramus, NJ: Prentice-Hall, 1970.

Ouseley, S. G. J. *The Power of the Rays: The Science of Colour-Healing*. London, UK: L. N. Fowler & Co., 1976.

——. *The Science of the Aura*. London, UK: L. N. Fowler & Co., 1973.

Pennick, Nigel. *The Complete Illustrated Guide to Runes*. Shaftesbury, UK: Element Books, 1999.

——. *Magickal Alphabets*. York Beach, ME: Samuel Weiser, 1992.

Petrie, William Flinders. *Amulets*. Warminster, UK: Aris & Phillips, Ltd., 1972.

Quirke, Stephen. *Ancient Egyptian Religion*. New York: Dover Publications, 1992.

Regardie, Israel. *How to Make and Use Talismans.* Wellingborough, UK: Aquarian Press, 1981.

Rosetree, Rose. *Aura Reading Through All Your Senses.* Sterling, VA: Women's Intuition Worldwide, 1996.

Sandoval, Annette. *The Directory of Saints: A Concise Guide to Patron Saints.* New York: Signet/Penguin, 1997.

Schulz, Mona Lisa. *Awakening Intuition.* New York: Three Rivers Press, 1998.

Sher, Barbara. *Wishcraft: How to Get What You Really Want.* New York: Ballantine Books, 1979.

Skelton, Robin. *Talismanic Magick.* York Beach, ME: Samuel Weiser, 1985.

Smith, Michael G. *Crystal Power.* St. Paul, MN: Llewellyn Publications, 1985.

———. *Crystal Spirit.* St. Paul, MN: Llewellyn Publications, 1990.

———, and Lin Westhorp. *Crystal Warrior: Shamanic Transformation and Projection of Universal Energy.* St. Paul, MN: Llewellyn Publications, 1993.

Snellgrove, Brian. *The Magick in Your Hands.* London, UK: The C. W. Daniel Company, 1997.

Thomas, William, and Kate Pavitt. *The Book of Talismans, Amulets, & Zodiacal Gems.* North Hollywood, CA: Wilshire Book Co., 1970.

Thompson, C. J. S. *Celtic Healing: The Healing Arts of Ancient Britain, Wales, and Ireland.* Edmonds, WA: Sure Fire Press, 1994.

Walker, Barbara G. *The Woman's Dictionary of Symbols & Sacred Objects.* San Francisco, CA: Harper & Row, 1988.

Walker, Morton. *The Power of Color.* Garden City, New York: Avery Publishing, 1989.

Webb, Marcus & Maria. *Healing Touch.* New York: Sterling Publishing, 1999.

Weinman, Ric A. *Your Hands Can Heal: Learn to Channel Healing Energy.* New York: E. P. Dutton, 1988.

Index

A

B

C

I

J

T

U

V

W

Y

Z